REFERENCE GUIDES IN LITERATURE

Everett Emerson, *Editor*

A Bibliography of Chaucer, 1964-1973

Lorrayne Y. Baird

G. K. HALL & CO., 70 LINCOLN STREET, BOSTON, MASS.

1977

Library of Congress Cataloging in Publication Data

Baird, Lorrayne Y.
   A bibliography of Chaucer, 1964-1973.

   (Reference guides in literature)
   "A continuation of William R. Crawford's Bibliography
of Chaucer, 1954-63."
   Includes indexes.
   1. Chaucer, Geoffrey, d. 1400--Bibliography.
I. Crawford, William R. Bibliography of Chaucer, 1954-
63. II. Title.
Z8164.B27   [PR1905]   016.821'1   77-374
ISBN 0-8161-8005-9

This publication is printed on permanent/durable acid-free paper
MANUFACTURED IN THE UNITED STATES OF AMERICA

for
Hildegard Schnüttgen

Contents

*See "General Prologue" in the index for the separate pilgrims

Contents

Contents

CONTENTS

Introduction

The past decade has witnessed a tremendous increase in Chaucer scholarship. The appearance in 1964-73 of nearly two hundred dissertations devoted wholly or partly to Chaucer, in comparison with about sixty in the decade previous, is a rough gauge of the increased interest and activity. This bibliography has been prepared for Chaucer scholars of all ranks as an aid in finding their way through this wealth of material.

Designed as a continuation of William R. Crawford's Bibliography of Chaucer, 1954-63, this work, with the following exceptions, uses his organization and methods. Numbered entries are used for the purpose of cross-reference. Source studies appear under the separate works to which they pertain. New or expanded categories include: (a) Festschriften and Collections, (b) Foreign Translations under Modernizations and Translations, (c) Literary and Aesthetic Backgrounds, (d) Music Backgrounds, (e) Recordings, Films, and Filmstrips, and (f) Musical Settings and Adaptations. Minor variations result from my perceptions which differ from Crawford's; courtly love studies, for example, appear under Literary and Aesthetic Backgrounds, rather than under Social Backgrounds. Appropriate references to Crawford and to his predecessor, D. D. Griffith (Bibliography of Chaucer, 1908-1953), appear throughout.

Within the decade covered by this Bibliography several reviews of scholarship have appeared: Robert W. Ackerman, 1668; Joyce Bazire and David Mills, 6; Morton W. Bloomfield, 172; D. S. Brewer, 178; J. A. Burrow, 2; William R. Crawford, 204; Richard L. Hoffman, 606; Charles Muscatine, 309; Helaine Newstead, 634.01; Beryl Rowland, 345. In addition, twenty-two reviews by various contributors appear in Beryl Rowland's Companion to Chaucer Studies, 60. Consequently, I have not felt it necessary to provide a review of scholarship such as Crawford's.

In the main part of the bibliography (1-1621), which attempts to be definitive, I have included new editions and reprints of earlier books and articles as well as a few items, mainly reviews, appearing after 1973. The Backgrounds section (1622-2125), is, of course, selective. Entries in this section, chosen on the basis of examination and book reviews, may have either specific or general relevance to Chaucer studies. In the main section I have attempted to add a dimension of selectivity by including abstract information and by annotation. The abstract is, however, not an infallible guide to the worth of an article, since MLA Abstracts, which is selective, did not begin until 1970; and since Abstracts of English Studies, 1964-74, which is not selective, did not include abstracts from all the journals and annuals which publish Chaucer Studies, including NM, ELH, AnM, UTQ, RUO and others. Annotations identify those books and articles of a general, introductory, or popular nature and those designed for undergraduates.

Despite my thoroughgoing attempt to look at every item itself, except dissertations, a few have escaped examination. These items and dissertations are prefaced with an asterisk (*) and followed by the source in which the item was found. Asterisks also accompany reviews not seen and publication information not extracted from the physical book or article, but discovered in bibliographic search.

In the bibliography proper, names of authors are listed as they appear on books and articles themselves; thus variants of an author's name may appear together in an order dictated by the author's works within a section. Expanded author names available from sources other than the physical work cited are indicated by brackets.

Editorial changes have been kept to a minimum, except that titles of Chaucer's works within an article, for example, are standardized by underlining, in order to avoid the confusion of the various methods found in the raw materials. Page numbers for books represent the sum of arabic and roman numeral pagination found in the original.

Cross references to the separate works of Chaucer include only writings about Chaucer. For editions consult the Subject Index or the section on Editions. Underlining distinguishes substantial from brief or casual references.

Abbreviations are those of MLA International Bibliography. Abbreviations not found in the MLA Master List conform to the usage in appropriate indexes, such as the Music Index, with formal modifications suitable to MLA style. Although Chaucer's works are not abbreviated in the annotations throughout this work, the standard abbreviations are included as a convenience to beginning scholars, and because a few appear in items cited.

An "Author Index" and a "Subject Index" have been provided. The existence of cross references is indicated in the Subject Index by the use of (+).

For the convenience of the user, I have taken an occasional liberty with form: background materials for The Nun's Priest's Tale (1234-1238), for instance, are included under the NPT, rather than being dispersed throughout the Backgrounds section.

Introduction

I acknowledge indebtedness to Thomas Kirby, Chairman of the Committee on Research and Bibliography of the Chaucer Group of the Modern
Language Association of America, for sending me reports of this committee; to Youngstown State University for a clerical assistance grant
and for providing the help of graduate assistants, Mary Ann Karas,
who helped lay the ground work, and Anna Eleftheriou, who helped with
bibliographic search, prepared the indexes and proofread; to Mary
Louise Quisenberry, who typed the final manuscript; to Barbara
Brothers, Head of the English Department, who arranged my regular
teaching schedule for optimum use of time; and to my husband Joseph L.
Baird, for consultation. My greatest debt of gratitude, however, is
to Hildegard Schnuttgen, Reference Librarian of Youngstown State
University, without whose efficient help with inter-library loans,
this bibliography could not have been done. The mere mention of the
kinds of help I have received can in no way give an indication of the
wonderful supportiveness and competence of those who helped.

Master List and Table of Abbreviations

A&A	Anelida and Arcite
A&S	Arts and Sciences (New York University)
ABäG	Amsterdamer Beiträge zur älteren Germanistik
AbFS	Abstracts of Folklore Studies
ABR	American Benedictine Review
ActaMus	Acta musicologica: Revue de la Société Internationale de Musicologie
AES	Abstracts of English Studies (no. 18 in this bibliography)
AHR	American Historical Review
AI	American Imago
AION-SG	Annali Istituto Universitario Orientale, Napoli, Sezione Germanica
AION-SL	Annali Istituto Universitario Orientale, Napoli, Sezione Linguistica
AKG	Archiv für Kulturgeschichte
Ambix:	Journal of the Society for the Study of Alchemy
AmChoralR	American Choral Review
AmOrg	The American Organist
AmR	American Recorder (New York)
AmRecG	American Recorder Guide
AMS	Journal of the American Musicological Society
AN&Q	American Notes and Queries (New Haven, Connecticut)
Ang	Anglia
Anglia (Kansai University, Osaka)	
AnM	Annuale Mediaevale (Duquesne University)
AnuMus	Annuario Musical
Apollo:	The Magazine of the Arts, new series (London)
Arcadia:	Zeitschrift für vergleichende Literaturwissenschaft (Berlin)
Archiv	Archiv für das Studium der Neueren Sprachen und Literaturen
ArchMus	Archiv für Musikwissenchaft
ArchR	Architectural Review
ArlQ	Arlington Quarterly
ArQ	Arizona Quarterly
Ars Organi:	Zeitschrift für das Orgelwesen
ArtB	Art Bulletin
ArtJ	Art Journal (New York)

AUBFA   Alexandria University Bulletin of the Faculty of
                      Arts
AULLA   Australian Universities Language and Literature
                      Association
AUMLA   Journal of the Australasian Universities Language and
                      Literature Association
AWR   Anglo-Welsh Review (Pembroke Dock, Wales)
BA   Books Abroad
Balcony: The Sydney Review
BaratR   Barat Review
BB   Bulletin of Bibliography
BC   Book Collector
BD   Book of the Duchess
BFH   Bulletin of the Faculty of Humanities (Seikei
                      University, Tokyo)
BHM   Bulletin of the History of Medicine
BHS   Bulletin of Hispanic Studies
BJRL   Bulletin of the John Rylands Library
BLA   Bibliographie Linguistic de l'Année...(no. 22 in this
                      bibliography)
BlakeS   Blake Studies
BNYPL   Bulletin of the New York Public Library
BRI   Book Review Index (no. 2.01 in this bibliography)
BRMMLA   Bulletin of the Rocky Mountain Modern Language
                      Association
BSUF   Ball State University Forum
BuR   Bucknell Review
BurM   Burlington Magazine (London)
BW   Book World (Chicago Tribune)
CahiersE   Cahiers Elisabéthains: Etudes sur la Pré-Renaissance
                      et la Renaissance Anglaises
C&L   Christianity and Literature
C&M   Classica et Mediaevalia
CamQ   Cambridge Quarterly
CarnetMus   Carnet Musical
CaSE   Carnegie Series in English
CCC   College Composition and Communication
CCTE   Conference of College Teachers of English of Texas
CE   College English
CEA   CEA Critic
CEJ   California English Journal
CF   Classical Folia
CH   Church History
ChauR   Chaucer Review (Pennsylvania State University)
ChCen   The Christian Century
CHLSSF   Commentationes Humanarum Litterarum Societas
                      Scientiarum Fennica
Choice (American Library Association)
CHR   Catholic Historical Review
Cithara (Saint Bonaventure University)
CJ   Classical Journal

CJL	Canadian Journal of Linguistics
CL	Comparative Literature
CLAJ	College Language Association Journal (Morgan State College, Baltimore)

Clavier, a Magazine for Pianists and Organists

ClassR	Classical Review, new series

Clio: An Interdisciplinary Journal of Literature, History, and the Philosophy of History (University of Wisconsin)

CLQ	Colby Library Quarterly
CLS	Comparative Literature Studies (University of Illinois)

Comitatus: Studies in Old and Middle English Literature

Connoisseur, The (London)

ContempR	Contemporary Review (London)

Costerus: Essays in English and American Language and Literature

CQR	Church Quarterly Review
CR	The Critical Review (Melbourne; Sydney)

Critic: A Catholic Review of Books and the Arts

Criticism: A Quarterly for Literature and the Arts (Wayne State University)

CritQ	Critical Quarterly (Manchester, England)
CSSH	Comparative Studies in Society and History: An International Quarterly (London)
CSSLL	Colorado Studies: Series in Language and Literature
CT	The Canterbury Tales
CurrentMus	Current Musicology
CYT	Canon's Yeoman's Tale
DA	Dissertation Abstracts
DAI	Dissertation Abstracts International [Supersedes DA in 1969]
DalR	Dalhousie Review
Diap	The Diapason
DQR	Dutch Quarterly Review of Anglo-American Letters
DrCrit	Drama Critique
DUJ	Durham University Journal, new series
DVLG	Deutsche Vierteljahrsschrift für Literaturwissenschaft und Geistesgeschichte
EA	Études Anglaises
E&S	Essays and Studies by Members of the English Association, new series
EarlyMus	Early Music
EconHistR	Economic History Review

Economist, The (London)

EHR	English Historical Review
EIC	Essays in Criticism (Oxford)
EigoS	Eigo Seinen [The Rising Generation] (Tokyo)
EJ	English Journal
ELH	Journal of English Literary History
ELN	English Language Notes (University of Colorado)
EM	English Miscellany
EMD	An English Miscellany (St. Stephen's College, Delhi)
EN	English Notes

Eng	English (London)
EngQ	English Quarterly (Canadian Council of Teachers of English, Toronto)
EngR	English Record
EngRev	English Review
Erasmus:	Speculum scientiarum, International Bulletin of Contemporary Scholarship (Wiesbaden)
ErasmusR	Erasmus Review: A Journal of the Humanities
ES	English Studies (Amsterdam)
ESA	English Studies in Africa (Johannesburg)
E-W	East-West Review
Expl	Explicator
Fabula:	Zeitschrift für Erzählforschung/Journal of Folktale Studies
FLett	Fiera Letteraria (Rome)
FMLS	Forum for Modern Language Studies (University of St. Andrews, Scotland)
FMod	Filología Moderna (Madrid)
FolkloreC	Folklore (Calcutta)
FrankT	Franklin's Tale
FriarT	Friar's Tale
FS	French Studies
GalpinSJ	The Galpin Society Journal (Edinburgh, Scotland)
GaR	Georgia Review
Gesta (International Center of Medieval Art, New Haven, Connecticut)	
GGA	Göttingische Gelehrte Anzeigen
GL	General Linguistics
GenProl	General Prologue
Greyfriar:	Siena Studies in Literature
GRM	Germanische-romanische Monatsschrift
GuitarR	The Guitar Review
HAB	Humanities Association Bulletin (Canada)
HCS	Hunter College Studies
HF	House of Fame
History:	The Journal of The Historical Association, new series
HisT	History Today
HSL	Hartford Studies in Literature: A Journal of Interdisciplinary Criticism
HudR	Hudson Review
HZ	Historische Zeitschrift
IBR	Internationale Bibliographie der Rezensionen (no. 11 in this bibliography)
IBRH	An Index to Book Reviews in The Humanities (no. 8.01 in this bibliography)
IBZ	Internationale Bibliographie der Zeitschriften Literatur (no. 12 in this bibliography)
ICLAP	International Comparative Literature Association Proceedings
II	International Index (no. 1856 in this bibliography)
IJES	Indian Journal of English Studies
IJSym	International Journal of Symbology
InF	Inozemna filogiya, L'vov

IntMus	International Musician
IQ	Italian Quarterly
IT	Index translationum (no. 10 in this bibliography)
Isis:	International Review Devoted to the History of Science and its Cultural Influences
JAAC	Journal of Aesthetics and Art Criticism
JAF	Journal of American Folklore
JAMA	Journal of the American Medical Association
JanL	Janua Linguarum (The Hague)
JAOS	Journal of the American Oriental Society
JBS	Journal of British Studies (Trinity College, Hartford, Connecticut)
JChurchMus	Journal of Church Music
JDH	Jahresverzeichnis der deutschen Hochschulschriften (no. 13 in this bibliography)
JEGP	Journal of English and Germanic Philology
JEH	Journal of Ecclesiastical History
JEconHist	Journal of Economic History
JEngL	Journal of English Linguistics
JHA	Journal for the History of Astronomy
JHI	Journal of the History of Ideas
JHM	Journal of the History of Medicine
JHP	Journal of the History of Philosophy
JMRS	Journal of Medieval and Renaissance Studies
JNT	Journal of Narrative Technique
JP	Journal of Philosophy
JR	Journal of Religion
JRME	Journal of Research in Music Education
JSA	Journal of the Society of Archivists
JTS	Journal of Theological Studies (London)
JWCI	Journal of the Warburg and Courtauld Institutes
JWH	Journal of World History
KCUJ	Kobe City University Journal
KFLQ	Kentucky Foreign Language Quarterly
KN	Kwartalnik Neofilologiczny (Warsaw)
KnT	Knight's Tale
L&P	Literature and Psychology (University of Hartford)
LangQ	Language Quarterly (University of South Florida)
Lang&S	Language and Style: An International Journal
Laographia:	Hellēnikē lāographikē hetaireia (Athens)
LauR	Laurel Review (West Virginia Wesleyan College)
LC	Library Chronicle (University of Pennsylvania)
LeedsSE	Leeds Studies in English
LGW	Legend of Good Women
LHR	Lock Haven Review (Lock Haven State College, Pennsylvania)
Library	The Library, fifth series
Listener, The	(British Broadcasting Corporation, London)
LitArts	Liturgical Arts (Concord, New Hampshire)
LJ	Library Journal
LT	Levende Talen

MA	Le Moyen Âge
MAE	Medium Aevum
M&H	Medievalia et Humanistica, 1970-new series, (Case Western Reserve University; 1973- North Texas State University)
M&L	Music and Letters (London)
ManT	Manciple's Tale
Manuscripta	(St. Louis University Library)
MassR	Massachusetts Review
McNR	McNeese Review (McNeese State College, Louisiana)
ME	Musikerziehung: Zeitschrift der Musikerzieher Oesterreichs
MedArch	Medieval Archaeology
MedH	Medical History
Mens en Mel	Mens en Melodie
MerT	Merchant's Tale
MF	Die Musikforschung
MH	Musikhandel: offizielles Fachblatt für den Handel mit Musikalien, Schallplatten, Musikinstrumenten und Zubehoer
MHRA	Modern Humanities Research Association
MI	Music Index (no. 2044 in this bibliography)
MilT	Miller's Tale
MLAA	Modern Language Association of America Abstracts (no. 16 in this bibliography)
MLJ	Modern Language Journal
MLN	Modern Language Notes
MLQ	Modern Language Quarterly
MLR	Modern Language Review
MLT	Man of Law's Tale
MonT	Monk's Tale
Moreana	(Angers)
Mosaic:	A Journal for the Comparative Study of Literature and Ideas (University of Manitoba)
MP	Modern Philology
MR	Massachusetts Review (University of Massachusetts)
MRS	Medieval and Renaissance Studies
MS	Mediaeval Studies (Toronto)
MSCS	Mankato State College Studies
MSE	Massachusetts Studies in English
MSpr	Moderna Sprak (Stockholm)
MSS	Manuscripts
Mus&Mus	Music and Musicians
MusDisc	Musica Discipline: A Yearbook of the History of Music
MusEdJ	Music Educators Journal
MusEvents	Musical Events
Musica:	Zweimonatsschrift für alle Gebiete des Musiklebens
Mus in Schule	Musik in der Schule: Zeitschrift für Theorie und Praxis des Musikunterrichts
MusJ	Music Journal
MusQ	Musical Quarterly

MusR	The Musical Review (Cambridge, England)
MusT	The Musical Times (London)
MusTcr	Music Teacher and Piano Student
Mus u Ges	Musik und Gesellschaft
Muzyka:	Kwartalnik poswiecony historii i teorii muzyki
N&Q	Notes and Queries, new series
NCarF	North Carolina Folklore
NCBEL	The New Cambridge Bibliography of English Literature (no. 19 in this bibliography)
NDEJ	Notre Dame English Journal
NEMLA Newsl:	A Publication of the Northeast Modern Language Association (formerly New York-Pennsylvania MLA)
Neophil	Neophilologus (Groningen)
NICEM	National Information Center for Educational Media (University of Southern California, Los Angeles, California, 90007)
NK	Narodna kultura (Sofia)
NM	Neuphilologische Mitteilungen: Bulletin of the Modern Language Society (Porthania University)
NMS	Nottingham Medieval Studies
Notes:	The Quarterly Journal of the Music Library Association (Ann Arbor)
NPT	Nun's Priest's Tale
NSt	New Statesman
NTg	De Nieuwe Taalgids
NwMSCS	Northwest Missouri State College Studies
NYHTB	New York Herald Tribune Book Review
NYRB	New York Review of Books
NYSJM	New York State Journal of Medicine
NZ	Neue Zeitschrift für Musik
NZZ	Neue Zürcher Zeitung
OJES	Osmania Journal of English Studies
OL	Orbis Litterarum
OrbisMus	Orbis Musicae: Studies in Musicology (Tel-Aviv University)
PardT	Pardoner's Tale
ParsT	Parson's Tale
PBA	Proceedings of the British Academy
PBSA	Papers of the Bibliographical Society of America
PCP	Pacific Coast Philology
PCTEB	Pennsylvania Council of Teachers of English Bulletin
PELL	Papers on English Language and Literature
Personalist:	An International Review of Philosophy (University of Southern California)
PF	Parliament of Fowls
PhR	Philosophical Review
PhysT	Physician's Tale
PLL	Papers on Language and Literature (formerly PELL)
PLPLS-LHS	Proceedings of the Leeds Philosophical and Literary Society, Literature and History Section
PMASAL	Papers of the Michigan Academy of Science, Arts, and Letters

PMLA	Publications of the Modern Language Association of America
PMLAB	PMLA International Bibliography (no. 17 in this bibliography)
PMMLA	Papers of the Midwest MLA
PPR	Philosophy and Phenomenological Research (Buffalo, New York)
PQ	Philological Quarterly
PriorT	Prioress' Tale
PSNLS	Publications of the Society for New Language Study
PULC	Princeton University Library Chronicle
QJS	Quarterly Journal of Speech
QQ	Queen's Quarterly
QR	Quarterly Review
R&MM	Recorder and Music Magazine (London)
RBelgeMus	Revue Belge de Musicologie
RBPH	Revue Belge de philologie et d'histoire (Brussels)
RdeMus	Revue de Musicologie
Reeve'sT	Reeve's Tale
REL	Review of English Litterature
Rendezvous:	Journal of Arts and Letters (Idaho State University)
RenP	Renaissance Papers
RenQ	Renaissance Quarterly
RES	Review of English Studies, new series
RLC	Revue de Littérature Comparée
RLV	Revue des Langues Vivantes (Bruxelles)
RMA	Royal Music Association Proceedings (Birmingham, England)
RN	Renaissance News
RoHum	Roczniki Humanistyczne (Lublin, Poland)
RomN	Romance Notes (University of North Carolina)
RPh	Romance Philology
RR	Romanic Review
RS	Research Studies (Washington State University)
RSH	Revue des Sciences Humaines
RUO	Revue de l'Université d'Ottawa
RUSE	Rutgers University Studies in English
SAB	South Atlantic Bulletin
Saga Book	(Viking Society for Northern Research)
SAQ	South Atlantic Quarterly
SatR	The Saturday Review
SB	Studies in Bibliography: Papers of the Bibliographical Society of the University of Virginia
SCB	South Central Bulletin
SciAmer	Scientific American
SCN	Seventeenth Century News
ScR	Strumenti Critici (Torino)
SchweizMus	Schweizerische Musikzeitung
Secolul:	revista de literatura universala (Bucharest, Romania)
SEL	Studies in English Literature, 1500–1900
SELit	Studies in English Literature (English Literary Society of Japan)

MASTER LIST AND TABLE OF ABBREVIATIONS

Seminar: A Journal of Germanic Studies (Victoria College, Toronto; and Newcastle University, New South Wales)
SEngL — Studies in English Literature (The Hague)
SewR — Sewanee Review
SFQ — Southern Folklore Quarterly
ShakS — Shakespeare Studies (University of Cincinnati)
ShT — Shipman's Tale
SHum — Studies in the Humanities
SIK — Studi Italici (Kyoto)
SJW — Shakespeare-Jahrbuch (Weimar)
SLitI — Studies in the Literary Imagination (Georgia State College)
SlovHud — Slovenska Hudba/Slovak Music (Bratislava, CSSR, Czechoslovakia)
SLUB — Studii de literatura universala (Bucharest)
SMC — Studies in Medieval Culture (Western Michigan University)
SN — Studia Neophilologica
SNT — Second Nun's Tale
SoQ — Southern Quarterly
SoR — Southern Review (Louisiana State University)
SoRA — Southern Review: An Australian Journal of Literary Studies (University of Adelaide)
SP — Studies in Philology
Spec — Speculum
Spect — Spectator
SpL — Spiegel der Letteren
Sprache — Die Sprache: Zeitschrift für Sprachwissenschaft (Wien)
SqT — Squire's Tale
SRen — Studies in the Renaissance
SSF — Studies in Short Fiction (Newberry College, South Carolina)
SSL — Studies in Scottish Literature (University of South Carolina)
StudiaMus — Studia Musicologica
Studies: An Irish Quarterly Review (Dublin)
StudiesMus — Studies in Music
SumT — Summoner's Tale
SUS — Susquehanna University Studies (Selingsgrove, Pennsylvania)
SvenskTid — Svensk Tidskrift för Musikforskning
Tablet (London and Brooklyn)
T&C — Troilus and Criseyde
Theoria: A Journal of Studies in the Arts, Humanities and Social Sciences
Thoth (Department of English, Syracuse University)
Thought: A Review of Culture and Idea
TLS — [London] Times Literary Supplement
Trivium (St. David's College, Lampeter, Cardiganshire, Wales)
TSB — Thoreau Society Bulletin
TSE — Tulane Studies in English
TSL — Tennessee Studies in Literature
TSLL — Texas Studies in Literature and Language

UCPES	University of California Publications, English Studies
UCTSE	University of Cape Town Studies in English
UES	Unisa English Studies
UMSE	University of Mississippi Studies in English
UNCSCL	University of North Carolina Studies in Comparative Literature
UNCSRLL	University of North Carolina Studies in Romance Languages and Literatures
Universitas	(Stuttgart)
UPortR	University of Portland Review
UR	University Review (Kansas City, Missouri)
UTDEMS	University of Tulsa Department of English Monograph Series
UTQ	University of Toronto Quarterly
Ventures:	Magazine of the Yale Graduate School
Viator:	Medieval and Renaissance Studies (Berkeley)
VJ	Vassar Journal of Undergraduate Series
VNM	Tijdschrift van de Vereniging voor Nederlandse Muziekgeschiedenis
VQR	Virginia Quarterly Review
WascanaR	Wascana Review (Regina, Saskatchewan)
WBEP	Weiner Beiträge zur Englischen Philologie
WBT	Wife of Bath's Tale
WCR	West Coast Review
WF	Western Folklore
WHR	Western Humanities Review
WSL	Wisconsin Studies in Literature
WSLL	Western Studies in Language and Literature (Ankara)
XUS	Xavier University Studies
YCGL	Yearbook of Comparative and General Literature
YES	Yearbook of English Studies (MHRA)
YR	Yale Review
YSE	Yale Studies in English
YWES	The Year's Work in English Studies (no. 6 in this bibliography
ZAA	Zeitschrift für Anglistik und Amerikanistik (East Berlin)
Zvuk:	Jugoslovenska muzicka revija

A Bibliography of Chaucer, 1964-1973

Bibliography

See Griffith, pp. 5-12; Crawford, pp. 3-6.

1   BAUGH, ALBERT C. Chaucer. Goldentree Bibliographies. New
        York: Appleton-Century-Crofts, 1968. 143 pp.

2   BURROW, J. A. "Chaucer, c. 1343-1400," in English Poetry:
        Select Bibliographical Guides. Edited by A. E. Dyson.
        London and New York: Oxford University Press, 1971,
        pp. 1-14.

2.01 BOOK REVIEW INDEX. Edited by Mildred Schlientz. Detroit,
        Book Tower: Gale Research Company. Vol. 1 (1965)--.

3   "CHAUCER RESEARCH," 1964-73. Reports No. 25, 26 of the
        Committee of Research and Bibliography of the Chaucer
        Group of the Modern Language Association of America.
        Edited by Thomas A. Kirby (Chairman), Martin M. Crow, and
        Charles S. Muscatine. Reports No. 27-33, ChauR, 1-8
        (1967-73); ChauR, 1 (1967), 186-99; ChauR, 2 (1968), 191-
        204; ChauR, 3 (1969), 204-22; ChauR, 4 (1970), 211-27;
        ChauR, 6 (1971), 64-79; ChauR, 7 (1972), 67-83; ChauR, 8
        (1973), 71-85.
            Abstr. in AES, 16 (1972-73), no. 1577.

4   "CHAUCER RESEARCH IN PROGRESS," compiled by Thomas A. Kirby.
        Published annually in NM, 70 (1969)--: NM, 70 (1969),
        545-55; NM, 71 (1970), 505 15; NM, 72 (1971), 517-25; NM,
        73 (1972), 708-15; NM, 74 (1973), 534-40.
            Abstr. in AES, 16 (1972-73), no. 333.

5   CRAWFORD, WILLIAM R. Bibliography of Chaucer 1954-63.
        Seattle and London: University of Washington Press, 1967.
        188 pp.
            First supplement to Griffith, 7 below.
            Reviews: Beryl Rowland, AN&Q, 6 (1967), 45-46; E. G.
        Stanley, N&Q, 15 (1968), 42; Paul Bacquet, EA, 21 (1968),
        300; TLS (22 February, 1968), p. 184; Rossell Hope Robbins,

Bibliography

Archiv, 205 (1969), 65–66; R. S. Rainbow, Jr., MP, 66
(1969), 273–74; P. M. Vermeer, ES, 52 (1971), 164–65.
See also: John Pilkington, Jr., "A Crawford Bibliography." UMSE, 4 (1963), 1-20.

6   THE ENGLISH ASSOCIATION. The Year's Work in English Studies.
Edited by various hands: beginning with 1964, by T. S.
Dorsch, C. G. Harlow, James Redmond, and others. London,
1921--(1964--).
Contains short descriptions of selected items. Authors
of the Chaucer sections are Joyce Bazire and David Mills.

7   GRIFFITH, DUDLEY DAVID. Bibliography of Chaucer 1908-1953.
Seattle: University of Washington Press, 1955. 416 pp.
See Crawford, p. 4.

8   HARTUNG, ALBERT E., ed. A Manual of the Writings in Middle
English, 1051-1500. Hamden, Connecticut: Shoe String
Press, 1973. 4 vols., 1313 pp.

8.01 AN INDEX TO BOOK REVIEWS IN THE HUMANITIES. Detroit and
Williamston, Michigan: Phillip Thompson. 1960--(1964--).

9   INTERNATIONAL GUIDE TO MEDIEVAL STUDIES: A Quarterly Index
to Periodical Literature. Darien, Connecticut: American
Bibliographic Service. Vol. 1 (1961)--.
Includes annotations of articles.

10   INTERNATIONAL INSTITUTE OF INTELLECTUAL COOPERATION. Index
translationum: Répertoire international des traductions.
New series. Paris. Vol. 1 (1948)--.

11   INTERNATIONALE BIBLIOGRAPHIE DER REZENSIONEN WISSENSCHAFTLICHER
LITERATUR [International Bibliography of Book Reviews of
Scholarly Literature]. Edited by Otto Zeller. Osnabrück:
Felix Dietrich Verlag, 1971--.

12   INTERNATIONALE BIBLIOGRAPHIE DER ZEITSCHRIFTEN-LITERATUR AUS
ALLEN GEBIETEN DES WISSENS [International Bibliography of
Periodical Literature Covering All Fields of Knowledge].
Edited by Otto Zeller. Osnabrück: Felix Dietrich Verlag,
1965-- for 1963/4--.

13   JAHRESVERZEICHNIS DER DEUTSCHEN HOCHSCHULSCHRIFTEN, 1885--.
Bearb. von der Deutschen Bücherei. Leipzig: Verlag für
Buch- und Bibliothekswesen, 1887--(1964--).
Lists German dissertations.

13.01 KIRBY, THOMAS. See 3 and 4 above.

14   THE MEDIAEVAL ACADEMY OF AMERICA. "Bibliography of American
         Periodical Literature," published quarterly in Speculum:
         A Journal of Mediaeval Studies, 1934--(1964--).
            Note also: "Books Received" in each issue of Speculum,
         and "Bibliography of Editions and Translations of Medieval
         Texts in Progress" by Louis L. Gioia in each January issue,
         beginning with 1973.

15   THE MODERN HUMANITIES RESEARCH ASSOCIATION. Annual Bibliog-
         raphy of English Language and Literature. Edited by
         Marjorie Rigby, Charles Nilon, John Horden, and James B.
         Misenheimer, Jr. Cambridge, 1920--(1964--).
            Notes reviews.

16   MODERN LANGUAGE ASSOCIATION OF AMERICA. Abstracts of Articles
         in Scholarly Journals. Compiled by John H. Fisher,
         Walter S. Achtert, and Eileen Mackesy. New York, 1970--.
            To be used in conjunction with MLA International Bibliog-
         raphy, 17 below.

17   MODERN LANGUAGE ASSOCIATION OF AMERICA. International Bibliog-
         raphy of Books and Articles on the Modern Languages and
         Literatures. Compiled by Paul A. Brown, Harrison T.
         Meserole, et al. New York, 1964--.
            See Crawford, p. 5.

18   NATIONAL COUNCIL OF TEACHERS OF ENGLISH. Abstracts of English
         Studies. Boulder, Colorado, 1964--.
            See Crawford, p. 5.

19   THE NEW CAMBRIDGE BIBLIOGRAPHY OF ENGLISH LITERATURE. Vol. I,
         600-1660. Edited by George Watson. Cambridge University
         Press, 1974.
            See pp. 557-628 for Chaucer bibliography.

20   QUARTERLY CHECK-LIST OF MEDIEVALIA: An International Subject
         Index of Current Books, Monographs, Brochures and Sepa-
         rates. Darien, Connecticut: American Bibliographic
         Service, 1958--(Vol. 7, no. 1, January, 1964--).

20.01 ROBBINS, ROSSELL HOPE. "The Chaucerian Apocrypha," in 8
         above, vol. 4, pp. 1286-1306.

Bibliography

For occasional Chaucer items, see also:

21 THE AMERICAN COMPARATIVE LITERATURE ASSOCIATION. Yearbook
    of Comparative and General Literature. Published at
    Indiana University in collaboration with The National
    Council of Teachers of English. Bloomington: Indiana
    University, nos. 13 (1964)--.

22 BIBLIOGRAPHIE LINGUISTIQUE DE L'ANNÉE...et complément des
    années précédentes. Publiée par le Comité International
    Permanent de Linguistes sous les auspices du Conseil
    International de la Philosophie et des Sciences Humaines.
    Utrecht, Antwerp: Editions Spectrum, 1949--(1964--).

23 BINDOFF, S[TANLEY] T[HOMAS] and JAMES T. BOULTON, eds.
    Research in Progress in English and Historical Studies in
    the Universities of the British Isles. London, Chicago:
    St. James Press, 1971. 117 pp.

24 COLEMAN, ARTHUR. Epic and Romance Criticism. A Checklist of
    Interpretations 1940-72 of English and American Epics and
    Metrical Romances. Vol. 1. New York: Watermill Pub-
    lishers, 1973. 414 pp.
        Includes obscure items, but is careless and unreliable.

25 ESSAY AND GENERAL LITERATURE INDEX. New York: Wilson,
    1934--(1964--).

26 THE MODERN HUMANITIES RESEARCH ASSOCIATION. The Year's Work
    in Modern Language Studies. Cambridge, 1931--(1964--).

27 STAFFORD, P. A., ed. International Medieval Bibliography.
    Directed by R. S. Hoyt and P. H. Sawyer. For 1968-69:
    4 Headingley Terrace, Leeds 6, England; Department of
    History, University of Minnesota, Minneapolis, Minnesota
    55455, USA. For 1970: Leeds: W. J. Maney, 1972.

28 ORTEGO, PHILIP DARRAUGH. "A Bibliography of Chaucer's French
    Sources." BB, 27 (1970), 72-76.

See also: 1718; 2043.

Festschriften and Collections

29 ATWOOD, E. BAGBY and ARCHIBALD A. HILL, eds. Studies in
    Language, Literature, and Culture of the Middle Ages and
    Later. Austin: University of Texas Press, 1969. 406 pp.

30 BESSINGER, JESS B., JR. and ROBERT P. CREED, eds.
    Franciplegius: Medieval and Linguistic Studies in Honor
    of Francis Peabody Magoun, Jr. New York: New York Uni-
    versity Press, 1965. 323 pp.

31 BLOOMFIELD, MORTON W. Essays and Explorations: Studies in
    Ideas, Language, and Literature. Cambridge, Massachusetts:
    Harvard University Press, 1970. 331 pp.
        Collection of Bloomfield's articles and reviews.

32 BOLTON, WHITNEY FRANK., ed. The Middle Ages. Sphere History
    of Literature in the English Language, 1. London:
    Barrie & Jenkins, 1970. 450 pp.

33 BRADDY, HALDEEN. Geoffrey Chaucer: Literary and Historical
    Studies. London; Port Washington: Kennikat, 1971.
    170 pp.
        Twenty-three literary and historical studies and five
    reviews, reprinted.
        Reviews: Hoyt Duggan, CEA, 35, iv (May, 1973), 28-32.

34 BRAHMER, MIECZYSLAW, STANISLAW HELSZTYŃSKI and JULIAN
    KRŻYZANOWSKI, eds. Studies in Language and Literature in
    Honour of Margaret Schlauch. Warsaw: Państwowe
    Wydawnictwo Naukowe, 1966; New York: Russell & Russell,
    1971. 483 pp.

35 BREWER, D. S. Chaucer and Chaucerians: Critical Studies in
    Middle English Literature. London: Nelson; University,
    *Alabama: University of Alabama, 1966. 278 pp.
        Nine new essays by various hands.
        Reviews: TLS (25 Aug., 1966), p. 765; R. M. Wilson,
    Eng, 16 (1966), 106-107; Kemp Malone, Spec, 42 (1967),
    358-62; Douglas Gray, N&Q, 15 (1968), 65-66; R. H. Robbins,

Festschriften and Collections

Archiv, 205 (1969), 67–68; P. M. Vermeer, ES, 52 (1971), 61–65; Martin Lehnert, ZAA, 18 (1970), 187–90.

36   BURROW, J. A., ed. Geoffrey Chaucer: A Critical Anthology.
        Baltimore, Maryland: Penguin, 1969.
        Excerpts and selections from fourteenth century to the
        present.
        Reviews: S. S. Hussey, N&Q, 17 (1970), 227–28; Gail M.
        Eifrig, Cresset, 34, iii (1971), 23.

37   CAWLEY, ARTHUR C., ed. Chaucer's Mind and Art. Edinburgh
        and London: Oliver and Boyd, 1969; New York: Barnes &
        Noble, 1970. 220 pp.
        Four new and six reprinted essays.
        Reviews: R. MacG. Dawson, DalR, 49 (1969), 429–30;
        D. Biggins, AUMLA, 33 (1970), 109–110; R. T. Davies, N&Q,
        17 (1970), 65–67; Morton W. Bloomfield, "Essays on
        Chaucer," YR, 60 (1971), 438–40.
        See also 373.

38   COLQUITT, BETSY FEAGAN, ed. Studies in Medieval, Renaissance,
        American Literature: A Festschrift (Honoring Troy C.
        Crenshaw, Lorraine Sherley, and Ruth Speer Angell).
        Fort Worth: Texas Christian University Press, 1971.
        205 pp.

39   DONALDSON, E. TALBOT. Speaking of Chaucer. London:
        Athlone Press; New York: W. W. Norton, 1970. 190 pp.
        Four new and eight reprinted essays.
        Reviews: TLS (4 September, 1970), p. 977; Morton W.
        Bloomfield, "Essays on Chaucer," YR, 60 (1971), 438–40;
        John A. Yunck, Criticism, 13 (1971), 420–22; J. R. Simon,
        EA, 25 (1972), 45–48; 54–55; D. S. Brewer, YES, 2 (1972),
        241–43.

40   DORSCH, T. S., ed. Essays and Studies 1972 in Honor of Beatrice
        White. Being Volume Twenty-Five of the New Series of
        Essays and Studies Collected for the English Association.
        New York: Humanities Press, 1972. 134 pp.

41   ELLIS, J. R., ed. Australasian Universities Language and
        Literature Association: Proceedings and Papers of the
        Thirteenth Congress Held at Monash University 12–18
        August 1970. Melbourne: AULLA and Monash University,
        1971. 493 pp.

42   EMERY, J. K., ed. University of Colorado Studies. Series in
        Language and Literature, 10. Boulder: University of
        Colorado Press, 1966.

43   ESCH, ARNO, ed. Chaucer und seine Zeit: Symposion für
     Walter F. Schirmer. Buchreihe der Anglia, Zeitschrift
     für englische Philologie, 14. Tübingen: Max Niemeyer,
     1968. 450 pp.

44   FOWLER, ROGER, ed. Essays on Style and Language: Linguistic
     and Critical Approaches to Literary Style. London:
     Routledge and Kegan Paul, 1966; *New York: Humanities
     Press, 1966. 197 pp.

45   GARDNER, JOHN and NICHOLAS JOOST, eds. Papers on the Art and
     Age of Geoffrey Chaucer. PLL, 3, Summer supplement
     (1967). Edwardsville and Carbondale, Illinois: Southern
     Illinois University, 1967. 109 pp.
        Reviews: Spec, 43 (1968), 392-93; F. C. DeVries,
     Neophil, 53 (1969), 99-101.

46   HAYDEN, DONALD E., ed. His Firm Estate: Essays in Honor of
     Franklin James Eikenberry by Former Students...UTDEMS, 2.
     Tulsa, Oklahoma: The University of Tulsa, 1967. 94 pp.

47   HOLMES, URBAN T., ed. Romance Studies in Memory of Edward
     Billings Ham. California State College Publications, 2.
     Hayward, California: California State College Press,
     1967. 169 pp.

48   HOY, MICHAEL and MICHAEL STEVENS. Chaucer's Major Tales.
     London: Norton Bailey, 1969. 178 pp.
        Seven new critical essays.

49   HUTTAR, CHARLES A., ed. Imagination and the Spirit: Essays
     in Literature and the Christian Faith Presented to
     Clyde S. Kilby. Grand Rapids, Michigan: Eerdmans, 1971.
     512 pp.

50   JOHNSON, WILLIAM C., JR. and LOREN C. GRUBER, eds. New Views
     on Chaucer: Essays in Generative Criticism. PSNLS, 1.
     Denver, Colorado: Society for New Language Study, 1973.
     50 pp.

51   KELLOGG, ALFRED L., et al. Chaucer, Langland, Arthur: Essays
     in Middle English Literature. New Brunswick, New Jersey:
     Rutgers University Press, 1972. 385 pp.
        Eight new and twelve reprinted essays (four on Chaucer).

52   KUHL, ERNEST P. Studies in Chaucer and Shakespeare. Edited
     by Elizabeth K. Belting. Beloit, Wisconsin: Belting
     Publications, 1971. 440 pp.
        Twenty-two reprinted essays on Chaucer (1913-1947).

Festschriften and Collections

53   LAWLOR, JOHN, ed. Patterns of Love and Courtesy: Essays in
     Memory of C. S. Lewis. Evanston, Illinois: Northwestern
     University Press; London: Edward Arnold, 1966. 206 pp.

54   MAEKAWA, SHUNICHI. Maekawa Shunichi Kyōju Kanreki Kinen-
     ronbunshū [Essays and Studies in Commemoration of Pro-
     fessor Shunichi Maekawa's Sixty-First Birthday]. Tokyo:
     Eihōsha, 1968. 382 pp.

55   MANDEL, JEROME and BRUCE A. ROSENBERG, eds. Medieval Liter-
     ature and Folklore Studies: Essays in Honor of Francis
     Lee Utley. New Brunswick, New Jersey: Rutgers
     University Press, 1970. 416 pp.

56   MITCHELL, JEROME and WILLIAM PROVOST, eds. Chaucer the Love
     Poet. Athens: University of Georgia Press, 1973.
     126 pp.

57   MUSTANOJA, TAUNO F. Studies Presented to Tauno F. Mustanoja
     on the Occasion of His Sixtieth Birthday. Special
     edition of NM, 73 (1972), i-ii. 496 pp.

58   NEWSTEAD, HELAINE, ed. Chaucer and His Contemporaries:
     Essays on Medieval Literature and Thought. Greenwich,
     Connecticut: Fawcett, 1968. 352 pp.
         Twenty reprinted essays, nine on Chaucer.

59   PEARSALL, D[EREK] A[LBERT] and R. A. WALDRON, eds. Medieval
     Literature and Civilization: Studies in Memory of G. N.
     Garmonsway. London: University of London, Athlone
     Press, 1969. 352 pp.
         Reviews: P. J. Franks, DUJ, 32 (1970), 70-72.

60   ROWLAND, BERYL, ed. Companion to Chaucer Studies. Toronto;
     New York: Oxford University Press, 1968. 409 pp.
         Twenty-two reviews of criticism.
         Reviews: R. MacG. Dawson, DalR, 48 (1968), 583-85;
     P. W. Rogers, QQ, 75 (1968), 751-53; TLS (15 May, 1969),
     p. 517; Sumner J. Ferris, AN&Q, 7 (1969), 77-78; F. C.
     DeVries, Neophil, 53 (1969), 334-35; R. T. Davies, RES,
     20 (1969), 477-79; Martin Lehnert, ZAA, 18 (1970),
     187-90; Dieter Mehl, Ang, 88 (1970), 535-37; Helaine
     Newstead, RPh, 24 (1970), 349-53; Hanspeter Schelp,
     Archiv, 207 (1970), 301-304; R. M. Wilson, YES, 1 (1971),
     216-18; J. R. Simon, EA, 25 (1972), 52-53.
         See also, 60.01.

Festschriften and Collections

60.01 RAMBLER, LINDA KAY. An Index to Beryl Rowland's Companion to
      Chaucer Studies. Bethlehem, Pennsylvania, 1970. 69 pp.
        Available from the author, C 201 Pattee Library,
      University Park, Pennsylvania, 16802.

61   SCHULZ, MAX F., WILLIAM D. TEMPLEMAN and CHARLES R. METZGER,
      eds. Essays in American and English Literature Presented
      to Bruce Robert McElderry, Jr. Athens, Ohio: Ohio
      University Press, 1968. 358 pp.

62   SULLIVAN, SHEILA, ed. Critics on Chaucer: Readings in
      Literary Criticism. London: Allen and Unwin; *Coral
      Gables, Florida: University of Miami Press, 1970.
      139 pp.
        Includes excerpts from Dryden, Arnold, Woolf, and
      modern critics.
        Reviews: A. C. Cawley, DUJ, 64 (1971), 70-71; S. S.
      Hussey, N&Q, 18 (1971), 72-73.

63   TREWEEK, A. P., ed. Australasian Universities Language and
      Literature Assocation: Proceedings and Papers of the
      Twelfth Congress Held at the University of Western
      Australia, 5-11 February, 1969. Sidney: AULLA, 1970.
      504 pp.

64   ZANDVOORT, R[EINARD] W[ILLEM]. English Studies Presented to
      R. W. Zandvoort on the Occasion of his Seventieth
      Birthday. ES, 45 (Supplement, 1964). 284 pp.

Life

See Griffith, pp. 13-27; Crawford, pp. 7-8.

65   BAUGH, ALBERT C.   "The Background of Chaucer's Mission to
        Spain," in 43, pp. 55-69.

66   BAUGH, ALBERT C.   "Chaucer the Man," in 60, pp. 1-19.

67   BOLTON, W. F.   "Chaucer's Life," in 32, chapter 5, part 1,
        pp. 159-62.
          Brief general survey.

68   BREWER, DEREK [STANLEY].   Chaucer in His Time.   London:
        Thomas Nelson, 1963.   243 pp.
          General culture of Chaucer's day.   See Crawford, p. 7.
          Reviews: George Holmes, Listener, 71 (1964), 729;
        TLS (11 June, 1964), p. 510; R. T. Davies, N&Q, 11 (1964),
        195-96; T. W. Craik, MLR, 60 (1965), 91; Donald W.
        Sutherland, Spec, 40 (1965), 128-29; P. Mroczkowski, MAE,
        34 (1965), 277-79.

69   CROW, MARTIN M[ICHAEL] and CLAIR C. OLSON, eds.   Chaucer Life-
        Records.   Oxford: Clarendon Press, 1966.   655 pp.
          Reviews: Beryl Rowland, AN&Q, 5 (1966), 29-31; TLS
        (22 September, 1966), p. 882; Morton W. Bloomfield, Spec,
        42 (1967), 365-66; Haldeen Braddy, JEGP, 66 (1967), 441-
        43; G. S. Ivy, DUJ, 28 (1967), 165-66; John Lawlor, RES,
        18 (1967), 450-51; D. S. Brewer, N&Q, 14 (1967), 36-37;
        Norman E. Eliason, SAQ, 66 (1967), 484-85; David M.
        Bevington, MP, 65 (1968), 369-70.

70   GARBÁTY, THOMAS JAY.   "Chaucer in Spain, 1366: Soldier of
        Fortune or Agent of the Crown?" ELN, 5 (1967), 81-87.
        Abstr. in AES, 12 (1969), no. 1487.

71   MAGOUN, FRANCIS P[EABODY].   A Chaucer Gazetteer.   Chicago
        and London: University of Chicago Press, 1961.   173 pp.
          See Crawford, p. 23.

12

Reviews: *Klaus Weimann, Archiv, 201 (1964), 136;
*P. Mertens-Fonck, RBPH, 42 (1964), 301; D. S. Brewer,
ES, 49 (1968) 147-48; Kelsie B. Harder, Names, 16 (1968),
66-67.

72   MITCHELL, JEROME. "Hoccleve's Supposed Friendship with
Chaucer." ELN, 4 (1966), 9-12. Abstr. in AES, 10 (1967)
no. 3263.

73   MITCHELL, JEROME. "Hoccleve's Tribute to Chaucer," in 43,
pp. 275-83.

74   OLSON, CLAIR. "Chaucer and Fourteenth-Century Society," in
60, pp. 20-37.

75   *PICHETTE, KATHRYN HOYE. "Chaucer's Lollard Friend, Sir
Richard Stury." DA, 29 (1969), 3584A. University of
Colorado, 1968. 113 pp.

76   SHUGRUE, MICHAEL. "The Urry Chaucer (1721) and the London
Uprising of 1384: A Phase in Chaucerian Biography."
JEGP, 65 (1966), 229-37. Abstr. in AES, 10 (1967),
no. 125.

77   STANLEY-WRENCH, MARGARET. Chaucer: Teller of Tales.
Tadworth, Surrey: The World's Works Ltd., The Press at
Kingswood, 1967. 192 pp.
    Originally published in the U.S.A. by Hawthorn Books,
Inc. as Teller of Tales, 1965.

78   WILLIAMS, GEORGE. "Chaucer and John of Gaunt," in 386,
chapter 2, pp. 20-55.

79   WINNY, JAMES. "Chaucer Himself," in 258, pp. 1-27.

79.01 WOOLF, VIRGINIA. "The Pastons and Chaucer," in 58,
pp. 218-34.
    Reprinted from The Common Reader by Virginia Woolf.
New York: Harcourt, Brace and World, 1925, 1953. Ex-
cerpt also reprinted in 62, pp. 17-22.

See also: 198, 206, 224, 255, 258, 317, 353, 379, 386, 387, 416,
684, 1595, 1596, 1683, 1640, 1699. For reprinted materials prior to
1964, see 33.

Manuscripts

See Griffith, pp. 28-40; Crawford, pp. 9-10.

80 CAMPBELL, JACKSON J. "Chaucer's Canterbury Tales." <u>PULC</u>,
    26 (1964), 5-6.
       Princeton Acquisition of the Tollemache Manuscript.

81 CHAUCER, GEOFFREY. <u>The Works, 1532, [of] Geoffrey Chaucer</u>,
    (with supplementary material from the editions of 1542,
    1561, 1598 and 1602). Introduction by D. S. Brewer.
    Menston: Scolar Press, 1969. 1000 pp.
       Facsimile reprint of first printed edition, London.

82 CROW, MARTIN MICHAEL. "John of Angoulême and His Chaucer
    Manuscript," in 38, pp. 33-44.
       Revised version of essay originally published in <u>Spec</u>,
    17 (1942), 86-99.

83 DAVIS, NORMAN. "Chaucer's <u>Gentilesse</u>: A Forgotten Manu-
    script, With Some Proverbs." <u>RES</u>, 20 (1969), 43-50.
    Abstr. in <u>AES</u>, 14 (1970-71), no. 2942.

84 DIX, WILLIAM S. "Four Notable Acquisitions." <u>PULC</u>, 26
    (Autumn, 1964), 3-15. Abstr. in <u>AES</u>, 8 (1965), no.
    1764.
       Acquisition of a fifteenth-century manuscript of
    Chaucer's <u>Canterbury Tales</u>.

85 DOYLE, A. I. and GEORGE B. PACE. "A New Chaucer Manuscript."
    <u>PMLA</u>, 83 (1968), 22-34. Abstr. in <u>AES</u>, 11 (1968),
    no. 2625.
       A manuscript of six short poems.

86 DUNLEAVY, GARETH W. "The Chaucer Ascription in Trinity Col-
    lege Dublin Ms D 2 8." <u>Ambix</u>, 12 (1965), 1-21.

87 EDDEN, VALERIS. "The Phillipps Manuscript of Chaucer's
    <u>Troilus and Criseyde</u>." <u>Library</u>, 27 (1972), 53. Abstr.
    in <u>AES</u>, 16 (1972-73), no. 1574.

88   EDWARDS, A. S. G. "The Case of the Stolen Chaucer Manuscript."
      BC, 21 (1972), 380-85. Abstr. in AES, 17 (1973-74),
      no. 382.
        On the Cardigan Manuscript.

89   ELLIOT, CHARLES. "The Reeve's Prologue and Tale in the
      Ellesmere and Hengwrt Manuscripts." N&Q, 11 (1964),
      167-70. Abstr. in AES, 7 (1964), no. 2246.

90   GORDON, JOHN D. "An Anniversary Exhibition. The Henry W.
      and Albert A. Berg Collection: 1940-1965." Parts 1, 2,
      and 3. BNYPL, 69 (October, November, December, 1965),
      537-54, 597-608, 665-77.
        The Third Edition of The Canterbury Tales, c. 1491.

91   HETHERINGTON, JOHN R. Chaucer, 1532-1602. Notes and facsim-
      ile texts designed to facilitate the identification of
      defective copies of the black-letter folio editions of
      1532, 1542, c. 1550, 1561, 1598 and 1602. Vernon House,
      Birmingham: The Author, 1964; reissued, 1967. 21 pp.

92   *KLINEDINST, LLOYD F. "The Scribal Art of Textual Transmis-
      sion: A Study of Fifteenth-Century Manuscript Tradition
      in Nineteen Manuscripts Containing Selected Canterbury
      Tales." DAI, 33 (1972), 725A. The University of
      Florida, 1971. 130 pp.

93   *MORGAN, M. C. "Dr. William Brewster of Hereford (1665-1715):
      A Benefactor to Libraries." MedH, 7, ii (April, 1964),
      137-48. Cited in AES, 12 (1969), no. 1600.

94   NICHOLS, ROBERT E., JR. "Chaucer's Fortune, Truth, and
      Gentilesse: The 'Last' Unpublished Manuscript Transcrip-
      tions." Spec, 44 (1969), 46-50. Abstr. in AES, 16
      (1972-73), no. 948.

95   PACE, GEORGE B. "The Chaucerian Proverbs." SB, 18 (1965),
      41-48. Abstr. in AES, 9 (1966), no. 286.

96   PACE, GEORGE B. "Speght's Chaucer and [Cambridge University
      Library] Ms Gg 4.27." SB, 21 (1968), 225-35. Abstr. in
      AES, 11 (1968), no. 2084.

97   SCHULZ, HERBERT C. The Ellesmere Manuscript of Chaucer's
      Canterbury Tales. San Marino, California: Huntington
      Library, 1965. 26 pp.
        Includes five pages of colored plates.

Manuscripts

98   SOUTHALL, RAYMOND. "The Devonshire Manuscript Collection of
       Early Tudor Poetry, 1532-41." RES, 15 (1964), 142-50.
       Manuscript containing fragments from Troilus and
       Criseyde.

See also: 240, 424, 544, 655, 681.

Editions with Notes

See Griffith, pp. 41-48; Crawford, pp. 11-14.

99   BAUGH, ALBERT C., ed. Chaucer's Major Poetry. New York: Appleton-Century-Crofts, 1963; London: Routledge and Kegan Paul, 1964. 615 pp.
     See Crawford, p. 11.
     Reviews: D. Fox, MLR, 59 (1964), 624-25; John Burrow, EIC, 14 (1964), 307-10.

100   BETHURUM, DOROTHY, ed. The Squire's Tale. Oxford: Clarendon Press, 1965. 102 pp.
     Reviews: R. W. Zandvoort, ES, 47 (1966), 164.

101   BREWER, D. S. and L. ELISABETH BREWER, eds. Troilus and Criseyde (abridged). Routledge English Texts. London: Routledge and Kegan Paul, 1969. 214 pp.

102   COGHILL, NEVILL and CHRISTOPHER TOLKIEN, eds. The Man of Law's Tale. Harrap's English Classics. London: Harrap, 1969. 176 pp.

103   COOK, DANIEL, ed. Troilus and Criseyde. Anchor Books, A524. Garden City, New York: Doubleday, 1966. 520 pp.
     Reviews: Robert E. Nichols, Jr., CCC, 18 (1967), 120-21.

104   *DICKERSON, ALBERT INSKIP, JR. "Chaucer's Book of the Duchess: A Critical Edition with Introduction, Variants, Notes, and Glossary." DA, 29 (1969), 2256A. University of North Carolina at Chapel Hill, 1968. 325 pp.

105   *GRIFFIN, RUSSELL MORGAN. "Chaucer's Lyrics: Selected and Edited with Commentary, Canon, and Text." DAI, 32 (1971), 1472A. Case Western Reserve University, 1970. 319 pp.

106   HALVERSON, JOHN, ed. Geoffrey Chaucer: The Canterbury Tales. Indianapolis and New York: Bobbs-Merrill, 1971. 461 pp.

Editions with Notes

107   HIEATT, CONSTANCE B., ed. The Miller's Tale. New York:
       Odyssey Press, 1970. 85 pp.

108   HODGSON, PHYLLIS, ed. General Prologue to the Canterbury
       Tales. London: Athlone Press, 1969. 220 pp., 4 plates.
       Reviews: R. T. Davies, N&Q, 17 (1970), 65-67.

109   HOWARD, DONALD R., ed., with the assistance of JAMES DEAN.
       The Canterbury Tales: A Selection. New York: New
       American Library, 1969. 458 pp.

110   HUSSEY, MAURICE, ed. The Canon's Yeoman's Prologue and Tale
       from The Canterbury Tales. Selected Tales from Chaucer.
       Cambridge University Press, 1965. 86 pp.
       Text based on Robinson's second edition.

111   HUSSEY, MAURICE, ed. The Merchant's Prologue and Tale.
       Selected Tales from Chaucer. London and New York:
       Cambridge University Press, 1965. 116 pp.
       Text based on Robinson's second edition.

112   HUSSEY, MAURICE, ed. The Nun's Priest's Prologue and Tale.
       Selected Tales from Chaucer. London and New York:
       Cambridge University Press, 1965. 96 pp.
         Reviews: Dieter Mehl, Ang, 83 (1965), 494-95;
       P. M. Vermeer, LT (April, 1966), 278-81.

113   KEE, KENNETH, ed. Geoffrey Chaucer: A Selection of His
       Works. College Classics in English. Toronto: Macmillan;
       New York: St. Martin's, 1966. 246 pp.

114   KING, FRANCIS and BRUCE STEELE, eds. Geoffrey Chaucer: The
       Prologue and Three Tales. Melbourne: Cheshire, 1969.
       218 pp.

115   KING, FRANCIS and BRUCE STEELE, eds. Selections from Geoffrey
       Chaucer's The Canterbury Tales. Melbourne: Cheshire,
       1969. 407 pp.

116   NICHOLS, STEPHEN G., JR., ed. Le Roman de la Rose. New York:
       Appleton-Century-Crofts, 1967. 202 pp.
         Pp. 153-97, a translation of fragment A, The Romaunt of
       the Rose, attributed to Chaucer.

117   PRATT, ROBERT A., ed. Geoffrey Chaucer: Selections from The
       Tales of Canterbury and Short Poems. Riverside Editions,
       B 41. Boston: Houghton Mifflin, 1966. 447 pp.
         Reviews: J. A. Burrow, N&Q, 14 (1967), 264-65.

Editions with Notes

118   REEVES, JAMES, ed. Lyric and Allegory. New York: Barnes &
           Noble, 1971. 174 pp.
           Contains selections from Chaucer.
           Reviews: Hoyt Duggan, CEA, 35, iv (May, 1973), 31.

119   ROOT, ROBERT KILBURN, ed. Troilus and Criseyde. New edition.
           Princeton: Princeton University Press; London: Oxford
           University Press, 1967. 668 pp.
           Originally published in 1926. See Griffith, p. 46.

120   SPEARING, A[NTHONY] C[OLIN], ed. The Franklin's Prologue and
           Tale. Selected Tales from Chaucer. London: Cambridge
           University Press, 1966. 128 pp.

121   SPEARING, A[NTHONY] C[OLIN], ed. The Knight's Tale. Selected
           Tales from Chaucer. London and New York: Cambridge Uni-
           versity Press, 1966. 223 pp.
           Text based on Robinson's second edition.

122   SPEARING, A[NTHONY] C[OLIN], ed. The Pardoner's Prologue and
           Tale. Selected Tales from Chaucer. London: Cambridge
           University Press, 1965. 107 pp.
           Reviews: P. M. Vermeer, LT (April, 1966), 278-81;
           Helmut Bonheim, Ang, 85 (1967), 212-13.

123   SUTHERLAND, RONALD. The Romaunt of the Rose and Le Roman de
           la Rose: A Parallel-Text Edition. Oxford: Blackwell,
           1967; Berkeley: University of California Press, 1968.
           241 pp.
           Published dissertation. See Crawford, p. 95 and DA,
           29 (1968), 1215A.
           Reviews: Rouben Cholakian, MLJ, 52 (1968), 528.

124   WINNY, JAMES. The Clerk's Prologue and Tale. Selected Tales
           from Chaucer. London and New York: Cambridge University
           Press, 1966. 121 pp.
           Text based on Robinson's second edition.

125   WINNY, JAMES. The General Prologue to the Canterbury Tales.
           Selected Tales from Chaucer. London: Cambridge Univer-
           sity Press, 1965. 142 pp.

126   WINNY, JAMES. The Miller's Prologue and Tale from the
           Canterbury Tales. Selected Tales from Chaucer. London:
           Cambridge University Press, 1971. 108 pp.

Editions with Notes

127   WINNY, JAMES. The Wife of Bath's Prologue and Tale. Selected
          Tales from Chaucer. London: Cambridge University Press,
          1965. 143 pp.
             Reviews: P. M. Vermeer, LT (April, 1966), 278-81.

See also:

128   REISS, EDMUND. "Editions and Translations of Chaucer Now in
          Print." CE, 26 (1965), 572-79.

See also: 424, 654, 996.

Modernizations and Translations

See Griffith, pp. 49–57; Crawford, pp. 15–17.

1. ENGLISH MODERNIZATIONS

129   COGHILL, NEVILL, ed. and trans. A Choice of Chaucer's Verse.
          London: Faber, 1972. 235 pp.
             Selections from Skeat's edition with facing paraphrases
          in verse.

130   COGHILL, NEVILL, trans. Troilus and Criseyde. Harmondsworth:
          Penguin, 1971. 357 pp.

131   STANLEY-WRENCH, MARGARET, ed. and trans. Troilus and
          Criseyde. London: Centaur Press, 1965. 328 pp.
             Reviews: "In Vulgari Eloquentia," TLS (15 April, 1965),
          p. 295.

132   WRIGHT, DAVID, trans. The Canterbury Tales. London: Barrie
          and Rockliff, 1964. 311 pp.
             Reviews: TLS (24 December, 1964), p. 1164.

133   WRIGHT, HERBERT G., ed. A Seventeenth-Century Modernisation
          of the First Three Books of Chaucer's "Troilus and
          Criseyde." The Cooper Monographs. Bern: Francke, 1960.
          240 pp.
             See Crawford, p. 17.
             Reviews: Martin Lehnert, ZAA, 14 (1966), 391–92.

2. FOREIGN TRANSLATIONS

Bulgaria

134   *SURBANOV, ALEKSANDĂR, trans. Kentărbărijski razkazi [The
          Canterbury Tales]. Sofija: Nar. kultura, 1970. 492 pp.
          Cited in IT (1970), no. 9085.

Modernizations and Translations

China

135   *CHANG, HSIU YA, trans. Chin Sang Tzǔ Ho Hu Li [Chanticleer
      and the fox]. Taipei: Kuo Yü Daily Press, 1965. 32 pp.,
      illustrated. Cited in IT (1965), no. 6392.

Czechoslovakia

136   *PRÍBUSOVÁ, MARGITA, trans. Canterburské poviedky [The Canter-
      bury Tales]. Bratislava: Mladé letá, 1969. 278 pp.,
      illustrated. Cited in IT (1969), no. 32059.

137   *VRBA, FRANTIŠEK. Canterburské povídky [Canterbury Tales].
      2 vols. Praha: Odeon, 1970. 435 pp. Cited in IT
      (1970), no. 34904.

Denmark

138   *BERGSØE, FLEMMING. Konen fra Bath [The Wife of Bath's Tale].
      København: Thanning & Appel, 1967. 70 pp., illustrated.
      Cited in IT (1967), no. 7379.

Finland

139   *MANNER, EEVA-LIISA. Canterburyn Kertomuksia [The Canterbury
      Tales: Tales from Chaucer]. Helsinki: Otava, 1966.
      192 pp. Cited in IT (1966), no. 12578.

France

140   SIMON, JEAN ROBERT. Troïle et Crisède (extr.). Paris:
      Aubier-Montaigne, 1970. 190 pp.
         Reviews: L. H. Somers, Les études classiques (Namur),
      38 (1970), 400.

Germany

141   *DIE CANTERBURY TALES. Köln: Hegner, 1969. 659 pp. Cited
      in IT (1969), no. 1802.

142   *DROESE, DETLEF. Canterbury-Erzählungen. Zurich: Manesse-
      Verlag, 1971. 567 pp., illustrated. Cited in IT (1971),
      no. 34601.

143   *HAUSMANN, WOLF and ALFRED KÜNNER. Singehell und der Fuchs
      [Chanticleer and the Fox]. Reinbek: Carlsen, 1968.
      18 pp., illustrated. Cited in IT (1970), no. 2840.

Foreign Translations

144   LEHNERT, MARTIN. Ausgewählte Canterbury Erzählungen. Halle:
       VEB Verlag, 1962. 208 pp.
       See Crawford, p. 16.
       Reviews: Herbert Voitl, Archiv, 201 (1964), 372-76.

145   *LEHNERT, MARTIN. Canterbury-Erzählungen (extr.). Berlin:
       Herbig, 1965; second edition, Rütten u. Loening, 1967.
       207 pp., illustrated. Cited in IT (1964), no. 1433; IT
       (1966), no. 1341; IT (1967), no. 1748.

Italy

146   *BARISONE, ERMANNO. Il racconti di Canterbury. Torino:
       U.T.E.T., 1967. 634 pp. Cited in IT (1968), no. 18473.

147   *MORRA, SILVANA. Il racconti di Canterbury. 2 vols. Milano:
       Ediz per il club del libro, 1962. Cited in IT (1965),
       no. 17934.

Netherlands

148   *BARNOUW, ADRIAAN J. Het boek van de hertogin. Het vogel
       parlement [The Book of the Duchess; The Parlement of
       Foulys: Two early poems]. Haarlem: Tjeenk Willink,
       1966-67. 70 pp. Cited in IT (1967), no. 24381.

149   *BARNOUW, ADRIAAN J. De vertellingen van de pelgrims naar
       Kantelberg [Canterbury Tales]. 2 vols. Utrecht:
       Spectrum, 1968. 563 pp., illustrated. Cited in IT
       (1968), no. 23570; IT (1969), no. 4617; IT (1971),
       no. 29528.

Romania

150   DUTESCU, DAN. Povestirile din Canterbury [Canterbury Tales].
       2 vols. Bucureşti: Editura pentru literatură universală,
       1965. 823 pp., illustrated.

Spain

151   *BONASTRE, JUAN CANTI. Cuentos de Canterbury. Barcelona:
       Bruguera, 1970. 555 pp. Cited in IT (1970), no. 13891.

152   *FERRER, JOSEFINA. Los Cuentos de Canterbury. Barcelona:
       Marte, 1967. 265 pp. Cited in IT (1967), no. 9602.

153   *Mª TRIANA, JOSÉ. Poesia menor. Madrid: Alberto Corazon,
       1970. 93 pp. Cited in IT (1970), no. 11865
       Includes the Miller's Tale.

Modernizations and Translations

154   *ORIOL, CARIDAD. Cuentos de Canterbury. Barcelona: Bruguera,
        1969.   447 pp.   Cited in IT (1969), no. 10485.

Sweden

155   *MJÖLNARENS BERÄTTELSE om den vackra Alison och den klipske
        scholaris [The Miller's Tale].   Göteborg: Rundqvist,
        1967.   38 pp., illustrated.   Cited in IT (1967),
        no. 29997.

156   *HALLQVIST, BRITT G. Tuppen och räven [Chanticleer and the
        fox].   Stockholm: Illustrationsförl.   Carlsen, 1968.
        36 pp., illustrated.   Cited in IT (1968), no. 28236.

157   JERNSTRÖM, HARALD. Två Canterbury sägner.   Stockholm:
        Sällsk.   Bokvännerna; Solna: Seelig, 1970.   92 pp.,
        illustrated.   Cited in IT (1970), no. 32631.

General Criticism

See Griffith, pp. 58-80; Crawford, pp. 18-29.

158   ANDO, SHINSUKI. "Some Problems in Chaucer's Description of
Women." SELit, 43 (October, 1966), 15-28.
In Japanese.

159   *APSTEIN, BARBARA. "Chaucer and the Gods." DAI, 32 (1971),
3240A. The City University of New York, 1971. 291 pp.

160   *BARGREEN, MELINDA LUETH. "The Author in His Work: The
Priest/Pupil Narrative Topos." DAI, 33 (1972), 2884A.
University of California, Irvine, 1972. 312 pp.

161   BATESON, F[REDERICK] W[ILSE]. A Guide to English Literature.
New York: Doubleday, 1965. 270 pp.
See especially chapters 1 and 2 (pp. 12-30, 31-45).
Excerpts are reprinted in 36, pp. 273-75.
Reviews: Charles Daves, SCN, 23 (1965), 36-37; AQ
21 (1965), 192; TLS (30 December, 1965), p. 1216;
Philip Hobsbaum, Listener, 74 (1965), 805; Daniel R.
Barnes, Cithara, 6 (November, 1966), 74-75; J. C. Maxwell,
NSt (11 March, 1966), p. 343.

162   BAUM, PAULL F[RANKLIN]. Chaucer: A Critical Appreciation.
Durham: Duke University Press; Cambridge University
Press, 1958. 229 pp.
See Crawford, p. 18.
Reviews: A. C. Cawley, ES, 47 (1966), 214-16.

163   BAUM, PAULL F[RANKLIN]. Chaucer's Verse. Durham, North
Carolina: Duke University Press; Cambridge University
Press, 1961. 144 pp.
See Crawford, p. 18.
Reviews: M. M. Crow, MP, 62 (1964), 60-62; E. Talbot
Donaldson, Spec, 39 (1964), 112-14; Gardiner Stillwell,
JEGP, 63 (1964), 141-47; Marie P. Hamilton, ArQ, 19
(1963), 271-74; P. J. Frankis, MAE, 35 (1966), 78-82;
A. C. Cawley, ES, 47 (1966), 214-16.

General Criticism

164   BEICHNER, PAUL E. "The Allegorical Interpretation of
       Medieval Literature." PMLA, 82 (1967), 33-38. Abstr. in
       AES, 10 (1967), no. 2105.
       Cites dangers of overuse of the allegorical method of
       criticism with reference to Chaucer. Reprinted in 58,
       pp. 112-23.

165   *BEKUS, ALBERT J. "Tradition and Innovation in the Prologues
       of Chaucer." DAI, 34 (1973), 1232A. Auburn University,
       1973. 308 pp.

166   *BERTOLOTTI, GEORGENE MARY. "Chaucer's Use of Classical
       Story." DAI, 33 (1973), 4330A. Brown University, 1972.
       218 pp.

167   *BISSON, LILLIAN MARIE (PERRAULT). "Chaucer's Use of the
       Student-Teacher Relationship as an Artistic Technique in
       His Early Poems." DAI, 30 (1970), 5400A. The Florida
       State University, 1969. 205 pp.

168   BLAKE, N. F. "Caxton and Chaucer." LeedsSE, 1 (1967), 19-36.

169   BLAKE, N. F. "Chaucer and the Alliterative Romances."
       ChauR, 3 (1969), 163-69. Abstr. in AES, 13 (1969-70),
       no. 2556.

170   BLAKE, N. F. "Chaucer in His Time," in 50, pp. 1-7. Abstr.
       in AES, 18 (1974-75), no. 747.

171   BLOOMFIELD, MORTON W. "Authenticating Realism and the
       Realism of Chaucer." Thought, 39 (1964), 335-58. Abstr.
       in AES, 10 (1967), no. 1103.
       Reprinted in 31, pp. 175-98.

172   BLOOMFIELD, MORTON, W. "The Gloomy Chaucer," in Veins of
       Humor. Edited by Harry Levin. Cambridge: Harvard Uni-
       versity Press, 1972, pp. 57-68. Abstr. in MLAA, 1
       (1973), no. 2755.
       Analyzes strategy of Chaucerian persona.

173   BOWDEN, MURIEL. A Reader's Guide to Geoffrey Chaucer. New
       York: Farrar, Straus and Giroux; Toronto: Ambassador
       Books, 1964; London: Thames and Hudson, 1965. 220 pp.
       Reviews: TLS (12 August, 1965), p. 698.

174   BOYD, BEVERLY. Chaucer and the Liturgy. Philadelphia:
       Dorrance, 1967. 95 pp.

Bibliography of Chaucer, 1964 - 1973

Reviews: Paul E. Beichner, C. S. C., Spec, 44 (1969),
115-16; H. Boone Porter, Jr., CH 38 (1969), 529;
E. Catherine Dunn, CHR, 57 (1971), 329-30.

175   BRADDY, HALDEEN. "Chaucer: Realism or Obscenity?" ArlQ, 2, i
(1969), 121-38. Abstr. in AES, 13 (1969-70), no. 3195.
Reprinted in 33, pp. 146-58.

176   BRADDY, HALDEEN. "Chaucer's Bawdy Tongue." SFQ, 30 (1966),
214-22.
Reprinted in 33, pp. 131-39.

177   BREWER, D. S. "Class Distinction in Chaucer." Spec, 43
(1968), 290-305. Abstr. in AES, 16 (1972-73), no. 945.

178   BREWER, D. S. "The Criticism of Chaucer in the Twentieth
Century," in 37, pp. 3-28.

179   BREWER, D. S. "Honour in Chaucer." E&S, 26 (1973), 1-19.

180   BREWER, D. S. "Images of Chaucer," in 35, pp. 240-70.
Chaucer's reputation.

181   BREZIANU, ANDREI. "Mediterana şi Anglia. Ulise-Crîmpeie
dintr-o reversiune metaforica" [The Mediterranean and
Great Britain. Ulysses--smithereens from a metaphorical
revision]. Secolul, 20 (1970), 276-82.
Passing references to Chaucer.

182   BROADBENT, JOHN BARCLAY. Poetic Love. London: Chatto and
Windus, 1964. 317 pp.
See especially chapters 1-3.

183   BROCKMAN, BENNETT A. "Medieval Songs of Innocence and
Experience: The Adult Writer and Literature for Children,"
in Children's Literature: The Great Excluded. Edited by
Francelia Butler. Storrs, Connecticut: Children's Lit-
erature Association, 1973, vol. 2, pp. 40-49.
Deals with the tale of Ugolino.

184   BRONSON, BERTRAND H[ARRIS]. In Search of Chaucer. Second
edition. Canadian University Publications. Toronto:
University Press; *London: Oxford University Press,
1965. 128 pp.
Originally published, 1959. See Crawford, p. 19. Part
of chapter 2, "In and Out of Dreams," is reprinted in 58,
pp. 126-42; "The Pardoner's Confession," in 1106,
pp. 15-22.
Reviews: M. Engelberghs, Kultuurleven, 34 (1967),
712-13.

General Criticism

185   BRUSENDORFF, AAGE. The Chaucer Tradition. Oxford University
       Press, 1969. 510 pp.
       Originally published 1925, reprinted.

186   BURGER, DOUGLAS A. "Chaucer's Narrative Pose: The Formative
       Phase." DA, 28 (1967), 619A. Lehigh University, 1966.
       245 pp.

187   BURNLEY, J. D. "Chaucer's Art of Verbal Allusion: Two
       Notes." Neophil, 56 (1972), 93-99.

188   BURROW, J[OHN] A[NTHONY]. Ricardian Poetry: Chaucer, Gower,
       Langland and the Gawain Poet. New Haven, Connecticut:
       Yale University Press, 1971. 174 pp.
       Reviews: R. M. Wilson, MLR, 67 (1972), 612-13;
       Morton W. Bloomfield, Spec, 48 (1973), 345-47; N. F. Blake,
       in 50, pp. 1-7 (see 170 above); Siegfried Wenzel, MAE, 42
       (1973), 93-95.

189   *CALDWELL, HARRY BOYNTON. "The Child Tragic Ballad: A Com-
       parison with Medieval Literary Tragedy--Boccaccio,
       Chaucer, Lydgate." DA, 29 (1968), 865A. Vanderbilt
       University, 1968. 215 pp.

190   CHESTERTON, G[ILBERT] K[EITH]. Chaucer. Second edition.
       London: Faber and Faber, 1959. 302 pp.
       See Crawford, p. 20.
       Reviews: A. Macdonald, DUJ, 25 (1964), 126-27.

191   CHIAPPELLI, CAROLYN. "Chaucer's Use of 'Solas.'" Comitatus,
       2 (1971), 91-92.

192   *CHIARENZA, FRANK JOHN. "Chaucer and the Medieval Amorous
       Complaint: A Study in the Evolution of a Poetic Genre."
       DAI, 31 (1970), 2337A. Yale University, 1956. 242 pp.

193   CLEMEN, WOLFGANG. Chaucers frühe Dichtung. Göttingen and
       Zurich: Vandenhoeck und Ruprecht, 1963. 246 pp.
       Enlarged edition of Der junge Chaucer. See Crawford,
       p. 20, and next entry.
       Reviews: W. F. Schirmer, Ang, 82 (1964), 240-42;
       Siegfried Wenzel, JEGP, 64 (1965), 165-66; W. Erzgräber,
       GGA, 219 (1967), 232-42.

194   CLEMEN, WOLFGANG. Chaucer's Early Poetry. Translated by
       C. A. M. Sym. New York: Barnes & Noble, 1964. 234 pp.
       See Crawford, p. 20, and entry above.
       Reviews: Dorothy Bethurum, Spec, 39 (1964), 510-13;
       John Lawlor, CritQ, 6 (1964), 90; M. C. Bradbrook, NSt,

67 (1964), 494-95; D. S. Brewer, Listener, 71 (1964),
490, 493; S. S. Hussey, N&Q, 11 (1964), 348-49; Paul
Bacquet, EA, 18 (1965), 66-67; T. W. Craik, MLR, 60
(1965), 240-41; F. C. DeVries, Neophil, 49 (1965), 81;
J. A. Burrow, MAE, 34 (1965), 152-54; *Hans Käsmann,
Archiv, 202 (1965), 289-92; David C. Fowler, MP, 64
(1966), 70-71; C. R. Barrett, AUMLA, No. 25 (1966),
pp. 112-13; *K. H. Göller, GRM, 46 (1966), 207-209. See
also C. Muscatine, MLQ, 25 (1964), 473-78.

195   COGHILL, NEVILL. "Canterbury Tales Translated: How Chaucer
       Became a Musical." MSS, 23 (1971), 93-102.
           See 2181 below.

196   COGHILL, NEVILL. Chaucer's Idea of What is Noble. Presiden-
       tial address, 1971. London: English Association, 1971.
       18 pp.
           Reviews: G. C. Britton, N&Q, 19 (1972), 272-73.

197   COGHILL, NEVILL. "Geoffrey Chaucer," in British Writers and
       Their Work, no. 1. Edited by Bonamy Dobree and
       J. W. Robinson. Lincoln: University of Nebraska Press,
       1963, pp. 1-68.
           Includes select bibliography.

198   COGHILL, NEVILL. The Poet Chaucer. Second edition. London,
       New York: Oxford University Press, 1968. 156 pp.

199   *CONDREN, EDWARD IGNATIUS. "The Metaphor of Love: A Critical
       Study of Chaucer's Early Poetry." DAI, 31 (1970),
       2338A-9A. University of Toronto, 1969.

200   *CONNELLY, WILLIAM JOSEPH. "Perspectives in Chaucer Criticism:
       1400-1700." DAI, 33 (1972), 721A. The University of
       Oklahoma, 1972. 306 pp.

201   CORSA, HELEN STORM. Chaucer: Poet of Mirth and Morality.
       Notre Dame, Indiana: University of Notre Dame Press,
       1964. 253 pp.
           Reviews: TLS (24 December, 1964), p. 1164; T. W. Craik,
       MLR, 60 (1965), 423-24; Gilbert G. Wright, Thought, 40
       (1965), 131-32; D. S. Brewer, N&Q, 12 (1965), 83.

202   *COWGILL, BRUCE KENT. "Chaucer and the Just Society: Concep-
       tions of Natural Law and the Nobility in the Parliament
       of Fowls, The Knight's Tale, and the Portraits of Miller
       and Reeve." DAI, 31 (1971), 5357A. University of
       Nebraska, 1970. 277 pp.

General Criticism

203 *CRAMPTON, GEORGIA RONAN. "The Protagonist as Sufferer: A
Critical Inquiry into a Topos in Chaucer and Spenser."
DA, 28 (1967), 2205A-6A. University of Oregon, 1967.
461 pp.

204 CRAWFORD, WILLIAM R. "The House of Chaucer's Fame." ChauR,
3 (1969), 191-203. Abstr. in AES, 13 (1969-70),
no. 2558.
Critical review of Chaucer studies published in 1967.

205 CURRY, WALTER CLYDE. Chaucer and the Medieval Sciences.
Second edition, revised, enlarged. New York: Barnes and
Noble; London: George Allen and Unwin, 1960. 393 pp.
See Griffith, p. 63; Crawford, p. 20. Excerpts
reprinted in 62, pp. 115-22.
Reviews: Thomas A. Kirby, ES, 49 (1968), 143-44.

206 D'ARDENNE, S. R. T. O. "Chaucer, the Englishman," in 43,
pp. 47-54.

207 *DAVIS, DARYL RICHARD. "Thematic Continuity in Chaucer's
Early Poetry." DAI, 31 (1970), 2379A. Indiana University, 1970. 207 pp.

208 *DAVIS, JULIE SYDNEY. "Creatures like Ourselves: The
Romantic Criticism of Chaucer." DAI, 33 (1973), 5118A.
Case Western Reserve University, 1973. 162 pp.

209 DELANY, SHEILA. "Undoing Substantial Connection: The Late
Medieval Attack on Analogical Thought." Mosaic, 5, iv
(Summer, 1972), 31-52. Abstr. in AES, 16 (1972-73),
no. 1583.
Argues that the allegorical mode was not suited to
Chaucer's poetic vision.

210 DELASANTA, RODNEY. "Chaucer and the Exegetes." SLitI, 4,
ii (1971), 1-10. Abstr. in AES, 15 (1971-72), no. 1658.

211 DE NEEF, A. LEIGH. "Robertson and the Critics." ChauR, 2
(1968), 205-34. Abstr. in AES, 16 (1972-73), no. 1584.

212 DIEKSTRA, F. N. M. Chaucer's Quizzical Mode of Exemplifi-
cation. Nijmegen: Dekker & Van de Vegt, 1973, 1974.
24 pp.
Treats the dislocated moralitas and willful incongruity
in Chaucer.

General Criticism

213   DONALDSON, E. TALBOT. "Chaucer and the Elusion of Clarity,"
        in 40, pp. 23-44. Abstr. in AES, 17 (1973-74), no. 23.

214   DONALDSON, E. TALBOT. "The Masculine Narrator and Four
        Women of Style," in 39, pp. 46-64.

215   DONALDSON, E. TALBOT. "Patristic Exegesis in the Criticism
        of Medieval Literature: The Opposition," in 39,
        pp. 134-53.

216   DONNER, MORTON. "Chaucer and His Narrators: The Poet's
        Place in His Poems." WHR, 27 (1973), 189-95.

217   DORRIS, GEORGE E. "The First Italian Criticism of Chaucer
        and Shakespeare." RomN, 6 (1965), 141-43. Abstr. in
        AES, 11 (1968), no. 2411.

218   DUGGAN, HOYT. "Scholar's Plenty." CEA, 35, iv (May, 1973),
        28-32. [Review article.]

219   *DUMITRESCU-BUŞULENGA, ZOE. "Literatura burlescă" [Burlesque
        literature], in Renaşterea, Umanismul şi dialogul
        artelor [Renaissance, Humanism and the dialogue of arts].
        Bucureşti: Albatros, 1971, pp. 165-67. Cited in MHRA
        (1972), no. 3036.

220   DUNLEAVY, GARETH W. "The Wound and the Comforter: the
        Consolations of Geoffrey Chaucer." PLL, 3 (Summer
        supplement, 1967), 14-27.

221   DUNNING, T. P. "Chaucer's Icarus-Complex: Some Notes on His
        Adventures in Theology," in English Studies Today, Third
        Series: Lectures and Papers Read at the Fifth Confer-
        ence of the International Association of Professors of
        English Held at Edinburgh and Glasgow August 1962.
        Edited by G. I. Duthie. Edinburgh: Edinburgh Univer-
        sity Press, 1964, pp. 89-106.

222   ^ELBOW, PETER HENRY. "Complex Irony in Chaucer." DAI, 30
        (1969), 2480A-1A. Brandeis University, 1969. 115 pp.

223   ELIASON, NORMAN E. "Chaucer the Love Poet," in 56, pp. 9-26.

224   ELLIOTT, R. W. V. "Chaucer's Reading," in 37, pp. 46-68.

225   ELLIOTT, R. W. V. "When Chaucer Swears," in 63, pp. 417-34.

General Criticism

226 *EMPRINGHAM, ANTOINETTE FLEUR. "Chaucerian Narrative and
        Gothic Style: A Study of the Legend of Good Women, the
        Monk's Tale, and the House of Fame." DAI, 33 (1973),
        5119A-20A. University of Southern California, 1973.
        154 pp.
            Analogies with medieval visual arts.

227 ENKVIST, NILS ERIK. Geoffrey Chaucer. Stockholm: Natur och
        Kultur, 1964. 88 pp.
            Reviews: Olof Sager, MSpr, 59 (1965), 441-42.

227.01 EVERETT, DOROTHY. "Some Reflections on Chaucer's 'Art
        Poetical,'" in 37, pp. 99-124.
            Reprinted from PBA, 36 (1950), 132-54.

228 FIFIELD, MERLE. "Chaucer the Theater-goer." PLL, 3 (Summer
        supplement, 1967), 63-70.
            Chaucer's references to miracle plays.

229 FLEMING, JOHN. "Gestes of Rome (Pierce the Ploughmans Crede
        45)." N&Q, 11 (1964), 210-11.
            Reference to a Tyrrwhitt note on Chaucer.

230 *FULWILER, LAVON BUSTER. "Image Progressions in Chaucer's
        Poetry: Exposition of a Theory of Creativity." DAI,
        32 (1972), 5181A-2A. Michigan State University, 1971.
        273 pp.

231 *GELLRICH, JESSE M. "Chaucer's Music of Love." DAI, 31
        (1971), 4713A. State University of New York at Buffalo,
        1970. 197 pp.
            Relationship of Chaucer's lovers' songs to sublime
        music.

232 *GILLMEISTER, HEINER. Discrecioun: Chaucer und die Via
        Regia. Bonn: Bouvier Verlag Herbert Grundmann, 1972.
        250 pp. Cited in YWES (1972), 110.

233 GREAVES, MARGARET. The Blazon of Honour: A Study in
        Renaissance Magnanimity. London: Methuen, 1964.
        142 pp.
            Studies in Chaucer's characters, pp. 37-45.

234 *GRENTHOT, JOAN SLOANE. "The Dream of Reality: A Study of
        Chaucer's Treatment of Love." Yale University Disser-
        tation, 1963. Cited in MHRA (1964), no. 2175.

235   GROSE, M. W. Chaucer. Literature in Perspective. London:
        Evans Brothers; New York: Arco, 1967.
        Popular introduction.

236   *HACKETHAL, MARIETTA. "Aufbau und Erzählstruktur der
        Erzählungen Chaucers." München Dissertation, 1966.
        Cited in JDH, 82, no. 6, p. 89, U6612220.

237   HALLIDAY, FRANK E. Chaucer and His World. London: Thames
        and Hudson, 1968; New York: Viking, 1968. 144 pp.

238   HALVERSON, JOHN. "Patristic Exegesis: A Medieval Tom
        Sawyer." CE, 27 (1965), 50-55.
        Spoof on patristic criticism as applied to Chaucer.

239   *HARIG, SISTER MARY LABOURÉ, S. N. D. "A Study of the Literary
        Garden Tradition and Chaucer." DAI, 32 (1972), 4565A.
        Case Western Reserve University, 1971. 255 pp.

240   *HART, JAMES P., JR. "Thomas Tyrwhitt (1730-86) as Annotator
        and Glossarist of Fragment A of The Canterbury Tales,
        and His Editorial Relations." DAI, 32 (1971), 2056A.
        University of Pennsylvania, 1971. 275 pp.

241   *HASELMAYER, LOUIS AUGUST, JR. "Chaucer and Medieval Verse
        Portraiture." DAI, 31 (1970), 2344A. Yale University,
        1937. 399 pp.

242   HASKELL, ANN S. "Lyric and Lyrical in the Works of Chaucer:
        The Poet in His Literary Context," in English Symposium
        Papers, 3. Edited by Douglas Shepard. Fredonia: State
        University of New York at Fredonia, 1972 [1973],
        pp. 1-45.

243   *HATCHER, JOHN SOUTHALL. "Chaucer's Imagery." DA, 29 (1969),
        3098A. University of Georgia, 1968. 290 pp.

244   HAYMES, EDWARD R. "Chaucer and the Romance Tradition." SAB,
        37, iv (1972), 35-43.

245   *HEIDTMANN, PETER WALLACE. "The Chaucerian Narrator." DA,
        25 (1965), 5905-06. The University of Wisconsin, 1965.
        238 pp.

246   HIEATT, CONSTANCE B. The Realism of Dream Visions: The
        Poetic Exploitation of the Dream-Experience in Chaucer
        and His Contemporaries. De Proprietatibus Litterarum,
        Series Practica, 2. The Hague: Mouton; New York:
        Humanities, 1967. 117 pp.

General Criticism

Anti-Robertsonian analysis.
Reviews: M.-M. Dubois, EA, 21 (1968), 408; Anne
Middleton, Spec, 44 (1969), 298-301; Wolfgang Weiss, Ang,
88 (1970), 537-9.

247 *HIGGS, ELTON DALE. "The Dream as a Literary Framework in the
Works of Chaucer, Langland and the Pearl Poet." DA, 27
(1966), 1030A. University of Pittsburgh, 1965. 182 pp.

248 HINTON, NORMAN. "Anagogue and Archetype: The Phenomenology
of Medieval Literature." AnM, 7 (1966), 57-73.
Response to "Robertsonianism."

249 *HIPOLITO, TERRANCE A. "Chaucer and the School of Chartres."
DAI, 31 (1971), 6551A. University of California, Los
Angeles, 1970. 525 pp.

250 HIRA, TOSHINORI. "Two Phases of Chaucer, Moral and Mortal,"
in 54, pp. 91-114.

251 HODAPP, MARION F[REEMAN]. "Algunas analogias entre el
Arcipreste de Hita y Geoffrey Chaucer," in El Arcipreste
de Hita: El Libro, el autor, la tierra, la epoca. Actas
del I Congreso Internacional sobre al Arcipreste de Hita.
Edited by Manuel Criado de Val. Barcelona: S. E. R. E.
S. A., pp. 285-308.
Suggests several similarities.

252 *HODAPP, MARION FREEMAN. "Two Fourteenth-Century Poets:
Geoffrey Chaucer and the Archpriest of Hita." DA, 29
(1968), 1897A. University of Colorado, 1968. 229 pp.

253 HOWARD, DONALD R. "Chaucer the Man." PMLA, 80 (1965),
337-43. Abstr. in AES, 9 (1966), no. 1243
Reprinted in 37, pp. 31-45.

254 HOWARD, DONALD R. The Three Temptations: Medieval Man in
Search of the World. Princeton: Princeton University
Press; *London: Oxford University Press, 1966. 328 pp.
Reviews: R. M. Wilson, Eng, 16 (1966), 106-107.

255 HOWARD, EDWIN J[OHNSTON]. Geoffrey Chaucer. Twayne English
Authors Series, 1. New York: Twayne, 1964. 219 pp.
Reviews: D. S. Brewer, N&Q, 12 (1965), 83; T. W. Craik,
MLR, 60 (1965), 589-90; Brinley Rhys, "Minstrels &
Mystics," SewR, 75 (1967), 337-45.

BIBLIOGRAPHY OF CHAUCER, 1964 - 1973

256   HUPPÉ, BERNARD F. and D. W. ROBERTSON, JR. Fruyt and Chaf:
       Studies in Chaucer's Allegories. Princeton, New Jersey:
       Princeton University Press, 1963.
          See Crawford, pp. 88, 95.
          Reviews: Donald R. Howard, Spec, 39 (1964), 537-41;
       R. T. Davies, MLR, 59 (1964), 625-27; Donald C. Baker,
       ELN, 2 (1963), 59-62; Robert O. Payne, CL, 15 (1964),
       272-76; Rosemary Woolf, EIC, 14 (1964), 301-307; D. S.
       Brewer, RES, 16 (1965), 304-305.

257   HUSSEY, MAURICE. Chaucer's World: A Pictorial Companion.
       London and New York: Cambridge University Press, 1967.
       172 pp.
          A pictorial companion to 258 below. 125 plates related
       to the works.
          Reviews: P. M. Vermeer, ES, 50 (1969), 607-608.

258   HUSSEY, MAURICE, A. C. SPEARING and JAMES WINNY. An Intro-
       duction to Chaucer. London: Cambridge University Press,
       1965. 199 pp.
          Reprinted with corrections in 1968.

259   HUSSEY, S. S. Chaucer: An Introduction. London: Methuen,
       1971. 244 pp.
          Reviews: G. C. Britton, N&Q, 19 (1972), 272-73;
       P. W. Rogers, QQ, 79 (1972), 416-17; C. S. Ivy, DUJ, 34
       (1972), 115-17; Dieter Mehl, Ang, 91 (1973), 249-52;
       Christian K. Zacher, Spec, 48 (1973), 757-60; D. S. Brewer,
       RES, 24 (1973), 61-63; R. M. Wilson, MLR, 68 (1973),
       147-48; Hoyt Duggan, CEA, 35, iv (May, 1973), 28-32.

260   HUSSEY, S. S. "The Minor Poems and the Prose," in 32,
       chapter 5, part 4, pp. 229-62.

261   HUXLEY, ALDOUS. "Exhumations I: Huxley's 'Chaucer.'" EIC,
       15 (1965), 6-21. Abstr. in AES, 8 (1965), no. 2227.
          Reprint of a 1920 essay.

262   ITO, MASAYOSHI. "Gower's Use of rime riche in Contessio
       Amantis: As Compared with his Practice in Mirour de
       L'Omme and with the Case of Chaucer." SELit, 46 (1969),
       29-44.

263   *JACOBSON, JOHN HOWARD. "The Church of Love in the Works of
       Chaucer and Gower." DAI, 31 (1970), 2347A. Yale Univer-
       sity, 1939. 320 pp.

General Criticism

264   *JAHN, JERALD DUANE. "The Elizabethan Epyllion: Its Art and
          Narrative Conventions." DAI, 33 (1972), 2331A. Indiana
          University, 1972. 416 pp.

265   *JANKOVIĆ, MIRA "Chaucerovi knjizevni razgovori o narativnoj
          formi" [Chaucer's literary conversation about narrative
          form]. Umjetnost rijeci, Zagreb, 13, i-ii (1969), 73-85.
          Cited in MHRA (1969), no. 2825.

266   JÄRV, HARRY. "Chaucers mänskliga komedi" [Chaucer's Human
          Comedy] in the author's Läsarmekanismer: Essäer och
          utblickar [Reader mechanisms: essays and outlooks].
          Staffanstorp: Cavefors, 1971, pp. 227-37.

267   JOHNSON, DUDLEY RAPELJE. "Chaucer and the Bible." DAI, 31
          (1971), 3506A. Yale University, 1941. 237 pp.

268   JOHNSON, W. C., JR. "Chaucer's Language of Inevitability,"
          in 50, pp. 17-27. Abstr. in AES, 18 (1974-75), no. 746.

269   JORDAN, ROBERT M. Chaucer and the Shape of Creation: The
          Aesthetic Possibilities of Inorganic Structure.
          Cambridge, Massachusetts: Harvard University Press;
          London: Oxford University Press, 1967.
              Reviews: R. MacG. Dawson, DalR, 48 (1968), 257-58;
          P. W. Rogers, QQ, 75 (1968), 751-53; Julia G. Ebel, CE,
          29 (1968), 572-76; Stephen Manning, ELN, 6 (1968),
          125-27; Bernard F. Huppé, Criticism, 11 (1969), 94-96;
          D. S. Brewer, N&Q, 16 (1969), 109-10; R. T. Davies, RES,
          20 (1969), 207-209; Richard L. Hoffman, Spec, 44 (1969),
          468-71; Alan T. Gaylord, JEGP, 68 (1969), 161-66; Sarah
          Appleton Weber, Thought, 44 (1969), 608-10; Francis Lee
          Utley, MLQ, 30 (1969), 284-91; W. Munson, CL, 22 (1970),
          70-75; Christopher Brookhouse, Style, 5 (1971), 203-205.

270   JORDAN, ROBERT M. "Chaucerian Narrative," in 60, pp. 85-102.
          Includes a review of scholarship and bibliography.

271   JORDAN ROBERT M. "Inorganic Art," in 62, pp. 38-41.
              Reprinted excerpts from Chaucer and the Shape of
          Creation, 269 above.

272   JOSIPOVICI, G. D. "Fiction and Game in The Canterbury Tales."
          CritQ, 7 (1965), 185-97. Abstr. in AES, 9 (1966),
          no. 1577.

273   JURSCHAX, GERTRUDE MARY. "Chaucer and Fourteenth-Century
          English Thought." DAI, 33 (1972), 1685A. Loyola Univer-
          sity of Chicago, 1972. 262 pp.

274   KAHRL, STANLEY J. "Allegory in Practice: A Study of Narra-
          tive Styles in Medieval Exempla." MP, 63 (1965),
          105-110.

275   KANE, GEORGE. The Autobiographical Fallacy in Chaucer and
          Langland Studies. Chambers Memorial Lecture. London:
          H. K. Lewis for University College, London, March 2, 1965.
          20 pp.
             Reviews: Barbara Raw, N&Q, 13 (1966), 194; TLS
          (20 January, 1966), 49; S. T. Knight, MAE, 36 (1967),
          282-85.

276   KEAN, P. M. Chaucer and the Making of English Poetry.
          2 vols. Vol. 1: Love Vision and Debate; Vol. 2: The
          Art of Narrative. London: Routledge and Kegan Paul,
          1972. 486 pp.
             Sees Chaucer in the context of the traditon of English
          poetry.
             Reviews: TLS (29 September, 1972), p. 1152; Hoyt
          Duggan, CEA, 35, iv (May, 1973), 28-32; Elizabeth R.
          Hatcher, Spec, 50 (1975), 323-27.

277   KELLOGG, ALFRED L. and ROBERT C. COX. "Chaucer's May 3 and
          Its Contexts," in 51, pp. 155-98.

278   KER, W. P. Form and Style in Poetry. Edited by R. W.
          Chambers, with an Introduction by J. Buxton. New edition.
          London: Macmillan, 1966. 407 pp.
             Originally published in 1928. See Griffith, pp. 121-22.

279   KHARENKO, M. F. "Dzhefri Choser i angliis'ka natsional'na
          mova" [Geoffrey Chaucer and the national English language].
          InF, 10 (1967), 41-47.

280   KIRBY, THOMAS A. "Arnold and Chaucer." NM, 73 (1972), 127-33.

281   KNIGHT, STEPHEN. "Chaucer--a Modern Writer?" Balcony, 2
          (1965), 37-43.

282   *KRANZ, GISBERT. "Chaucers Frömmigkeit. Zur Religiosität des
          gebildeten Laien im 14. Jahrhundert." Begegnung, 20
          (1965), 45-48. Cited and abstr. in AES, 8 (1965), no.
          2200.

283   LANHAM, RICHARD A. "Game, Play, and High Seriousness in
          Chaucer's Poetry." ES, 48 (1967), 1-24. Abstr. in AES,
          11 (1968), no. 1912.

General Criticism

284   LAWLOR, JOHN. Chaucer. London: Hutchinson, 1968; New York:
      Harper, 1969. 181 pp.
         Reviews: TLS (15 May, 1969), p. 517.

285   LAWLOR, JOHN. "The Earlier Poems," in 35, pp. 39-64.

286   LEHNERT, MARTIN. "Shakespeare und Chaucer." SJW, 103 (1967),
      7-39. Abstr. in AES, 10 (1967), no. 3143.

287   *LEICESTER, HENRY MARSHALL, JR. "The Rhetorical Moment:
      Studies in the Development of the First-Person Narrative
      Mode in Chaucer's Poetry." DA, 28 (1967), 1052A. Yale
      University, 1967. 461 pp.

288   *LEONARD, FRANCES MCNEELY. "Comedy in Allegory: A Study of
      Vision and Technique in the Chaucer Tradition from The
      Book of the Duchess to The Faerie Queene." DAI, 33
      (1973), 6316A-17A. University of Kansas, 1972. 257 pp.

289   *LOCKHART, ADRIENNE ROSEMARY. "The Draf of Storyes: Chaucer
      as Non-Narrative Poet." DAI, 33 (1973), 3592A. The
      Pennsylvania State University, 1972. 156 pp.

290   LOOMIS, DOROTHY B. "Chaucer and Shakespeare," in 37,
      pp. 166-90.

291   MAGOUN, FRANCIS P., JR. A Chaucer Gazetteer. Chicago:
      University of Chicago Press; Uppsala: Almqvist and
      Wiksell, 1961.
         See Crawford, pp. 23-24.
         Reviews: Klaus Weimann, Archiv, 201 (1964), 136;
      P. Mertens-Fonck, RBPH, 42 (1964), 301; D. S. Brewer,
      ES, 49 (1968), 147-48; Kelsie B. Harder, Names, 16
      (1968), 66-67.

292   MARKMAN, ALAN. "The Concern of Chaucer's Poetry." AnM, 7
      (1966), 90-103.

293   *MASUI, MICHIO. Chaucer Kenkyu. [Study of Chaucer]. Tokyo:
      Kenkyusha, 1973. 362 pp. Cited in PMLAB (1973), no.
      2772.
         In Japanese.

294   MASUI, MICHIO. "Chaucer no yasashisa to nagusame no shudai"
      [Themes of gentleness and consolation in Chaucer].
      EigoS, 117 (1971), 550-52.
         In Japanese.

295   MASUI, MICHIO. "Chaucer's Tenderness and the Theme of Conso-
          lation." NM, 73, (1972), 214-21.

296   *MASUI, MICHIO. Studies in Chaucer. Tokyo: Kenkyusha, 1963.
          362 pp. Cited in MHRA (1965), no. 2522.
          In Japanese.

297   MATHEW, GERVASE. The Court of Richard II. London: John
          Murray, 1968. 238 pp., 29 plates.
          See chapter 4, pp. 62-74 on Geoffrey Chaucer.

298   MATTHEWS, WILLIAM. "A New Preface to Western Medieval Litera-
          ture," RPh, 17 (1964), 634-42. Abstr. in AES, 12 (1969),
          no. 1325.
          Review article.

299   *McCABE, JOHN DONALD. "The Comic in the Poetry of Chaucer:
          Congruence of 'Sentence' and 'Solaas.'" DAI, 30 (1969),
          285A. University of Minnesota, 1968. 143 pp.

300   CANCELLED

301   *McCRAY, CURTIS LEE. "Chaucer and Lydgate, and the Uses of
          History." DA, 29 (1969), 4461A-62A. The University of
          Nebraska, 1968. 266 pp.
          Chaucer's use of Theban history.

302   *McNAMARA, JOHN FRANCIS. "Responses to Ockhamist Theology in
          the Poetry of the Pearl-Poet, Langland, and Chaucer." DA,
          29 (1969), 3148A-49A. Louisiana State University, 1968.
          198 pp.

303   MEHL, DIETER. Geoffrey Chaucer: Eine Einführung in seine
          erzählenden Dichtungen. Grundlagen der Anglistik und
          Amerikanistik, 7. Berlin: Erich Schmidt Verlag, 1973.
          226 pp.

304   MILLS, JOHN. "Chaucer's Low Seriousness." Paunch, 27
          (October, 1966), 39 57. Abstr. in AES, 10 (1967),
          no. 2098.

305   MOGAN, JOSEPH J., JR. Chaucer and the Theme of Mutability.
          De Proprietatibus Litterarum, Series Practica, 3.   The
          Hague, Paris: Mouton, 1968. 190 pp.
          Reviews: Edmund Reiss, Spec, 46 (1971), 175-76;
          J. R. Simon, Erasmus, 25 (1973), 165-67.

General Criticism

306   MURPHY, JAMES J. "A New Look at Chaucer and the Rhetoricians."
       RES, 15 (1964), 1-20. Abstr. in AES, 7 (1964), no. 1871.
       Excerpts reprinted in 62, pp. 31-38.
          Challenges Manly, "Chaucer and the Rhetoricians." See
       Griffith, p. 123.

307   MURTAUGH, DANIEL M. "Women and Geoffrey Chaucer." ELH, 38
       (1971), 473-92.

308   MUSCATINE, CHARLES. Chaucer and the French Tradition: A
       Study in Style and Meaning. New edition. Berkeley and
       Los Angeles: University of California Press; London:
       Cambridge University Press, 1964. 282 pp.
          Originally published in 1957. See Crawford, p. 24.

309   MUSCATINE, CHARLES. "Chaucer in an Age of Criticism." MLQ,
       25 (1964), 473-78.
          Review article.

310   MUSCATINE, CHARLES. Poetry and Crisis in the Age of Chaucer.
       Notre Dame: University of Notre Dame Press, 1972.
       175 pp.
          Reviews: N. F. Blake, in 50 (PSNLS, 1 [1973]), 1-7;
       Jerome Mitchell, NDEJ, 8 (1972), 50-51.

311   NIST, JOHN R. "The Art of Chaucer: Pathedy." TSL, 11
       (1966), 1-10. Abstr. in AES, 10 (1967), no. 2177.

312   NORTH, J. D. "Kalenderes Enlumyned Ben They: Some Astro-
       nomical Themes in Chaucer." RES, 20 (1969), 129-54;
       257-83, 418-44. [Parts I, II, and III.] Abstr. in AES,
       14 (1970-71), nos. 2945, 2946 and 2947.
          Smyser, 359, disagrees.

313   NORTH, J. D. Kalenderes Enlumyned Ben They: Some Astro-
       nomical Themes in Chaucer. Oxford: Museum of the History
       of Science, 1969.
          Reprinted from RES, 312 above.
          Reviews: A. J. Meadows, JHA, 2 (1971), 45.

314   OIJI, TAKEO. Chaucer to sono Shuhen [Chaucer and his circle].
       Tokyo: Bunrishoin, 1968. 281 pp.
          In Japanese.

315   OLSON, CLAIR C. "Chaucer and Fourteenth-Century Society,"
       in 60, pp. 20-37.

316   OLSON, GLENDING. "Deschamps' Art de dictier and Chaucer's
          Literary Environment." Spec, 48 (1973), 714-23. Abstr.
          in MLAA (1973), no. 2775.

317   O'NEIL, YNEZ VIOLÉ. "Chaucer and Medicine." JAMA, 208
          (1969), 78-82.

318   *OVERBECK, M. PATRICIA T.   "The Lyf So Short—Studies in
          Chaucer's Dream Visions." DAI, 30 (1970), 2977A.
          University of Cincinnati, 1969.   157 pp.

319   OWEN, CHARLES A., JR. "The Problem of Free Will in Chaucer's
          Narratives." PQ, 46 (1967), 433-56. Abstr. in AES, 15
          (1971-72), no. 721.

320   PATCH, HOWARD R. "The Subjects of Chaucer's Poetry," in 30,
          pp. 255-64.

321   PAYNE, ROBERT O. The Key of Remembrance. New Haven and
          London: Yale University Press for the University of
          Cincinnati, 1963.   258 pp.
             See Crawford, p. 25.
             Reviews: R. T. Davies, MLR, 59 (1964), 625-27;
          Paull F. Baum, ELN, 1 (1964), 219-20; Morton W. Bloomfield,
          CL, 16 (1964), 283-85; Gardiner Stillwell, JEGP, 63
          (1964), 332-36; Elizabeth Salter, N&Q, 11 (1964), 109;
          Rosemary Woolf, CritQ, 7 (1965), 290-91.

322   PEARSALL, DEREK. "Gower's Narrative Art." PMLA, 81 (1966),
          475-84.
             Comparisons with Chaucer's art.

323   *PEAVLER, JAMES MARTIN. "Chaucer's 'Natural' Astronomy."
          DAI, 32 (1971), 3264A-65A. University of Missouri,
          Columbia, 1971.   147 pp.

324   *PECK, RUSSELL ALBERT. "Number Symbolism and the Idea of
          Order in the Works of Geoffrey Chaucer." DA, 24 (1964),
          2894-95. Indiana University, 1963.   229 pp.

325   *POTTER, JOYCE ELIZABETH. "Chaucer's Use of the Pagan God
          Jove." DAI, 33 (1972), 1147A. Duke University, 1972.
          303 pp.

326   *PRASAD, PRAJAPATI. "The Order of Complaint: A Study in
          Medieval Tradition." DA, 26 (1966), 3930. The Univer-
          sity of Wisconsin, 1965.   359 pp.

General Criticism

327   PRESSON ROBERT K. "The Aesthetic of Chaucer's Art of Con-
         trast." EM, 15 (1964), 9-23. Abstr. in AES, 9 (1966),
         no. 134.

328   PRESSON, ROBERT K. "Two Types of Dreams in the Elizabethan
         Drama and Their Heritage: Somnium Animale and the Prick-
         of-Conscience." SEL, 7 (1967), 239-56. Abstr. in AES,
         10 (1967), no. 3176.

329   *PULLIAM, WILLENE. "The Relationship of Geoffrey Chaucer's
         Works to the Anti-feminist Tradition." DA, 28 (1968),
         3646A-47A. Tulane University, 1967. 343 pp.

330   RAJIVA, STANLEY F. "The Eternal Anti-Feminine: An Essay on
         Feminism and Anti-Feminism in Chaucer." IJES, 12 (1971),
         1-21.

331   *RAMSEY, ROY VANCE. "Tradition and Chaucer's Unfaithful
         Woman." DA, 25 (1964), 3557. The University of Oklahoma,
         1964. 459 pp.

332   RAMSON, W. S. "In Praise of Chaucer," in 63, pp. 456-76.

333   *REED, GAIL HELEN VIETH. "Chaucer's Women: Commitment and
         Submission." DAI, 34 (1974), 4215A-16A. The University
         of Nebraska, Lincoln, 1973. 198 pp.

334   REGAN, CHARLES LIONEL. "Chaucer's 'I Passe.'" Greyfriar,
         14 (1973), 3-14.

335   REISS, EDMUND. "Chaucer's Parodies of Love," in 56,
         pp. 27-44.

336   REXROTH, KENNETH. "Chaucer." SatR (25 December, 1965),
         p. 23.

337   RHYS, BRINLEY. "A Preface to Chaucer." SewR, 72 (1964),
         335-41.
            Review article on D. W. Robertson, A Preface to Chaucer,
         339 below.

338   RHYS, BRINLEY. "Minstrels and Mystics." SewR, 75 (1967),
         337-45.

339   ROBERTSON, D. W., JR. A Preface to Chaucer: Studies in
         Medieval Perspectives. Princeton, New Jersey: Princeton
         University Press; London: Oxford University Press, 1962.
         See Crawford, p. 26.

Reviews: R. T. Davies, MLR, 59 (1964), 255–57; Brinley
Rhys, SewR, 72 (1964), 335–41; David C. Fowler, MLQ, 25
(1964), 117–20; Robert O. Payne, CL, 15 (1963), 269–71;
John Lawlor, RES, 15 (1964), 415–18; Guy Bourquin, EA,
18 (1965), 65–66; John MacQueen, FMLS, 2 (1966), 155–59;
F. Parmisano, O. P., MAE, 35 (1966), 273–79; see also
DeNeef, 211 above; Kahrl, 274 above; Matthews, 298 above;
Rhys, 337 above; Utley, 373, 375 below.

340   ROBINSON, IAN. Chaucer and the English Tradition. London
      and New York: Cambridge University Press, 1972. 307 pp.
      Rejects principles of historical criticism.
      Reviews: Donald Davie, EIC, 22 (1972), 429–36; G. S.
      Ivy, DUJ, 34 (1972), 115–17; Hoyt Duggan, CEA, 35, iv
      (May, 1973), 28–32; N. F. Blake, in 50, (PSNLS, 1 [1973]),
      107; Bernard Huppé, Criticism, 15 (1973), 69–70; Dieter
      Mehl, Ang, 91 (1973), 252–55; Marjorie Rigby, RES, 24
      (1973), 321–23; A. C. Spearing, MAE, 42 (1973), 282–85;
      C. A. Owen, Spec, 49 (1974), 148–51.

341   ROSS, THOMAS W. Chaucer's Bawdy. New York: Dutton;
      Toronto and Vancouver: Clarke, Irwin and Co., 1972.
      256 pp.
      Reviews: Paul E. Beichner, NDEJ, 8 (1972), 52–54.

342   ROWLAND, BERYL. "Aspects of Chaucer's Use of Animals."
      Archiv, 201 (1964), 110–14. Abstr. in AES, 8 (1965),
      no. 2832.

343   ROWLAND, BERYL. Blind Beasts: Chaucer's Animal World.
      Kent, Ohio: Kent State University Press, 1971. 204 pp.
      Reviews: P. W. Rogers, QQ, 79 (1972) 416–17; J. R.
      Schoeck, AN&Q, 10 (1972), 91–92; Hoyt Duggan, CEA, 35,
      iv (May, 1973), 28–32; D. S. Brewer, MLR, 68 (1973),
      630–34; Dieter Mehl, Ang, 91 (1973), 255–57; Alison M.
      Wilson, MAE, 42 (1973), 91–93; Edmund Reiss, Spec, 49
      (1974), 151–53; David E. Lampe, ELN, 10 (1973), 226–28.

344   ROWLAND, BERYL. "Chaucer's Imagery," in 60, pp. 103–22.

345   ROWLAND, BERYL. "Contemporary Chaucer Criticism." Eng,
      22 (1973), 3–10. Abstr. in AES, 18 (1974–75), no. 748.

346   ROWLAND, BERYL. "The Horse and Rider Figure in Chaucer's
      Works." UTQ, 35 (1966), 246–59. Abstr. in AES, 10
      (1967), no. 3522.

General Criticism

347   ROWLAND, BERYL. "The Mill in Popular Metaphor from Chaucer
       to the Present Day." SFQ, 33 (1969), 69-79.

348   SALTER, ELIZABETH. "Medieval Poetry and the Visual Arts."
       E&S, 22 (1969), 16-32.

349   SARNO, RONALD A., S. J. "Chaucer and the Satirical Tradi-
       tion." CF, 21 (1967), 41-61.

350   SCHAAR, CLAES. The Golden Mirror: Studies in Chaucer's
       Descriptive Technique and its Literary Background. Acta
       Regiae Societatis Humaniorum Litterarum Lundensis, 54.
       Photographic Reprint with an Index. Lund: Gleerup,
       1967. 565 pp.
          Originally published in 1955. See Crawford, pp. 26-27.

351   *SCHEPER, GEORGE LOUIS. "The Spiritual Marriage: The
       Exegetic History and Literary Impact of the Song of Songs
       in the Middle Ages." DAI, 32 (1972), 3963A. Princeton
       University, 1971. 1034 pp.

352   SCHIRMER, RUTH. "Umgang mit einer Konkordanz und
       Werkinterpretation." NZZ (9 April, 1972), p. 52.
          Playful examination of the potentials of the concor-
       dance in literary interpretations, applied to Troilus
       and Criseyde.

353   SCHLAUCH, MARGARET. English Medieval Literature and Its
       Social Foundations. London: Oxford University Press;
       Warsaw: Panstwowe Wydawnictwo Naukowe, 1967. 382 pp.
          Originally published in 1956. See Crawford, p. 27.

354   SCHOECK, RICHARD J. and JEROME TAYLOR, eds. Chaucer Crit-
       icism: The Canterbury Tales. Notre Dame, Indiana:
       University of Notre Dame Press, 1960, 1961. 320 pp.
          See Crawford, p. 27.
          Reviews: Thomas A. Kirby, ES, 49 (1968), 143-44.

355   *SCRIVNER, BUFORD, JR. "Chaucer's Early Poetry: A Study of
       Imagery in Relation to Theme and Structure." DAI, 33
       (1972), 2905A. The Florida State University, 1972.
       269 pp.

356   SHARMA, GOVIND NARAYAN. "Dreams in Chaucer." IJES, 6
       (1965), 1-18.

357   SILVERSTEIN, THEODORE. "Allegory and Literary Form." PMLA,
           82 (1967), 28-32. Abstr. in AES, 10 (1967), no. 2104.

358   SINGH, BRIJRAJ. "Chaucer as a Poet of Love." RUSE, 6
           (1972), 1-11.

359   SMYSER, HAMILTON M. "A View of Chaucer's Astronomy." Spec,
           45 (1970), 359-73. Abstr. in AES, 16 (1972-73), no. 949.

360   SOUTHWORTH, JAMES G. "Chaucer: A Plea for a Reliable Text."
           CE, 26 (1964), 173-79. Abstr. in AES, 8 (1965), no. 976.
           Reprinted, revised in 37, pp. 86-96.

361   SPEARING, A. C. "An Audience of Listeners," in 363,
           pp. 16-25.
           Reprinted in 62, pp. 22-26.

362   SPEARING, A. C. "Chaucer the Writer," in 258, chapter 5,
           pp. 115-52.

363   SPEARING, A. C. Criticism and Medieval Poetry. London:
           Edward Arnold; *New York: Barnes & Noble, 1964; second
           edition, 1972. 207 pp.
           Excerpts reprinted in 62, pp. 22-26.
           Reviews: Olof Sager, MSpr, 59 (1965), 69-70; Richard
           Hamilton Green, Spec, 40 (1965), 549-53; J. P. Pritchard,
           BA, 39 (1965), 459; John Finlayson, QQ, 72 (1965),
           211-12; D. S. Brewer, N&Q, 12 (1965), 111; J. A. Burrow,
           MAE, 34 (1965), 274-77; Stephen Manning, ELN, 2 (1965),
           221-22; Roger Fowler, CritQ, 7 (1965), 198-99.

364   SPEIRS, JOHN. Chaucer the Maker. New Edition. London:
           Faber and Faber, 1964. 224 pp.
           Originally published in 1951, 1960. See Griffith,
           p. 77, Crawford, p. 28.

365   *STAINTON, ALBERT PETER. "The Time Motif in the Medieval
           Lyric." DAI, 32 (1971), 3272A. Rutgers University,
           1971. 167 pp.
           Treats Chaucer's lyrics.

366   STEADMAN, JOHN M. "'Courtly Love' as a Problem of Style,"
           in 43, pp. 1-33.

367   *STEVENSON, ALLAN. "Tudor Roses from John Tate." SB, 20
           (1967), 15-34. Abstr. in AES, 10 (1967), no. 2137.

General Criticism

368   STROHM, PAUL. "Jean of Angoulême: A Fifteenth Century
Reader of Chaucer." NM, 72 (1971), 69-76.

369   TATLOCK, J. S. P. The Mind and Art of Chaucer. New York:
Gordian, 1966. 123 pp.
Originally published in 1950. See Griffith, p. 78.

370   THOMPSON, MEREDITH. "Current and Recurrent Fallacies in
Chaucer Criticism," in 61, pp. 141-64.

371   THOMSON, PATRICIA. "Wyatt's Boethian Ballade." RES, 15
(1964), 262-67.

372   TUREK, RICHARD. "Thoreau and Chaucer's Dream." TSB, 103
(1968), 1.

373   UTLEY, FRANCIS LEE. "Chaucer and Patristic Exegesis," in
37, pp. 69-85.
Reprinted from RPh, 19 (1965), 250-60, entered 375,
below under a different title.

374   UTLEY, FRANCIS LEE. "Must We Abandon the Concept of Courtly
Love?" M&H, 3 (1972), 299-324.

375   UTLEY, FRANCIS LEE. "Robertsonianism Redivivus." RPh, 19
(1965), 250-60.
Review article on D. W. Robertson, A Preface to
Chaucer, 339 above. Reprinted in 37, pp. 69-85.

376   VAN DUZEE, MABEL. A Medieval Romance of Friendship: Eger
and Grime. Selected Papers in Literature and Criticism,
2. New York: Burt Franklin, 1963. 206 pp.
See pp. 125-31 for an analysis of Chaucer's connections
with and references to Anne of Bohemia, Queen of Richard
II.

377   *VON KREISLER, NICOLAI ALEXANDER. "The Achievement of
Chaucer's Love-Visions." DA, 29 (1968), 1882A. The
University of Texas at Austin, 1968. 171 pp.

378   VON KREISLER, NICOLAI. "A Recurrent Expression of Devotion
in Chaucer's Book of the Duchess, Parliament of Fowls,
and Knight's Tale." MP, 68 (1970), 62-64. Abstr. in
AES, 14 (1970-71), no. 1648.

379   WAGENKNECHT, EDWARD C. The Personality of Chaucer. Norman:
University of Oklahoma Press, 1968. 168 pp.
Reviews: P. W. Rogers, QQ, 75 (1968), 751-53; TLS
(15 May, 1969), p. 517.

380   *WALLER, MARTHA S. "Chaucer and the History of Rome." DAI,
        34 (1973), 1942A. Indiana University, 1973. 333 pp.

381   *WALTERS, GERTRUD. "Grundtypen der Erzähl- und
        Darstellungstechnik bei Chaucer." München Dissertation,
        1964. Cited in JDH, 80, v (1964), p. 487, no. U649395.

382   *WASS, ROSEMARY THÉRÈSE ANN. "Chaucer and Late Medieval
        Scholasticism: A Preliminary Study of Individuality and
        Experience." DAI, 34 (1974), 5128A. University of
        Cincinnati, 1973. 229 pp.

383   WATTS, ANN CHALMERS. "Chaucerian Selves--Especially Two
        Serious Ones." ChauR, 4 (1970), 229-41. Abstr. in AES,
        15 (1971-72), no. 722.

384   WHITE, BEATRICE. "Poet and Peasant," in The Reign of Richard
        II: Essays in Honour of May McKisack. Edited by
        F. R. H. DuBoulay and Caroline M. Barron. London: The
        Athlone Press, 1971, pp. 58-75.
        References to Chaucer's Literary treatment of the poor.

385   WHITMAN, F[RANK] H. "Exegesis and Chaucer's Dream Visions."
        ChauR, 3 (1969), 229-38. Abstr. in AES, 13 (1969-70),
        no. 2557.

386   WILLIAMS, GEORGE G. A New View of Chaucer. Durham, North
        Carolina: Duke University Press, 1965. 209 pp.
        Argues much of Chaucer's poetry reflects personalities
        he knew, especially John of Gaunt and his circle.
        Reviews: John R. Willingham, LJ, 90 (1965), 2142;
        Dieter Mehl, Ang, 83 (1965), 495-98; Albert C. Baugh,
        JEGP, 65 (1966), 586-89; Derek Pearsall, MAE, 35 (1966),
        149-50; H. L. Rogers, AUMLA, 26 (1966), 313-14; Edmund
        Reiss, CE, 27 (1966), 649; Stanley B. Greenfield, ELN,
        3 (1966), 300-303; F. C. DeVries, Neophil, 50 (1966),
        200-203; D. S. Brewer, RES, 18 (1967), 490; Paule
        Mertens-Fonck, MA, 74 (1968), 360-63.

387   WILSON, WILLIAM S. "Days and Months in Chaucer's Poems."
        AN&Q, 4 (1966), 83-84. Abstr. in AES, 17 (1973-74),
        no. 2612.

388   WIMSATT, JAMES I. Allegory and Mirror: Tradition and
        Structure in Middle English Literature. New York:
        Pegasus, 1970. 237 pp.
        See especially chapter 7, "The Mirror of Society:
        Chaucer's Canterbury Tales," pp. 163-89.

General Criticism

389   WINNY, JAMES. Chaucer's Dream Poems. London: Chatto &
       Windus, 1973. 158 pp.

390   WOOD, CHAUNCEY. "Chaucer and Astrology," in 60, pp. 176-91.

391   WOOD, CHAUNCEY [DERBY]. Chaucer and the Country of the
       Stars: Poetic Uses of Astrological Imagery. Toronto:
       Saunders; Princeton: Princeton University Press, 1970.
       337 pp., 32 plates.
          Based on the author's doctoral dissertation, 392
       below.
          Reviews: Nan Cooke Carpenter, GaR, 24 (1970), 511-13;
       R. MacG. Dawson, DalR, 50 (1970), 271-73; J. D. North,
       RES, 22 (1971), 471-74; J. A. W. Bennett, UTQ, 41 (1972),
       174-75; TLS (20 October, 1970), p. 1140; VQR, 56 (1970),
       xcviii; John M. Steadman, JEGP, 71 (1972), 113-16;
       R. M. Wilson, Eng, 19 (1970), 97-98.

392   WOOD, CHAUNCEY DERBY. "Chaucer's Use of Astrology for
       Poetic Imagery." DA, 25 (1964), 2970. Princeton
       University, 1963. 390 pp.
          Published as 391 above.

393   YOSHIDA, SHINGO. Chaucer. Tokyo: Apollonsha, 1966. 295 pp.
       In Japanese.

394   ZANCO, AURELIO. Chaucer e il suo mondo. Second edition,
       revised and corrected. Torino: G. B. Petrini, 1965.
       274 pp.
          Originally published in 1955. See Crawford, p. 29.

See also: 403, 442, 500, 506, 1151, 1733, 1748, 1832, 1842, 1942.
For reprinted articles prior to 1964, see 31.

Literary Relations and Sources

See Griffith, pp. 81–99; Crawford, pp. 30–35.

395   BENSON, LARRY D. The Literary Context of Chaucer's Fabliaux.
        Indianapolis and New York: Bobbs-Merrill, 1971. 410 pp.
        Analogues of Chaucer's fabliaux-texts and translations.
        Reviews: R. M. Wilson, MLR, 68 (1973), 147–48; Helen
        Cooper, MAE, 42 (1973), 285–86.

396   BRADDY, HALDEEN. "The French Influence on Chaucer," in 60,
        pp. 123–38.

397   *BRENNAN, JOHN PATRICK, JR. "The Chaucerian Text of Jerome
        Adversus Jovinianum: An Edition Based on Pembroke College,
        Cambridge, MS 234." DA, 28 (1968), 4622A–23A. University
        of California, Davis, 1967. 353 pp.

398   CLOGAN, PAUL M. "Chaucer and the Thebaid Scholia." SP, 61
        (1964), 599–615. Abstr. in AES, 8 (1965), no. 1236.

399   CLOGAN, PAUL M. "Chaucer's Use of the Thebaid." EM, 18
        (1967), 9–31. Abstr. in AES, 12 (1969), no. 391.

400   CUMMINGS, HUBERTIS M. The Indebtedness of Chaucer's Works
        to the Italian Works of Boccaccio: A Review and Summary.
        New York: Haskell House, 1965. 202 pp.
        Originally published in 1916. See Griffith, p. 84.

401   DEAN, NANCY. "Chaucer's Complaint, a Genre Descended from
        the Heroides." CL, 19 (1967), 1–27. Abstr. in AES, 11
        (1968), no. 1868.

402   *DEAN, NANCY. "Studies in Chaucer's Use of Ovid in Selected
        Early Poems." DA, 27 (1966), 1334A. New York University,
        1963. 522 pp.

403   DELASANTA, RODNEY. "James Smith and Chaucer." EIC, 22 (1972),
        221–25.
        Response to James Smith, 418 below.

49

Literary Relations and Sources

404   GARBÁTY, THOMAS JAY. "Pamphilus, De Amore: An Introduction
       and Translation." ChauR, 2 (1967), 108-34. Abstr. in
       AES, 16 (1972-73), no. 1589.

405   GARDNER, AVERIL. "Chaucer and Boethius: Some Illustrations
       of Indebtedness." UCTSE, 2 (1971), 31-38.

406   GERRITSEN, W. P. "Galfredus de Vino Salvo en de
       Middelnederlandse bewerkers van epische poezie." NTg,
       56 (1963), 25-32.

407   *GUERIN, RICHARD STEPHEN. "The Canterbury Tales and Il
       Decamerone." DA, 28 (1967), 1396A. University of
       Colorado, 1966. 288 pp.
          Questions the view that Chaucer did not know the
       Decameron.

408   *HALABY, RAOUF JAMIL. "Arabic Influences on Chaucer: Specula-
       tive Essays on a Study of a Literary Relationship." DAI,
       34 (1974), 5911A-12A. East Texas State University, 1973.
       203 pp.

409   HOFFMAN, RICHARD L. "The Influence of the Classics on
       Chaucer," in 60, pp. 162-75.

410   JEFFERSON, BERNARD L. Chaucer and the Consolation of
       Philosophy of Boethius. New York: Haskell House, 1965.
       173 pp.
          Reprint of the author's thesis, originally published
       in 1917. See Griffith, p. 88. Excerpts included in 62,
       pp. 92-96.

411   *LEWIS, ROBERT ENZER. "Chaucer and Pope Innocent III's
       De Miseria Humane Conditionis." DA, 25 (1965), 7246-47.
       University of Pennsylvania, 1964. 451 pp.

412   LOOMIS, DOROTHY BETHURUM. "The Venus of Alanus de Insulis
       and the Venus of Chaucer," in Philological Essays:
       Studies in Old and Middle English Language and Literature
       in Honor of Herbert Dean Merritt. Janua Linguarum,
       Series maior, 37. Edited by James L. Rosier. The Hague,
       Mouton, 1970, pp. 182-95. Abstr. in AES, 15 (1971-72),
       no. 2894.

413   *LOPRESTI, VINCENT AUGUST. "Chaucer's Treatment of the Gods
       in Relation to Source, Analogue, and Tradition." DA, 28
       (1967), 636A. The University of Wisconsin, 1966. 237 pp.

Literary Relations and Sources

414   *MEECH, SANFORD BROWN. "Chaucer and Mediaeval Ovidiana."
          DAI, 31 (1970), 2350A. Yale University, 1929. 529 pp.

415   *PAGE, CURTIS CARLING. "Chaucer's Testimony Concerning His
          Sources." DAI, 31 (1970), 2362A. Yale University,
          1947. 434 pp.

416   PRATT, ROBERT A. "Chaucer and the Hand That Fed Him." Spec,
          41 (1966), 619-42. Abstr. in AES, 16 (1972-73), no. 29.
          Chaucer's use of Communiloquium sive summa collationum
          of John of Wales.

417   RUGGIERS, PAUL G. "The Italian Influence on Chaucer," in 60,
          pp. 139-61.

418   SMITH, JAMES. "Chaucer, Boethius and Recent Trends in
          Criticism." EIC, 22 (1972), 4-32.
          A lecture delivered at the University of Bristol. See
          403 above for dissenting opinion.

419   *WEBER, BARBARA JEAN (DRUM). "A Comparative Study of the Dido
          Theme in Virgil, Ovid, and Chaucer." DAI, 31 (1970),
          2363A-4A. The Florida State University, 1970. 131 pp.

420   WIMSATT, JAMES I. "Chaucer and the Canticle of Canticles,"
          in 56, pp. 66-90.

421   WITLIEB, BERNARD L. "Chaucer and a French Story of Thebes."
          ELN, 11 (1973), 5-9. Abstr. in MLAA (1973), no. 2790.

422   *WITLIEB, BERNARD L. "Chaucer and the Ovide moralisé." DAI,
          31 (1970), 1245A. New York University, 1970. 333 pp.

423   WITLIEB, BERNARD L. "Chaucer and Ovide moralisé." N&Q, 17
          (1970), 202-207. Abstr. in AES, 14 (1970-71), no. 349.

See also Source Studies under separate works: 679-81, 807-808, 833-
34, 870-74, 927-35, 947, 962, 988-89, 1034-38, 1081, 1135-37, 1145-49,
1188-89; 1198-99, 1239-45, 1251, 1288-90, 1298-99, 1336-43, 1369-71,
1380-83, 1406-07, 1568-85, 1604, 699, 741, 747, 754, 837. Further
cross references follow these numbers. Under some works, Source
Studies contain only cross references. For completeness all numbers
should be consulted.

See also: 28, 166, 188, 220, 224, 267, 312, 350, 492, 493, 554, 555,
563, 572, 588, 652, 670, 679, 680, 1184, 1748.

Influence and Allusions

See Griffith, pp. 100-16; Crawford, pp. 36-41.

424 ALDERSON, WILLIAM L[EWIS] and ARNOLD C. HENDERSON. Chaucer
and Augustan Scholarship. UCPES, 35. Berkeley: University of California Press, 1970. 284 pp.
Reviews: H. Neville Davies, YES, 2 (1972), 245-46;
Sylvia Wallace Holton, SN, 44 (1972), 171-73.

425 ANDERSON, JUDITH H. "'Nat worth a boterflye': Muiopotmos
and The Nun's Priest's Tale." JMRS, 1 (1971), 89-106.

426 *ARTHURS, JUDITH GOTT. "Edmund Spenser and Dan Chaucer: A
Study of the Influence of The Canterbury Tales on The
Faerie Queen." DAI, 34 (1973), 3334A. University of
Arkansas, 1973. 187 pp.

427 BAWCUTT, PRISCILLA. "Dunbar's Tretis of the Tua Mariit Wemen
and the Wedo 185-187 and Chaucer's Parson's Tale." N&Q,
11 (1964), 332-33. Abstr. in AES, 8 (1965), no. 1721.

428 BAWCUTT, PRISCILLA. "Gavin Douglas and Chaucer." RES, 21
(1970), 401-21.

429 BENSON, C. DAVID. "Chaucer's Influence on the Prose Sege of
Troy." N&Q, 18 (1971), 127-30. Abstr. in AES, 15
(1971-72), no. 43.

430 *BIRD, ROGER ANTHONY. "Dryden's Medieval Translations." DAI,
30 (1970), 4397A. University of Minnesota, 1969.
219 pp.

431 BLEETH, KENNETH A. "Wyatt and Chaucer's 'lusty leese.'"
N&Q, 18 (1971), 214.

432 BRYANT, JAMES C. "The Pardoner and the Friar as Reformation
Polemic." RenP (1972), pp. 17-24.
Similarities between John Heywood's The Pardoner and the
Friar and Chaucer's Pardoner's Prologue.

Influence and Allusions

433   DEAN, CHRISTOPHER. "Henryson's Testament of Cresseid, 188."
Expl, 31 (1972), Item 21. Abstr. in AES, 17 (1973-74),
no. 1584.

434   *DORMAN, PETER J. "Chaucer's Reputation in the Restoration
and Eighteenth Century." DAI, 32 (1972), 5734A. New
York University, 1971. 694 pp.

435   DYER, FREDERICK B., JR. "The Destruction of Pandare," in
1564-1964: Shakespeare Encomium. The City College Papers,
I. Edited by Anne Paolucci. New York: The City College,
1964, pp. 123-33.

436   EDDY, ELIZABETH ROTH. "Sir Thopas and Sir Thomas Norny:
Romance Parody in Chaucer and Dunbar." RES, 22 (1971),
401-409. Abstr. in MLAA (1973), no. 2136.

437   *EDDY, ELIZABETH ROTH. "Studies on William Dunbar." DAI, 33
(1973), 6906A-7A. University of Washington, 1972.
237 pp.

438   ELIASON, NORMAN E. "Chaucer's Fifteenth-Century Successors."
MRS, 5 (1971), 103-21.

439   FLETCHER, HARRIS. "A Chaucer Allusion (Latin), 1619." N&Q,
13 (1966), 254. Abstr. in AES, 10 (1967), no. 254.
Abstr. in AES, 10 (1967), no. 209.

440   FOX, DENTON. "Chaucer's Influence on Fifteenth-Century
Poetry," in 60, pp. 385-402.

441   FOX, DENTON. "The Scottish Chaucerians," in 35, pp. 164-200.

442   *GLUCK, FLORENCE. "The Minor Poems of Stephen Hawes." DA,
27 (1967), 3426A-27A. Western Reserve University, 1966.
292 pp.
Makes comparisons between Hawes and Chaucer.

443   GOLDEN, SAMUEL A. "Chaucer in Minsheu's Guide into the
Tongues." ChauR, 4 (1970), 49-54. Abstr. in MLAA (1970),
no. 1776 and AES, 13 (1969-70), no. 2872.
Over fifty newly discovered seventeenth century allusions to Chaucer.

444   HARWARD, VERNON. "Hary's Wallace and Chaucer's Troilus and
Criseyde." SSL, 10 (1972), 48-50.

Influence and Allusions

445   HEUSTON, EDWARD F. "Chaucer Sprig in Wordsworth's Liberty," N&Q, 11 (1964), 20-21.

446   *INGHAM, MURIEL BRIERLEY. "Some Fifteenth-Century Images of Death and Their Background." DA, 28 (1968), 4132A-33A. University of California, Riverside, 1967. 193 pp. Notes "positive" attitudes toward death in the Canterbury Tales and Troilus and Criseyde.

447   LAMPE, DAVID E. "Tradition and Meaning in The Cuckoo and the Nightingale." PLL, 3 (Summer supplement, 1967), 49-62. Suggests influence of the Knight's Tale on Sir John Clanvowe's poem.

448   *LEVY, ROBERT ALLEN. "Dryden's Translation of Chaucer: A Study of the Means of Re-creating Literary Models." DAI, 34 (1974), 5108A-09A. The University of Tennessee, 1973. 298 pp.

449   LOOMIS, DOROTHY BETHURUM. "Chaucer and Shakespeare," in 37, pp. 166-90.

450   *LYNN, KAREN. "Computational Prosodics: The Decasyllabic Line from Chaucer to Skelton." DAI, 34 (1974), 4210A. University of Southern California, 1973. 381 pp.

451   LYONS, JOHN O. "James Joyce and Chaucer's Prioress." ELN, 2 (1964), 127-32. Abstr. in AES, 8 (1965), no. 2915.

452   MacDONALD, DONALD. "Chaucer's Influence on Henryson's Fables: The Use of Proverbs and Sententiae." MAE, 39 (1970), 21-27. Abstr. in AES, 17 (1973-74), no. 1000.

453   MacDONALD, DONALD. "Henryson and Chaucer: Cock and Fox." TSLL, 8 (1967), 451-61.

454   MANZALAOUI, MAHMOUD. "George Wither and Chaucer's Troilus and Criseyde, I, 813 ff." N&Q, 11 (1964), 92.

455   MAXWELL, J. C. "The Ancient Mariner and The Squire's Tale." N&Q, 13 (1966), 224.

456   MAXWELL, J. C. "An Echo of Chaucer in The Kingis Quair." N&Q, 11 (1964), 172. Abstr. in AES, 7 (1964), no. 2249.

457   MAXWELL, J. C. and DOUGLAS GRAY. "An Echo of Chaucer." N&Q, 16 (1969), 170.

Influence and Allusions

458 MIDDLETON, ANNE. "The Modern Art of Fortifying: Palamon and
     Arcite as Epicurean Epic." ChauR, 3 (1968), 124-43.

459 MINER, EARL. "Chaucer in Dryden's Fables," in Studies in
     Criticism and Aesthetics, 1660-1800: Essays in Honor of
     Samuel Holt Monk. Edited by Howard Peter Anderson and
     John S. Shea. Minneapolis: University of Minnesota
     Press, 1967, pp. 58-72.

460 MITCHELL, JEROME. "Hoccleve's Tribute to Chaucer," in 43,
     pp. 275-83.

461 NATHAN, LEONARD E. "Tradition and Newfangleness in Wyatt's
     They Fle From Me." ELH, 32 (1965), 1-16.

462 PACE, GEORGE B. "Giraldi on Chaucer." ChauR, 7 (1973),
     295-96. Abstr. in AES, 17 (1973-74), no. 2896 and MLAA
     (1973), no. 2776.

463 PEARSALL, DEREK. "The English Chaucerians," in 35, pp. 201-39.
     Lydgate, Hoccleve, and others.

464 PHILLIPS, NORMA. "Observations on the Derivative Method of
     Skelton's Realism." JEGP, 65 (1966), 19-35. Abstr. in
     AES, 10 (1967), no. 120.

465 PRESSON, ROBERT K. "Two Types of Dreams in the Elizabethan
     Drama, and their Heritage: Somnium Animale and the
     Pricke-of-Conscience." SEL, 7 (1967), 239-56.

466 *PRIMEAU, RONALD R. "Keats's Chaucer: Realism and Romanticism
     in the English Tradition." DAI, 32 (1972), 4575A. Uni-
     versity of Illinois, Urbana-Champaign, 1971. 279 pp.
     Keats's use of Chaucer's dream visions.

467 RAIZIS, M. BYRON. "Nikos Kazantzakis and Chaucer." CLS,
     6 (1969), 141-47. Abstr. in AES, 13 (1969-70), no. 756.

468 ROBBINS, ROSSELL HOPE. "A Late-Sixteenth Century Chaucer
     Allusion (Douce MS 290)." ChauR, 2 (1967), 135-37.
     Abstr. in AES, 16 (1972-73), no. 1578.

469 ROBBINS, ROSSELL HOPE. "A New Chaucer Analogue: The Legend
     of Ugolino." Trivium, 2 (1967), 1-16. Abstr. in AES,
     11 (1968), no. 335.
     Newly discovered Middle English poem (c. 1500), which
     expands Chaucer's tale of Ugolino.

Influence and Allusions

470   ROHR, M. R. "Gascoigne and 'my master Chaucer.'" <u>JEGP</u>, 67
        (1968), 20-31. Abstr. in <u>AES</u>, 12 (1969), no. 1553.

471   *ROKUTANDA, OSAMU. "L'incontro del Chaucer e la letteratura
        italiana." <u>SIK</u>, 17 (1969), 63-77. Cited in <u>PMLAB</u> (1971),
        no. 2215.
        Chaucer's influence on Italian literature.

472   SCATTERGOOD, V. J. "The Authorship of <u>The Boke of Cupide</u>."
        <u>Ang</u>, 82 (1964), 137-45. Abstr. in <u>AES</u>, 9 (1966),
        no. 1512.

473   SCHAAR, CLAES. "Conventional and Unconventional in the
        Descriptions of Scenery in Shakespeare's Sonnets." <u>ES</u>,
        45 (1964), 142-49. Abstr. in <u>AES</u>, 7 (1964), no. 2416.
        See especially p. 144 for a note on the <u>General
        Prologue</u>.

474   SCHEPS, WALTER. "Chaucerian Synthesis: the Art of <u>The
        Kingis Quair</u>." <u>SSL</u>, 8 (1971), 143-65. Abstr. in <u>AES</u>,
        16 (1972-73), no. 626.

475   SCHLAUCH, MARGARET. "The Doctrine of 'Vera Nobilitas' as
        Developed after Chaucer." <u>KN</u>, 17 (1970), 119-27.

476   SPEARING, A. C. "Conciseness and <u>The Testament of Cresseid</u>,"
        in his <u>Criticism and Medieval Poetry</u>, 363, above, chap-
        ter 7, pp. 157-92.

477   STAFFORD, T. J. "Middleton's Debt to Chaucer in <u>The Change-
        ling</u>." <u>BRMMLA</u>, 22 (1968), 208-13.

478   STEVENS, MARTIN. "Juliet's Nurse: Love's Herald." <u>PLL</u>, 2
        (1966), 195-206.

479   STOUCK, MARY-ANN. "Chaucer's Pilgrims and Cather's Priests."
        <u>CLQ</u>, 9 (1972), 531-37.

480   STROHM, PAUL. "Jean of Angoulême: A Fifteenth Century
        Reader of Chaucer." <u>NM</u>, 72 (1971) 69-76.

481   TAYLOR, ERIC F. "<u>The Knight's Tale</u>: A New Source for
        Spenser's <u>Muiopotmos</u>." <u>RenP</u> (1965), pp. 57-63. Abstr.
        in <u>AES</u>, 10 (1967), no. 567.

482   TENFELDE, NANCY L. "Longfellow's <u>Chaucer</u>." <u>Expl</u>, 22 (1964),
        Item 55.

Influence and Allusions

483   THOMPSON, PATRICIA. "Wyatt's Boethian Ballade." RES, 15
          (1964), 262-67. Abstr. in AES, 8 (1965), no. 2700.

484   TOOLE, WILLIAM B., III. "Wit and Symbol: The Prior's Niece
          and the Structure of Fra Lippo Lippi." SAB, 35, ii
          (March, 1970), 3-8.

485   WAWN, ANDREW N. "Chaucer, Wyclif and the Court of Apollo."
          ELN, 10 (1972), 15-20. Abstr. in AES, 17 (1973-74),
          no. 1580.
          William Vaughn's representation of Chaucer as arch-
          Protestant and Wyclif's master.

486   WAX, JUDITH. "The Waterbury Tales." New Republic
          (15 September, 1973), pp. 24-25. Reprinted in Time
          (24 September, 1973), p. 20.
          Pseudo-Chaucerian parody of Watergate.

487   WHITE, ROBERT B., JR. "An Eighteenth Century Allusion to
          Chaucer's Cook's Tale." ELN, 7 (1970), 190-92.

488   WINTER, J. L. "Browning's Piper." N&Q, 14 (1967), 373.
          Abstr. in AES, 11 (1968), no. 1359.
          Suggests Browning may have modeled his Pied Piper on
          Chaucer's Pardoner.

See also: 36, 189, 217, 255, 301, 617, 1211, 1237, 1300, 1342, 1451,
1504, 1570, 1580, 1581, 1591.

Style Including Versification and Puns

See Griffith, pp. 116-27; Crawford, pp. 42-47.

489   ADAMS, PERCY G. "Chaucer's Assonance." _JEGP_, 71 (1972), 527-39. Abstr. in _MLAA_ (1972), no. 2647.

490   *ANDREAS, JAMES ROBERT. "The Noble Rhetor: Chaucer and Medieval Poetic Traditions." _DAI_, 34 (1974), 5088A. Vanderbilt University, 1973. 485 pp.

491   BALTZELL, JANE. "Rhetorical Amplification and Abbreviation and the Structure of Medieval Narrative." _PCP_, 2 (1967), 32-39.

492   *BICKFORD, CHARLES GRAY. "The Influence of Rhetoric on Chaucer's Portraiture." _DAI_, 34 (1974), 5091A. University of Pennsylvania, 1973. 245 pp.

493   BREWER, D. S. "The Relationship of Chaucer to the English and European Traditions," in 35, pp. 1-38. Excerpts reprinted in 62, pp. 41-47.

494   BROOKHOUSE, CHRISTOPHER. "Chaucer's _Impossibilia_." _MAE_, 34 (1965), 40-42. Abstr. in _AES_, 10 (1967), no. 3029.

495   CHRISTOPHERSEN, PAUL. "The Scansion of Two Lines in Chaucer." _ES_, 45, Supplement (1964), 146-50. Abstr. in _AES_, 9 (1966), no. 1138.
        Examines _Canterbury Tales_ A49 and A173.

496   *COMBS, BRUCE ELMER. "A Linguistic Analysis of Rime with Studies in Chaucer, Donne, and Pope." _DAI_, 30 (1970), 4963A. University of Oregon, 1969. 129 pp.

497   *DAALDER, JOOST. "Chaucer's Prosody." _AUMLA_, 37 (May, 1972), 73-75. Cited and abstr. in _AES_, 16 (1972-73), no. 2176.
        Review article. See 513.

Style Including Versification and Puns

498   *DAYE, MARY LOUISE. "The Rhetoric of Narration: A Study of
          Narrative Intrusion in Chaucer's Tales of the Squire,
          Manciple, Merchant and Nun's Priest." DA, 29 (1968),
          563A-4A. The University of Wisconsin, 1968. 201 pp.

499   FIFIELD, MERLE. Theoretical Techniques for the Analysis of
          Variety in Chaucer's Metrical Stress. Ball State
          Monograph, 23. Muncie, Indiana: Ball State University,
          1973. 47 pp.

500   *GEISSMAN, ERWIN WILLIAM. "The Style and Technique of
          Chaucer's Translations from French." DAI, 30 (1969),
          320A. Yale University, 1952. 329 pp.

501   HALLE, MORRIS and SAMUEL JAY KEYSER. "Chaucer and the Study
          of Prosody." CE, 28 (1966), 187-219. Abstr. in AES,
          10 (1967), no. 1910.
             See also 503 and 522.

502   *HARRISON, BENJAMIN SAMUEL. "The Colors of Rhetoric in
          Chaucer." DA, 27 (1966), 1786A. Yale University, 1932.
          373 pp.

503   HASCALL, DUDLEY L. "Some Contributions to the Halle-Keyser
          Theory of Prosody." CE, 30 (1969), 357-65.
             Refutation of theories of Halle and Keyser, 501 above.

504   HINTON, NORMAN D. "More Puns in Chaucer." AN&Q, 2 (1964),
          115-16. Abstr. in AES, 9 (1966), no. 1472.

505   ITO, MASAYOSHI. "Gower's Use of rime riche in Confessio
          Amantis: As Compared with his Practice in Mirour de
          l'Omme and with the Case of Chaucer." SELit, 46 (1969),
          29-44.

506   JORDAN, ROBERT M. "Chaucerian Narrative," in 60, pp. 85-102.

507   *LEICESTER, HENRY MARSHALL, JR. "The Rhetorical Moment:
          Studies in the Development of the First-Person Narrative
          Mode in Chaucer's Poetry." DA, 28 (1967), 1052A-3A.
          Yale University, 1967. 461 pp.

508   MUSTANOJA, TAUNO F. "Chaucer's Prosody," in 60, pp. 58-84.

509   NORTON-SMITH, J. "Chaucer's Epistolary Style," in 44,
          pp. 157-65.

Style Including Versification and Puns

510   OWEN, CHARLES A., JR. "'Thy Drasty Rymyng....'" SP, 63
       (1966), 533-64. Abstr. in AES, 10 (1967), no. 3193.

511   PAYNE, ROBERT O. "Chaucer and the Art of Rhetoric," in 60,
       pp. 38-57.

512   PYLE, FITZROY. "Chaucer's Prosody." MAE, 42 (1973), 47-56.
       Criticism of Ian Robinson, 513 below.

513   ROBINSON, IAN. Chaucer's Prosody: A Study of the Middle
       English Verse Tradition. London: Cambridge University
       Press, 1971. 251 pp.
          Reviews: R. T. Davies, RES, 23 (1972), 190-92;
       J. A. Burrow, CamQ, 5 (1971), 389-93; *A. C. Cawley, DUJ,
       23 (1972), 158-60; H. H. Meier, DQR, 2 (1972), 127-29;
       J. R. Simon, EA, 25 (1972), 45-65; G. S. Fraser, Lang&S,
       5 (1972), 313-15; Joost Daalder, AUMLA, 37 (May, 1972),
       73-75; Charles A. Owen, Jr., Spec, 49 (1974), 148-51.
       See also 512.

514   *RUFF, JOSEPH RUSSELL. "Occupatio in the Poetry of Chaucer."
       DAI, 32 (1971), 3328A. University of Pittsburgh, 1971.
       212 pp.

515   *SABIN, MARIE NOONAN. "Chaucer's Styles: A Study of the
       Rhetorical Relationships Between the Tales of the Knight
       and the Miller, the Wife of Bath and the Clerk, and the
       Monk and the Nun's Priest." Yale University Dissertation,
       1964. Cited in MHRA (1965), no. 2547.

516   SAMUELS, M. L. "Chaucerian Final '-e.'" N&Q, 19 (1972),
       445-48. Abstr. in AES, 17 (1973-74), no. 2897.

517   SCHLAUCH, MARGARET. "The Art of Chaucer's Prose," in 35,
       pp. 140-63.

518   SUDO, JUN. "Some Specific Rime-Units in Chaucer." SELit,
       45 (1969), 221-36.

519   *SYMES, KEN MICHAEL. "The Narrative Techniques of Chaucer's
       Fabliaux." DA, 28 (1968), 3650A-51A. The University of
       New Mexico, 1967. 160 pp.

520   WEESE, WALTER EUGENE. "Word-Order as a Factor of Style in
       Chaucer's Poetry." DAI, 31 (1971), 4138A. Yale Univer-
       sity, 1950. 218 pp.

Style Including Versification and Puns

521   *WEIDENBRÜCK, ADOLPH W. "Chaucers Sprichwortpraxis: Eine
        Form-und Funktionsanalyse." Bonn Dissertation, 1970.
        Cited in BLA (1970), no. 7734.

522   WIMSATT, W. K. "The Rule and the Norm: Halle and Keyser on
        Chaucer's Meter." CE, 31 (1970), 774-88.
            Reprinted in Literary Style: A Symposium. Edited by
        Seymour Chatman. New York: Oxford University Press,
        1971, pp. 197-215. See also pp. 215-20 in the book for
        "Discussion of Wimsatt's Paper."

See also: 170, 187, 188, 213, 308, 321, 360, 523, 529, 538, 544,
552, 560, 576, 588, 595, 657, 749, 756, 722, 710, 913, 1009, 1141,
1172, 1178, 1184, 1212, 1272, 1282, 1310, 1315, 1316, 1321, 1411,
1492, 1493, 1496, 1550, 1557, 1560, 1586, 1594, 1611.

Language and Word Studies

See Griffith, pp. 128-50; Crawford, pp. 48-51.

523   BAUER, GERO. "Historisches Präsens und Vergegenwärtigung des epischen Geschehens: Ein erzähltechnischer Kunstgriff Chaucers." Ang, 85 (1967), 138-60.

524   BAUER, GERO. Studien zum System und Gebrauch der "Tempora" in der Sprache Chaucers und Gowers. WBEP, 73. Wien: Wilhelm Braumüller, 1970. 165 pp.
      Reviews: *Rüdiger Zimmerman, Die Sprache, 17 (1971), 185; K. C. Phillipps, ES, 53 (1972), 456-58.

525   BERMAN, ARLENE. "The Relative Clause Construction in Old and Middle English," in Mathematical Linguistics and Automatic Translation. Report No. NSF-26 to The National Science Foundation. Cambridge, Massachusetts: Aiken Computation Laboratory of Harvard University, 1970. 43 pp.

526   BIGGINS, D[ENNIS]. "A Chaucerian Crux: 'Spiced Conscience,' CT I (A) 526, III (D) 435." ES, 47 (1966), 169-80. Abstr. in AES, 10 (1967), no. 2354.

527   DEAN, CHRISTOPHER. "Chaucer's Use of Function Words with Substantives." CJL, 9, ii (1964), 67-74. Abstr. in AES, 9 (1966), no. 49 and in AES, 14 (1970-71), no. 2619.

528   EDMONDS, JOSEPH. "The Derived Nominals, Gerunds, and Participles in Chaucer's English," in Issues in Linguistics: Papers in Honor of Henry and Renée Kahane. Edited by Braj B. Kachru et al. Chicago: University of Illinois Press, 1973, pp. 185-98.

529   ELIASON, NORMAN E. The Language of Chaucer's Poetry: An Appraisal of the Verse, Style and Structure. Anglistica, 17. Copenhagen: Rosenkilde and Hagger, 1972. 250 pp.

Language and Word Studies

Reviews: R. M. Wilson, MLR, 68 (1973), 889; D. S.
Brewer, RES, 25 (1974), 74-76; Charles A. Owen, Jr.,
Spec, 49 (1974), 727-30.

530   FISIAK, JACEK. The Morphemic Structure of Chaucer's English.
Alabama Linguistic and Philological Series, 10. Univer-
sity, Alabama: University of Alabama Press, 1965.
125 pp.
Reviews: Norman Davis, RES, 18 (1967), 303-305;
J. Boswinkel, ES, 49 (1968), 244-45.

531   FREY, EDGAR. Die Verben des Transportfelds bei Chaucer und
König Alfred dem Grossen: Untersuchung über das
Nebeneinander sprachlicher Begriffe im semantischen Feld.
Zurich: Verlag P. G. Keller, 1967. 300 pp.

532   HANKEY, CLYDE T. "Defining-Context, Associations Sets and
Glosing Chaucer." SMC, 7, ii (April, 1964), 69-73.

533   KERKHOF, JELLE. Studies in the Language of Geoffrey Chaucer.
Leidse germanistische en anglistische reeks, 5. Leiden:
Universitaire Pers, 1966. 251 pp.
Also as Leiden Doctoral Dissertation, 1966.

534   KHARENKO, M. F. "Dzhefri Choser i angliis'ka natsional'na
mova" [Geoffrey Chaucer and the National English
Language]. InF, 2 (1967), 41-47.

535   KHARENKO, M. F. "Spivvidnoshennya zalozshenogo ta
pervinnogo elementiv u slovniku 'Kenterberiis'kikh
opovidan' Dzh. Chosera" [Vocabulary of the Canterbury
Tales]. InF, 2 (1967), 23-30.
Accompanied by an English summary.

536   *KIRWIN, WILLIAM JAMES, JR. "Inflectional and Principal
Syntactic Classes in Chaucer's Canterbury Tales." University of Chicago Dissertation, 1964. Cited in MHRA
(1965), no. 2511.

537   KIVIMAA, KIRSTI. Clauses in Chaucer Introduced by Conjunc-
tions with Appended "That". CHLSSF, 43:1. Helsinki:
Societas Scientiarum Fennica, 1968. 75 pp. Abstr. in
AES, 15 (1971-72), no. 2530.

538   KIVIMAA, KIRSTI. The Pleonastic "That" in Relative and
Interrogative Construction in Chaucer's Verse. CHLSSF,
39:3. Helsinki: Societas Scientiarum Fennica, 1966.
39 pp. Abstr. in AES, 15 (1971-72), no. 2529.
Reviews: Broder Carstensen, Archiv, 207 (1970), 301.

Language and Word Studies

538.01 KUHN, SHERMAN M. and JOHN REIDY, eds. Middle English Diction-
ary. Vol. 4: G to H. Ann Arbor: University of Michigan
Press, 1965-67.
See Griffith, p. 134.
Reviews: B. D. H. Miller, MAE, 42 (1973), 73-81.

539   MASUI, MICHIO. The Structure of Chaucer's Rime Words: An
Exploration into the Poetic Language of Chaucer. Tokyo:
Kenkyusha, 1964. 393 pp.
Reviews: Guy Bourquin, EA, 18 (1965), 301-302;
Tauno F. Mustanoja, NM, 66 (1965), 262-63; E. G. Stanley,
N&Q, 12 (1965), 389-90; Margaret Schlauch, KN, 12 (1965),
102-103; Thomas A. Kirby, ES, 51 (1970), 450-51.

540   MASUI, YOSHIO "Chusei kara mita Renaissance no Gengo to
Hyogen--Chaucer to Shakespeare" [Language and Expression
in the Renaissance from Viewpoint of Middle Ages--Chaucer
and Shakespeare]. EigoS, 119 (1973), 388-90.

541   MERSAND, JOSEPH. Chaucer's Romance Vocabulary. Port Washington, New York: Kennikat, 1968. 184 pp.
Reprint of 1939 edition. See Griffith, p. 136.

542   MIURA, TSUNESHI. "Arrangement of Two or More Attributive
Adjectives in Chaucer." Anglica, 6:i-ii (1966), 1-23.

543   ONO, SHIGERU. "Chaucer's Variants and What They Tell Us:
Fluctuation in the Use of Modal Auxiliaries." SELit
English number (1969), 51-74.

544   ONO, SHIGERU. "Gengo, Buntai, Shahon--Chaucer no baai"
[Language, Style, MSS--The Case of Chaucer]. EigoS,
114 (1968), 456-57.
In Japanese.

545   POTTER, SIMEON. "Chaucer's Untransposable Binominals."
NM, 73 (1972), 309-14.

546   *SMITH, CHARLES CAMPBELL. "Noun + Noun Compounds in the Works
of Geoffrey Chaucer." DAI, 32 (1972), 5769A. New York
University, 1971. 156 pp.

547   SMYSER, H. M. "Chaucer's Use of Gin and Do." Spec, 42
(1967), 68-83. Abstr. in AES, 16 (1972-73), no. 30.

548   SPEARING, A. C. "Chaucer's Language," in 258, chapter 4,
pp. 89-114.

Language and Word Studies

549   SVARTVIK, JAN and RANDOLPH QUIRK. "Types and Uses of Non-
            Finite Clause in Chaucer." ES, 51 (1970), 393-411.

550   TENGSTRAND, ERIK. "A Special Use of Old English ōþer after
            swilce." SN, 37 (1965), 382-92.
            Note on Canterbury Tales I (A) 1307-09.

551   TOPLIFF, DELORES E. "Analysis of Singular Weak Adjective
            Inflection in Chaucer's Works." JEngL, 4 (1970), 78-89.
            Abstr. in MLAA (1970), no. 1833.

552   *WOLFF, EDWARD J. "Chaucer's Normalized Diction: A Comparison
            of Recurring Phrases in Chaucer and Beowulf to Determine
            the Validity of the Magoun Thesis." DA, 27 (1967),
            3022A-23A. Michigan State University, 1966. 122 pp.

553   WORTHINGTON, MARTHA G. "The Compound Past Tense in Old
            French Narrative Poems." RPh, 19 (1966), 397-417.
            Chaucer's use of tense in Knight's Tale and Clerk's
            Tale.

See also: 258, 489, 493, 496, 499, 503, 620, 650, 656, 820, 940,
1120, 1124, 1154, 1170, 1184, 1185, 1275, 1297, 1360, 1366, 1511,
1531, 1541, 1618, 2128, 2143.

The Canterbury Tales

GENERAL

See Griffith, pp. 151-63; Crawford, pp. 52-54.

554   ADAMS, GEORGE R. AND BERNARD S. LEVY. "Good and Bad Fridays and May 3 in Chaucer." ELN, 3 (1966), 245-48. Abstr. in AES, 10 (1967), no. 1686.

555   ANDERSEN, JENS KR. "An Analysis of the Framework Structure of Chaucer's Canterbury Tales." OL, 27 (1972), 179-201. Abstr. in AES, 17 (1973-74), no. 1905.

556   *BALTZELL, JANE LUCILE. "An Explanation of Medieval Poetic with Special Reference to Chaucer." DA, 26 (1966), 4622. University of California, Berkeley, 1965. 535 pp. Analyses of Tales of the Miller, Prioresse, Physician, Merchant, and Clerk.

557   BARTHOLOMEW, BARBARA. Fortuna and Natura: A Reading of Three Chaucer Narratives. Studies in English Literature, 16. London and Paris: The Hague: Mouton, 1966. 112 pp. Reviews: Helmut Bonheim, Ang, 85 (1967), 459-60; P. M. Vermeer, LT, 240 (1967), 405-407; A. G. Rigg, RES 18 (1967), 448-50.

558   BERGNER, HEINZ. "Das Fabliau in der mittelenglischen Literatur." Sprachkunst, 3 (1972), 298-312.

559   *BERNAOLA, M. ANGELES. "The Two Pilgrimages--A Comparative Study of Chaucer and Langland." Universidad de Duesto: M. A. Thesis, 1972. Cited in MHRA (1972), no. 3001.

560   BIGGINS, DENNIS. "Sym(e)kyn/simia: The Ape in Chaucer's Millers." SP, 65 (1968), 44-50.

561   *BOWKER, ALVIN WILLINGTON. "A Jape of Malice: The Dark Spirit of Chaucer's Fabliaux." DAI, 34 (1973), 3336A. State University of New York at Buffalo, 1973. 357 pp.

BIBLIOGRAPHY OF CHAUCER, 1964 - 1973

562   BRADDY, HALDEEN. "Chaucer's Bilingual Idiom." SFQ, 32
       (1968), 1-6.
           Bawdy slang from French and Anglo-Saxon. Article is
       reprinted in 33, pp. 140-45.

563   BREWER, D. S. "The Fabliaux," in 60, pp. 247-67.

564   *BRONDELL, WILLIAM JOHN. "The Moral Vision in The Canterbury
       Tales." DA, 25 (1965), 5901-02. University of Missouri,
       1964. 210 pp.

565   BROOKHOUSE, CHRISTOPHER. "The Confessions of Three Pilgrims."
       LauR, 8 (1968), 49-56.
           Treats the Pardoner's Tale, the Wife of Bath's Tale
       and the Canon's Yeoman's Tale.

566   *BUERMANN, THEODORE BARRY. "Chaucer's 'Book of Genesis' in
       The Canterbury Tales: The Biblical Schema of the First
       Fragment." DA, 28 (1968), 5009A-10A. University of
       Illinois, 1967. 437 pp.

567   BURGESS, ANTHONY. "Whan that Aprille." Horizon, 13:2 (1971),
       45-59. Abstr. in AES, 17 (1973-74), no. 381.
           New illustrations of five Canterbury Tales.

568   *CANNON, THOMAS F., JR. "Chaucer's Pilgrims as Artists." DAI,
       34 (1974), 4190A-91A. University of Virginia, 1973.
       137 pp.

569   CLARK, JOHN W. "'This Litel Tretys' Again." ChauR, 6 (1971),
       152-56. Abstr. in AES, 15 (1971-72), no. 2845 and in
       MLAA (1971), no. 2121.

570   COGHILL, NEVILL. "Chaucer's Narrative Art in The Canterbury
       Tales," in 35, pp. 114-39.

571   *COOK, JAMES WYATT. "Character Projection in Chaucer's
       Canterbury Tales: A Narrative and Characterizing Device."
       Wayne State University Dissertation, 1964. Cited in
       MHRA (1965), no. 2461.

572   *COOKE, THOMAS D. "The Comic Climax in the Old French and
       Chaucerian Fabliaux." DAI, 31 (1970), 1754A. University
       of Pittsburgh, 1969. 226 pp.

573   COURTNEY, NEIL. "Chaucer's Poetic Vision." CR, 8 (1965),
       129-40. Abstr. in AES, 11 (1968), no. 67.
           Chaucer's realism and the pilgrimage motif.

Canterbury Tales

574   COX, LEE SHERIDAN. "A Question of Order in the Canterbury
        Tales." ChauR, 1 (1967), 228-52. Abstr. in AES, 14
        (1970-71), no. 2940.

575   CRAIK, T. W. The Comic Tales of Chaucer. London: Methuen,
        1963. 156 pp.
             Reviews: John Burrow, CritQ, 6 (1964), 180-81;
        D. S. Brewer, Listener, 71 (1964), 31; Nevill Coghill,
        N&Q, 11 (1964), 196-97; Martin Lehnert, ZAA, 13 (1965),
        180-82.

576   *CROWTHER, JOAN DOROTHY WHITEHEAD. "Word and Deed: A Study
        of Style in Seven of the Canterbury Tales." DA, 28
        (1968), 4122A. Bryn Mawr College, 1967. 216 pp.

577   DELASANTA, RODNEY. "The Horsemen of the Canterbury Tales."
        ChauR, 3 (1968), 29-36. Abstr. in AES, 17 (1973-74),
        no. 692.

578   DELASANTA, RODNEY. "The Theme of Judgment in The Canterbury
        Tales." MLQ, 31 (1970), 298-307. Abstr. in MLAA (1970),
        no. 1764.

579   *DILLARD, NANCY FREY. "The English Fabular Tradition:
        Chaucer, Spenser, Dryden." DAI, 34 (1974), 7186A. The
        University of Tennessee, 1973. 220 pp.

580   *DIMARCO, VINCENT JOSEPH. "Literary and Historical Researches
        Respecting Chaucer's Knight and Squire." DAI, 33 (1972),
        1677A. University of Pennsylvania, 1972. 414 pp.

581   DONALDSON, E. T. "Chaucer, Canterbury Tales, D117: A Critical
        Edition." Spec, 40 (1965), 626-33.
             Reprinted in 39, pp. 119-30.

582   DONALDSON, E. T. "The Ordering of the Canterbury Tales,"
        in 55, pp. 193-204.

583   DRUCKER, TRUDY. "Some Medical Allusions in The Canterbury
        Tales." NYSJM, 68 (1968), 444-47.

584   *DUKE, ELIZABETH ANNE FOSTER. "Evolution of the Text of
        Chaucer's Canterbury Tales: 1477-1775." DA, 29 (1969),
        3971A. The University of Iowa, 1968. 271 pp.

585   ELIASON, NORMAN E. "Personal Names in the Canterbury Tales."
        Names, 21 (1973), 137-52.

BIBLIOGRAPHY OF CHAUCER, 1964 - 1973

586   *EVERS, JIM W. "Some Implications of Chaucer's Use of Astrol-
           ogy in the Canterbury Tales." DAI, 32 (1972), 4561A.
           Duke University, 1971. 344 pp.

587   FISHER, JOHN H. "Chaucer's Last Revision of the Canterbury
           Tales." MLR, 67 (1972), 241-51. Abstr. in AES, 18
           (1974-75), no. 39.

588   FISHER, JOHN H. "The Three Styles of Fragment I of the
           Canterbury Tales." ChauR, 8 (1973), 119-27. Abstr. in
           MLAA (1973), no. 2811.

589   FROST, WILLIAM. "What Is a Canterbury Tale?" WHR, 27
           (1973), 39-59. Abstr. in AES, 17 (1973-74), no. 2249
           and in MLAA (1973), no. 2817.

590   *GALEWSKI, BARBRO. "Simplicity and Directness in Chaucer's
           Canterbury Tales." Uppsala University Dissertation,
           1970. Cited in MHRA (1970), no. 2911.

591   GARBÁTY, THOMAS JAY. "The Monk and the Merchant's Tale:
           An Aspect of Chaucer's Building Process in the Canterbury
           Tales." MP, 67 (1969), 18-24. Abstr. in AES, 13
           (1969-70), no. 2549.

592   GAYLORD, ALAN T. "Sentence and Solaas in Fragment VII of
           the Canterbury Tales: Harry Bailey as Horseback Editor."
           PMLA, 82 (1967), 226-35. Abstr. in AES, 10 (1967),
           no. 2852.

593   GARDNER, JOHN. "The Case Against the 'Bradshaw Shift'; or,
           the Mystery of the Manuscript in the Trunk." PLL, 3
           (Summer supplement, 1967), 80-106.

594   GRIFFITH, RICHARD R. A Critical Study Guide to Chaucer's
           The Canterbury Tales. Totowa, New Jersey: Littlefield,
           Adams and Co., 1968. 159 pp.
           Undergraduate guide.

595   *GROSSMAN, JUDITH S. "Convention and Innovation: Two Essays
           on Style in the Canterbury Tales." DA, 29 (1969),
           2709A-10A. Brandeis University, 1968. 213 pp.

596   *GRUBER, LOREN CHARLES. "Isolation in Old English Elegies
           and the Canterbury Tales: A Contribution to the Study
           of the Continuity of English Poetry." DAI, 33 (1972),
           2891A-92A. University of Denver, 1972. 168 pp.

Canterbury Tales

597   *HAINES, RAYMOND MICHAEL. "Fortune, Nature, and Grace in
         Chaucer's Canterbury Tales." DAI, 32 (1972), 3952A.
         Ohio State University, 1971. 317 pp.

598   HANNING, ROBERT W. "Uses of Names in Medieval Literature."
         Names, 16 (1968), 325-38.
            General information on names in the Canterbury Tales.

599   *HANSON, THOMAS BRADLEY. "Stylized Man: The Poetic Use of
         Physiognomy in Chaucer's Canterbury Tales." DAI, 31
         (1970), 1278A. The University of Wisconsin, 1970.
         236 pp.

600   HARLOW, BENJAMIN C. "Chaucer's Host: The Character of
         Harry Bailly." NcNR, 19 (1968), 36-47. Abstr. in AES,
         15 (1971-72), no. 2846.

601   *HART, JAMES PAXTON, JR. "Thomas Tyrwhitt (1730-1786) as
         Annotator and Glossarist of Fragment A of The Canterbury
         Tales, and His Editorial Relations." DAI, 32 (1971),
         2056A. University of Pennsylvania, 1971. 275 pp.

602   HASKELL, ANN S. "The Golden Ambiguity of the Canterbury
         Tales." ErasmusR, 1, i (1971), 1-9.

603   *HATTON, THOMAS JENISON. "The Canterbury Tales and Late
         Fourteenth Century Chivalry: Literature Stylization and
         Historical Idealism." DA, 27 (1966), 456A. The Univer-
         sity of Nebraska, 1966. 201 pp.

604   *HIPOLITO, TERRANCE ARNOLD. "Chaucer and the School of
         Chartres." DAI, 31 (1971), 6551A. University of
         California, Los Angeles, 1970. 525 pp.
            Proposes a unity for the Canterbury Tales on Chartrian
         principles.

605   HODGE, JAMES L. "The Marriage Group: Precarious Equilib-
         rium." ES, 46 (1965), 289-300. Abstr. in AES, 9 (1966),
         no. 2568.

606   HOFFMAN, RICHARD LESTER. "The Canterbury Tales," in Critical
         Approaches to Six Major English Works. Edited by
         Robert M. Lumiansky and Herschel Baker. Philadelphia:
         University of Pennsylvania Press; *London: Oxford
         University Press, 1968, pp. 41-80.
            Reviews scholarship and classical influence on the
         Canterbury Tales.
            Review of Critical Approaches...: TLS (25 September,
         1969), p. 1067.

607   HOLBROOK, DAVID. "Chaucer's Debate on Marriage," in his
      Quest for Love. Alabama: University of Alabama Press,
      1965, pp. 114-26.

608   HOWARD, DONALD R. "The Canterbury Tales: Memory and Form."
      ELH, 38 (1971), 319-28.

609   *HUBER, JOAN RAPHAEL. "Chaucer's Concept of Death in The
      Canterbury Tales." DA, 28 (1967), 1397A. University of
      Pittsburgh, 1967. 240 pp.

610   HUPPÉ, BERNARD F. A Reading of the Canterbury Tales.
      Binghamton: State University of New York Press, 1964.
      245 pp.
        Reviews: Ben W. Fuson, LJ, 90 (1965), 124; John Lawlor,
      RES, 17 (1966), 304-306; Christian Enzensberger, Ang, 84
      (1966), 96-98; Herbert K. Tjossem, CE, 27 (1966), 515;
      A. C. Spearing, MAE, 36 (1967), 195-99; Valerie Edden,
      MLR, 62 (1967), 306-308; Albert C. Baugh, ES, 48 (1967),
      435-38.

611   JAMAIS, CHRISTINO. "Chaucer, The Canterbury Tales: Forever
      England," in World Literature. Edited by Dionisia A.
      Riola. General Education Journal (Quezon City), 13
      (1968), 69-80.

612   JANKOVIĆ, MIRA. "Chaucerovi knjizevni razgovori o narativnoj
      formi" [Chaucer's literary conversation about narrative
      form]. Umjetnost rijeci (Zagreb, Yugoslavia), 13, i-ii
      (1969), 73-85.

613   JOSEPH, GERHARD. "Chaucerian 'Game'-'Ernest' and the
      'Argument of Herbergage' in The Canterbury Tales." ChauR,
      5 (1970), 83-96. Abstr. in AES, 15 (1971-72), no. 714
      and in MLAA (1971), no. 2176.

614   JOSIPOVICI, G. D. "Fiction and Game in The Canterbury Tales."
      CritQ, 7 (1965), 185-97. Abstr. in AES, 9 (1966),
      no. 1577.
        Excerpts reprinted in 1106.

615   KASKE, R. E. "Chaucer's Marriage Group," in 56, pp. 45-65.

616   *KEEN, WILLIAM PARKER. "A Study of the Host in the Canterbury
      Tales." DA, 28 (1968), 4133A-34A. Lehigh University,
      1967. 222 pp.

Canterbury Tales

617   KIRALIS, KARL. "William Blake as an Intellectual and
       Spiritual Guide to Chaucer's Canterbury Pilgrims."
       BlakeS, 1 (1969), 139-90.

618   KNAPP, DANIEL. "The Relyk of a Seint: A Gloss on Chaucer's
       Pilgrimage." ELH, 39 (1972), 1-26.

618.01*KNIGHT, STEPHEN. Ryming Craftily: Meaning in Chaucer's
       Poetry. Sydney, Australia: Angus and Robertson, 1973.
       265 pp. Verified, BIP: Authors (1975), p. 1657.

619   KNOX, NORMAN. "The Satiric Pattern of The Canterbury Tales,"
       in Six Satirists. By A. Fred Sochatoff, Norman Knox,
       et al. CaSE, 9. Pittsburgh, Pennsylvania: Carnegie
       Institute of Technology, 1965, pp. 17-34. Abstr. in AES,
       10 (1967), no. 851.

620   KOLINSKY, MURIEL. "Pronouns of Address and the Status of
       Pilgrims in the Canterbury Tales." PLL, 3 (Summer
       supplement, 1967), 40-48.

621   LUMIANSKY, R. M. "Two Notes on the Canterbury Tales,"
       in 34, pp. 227-32.
       I. The Position of Fragment VI.
       II. A Dietary Lecture for the Monk.

622   MacDONALD, DONALD. "Proverbs, Sententiae, and Exempla in
       Chaucer's Comic Tales: The Function of Comic Misapplica-
       tion." Spec, 41 (1966), 453-65. Abstr. in AES, 16
       (1972-73), no. 28.

623   MACLAINE, ALLAN H. The Student's Comprehensive Guide to the
       Canterbury Tales. Woodbury, New York: Barron's Educa-
       tional Series, 1964. 300 pp.

624   MARKS, JASON. "Tales from Chaucer as Projections of Their
       Tellers' Needs." DAI, 32 (1971), 1480A. New York
       University, 1971. 466 pp.

625   MARTIN, WILLIAM EUGENE. "Concepts of Sovereignty in The
       Canterbury Tales." DAI, 32 (1972), 5236A. University
       of Pittsburgh, 1971. 189 pp.

626   McCANN, GARTH A. "Chaucer's First Three Tales: Unity in
       Trinity." BRMMLA, 27 (1973), 10-16.

627   MEHL, DIETER. "Erscheinungsformen des Erzählers in Chaucers:
       Canterbury Tales," in 43, pp. 189-206.

628   MILLER, ROBERT P. "Allegory in the Canterbury Tales," in
       60, pp. 268-90.

629   MOGAN, JOSEPH J., JR. "Chaucer and the Bona Matrimonii."
       ChauR, 4 (1970), 123-41. Abstr. in AES, 14 (1970-71),
       no. 697 and in MLAA (1970), no. 1804.

630   *MOLHOVA, ŽANA. "Džefri Cosăr 1340-1400" [Geoffrey Chaucer
       1340-1400], in Džefri Cosăr. Kentărbărijski razkazi
       [The Canterbury Tales]. NK (1970), 7-22. Cited in MHRA
       (1970), no. 2948. Unavailable.

631   MOORMAN, CHARLES. "The Philosophical Knights of The
       Canterbury Tales." SAQ, 64 (1965), 87-99. Abstr. in
       AES, 8 (1965), no. 1816.

632   MULVEY, MINA. The Canterbury Tales: Analytic Notes. New
       York: American, 1965. 136 pp.

633   MUSCATINE, CHARLES. "The Canterbury Tales: Style of the Man
       and Style of the Work," in 35, pp. 88-113.

634   *MYERS, DORIS EVALINE THOMPSON. "The Artes Praedicandi and
       Chaucer's Canterbury Preachers." DA, 28 (1967),
       2215A-16A. The University of Nebraska, 1967. 221 pp.

634.01 NEWSTEAD, HELAINE. "Chaucer's Canterbury Tales," in 659.01,
       pp. 97-107.

635   *NICHOLS, NICHOLAS PETE. "Discretion and Marriage in the
       Canterbury Tales." DAI, 32 (1971), 3263A. Columbia
       University, 1971. 377 pp.

636   NIST, JOHN. "Chaucer's Apostrophic Mode in The Canterbury
       Tales." TSL, 15 (1970), 85-98. Abstr. in AES, 14
       (1970-71), no. 2941 and in MLAA (1970), no. 1805.

637   *OLSON, GLENDING ROBERT. "The Cultural Context of Chaucer's
       Fabliaux." DAI, 30 (1969), 1145A-46A. Stanford Univer-
       sity, 1969. 321 pp.

638   OWEN, CHARLES A., JR. "The Design of The Canterbury Tales,"
       in 60, pp. 192-207.

639   PAGE, BARBARA. "Concerning the Host." ChauR, 4 (1970),
       1-13. Abstr. in MLAA (1970), no. 1811.

Canterbury Tales

640   PEARSALL, DEREK A. "The Canterbury Tales," in 32, chapter
      5, part 2, pp. 163-94.

641   RAMSEY, VANCE. "Modes of Irony in the Canterbury Tales," in
      60, pp. 291-312.

642   REISS, EDMUND. "The Pilgrimage Narrative and the Canterbury
      Tales." SP, 67 (1970), 295-305. Abstr. in MLAA (1970),
      no. 1817.

643   RICHARDSON, CYNTHIA C. "The Function of the Host in The
      Canterbury Tales." TSLL, 12 (1970), 325-44. Abstr. in
      MLAA (1970), no. 1818.

644   RICHARDSON, JANETTE. Blameth Nat Me: A Study of Imagery in
      Chaucer's Fabliaux. SEngL, 58. Paris; The Hague:
      Mouton, 1970. 186 pp.
        Reviews: John V. Fleming, Spec, 47 (1972), 797-99;
      Betty Hill, MAE, 41 (1972), 270-72.

645   ROBBINS, ROSSELL HOPE. "The English Fabliau: Before and
      After Chaucer." MSpr, 64 (1970), 231-44. Abstr. in AES,
      15 (1971-72), no. 982.

646   ROBINSON, IAN. "Chaucer's Religious Tales." CR, 10 (1967),
      18-32. Abstr. in AES, 14 (1970-71), no. 30.

647   RODAX, YVONNE. The Real and the Ideal in the Novella of
      Italy, France, and England. Chapel Hill: University of
      North Carolina Press, 1968. 138 pp.
        See chapter 2. "The Worlds of the Canterbury Tales."
        Reviews: Joseph Frank, RenQ, 23 (1970), 177-78.

648   ROSENBERG, BRUCE ALAN. "Reason and Revelation in the
      Canterbury Tales." DA, 26 (1965), 1654. The Ohio State
      University, 1965. 161 pp.

649   ROTZLER, WILLY. "Chaucer's Canterbury Tales." DU:
      Kulturelle Monatschrift (Zurich), 27 (January, 1967),
      226-28.
        General remarks.

650   ROUCAUTE, DANIELLE. "Champ sémantique de l'erotique dans les
      Contes de Canterbury de Chaucer." CahiersE, 1 (1972),
      3-24.
        Includes linguistic charts.

651   RUGGIERS, PAUL G. The Art of the Canterbury Tales. Madison
        and Milwaukee: University of Wisconsin Press, 1965.
        283 pp.
            Excerpts reprinted in 62, pp. 111-14.
            Reviews: Robert F. Cayton, LJ, 90 (1965), 3454;
        Choice, 2 (1965), 388; Donald C. Baker, BA, 40 (1966),
        86; Herbert K. Tjossem, CE, 27 (1966), 515; Donald F.
        Chapin, HAB, 17 (1966), 70-71; Albert C. Baugh, ES, 48
        (1967), 546-48; Sylvia Wallace Holton, SN, 41 (1969),
        176-79.

652   RUGGIERS, PAUL G. "Notes Toward a Theory of Tragedy in
        Chaucer." ChauR, 8 (1973), 89-99. Abstr. in MLAA (1973),
        no. 2782.

653   RUTLEDGE, SHERYL P. "Chaucer's Zodiac of Tales." Costerus,
        9 (1973), 117-43. Abstr. in AES, 17 (1973-74), no. 2611.

654   RYDLAND, KURT. "The Meaning of 'Variant Reading' in the
        Manly-Rickert Canterbury Tales: A Note on the Limi-
        tations of the Corpus of Variants." NM, 73 (1972),
        805-14.

655   *SAITO, MOTHER MASAKO, R. S. C. J. "The Archetype of Bondage:
        Five Clusters of Imagery in the Canterbury Tales." DA,
        25 (1964), 1897. Fordham University, 1964. 123 pp.

656   *SAMPSON, GLORIA MARIE PAULIK. "Social Systems and Lexical
        Features: Pronominal Usage in the Canterbury Tales."
        DAI, 31 (1970), 747A. The University of Michigan, 1969.
        121 pp.

657   *SANDERS, BARRY R. "Double-Entendres in The Canterbury Tales."
        DA, 28 (1967), 1058A. University of Southern California,
        1967. 123 pp.

658   *SCHAEFER, WILLENE. "The Evolution of a Concept: Gentilesse
        in Chaucer's Poetry." DA, 27 (1967), 3850A-51A.
        Louisiana State University, 1966. 248 pp.
            Would substitute "Gentilesse Group" for "Marriage
        Group."

659   *SCHILDGEN, BRENDA DEEN. "The Conflict Between Art and
        Morality in Two Fourteenth-Century Poets: Juan Ruiz and
        Geoffrey Chaucer." DAI, 33 (1973), 4362A. Indiana
        University, 1972. 265 pp.
            Chaucer's ambivalence toward art and morality in the
        Canterbury Tales.

Canterbury Tales

659.01 SEVERS, J. BURKE, ed. Recent Middle English Scholarship and
       Criticism: Survey and Desiderata. Pittsburgh, Pennsyl-
       vania: Duquesne University Press; Louvain: E.
       Nauwelaerts, 1971. 107 pp.
          See especially the review by Helaine Newstead,
       pp. 97-105, on Chaucer's Canterbury Tales.

660   SEVERS, J. BURKE. "The Tales of Romance," in 60, pp. 229-46.

661   *SHILKETT, CAROL LEE. "Chaucerian Realist: A Study of
       Mimesis in the Canterbury Pilgrimage." DAI, 33 (1973),
       5141A. Michigan State University, 1972. 263 pp.

662   SILVIA, D. S. "Geoffrey Chaucer on the Subject of Men,
       Women, and Gentilesse." RLV, 33 (1967), 227-36.

663   STAMBUSKY, ALAN A. "Chaucer and Molière: Kindred Patterns of
       the Dramatic Impulse in Human Comedy." Lock Haven Bulle-
       tin (Lock Haven State College, Pennsylvania), Series i,
       No. 5 (1965), 43-60.

664   STROHM, PAUL. "Some Generic Distinctions in the Canterbury
       Tales." MP, 68 (1971), 321-28. Abstr. in AES, 15
       (1971-72), no. 1290.

665   *THOMAS, FREDERICK BRYCE. "Thomas Tyrwhitt and The Canterbury
       Tales." DA, 28 (1967), 1088A. Fordham University, 1967.
       238 pp.
          Evaluates Tyrwhitt's scholarship in his 1775-78
       edition.

666   THUNDYIL, ZACHARIAS. "The Moral Chaucer." C&L, 20, iii
       (1971), 12-16.

667   *TISDALE, CHARLES PRESSLEY ROBERTS. "The Medieval Pilgrimage
       and Its Use in The Canterbury Tales." DAI, 30 (1970),
       4958A. Princeton University, 1969. 301 pp.

668   UTLEY, FRANCIS LEE. "Some Implications of Chaucer's Folk
       Tales." Laographia, 22 (1965), 588-99.

669   WEISSMAN, HOPE PHYLLIS. "Chaucer's Bad Tales: The Aesthetic
       Forms of Late Medieval Pathos and the Tradition of Sermo
       Humilis." DAI, 34 (1973), 3362A. Columbia University,
       1973. 637 pp.

670   WEST, MICHAEL D. "Dramatic Time, Setting, and Motivation in
       Chaucer." ChauR, 2 (1968), 172-87. Abstr. in AES, 16
       (1972-73), no. 1568.

671   WHITE, BEATRICE. "Decline and Fall of Interjections." NM,
          64 (1963), 356-72.
             See especially pp. 358-62. Treats swearing and oaths
          in the Canterbury Tales.

672   WHITTOCK, TREVOR. A Reading of the Canterbury Tales. London:
          Cambridge University Press, 1968. 315 pp.
             Reviews: R. T. Davies, RES, 20 (1969), 477-79; TLS
          (15 May, 1969), p. 517; Robert M. Jordan, JEGP, 69 (1970),
          165-67; H. L. Rogers, AUMLA, 33 (1970), 110-12; Dieter
          Mehl, Ang, 89 (1971), 254-57; Edmund Reiss, Spec, 46
          (1971), 197-99.

673   *WILLIAMS, CLEM C., JR. "The Genre and Art of the Old French
          Fabliaux: A Preface to the Study of Chaucer's Tale of
          the Fabliau Type." DA, 28 (1968), 3161A. Yale Univer-
          sity, 1961. 160 pp.

674   WILLIAMS, GEORGE. "Many Sondry Werkes," in 386, chapter 9,
          pp. 152-66.
             Evidence for Chaucer's connections with John of Gaunt
          appearing in Canterbury Tales and minor poems.

675   WILSON, JAMES H. "The Pardoner and the Second Nun: A Defense
          of the Bradshaw Order." NM, 74 (1973), 292-96.

676   WIMSATT, JAMES I. "The Mirror of Society: Chaucer's
          Canterbury Tales," in 388, pp. 163-89.

677   WOO, CONSTANCE and WILLIAM MATTHEWS. "The Spiritual Purpose
          of the Canterbury Tales." Comitatus, 1 (1970), 85-109.

678   WOOD, CHAUNCEY. "The April Date as a Structural Device in
          The Canterbury Tales." MLQ, 25 (1964), 259-71. Abstr.
          in AES, 9 (1966), no. 223.

See also: 171, 173, 174, 182, 185, 188, 190, 201, 225, 226, 239,
243, 245, 246, 251, 255, 257, 259, 269, 273, 276, 283, 284, 287, 289,
296, 299, 302, 303, 304, 305, 308, 312, 319, 321, 329, 333, 339, 346,
353, 354, 357, 359, 363, 364, 369, 382, 388, 391, 498, 513, 514, 523,
535, 536, 604, 763, 793, 1087, 1291, 1649, 1683, 1699, 1711, 1727,
1729, 1733, 1759, 1770, 1798, 1804, 1832, 1839, 1855, 1862, 1880,
2018, 2032, 2033, 2066, 2139, 2141, 2142, 2156-59+.

Canterbury Tales

Canterbury Tales: Source Studies

679   *HOFFMAN, RICHARD LESTER. "Ovid and The Canterbury Tales."
          DA, 25 (1965), 5280. Princeton University, 1964. 297 pp.
          See 680.

680   HOFFMAN, RICHARD L. Ovid and The Canterbury Tales. Philadel-
          phia: University of Pennsylvania, 1966. 229 pp.
          Based on the author's doctoral dissertation. See 679.
          Reviews: Christopher Brookhouse, Spec, 43 (1968),
          512-15.

681   SILVIA, DANIEL S., JR. "Glosses to the Canterbury Tales
          from St. Jerome's Epistola Adversus Jovinianum." SP,
          62 (1965), 28-39. Abstr. in AES, 9 (1966), no. 611.

See also Source Studies for individual tales of the Canterbury Tales
listed at the end of each tale.

See also: 395, 400, 407, 606, 1748.

GENERAL PROLOGUE

        See Griffith, pp. 163-67; Crawford, pp. 55-56.

682   ADAMS, GEORGE R. "Sex and Clergy in Chaucer's General
          Prologue." L&P, 18 (1968), 215-22.

683   BADENDYCK, J. LAWRENCE. "Chaucer's Portrait Technique and
          the Dream Vision Tradition." EngR, 21 (1970), 113-25.
          Abstr. in AES, 14 (1970-71), no. 2289.

684   BHATTACHERJE, M. M. Pictorial Poetry. Folcroft, Pennsyl-
          vania: Folcroft Press, 1969. 182 pp.
          Originally published in 1954. Contains general notes
          on "realism" in the General Prologue. See pp. 18-26,
          "Chaucer."

685   BOWDEN, MURIEL AMANDA. A Commentary on the General Prologue
          to The Canterbury Tales. Second edition with additional
          matter and a new preface. New York: McMillan, 1967.
          341 pp.
          Originally published in 1948. See Griffith, p. 164.
          Excerpts reprinted in 67, pp. 97-104.

686   BRIGHT, J. C. and P. M. BIRCH. Four Essays on Chaucer.
       Sydney: William Brooks and Co., 1967. 48 pp.
       1. Chaucer, Society and the General Prologue.
       2. Chaucer and Medieval Thought.
       3. Chaucer and Medieval Tradition.
       4. Chaucer and his Pilgrims.

687   COGHILL, NEVILL. "The Prologue to the Canterbury Tales,"
       in 198, pp. 85-94. Reprinted in 58, pp. 164-73.

688   DALEY, A. STUART. "Chaucer's 'Droghte of March' in Medieval
       Farm Lore." ChauR, 4 (1970), 171-79. Abstr. in AES, 14
       (1970-71), no. 1974 and MLAA (1970), no. 1762.

689   FARINA, PETER M. "The Twenty-Nine Again: Another Count of
       Chaucer's Pilgrims." LangQ, 9, iii-iv (1971), 29-32.

690   HIGDON, DAVID LEON. "Diverse Melodies in Chaucer's General
       Prologue." Criticism, 14 (1972), 97-108. Abstr. in
       AES, 17 (1973-74), no. 17 and MLAA (1972), no. 2708.
       Symbolic and iconographic associations of music and
       musical instruments in the General Prologue.

691   KIRBY, THOMAS A. "The General Prologue," in 60, pp. 208-28.

692   KNIGHT, STEPHEN. "Chaucer--a Modern Writer?" Balcony, 2
       (1965), 37-43. Abstr. in AES, 17 (1973-74), no. 2607.

693   LAGUARDIA, ERIC. "Figural Imitation in English Renaissance
       Poetry." ICLAP, Fribourg (1966), 844-54.
       Argues the General Prologue figurally emphasizes expe-
       rience over essence.

694   LENAGHAN, R. T. "Chaucer's General Prologue as History and
       Literature." CSSH, 12 (1970), 73-82.

695   MANN, JILL. Chaucer and Medieval Estates Satire: The Liter-
       ature of Social Classes and the General Prologue to the
       Canterbury Tales. New York and London: Cambridge Uni-
       versity Press, 1973. 348 pp.

696   ROGERS, P. BURWELL. "The Names of the Canterbury Pilgrims."
       Names, 16 (1968), 339-46. Abstr. in AES, 17 (1973-74),
       no. 2250.

697   SPENCER, WILLIAM. "Are Chaucer's Pilgrims Keyed to the
       Zodiac?" ChauR, 4 (1970), 147-70. Abstr. in AES, 14
       (1970-71), no. 1976 and MLAA (1970), no. 1827.

Canterbury Tales

698   STEVENS, MICHAEL. "The General Prologue," in 48, pp. 1-21.

See also: 108, 132, 162, 163, 165, 201, 239, 255, 259, 296, 303,
308, 339, 340, 343, 353, 369, 391, 459, 479, 513, 566, 577, 578, 594,
595, 608, 610, 620, 640, 645, 647, 653, 678, 680, 940, 1683, 1819,
2133, 2134, 2135, 2136, 2160-68+.

General Prologue: Source Studies

699   REA, JOHN A. "An Old French Analogue to General Prologue
          1-18." PQ, 46 (1967), 128-30. Abstr. in AES, 14
          (1970-71), no. 1975.

Knight, Lines 43-78

          See Griffith, pp. 167-68; Crawford, pp. 56-57.

700   EBNER, DEAN. "Chaucer's Precarious Knight," in 49, pp. 87-100.

701   ENGEL, CLAIRE-ELAINE. "Les croisades du chevalier." RSH,
          120 (1965), 577-85.

702   GÖRLACH, MANFRED. "Canterbury Tales Prologue, 60: The
          Knight's Army." N&Q, 20 (1973), 363-65. Abstr. in AES,
          18 (1974-75), no. 1039.

703   HATTON, THOMAS J. "Chaucer's Crusading Knight, A Slanted
          Ideal." ChauR, 3 (1968), 77-87. Abstr. in AES, 17
          (1973-74), no. 685.

704   MITCHELL, CHARLES. "The Worthiness of Chaucer's Knight."
          MLQ, 25 (1964), 66-75. Abstr. in AES, 8 (1965), no. 448.

See also: 386, 495, 580, 603, 624, 631, 683, 695, 697, 1683, 1799.

Squire, Lines 79-100

          See Griffith, p. 168; Crawford, p. 57.

705   WOOD, CHAUNCEY. "The Significance of Jousting and Dancing
          as Attributes of Chaucer's Squire." ES, 52 (1971),
          116-18.

See also: 580, 683, 695, 697, 1683, 1699, 1860, 1874.

Squire: Source Studies

706   FLEMING, JOHN V. "Chaucer's Squire, the Roman de la Rose,
        and the Romaunt." N&Q, 14 (1967), 48-49. Abstr. in AES,
        10 (1967), no. 2763.

Yeoman, Lines 101-17

            See Griffith, p. 168; Crawford, p. 57.

707   TEST, GEORGE A. "Archers' Feathers in Chaucer and Ascham."
        AN&Q, 2 (1964), 67-68. Abstr. in AES, 9 (1966), no. 1465.

See also: 695, 697.

Prioress, Nun, and Three Priests, Lines 118-64.

            See Griffith, pp. 168-72; Crawford, pp. 57-58.

708   COPLAND, R. A. "A Line from Chaucer's Prologue to the
        Canterbury Tales." N&Q, 17 (1970), 45-46. Abstr. in
        AES, 13 (1969-70), no. 3190.

709   FISHER, JOHN HURT. "Embarrassment of Riches." CLAJ, 7
        (1963), 1-12. Abstr. in AES, 10 (1967), no. 388.
            Portrait of Prioress seen as criticism of an institu-
        tion rather than an individual.

710   FOSTER, BRIAN. "Chaucer's 'Seynt Loy': An Anglo-French Pun?"
        N&Q, 15 (1968), 244-45. Abstr. in AES, 11 (1968), no.
        3310.

711   FRIEDMAN, JOHN BLOCK. "The Prioress's Beads 'Of Smal Coral.'"
        MAE, 39 (1970), 301-305. Abstr. in AES, 18 (1974-75),
        no. 744.

712   KNIGHT, S. T. "'Almoost a Spanne Brood.'" Neophil, 52
        (1968), 178-80. Abstr. in AES, 13 (1969-70), no. 1114.

713   KNOEPFLMACHER, U. C. "Irony Through Scriptural Allusion:
        A Note on Chaucer's Prioresse." ChauR, 4 (1970), 180-83.
        Abstr. in AES, 14 (1970-71), no. 1980 and in MLAA (1970),
        no. 1787.

Canterbury Tales

714   LEE, DWIGHT A. "Chaucer's Prioress and Saint Venus." MSCS,
           3 (1968), 69-75. Abstr. in AES, 13 (1969-70), no. 3193.

715   MADELEVA, SISTER M. Chaucer's Nuns and Other Essays. Port
           Washington, New York: Kennikat, 1965. 215 pp. See
           pp. 1-42.

716   REID, T. B. W. "Chaucer's 'Ferthing of Grece.'" N&Q, 11
           (1964), 373-74. Abstr. in AES, 8 (1965), no. 1735.

717   SIMONS, RITA DANDRIDGE. "The Prioress's Disobedience of the
           Benedictine Rule." CLAJ, 12 (1968), 77-83.

See also: 174, 214, 339, 382, 386, 680, 695, 696, 697, 1153, 1163,
1849, 1874, 1886.

Monk, Lines 165-207

           See Griffith, pp. 172-73; Crawford, p. 58.

718   BERNDT, DAVID E. "Monastic Acedia and Chaucer's Characteriza-
           tion of Daun Piers." SP, 68 (1971), 435-50. Abstr. in
           MLAA (1971), no. 2108.

719   BROWN, JOELLA OWENS. "Chaucer's Daun Piers: One Monk or
           Two?" Criticism, 6 (1964), 44-52.

720   FARINA, PETER M. "Two Notes on Chaucer." LangQ, 10, iii-iv
           (1972), 23-26.
               See 1. "The 'keepere of the celle,'" on the General
           Prologue, 172.

721   GILLMEISTER, HEINER. "Chaucers Mönch und die 'Reule of Seint
           Maure or of Seint Beneit.'" NM, 69 (1968), 222-32.
           Abstr. in AES, 15 (1971-72), no. 1649.

722   GRENNEN, JOSEPH E. "Chaucer's Monk: Baldness, Venery, and
           Embonpoint." AN&Q, 6 (1968), 83-85.

723   GRENNEN, JOSEPH E. "Chaucerian Portraiture: Medicine and
           the Monk." NM, 69 (1968), 569-74. Abstr. in AES, 15
           (1971-72), no. 1650.

724   REISS, EDMUND. "The Symbolic Surface of the Canterbury Tales:
           The Monk's Portrait." ChauR, 2 (1968), 254-72; and ChauR,
           3 (1968), 12-28. Abstr. in AES, 16 (1972-73), no. 1558.
           Treats symbolic value of "realistic" details.

725   SEQUEIRA, ISAAC. "Clerical Satire in the Portrait of the Monk and the Prologue to The Monk's Tale," in Literary Studies: Homage to Dr. A. Sivaramasubramonia Aiyer. Edited by K. P. K. Menon, M. Manuel, and K. Ayyappa Paniker. Trivandrum: St. Joseph's Press for the Dr. A. Sivaramasubramonia Aiyer Memorial Committee, 1973, pp. 34-43.

726   USSERY, HULING E. "The Status of Chaucer's Monk: Clerical, Official, Social, and Moral." TSE, 17 (1969), 1-30. Abstr. in AES, 14 (1970-71), no. 1028.

727   WAILES, STEPHEN L. "The Hunt of the Hare in Das Häslein." Seminar, 5 (1969), 92-101.
        Classical and medieval background for the hare as symbol of lechery.

728   WHITE, ROBERT B., JR. "Chaucer's Daun Piers and the Rule of St. Benedict: The Failure of an Ideal." JEGP, 70 (1971), 13-30. Abstr. in MLAA (1971), no. 2242.

See also: 232, 276, 343, 379, 495, 591, 621, 695, 696, 697, 1214, 1642.

Monk: Source Studies

See 680.

Friar, Lines 208-69

        See Griffith, pp. 173-74; Crawford, p. 58.

729   JEFFREY, DAVID LYLE. "The Friar's Rent." JEGP, 70 (1971), 600-606. Abstr. in MLAA (1971), no. 2176.

730   PEARCY, ROY J. "The Marriage Costs of Chaucer's Friar." N&Q, 17 (1970), 124-25. Abstr. in AES, 13 (1969-70), no. 3191.

731   SZÖVÉRFFY, JOSEPH. "Chaucer's Friar and St. Nicholas (Prologue 212)." N&Q, 16 (1969), 166-67. Abstr. in AES, 13 (1969-70), no. 752.

See also: 340, 695, 696, 697, 960, 1728, 1779, 1820.

Canterbury Tales

Friar: Source Studies

See 730.

Merchant, Lines 270-84

> See Griffith, pp. 174-75; Crawford, p. 59.

732   CRANE, JOHN KENNY. "An Honest Debtor?: A Note on Chaucer's
       Merchant, Line A276." ELN, 4 (1966), 81-85. Abstr. in
       AES, 11 (1968), no. 419.

733   PARK, B. A. "The Character of Chaucer's Merchant." ELN, 1
       (1964), 167-75. Abstr. in AES, 8 (1965), no. 1268.

See also: 695, 697, 993, 1699.

Clerk, Lines 285-308

> See Griffith, pp. 175-76; Crawford, p. 59.

734   USSERY, HULING E. "Fourteenth-Century English Logicians:
       Possible Models for Chaucer's Clerk." TSE, 18 (1970),
       1-15. Abstr. in AES, 14 (1970-71), no. 1027 and in
       MLAA (1970), no. 1835.

735   USSERY, HULING E. "How Old is Chaucer's Clerk?" TSE, 15
       (1967), 1-18. Abstr. in AES, 11 (1968), no. 1054.

See also: 624, 695, 697.

Clerk: Source Studies

736   FLEMING, JOHN. "Chaucer's Clerk and John of Salisbury."
       ELN, 2 (1964), 5-6. Abstr. in AES, 8 (1965), no. 2887.

737   WOOD, CHAUNCEY. "Chaucer's Clerk and Chalcidus." ELN, 4
       (1967), 166-72. Abstr. in AES, 11 (1968), no. 906.

Sergeant of the Law, Lines 309-30

        See Griffith, p. 176.

738   BAUGH, ALBERT C. "Chaucer's Serjeant of the Law and the
       Year Books," in Mélanges de Langue et de Littérature du
       Moyen Age et de la Renaissance offerts à Jean Frappier--
       par ses collègues, ses élèves et ses amis. Publications
       Romanes et Françaises, 112. 2 vols. Genève: Librarie
       Droz, 1970, Vol. 1, pp. 65-76.

739   LAMBKIN, MARTHA DAMPF. "Chaucer's Man of Law as Purchasour."
       Comitatus, 1 (1970), 81-84.

See also: 386, 624, 695, 697, 854, 1809.

Franklin, Lines 331-60

        See Griffith, pp. 176-77; Crawford, p. 59.

740   PEARCY, ROY J. "Chaucer's Franklin and the Literary Vavasour."
       ChauR, 8 (1973), 33-59. Abstr. in MLAA (1973), no. 2840.

See also: 386, 695, 697, 1874.

Franklin: Source Studies

741   FRANKIS, P. J. "Chaucer's 'Vavasour' and Chrétien de Troyes."
       N&Q, 15 (1968), 46-47. Abstr. in AES, 11 (1968),
       no. 2568.

Tradesmen, Lines 361-78

        See Griffith, p. 177; Crawford, p. 59.

See: 386, 695, 697.

Cook, Lines 379-87

        See Griffith, pp. 177-78; Crawford, p. 60.

See: 33, 695, 696, 697.

Canterbury Tales

Shipman, Lines 388-410

        See Griffith, p. 178; Crawford, p. 60.

See: 683, 695, 697.

Physician, Lines 411-44

        See Griffith, pp. 179-80; Crawford, p. 60.

742   *RAYMOND, R. W. "The Physician: Chaucer's Neglected Pilgrim."
       Icarus, 19 (1969). Cited in NCBEL, p. 575. Unlocatable.

743   REGENOS, GRAYDON W. "The Doctor in Nigellus Wireker and
       Chaucer," in Classical, Medieval and Renaissance Studies
       in Honor of Berthold Louis Ullman. Edited by Charles
       Henderson, Jr. 2 vols. Roma: Edizioni di storia e
       letterature, 1964, vol. 2, pp. 41-46.

744   ROBBINS, ROSSELL HOPE. "The Physician's Authorities," in
       34, pp. 335-41.

745   USSERY, HULING E. Chaucer's Physician: Medicine and Litera-
       ture in Fourteenth-Century England. TSE Monographs, 19.
       New Orleans, Louisiana: Tulane University Press, 1971.
       158 pp. Abstr. in AES, 17 (1973-74), no. 2609.
       Reviews: Joseph E. Grennen, Spec, 49 (1974), 158-59.

See also: 317, 695, 697, 1082, 1642, 1994.

Wife of Bath, Lines 445-76

        See Griffith, p. 180; Crawford, p. 60.

746   GARBÁTY, THOMAS JAY. "Chaucer's Weaving Wife." JAF, 81
       (1968), 342-46.

See also: 213, 382, 695, 696, 697, 1699.

Wife of Bath: Source Studies

747   HOFFMAN, RICHARD L. "The Wife of Bath as Student of Ovid."
       N&Q, 11 (1964), 287-88.
          The Wife was a literal-minded student of Ovid.

See also: 680.

Parson, Lines 477-528

      See Griffith, pp. 180-81; Crawford, pp. 60-61.

748   FLEMING, JOHN. "The 'Figure' of Chaucer's Good Parson and a
        Reprimand by Grosseteste." N&Q, 11 (1964), 167. Abstr.
        in AES, 7 (1964), no. 2245.

See also: 174, 459, 526, 695, 697, 1862, 1976.

Parson: Source Studies

See: 748.

Plowman, Lines 529-41

See: 695, 697.

Miller, Lines 542-66

      See Griffith, pp. 181-82; Crawford, p. 61.

749   McCRACKEN, SAMUEL. "Chaucer's Canterbury Tales, A. 565-566."
        Expl, 23 (1965), Item 55.
        Pun on town/tune.

750   REISS, EDMUND. "Chaucer's Miller, Pilate, and the Devil."
        AnM, 5 (1964), 21-25.

751   SCOTT, KATHLEEN L. "Sow-and-Bagpipe Imagery in the Miller's
        Portrait." RES, 18 (1967), 287-90. Abstr. in AES, 12
        (1969), no. 1060.

See also: 202, 560, 695, 696, 697, 1683, 1862

Manciple, Lines 567-86

      See Griffith, p. 182; Crawford, p. 61

See: 695, 697.

Canterbury Tales

Reeve, Lines 587-622

> See Griffith, p. 182; Crawford, p. 61.

See: 202, 386, 695, 697.

Summoner, Lines 623-68

> See Griffith, pp. 182-83; Crawford, pp. 61-62.

752   BIGGINS, D[ENNIS]. "Chaucer's Summoner: 'Wel Loved He
         Garleek, Oynons, and eek Lekes,' C T I, 634." N&Q, 11
         (1964), 48. Abstr. in AES, 7 (1964), no. 1472.

753   PELTOLA, NIILO. "Chaucer's Summoner--'Fyr-reed Cherubynnes
         Face.'" NM, 69 (1968), 560-68. Abstr. in AES, 15
         (1971-72), no. 1652.

See also: 317, 340, 695, 697, 754, 1728.

Summoner: Source Study

754   WOOD, CHAUNCEY. "The Sources of Chaucer's Summoner's
         'Garleek, Onyons, and eek Lekes.'" ChauR, 5 (1971),
         240-44. Abstr. in AES, 15 (1971-72), no. 711 and MLAA
         (1971), no. 2248.

See also: 752.

Pardoner, Lines 669-714

> See Griffith, pp. 183-84; Crawford, p. 62.

755   GAFFORD, CHARLOTTE K. "Chaucer's Pardoner and Haze Motes of
         Georgia," in Essays in Honor of Richebourg Gaillard
         McWilliams. Special issue of Birmingham-Southern
         College Bulletin, 63, ii (1970), 9-12.
         A comparison.

756   KIEHL, JAMES M. "Dryden's Zimri and Chaucer's Pardoner:
         A Comparative Study of Verse Portraiture." Thoth, 6
         (1965), 3-12.

757   ROWLAND, BERYL. "Animal Imagery and the Pardoner's Abnor-
          mality." Neophil, 48 (1964), 56-60. Abstr. in AES, 8
          (1965), no. 2058.

758   SCHWEITZER, EDWARD C., JR. "Chaucer's Pardoner and the Hare."
          ELN, 4 (1967), 247-50. Abstr. in AES, 11 (1968),
          no. 919.

See also: 340, 382, 488, 624, 695, 697, 1116, 1130, 1927, 1975.

Chaucer the Pilgrim

See Crawford, p. 63.

759   DONALDSON, E. TALBOT. "Chaucer the Pilgrim," in 39,
          pp. 1-12.
              Reprint of article in PMLA, 69 (1954), 928-36.

760   RUGGIERS, PAUL. "The Narrator: the Pilgrim as Poet," in 62,
          pp. 111-14.
              Reprint from 651, pp. 17-23.

See also: 610, 624, 1180.

The Host

761   DELASANTA, RODNEY. "The Bartenders in Eliot and Chaucer."
          NM, 72 (1971), 60-61.

762   KEEN, WILLIAM. "'To Doon Ye Ese': A Study of the Host in
          the General Prologue of the Canterbury Tales." Topic,
          17 (1969), 5-18. Abstr. in AES, 14 (1970-71), no. 1026.

763   WILLIAMS, CELIA ANN. "The Host - England's First Tour
          Director." EJ, 57 (1969), 1149-50, 1214.

See also: 600, 616, 639, 643, 696, 1131, 1190, 1192.

Canterbury Tales

THE KNIGHT'S TALE

See Griffith, pp. 184-92; Crawford, pp. 63-65.

764   BAWCUTT, PRISCILLA. "The Lark in Chaucer and Some Later
       Poets." YES, 2 (1972), 5-12.

765   BEIDLER, PETER G. "Chaucer's Knight's Tale and Its Teller."
       EngR, 18 (1968), 54-60. Abstr. in AES, 11 (1968), no. 2504.

766   BENSON, C. DAVID. "The Knight's Tale as History." ChauR, 3
       (1968), 107-23. Abstr. in AES, 17 (1973-74), no. 682.

767   BLAKE, KATHLEEN A. "Order and the Noble Life in Chaucer's
       Knight's Tale?" MLQ, 34 (1973), 3-19. Abstr. in MLAA
       (1973), no. 2799.

768   BOLTON, W. F. "The Topic of the Knight's Tale." ChauR, 1
       (1967), 217-27. Abstr. in AES, 14 (1970-71), no. 2939.

769   BROOKS, DOUGLAS and ALASTAIR FOWLER. "The Meaning of
       Chaucer's Knight's Tale." MAE, 39 (1970), 123-46.
       Abstr. in AES, 18 (1971), no. 38.

770   CAMERON, ALLEN BARRY. "The Heroine in The Knight's Tale."
       SSF, 5 (1968), 119-27. Abstr. in AES, 12 (1969), no. 639.

771   COZART, WILLIAM R. "Chaucer's Knight's Tale: A Philosophical
       Re-Appraisal of a Medieval Romance." in Medieval Epic to
       the Epic Theater of Brecht. University of Southern Cali-
       fornia Studies in Comparative Literature, 1. Edited by
       Rosario P. Armato and John M. Spalek. Los Angeles: Uni-
       versity of Southern California Press, 1968, pp. 25-34.
       Abstr. in AES, 15 (1971-72), no. 2528.

772   DEAN, CHRISTOPHER. "Imagery in the Knight's Tale and the
       Miller's Tale." MS, 31 (1969), 149-63.

773   DEAN, CHRISTOPHER. "The 'Place' in The Knight's Tale." N&Q,
       13 (1966), 90-92. Abstr. in AES, 9 (1966), no. 3101.

774   DELASANTA, RODNEY. "Uncommon Commonplaces in The Knight's
       Tale." NM, 70 (1969), 683-90. Abstr. in AES, 17
       (1973-74), no. 2608.

775   ELBOW, PETER H. "How Chaucer Transcends Oppositions in the
       Knight's Tale." ChauR, 7 (1972), 97-112. Abstr. in
       AES, 17 (1973-74), no. 2884 and in MLAA (1972), no. 2696.

The Knight's Tale

776   FIFIELD, MERLE. "The Knight's Tale: Incident, Idea, Incor-
       poration." ChauR, 3 (1968), 95-106. Abstr. in AES, 17
       (1973-74), no. 683.

777   FLETCHER, P. C. B. "The Role of Destiny in The Knight's
       Tale." Theoria, 26 (1966), 43-50.

778   FOSTER, EDWARD E. "Humor in the Knight's Tale." ChauR, 3
       (1968), 88-94. Abstr. in AES, 17 (1973-74), no. 684.

779   GRUBER, LOREN C. "The Wanderer and Arcite: Isolation and
       the Continuity of the English Elegiac Mode," in Four
       Papers for Michio Masui. PSNLS, 1, i (September, 1972).
       Denver, Colorado: Society for New Language Study, 1972,
       pp. 1-10. Abstr. in AES, 17 (1973-74), no. 378.

780   HALLER, ROBERT S. "The Knight's Tale and the Epic Tradition."
       ChauR, 1 (1966), 67-84. Abstr. in AES, 13 (1969-70), no. 348.

781   HARGEST-GORZELAK, ANNA. "A Brief Comparison of the Knight's
       Tale and Sir Gawain and The Green Knight." RoHum, 15,
       iii (1967), 91-102.

782   HARRINGTON, DAVID V. "Rhetoric and Meaning in Chaucer's
       Knight's Tale." PLL, 3 (Summer supplement, 1967), 71-79.

783   HELTERMAN, JEFFREY. "The Dehumanizing Metamorphoses of The
       Knight's Tale." ELH, 38 (1971), 493-511.

784   HERZ, JUDITH SCHERER. "Chaucer's Elegiac Knight." Criticism,
       6 (1964), 212-24.

785   HOFFMAN, RICHARD L. "Mercury, Argus, and Chaucer's Arcite:
       Canterbury Tales I (A) 1384-90." N&Q, 12 (1965), 128-29.
       Abstr. in AES, 9 (1966), no. 452.

786   HOFFMAN, RICHARD L. "Two Notes on Chaucer's Arcite." ELN,
       4 (1967), 172-75. Abstr. in AES, 11 (1968), no. 907.

787   INGLE, PATRICIA. "'In the Glasynge Ywrought': The Knight's
       Tale as a Stained-Glass Window." CCTE, 31 (1966), 26.
       Abstract of a paper.

788   KUROSE, TAMOTSU. "Rhetorical Use of 'Jupiter' in Medieval
       and Elizabethan Literature." Anglica (March, 1964),
       1-34.

789   *LEVINE, DON ERIC. "The Style of Morality." DAI, 33 (1972),
       1143A. Princeton University, 1972. 349 pp.
       Elucidates the Knight's Tale by reference to the
       Narcissus episode in the Roman de la Rose.

Canterbury Tales

790   LOOMIS, DOROTHY BETHURUM. "Saturn in Chaucer's Knight's
       Tale," in 43, pp. 149-61.

791   MARKLAND, MURRAY F. "The Order of The Knight's Tale and The
       Tempest." RS, 33 (March, 1965), 1-10. Abstr. in AES,
       10 (1967), no. 1803.

792   MEIER, T. K. "Chaucer's Knight as 'Persona': Narration as
       Control." EM, 20 (1969), 11-21. Abstr. in AES, 14
       (1970-71), no. 28.

793   PENNINGER F. ELAINE. "Chaucer's Knight's Tale and the Theme
       of Appearance and Reality in The Canterbury Tales." SAQ,
       63 (1964), 398-405. Abstr. in AES, 8 (1965), no. 1806.

794   RUMBLE, T. C. "Chaucer's Knight's Tale, 2680-83." PQ, 43
       (1964), 130-33. Abstr. in AES, 8 (1965), no. 2302.

795   SCHMIDT, A. V. C. "The Tragedy of Arcite: A Reconsideration
       of the Knight's Tale." EIC, 19 (1969), 107-17. Abstr.
       in AES, 13 (1969-70), no. 753.

796   STEVENS, MICHAEL. "The Knight's Tale," in 48, pp. 23-37.

797   TATELBAUM, LINDA. "Venus' Citole and the Restoration of
       Harmony in Chaucer's Knight's Tale." NM, 74 (1973),
       649-64.

798   *THURSTON, PAUL THAYER. "Artistic Ambivalence in Chaucer's
       Knight's Tale." DA, 29 (1968), 882A. The University
       of Florida, 1961. 375 pp.
          See 799 below.

799   THURSTON, PAUL T. Artistic Ambivalence in Chaucer's Knight's
       Tale. Gainesville: University of Florida Press, 1968.
       250 pp.
          Published dissertation. See 798 above.
          Reviews: Alfred David, Spec, 45 (1970), 498-500;
       R. T. Davies, N&Q, 17 (1970), 65-67; Alan T. Gaylord,
       JEGP, 69 (1970), 167-69; R. M. Wilson, YES, 1 (1971),
       216-18.

800   TRIPP, RAYMOND P., JR. "The Knight's Tale and the Limita-
       tions of Language (The Boundaries Which Words Are)."
       Rendezvous, 6, i (1971), 23-28.

801   *VAN, THOMAS ANTHONY. "A Critical Reading of Chaucer's
       Knight's Tale with the Aid of Boccaccio's Teseida." DA,
       28 (1967), 697A. Duke University, 1966. 381 pp.

802   VAN, THOMAS A. "Second Meanings in Chaucer's Knight's Tale."
        ChauR, 3 (1968), 69-76. Abstr. in AES, 17 (1973-74),
        no. 686.

803   VAN, THOMAS A. "Theseus and the 'Right Way' of the Knight's
        Tale." SLitI, 4, ii (October, 1971), 83-100. Abstr. in
        AES, 15 (1971-72), no. 1648.

804   VANN, J. DON. "A Character Reversal in Chaucer's Knight's
        Tale." AN&Q, 3 (1965), 131-32. Abstr. in AES, 10 (1967),
        no. 1566.

805   WALDRON, R. A. "Knight's Tale A1037: 'fressher than the
        May.'" ES, 46 (1965), 402-406.

806   WESTLUND, JOSEPH. "The Knight's Tale as an Impetus for
        Pilgrimage." PQ, 43 (1964), 526-37. Abstr. in AES, 8
        (1965), no. 2321.

See also: 121, 132, 162, 169, 173, 182, 190, 196, 198, 201 (and
Brewer's review), 202, 203, 205, 214, 222, 225, 226, 231, 239, 255,
259, 264, 268, 269, 276, 277, 301, 305, 308, 312, 319, 324, 325,
339, 340, 343, 350, 364, 369, 378, 386, 387, 391, 412, 413, 426,
430, 447, 458, 459, 481, 513, 514, 515, 550, 554, 557, 566, 580,
583, 595, 596, 603, 610, 613, 624, 625, 626, 628, 631, 635, 640,
647, 651, 653, 660, 666, 672, 1039, 1468, 1561, 1602, 1679, 1683,
1746, 1757.01, 1759, 1799, 1839, 1843, 1850, 1987, 2145, 2158.

The Knight's Tale: Source Studies

807   HOFFMAN, RICHARD L. "The Felaweshipe of Chaucer's Love and
        Lordshipe." C&M, 25 (1964), 263-73.

808   HOFFMAN, RICHARD L. "Ovid and Chaucer's Myth of Theseus and
        Pirithoüs." ELN, 2 (1965), 252-57. Abstr. in AES, 10
        (1967), no. 1186.

See also: 398, 399, 400, 408, 421, 554, 606, 680, 780, 784, 785,
801, 803.

THE MILLER'S TALE

See Griffith, pp. 192–95; Crawford, pp. 66–67.

809   BENTLEY, JOSEPH. "Chaucer's Fatalistic Miller." SAQ, 64
      (1965), 247–53. Abstr. in AES, 9 (1966), no. 1787.

810   BLOOMFIELD, MORTON W. "The Miller's Tale––an UnBoethian
      Interpretation," in 55, pp. 205–11.

811   BRATCHER, JAMES T. and NICOLAI A. VON KREISLER. "The
      Popularity of the Miller's Tale." SFQ, 35 (1971),
      325–35. Abstr. in MLAA (1971), no. 2111.

812   BROWN, WILLIAM J. "Chaucer's Double Apology for the Miller's
      Tale," in 42, pp. 15–22. Abstr. in AES, 10 (1967), no.
      3511.

813   BURKHART, ROBERT E. "Chaucer's Absolon: A Sinful Parody of
      the Miller." Cithara, 8 (1969), 47–54. Abstr. in AES,
      13 (1969–70), no. 754.

814   DONALDSON, E. TALBOT. "Idiom of Popular Poetry in the
      Miller's Tale," in 39, pp. 13–29; also reprinted in 58,
      pp. 174–89.
          Originally published in English Institute Essays, 1950.

815   GELLRICH, JESSE M. "Nicholas' 'Kynges Noote' and 'Melodye.'"
      ELN, 8 (1971), 249–52.

816   HANSON, THOMAS B. "Physiognomy and Characterization in the
      Miller's Tale." NM, 72 (1971), 477–82.

817   HATTON, THOMAS J. "Absolon, Taste, and Odor in The Miller's
      Tale." PLL, 7 (1971), 72–75. Abstr. in AES, 14
      (1970–71), no. 2616 and in MLAA (1971), no. 2167.

818   HENCH, ATCHESON L. "Chaucer's Miller's Tale, 3226." ELN, 3
      (1965), 88–92. Abstr. in AES, 10 (1967), no. 1218.

819   HILL, BETTY. "Chaucer: The Miller's and Reeve's Tales."
      NM, 74 (1973), 665–75.

820   LEWIS, ROBERT E. "Alisoun's 'Coler': Chaucer's Miller's
      Tale 11. 3239, 3242, 3265." MS, 32 (1970), 337–39.
      Abstr. in AES, 16 (1972–73), no. 2467.

821   MacDONALD, ANGUS. "Absolon and St. Neot." Neophil, 48 (1964),
       235-37. Abstr. in AES, 8 (1965), no. 3005.

822   McCRACKEN, SAMUEL. "Miller's Tale [I(A)3384]." N&Q, 20
       (1973), 283. Abstr. in AES, 18 (1974-75), no. 1040.

823   MILLER, ROBERT P. "The Miller's Tale as Complaint." ChauR,
       5 (1970), 147-60. Abstr. in AES, 15 (1971-72), no. 701
       and in MLAA (1971), no. 2201.

824   MORGAN (sic), JOSEPH J., JR. "The Mutability Motif in The
       Miller's Tale." AN&Q, 8 (1969), 19.
            Correct name is Joseph J. Mogan, Jr.

825   MULLANY, PETER F. "Chaucer's Miller and 'Pilates Voys.'"
       AN&Q, 3 (1964), 54-55. Abstr. in AES, 9 (1966), no. 1495.

826   NOVELLI, CORNELIUS. "Absolon's 'Freend so Deere': A Pivotal
       Point in the Miller's Tale." Neophil, 52 (1968), 65-69.
       Abstr. in AES, 13 (1969-70), no. 1120.

827   POTEET, DANIEL P., II. "Avoiding Women in Times of Afflic-
       tion: An Analogue for the Miller's Tale, A 3589-91."
       N&Q, 19 (1972), 89-90. Abstr. in AES, 16 (1972-73),
       no. 330.

828   REISS, EDMUND. "Daun Gerveys in the Miller's Tale." PLL,
       6 (1970), 115-24. Abstr. in AES, 14 (1970-71), no. 692
       and in MLAA (1970), no. 1816.

829   ROWLAND, BERYL. "Alison Identified (The Miller's Tale, 3234)."
       AN&Q, 3 (1964), 3-4, 20-21, 39. Abstr. in AES, 9 (1966),
       nos. 1480, 1486, 1493.

830   ROWLAND, BERYL B. "The Play of the Miller's Tale: A Game
       Within a Game." ChauR, 5 (1970), 140-46. Abstr. in AES,
       15 (1971-72), no. 702 and in MLAA (1971), no. 2219.

831   THRO, A. BOOKER. "Chaucer's Creative Comedy: A Study of the
       Miller's Tale and the Shipman's Tale." ChauR, 5 (1970),
       97-111. Abstr. in AES, 15 (1971-72), no. 715 and in MLAA
       (1971), no. 2229.

832   WENZEL, SIEGFRIED. "Two Notes on Chaucer and Grosseteste."
       N&Q, 17 (1970), 449-51. Abstr. in AES, 14 (1970-71),
       no. 2290.
            On the Canterbury Tales, A.3485; D.1825ff.

Canterbury Tales

See also: 132, <u>164</u>, 190, 198, <u>201</u>, <u>205</u>, <u>225</u>, <u>226</u>, <u>231</u>, 255, 259,
<u>269</u>, <u>276</u>, 296, <u>308</u>, 331, <u>339</u>, 340, <u>343</u>, 364, 369, 379, <u>386</u>, <u>391</u>, <u>395</u>,
407, <u>515</u>, 519, 556, <u>561</u>, <u>563</u>, <u>566</u>, <u>567</u>, <u>575</u>, <u>576</u>, 588, 596, <u>610</u>, 613,
<u>622</u>, 626, 629, 635, <u>637</u>, <u>640</u>, <u>643.01</u>, 644, <u>647</u>, <u>651</u>, 653, 672, <u>677</u>,
<u>750</u>, <u>772</u>, 844, <u>1125</u>, <u>1280</u>, 1722, 1790, 2169+.

The Miller's Tale: Source Studies

833   HOFFMAN, RICHARD L. "Ovid's <u>Ictibus Agrestis</u> and the <u>Miller's
       Tale</u>." <u>N&Q</u>, 11 (1964), 49–50. Abstr. in <u>AES</u>, 7 (1964),
       no. 1474.

834   PEARCY, ROY J. "A Minor Analogue to the Branding in <u>The
       Miller's Tale</u>." <u>N&Q</u>, 16 (1969), 333–35. Abstr. in <u>AES</u>,
       13 (1969–70), no. 1501.

See also: <u>680</u>, <u>825</u>, 827, 832, 1736.01.

THE REEVE'S PROLOGUE AND TALE

       See Griffith, pp. 195–97; Crawford, pp. 67–68.

835   BAIRD, JOSEPH L. "Law and the <u>Reeve's Tale</u>." <u>NM</u>, 70 (1969),
       679–83.

836   BREWER, DEREK S. "The <u>Reeve's Tale</u> and the King's Hall,
       Cambridge." <u>ChauR</u>, 5 (1971), 311–17. Abstr. in <u>AES</u>, 15
       (1971–72), no. 704 and in <u>MLAA</u> (1971), no. 2112.

837   BURBRIDGE, ROGER T. "Chaucer's <u>Reeve's Tale</u> and the Fabliau
       <u>Le meunier et les .II. clers</u>." <u>AnM</u>, 12 (1971), 30–36.
       Abstr. in <u>MLAA</u> (1971), no. 2116.

838   CORREALE, ROBERT M. "Chaucer's Parody of Compline in the
       <u>Reeve's Tale</u>." <u>ChauR</u>, 1 (1967), 161–66. Abstr. in <u>AES</u>,
       13 (1969–70), no. 2866.

839   DELANY, SHEILA. "Clerks and Quiting in the <u>Reeve's Tale</u>."
       <u>MS</u>, 29 (1967), 351–56. Abstr. in <u>AES</u>, 12 (1969),
       no. 1253.

840   FRANK, ROBERT W., JR. "The Reeve's Tale and the Comedy of
       Limitation," in <u>Directions in Literary Criticism</u>:

The Reeve's Prologue and Tale

Contemporary Approaches to Literature. Festschrift for
Henry W. Sams. Edited by Stanley Weintraub and Philip
Young. University Park and London: Pennsylvania State
University Press, 1973, pp. 53-69.

841   FRIEDMAN, JOHN B. "A Reading of Chaucer's Reeve's Tale."
      ChauR, 2 (1967), 8-19. Abstr. in AES, 15 (1971-72), no. 37.

842   GARBÁTY, THOMAS JAY. "Satire and Regionalism: The Reeve and
      His Tale." ChauR, 8 (1973), 1-8. Abstr. in MLAA (1973),
      no. 2820.

843   GOSSELINK, ROBERT. "The Miller's Wife in Chaucer's Reeve's
      Tale." EngQ 6, i (Spring, 1973), 59-66. Abstr. in AES,
      18 (1974-75), no. 745.

844   HARVEY, R. W. "The Reeve's Polemic." WascanaR, 2, i (1967),
      62-73. Abstr. in AES, 10 (1967), no. 3611.

845   LANCASHIRE, IAN. "Sexual Innuendo in the Reeve's Tale."
      ChauR, 6 (1972), 159-70. Abstr. in AES, 16 (1972-73),
      no. 1563 and in MLAA (1972), no. 2720.

846   OLSON, GLENDING. "The Reeve's Tale and Gombert." MLR, 64
      (1969), 721-25. Abstr. in AES, 13 (1969-70), no. 2867.
      Parallels from Bodel's Gombert.

847   WILSON, ROBERT C. "Chaucer's The Reeve's Tale." Expl, 24
      (1965), Item 32. Abstr. in AES, 11 (1968), no. 2159.

See also: 89, 132, 198, 201, 205, 231, 308, 343, 347, 395, 407, 519,
560, 561, 563, 566, 575, 576, 588, 613, 622, 626, 635, 637, 640, 644,
647, 651, 653, 672, 761, 819, 1536, 1800, 1820, 1880, 2145, 2156,
2169, 2181.

The Reeve's Tale: Source Studies

See: 837, 846

THE COOK'S PROLOGUE AND TALE

See Griffith, pp. 197-98; Crawford, p. 68.

848   BIGGINS, DENNIS. "Erroneous Punctuation in Chaucer CT I (A)
      4394-96." PQ, 44 (1965), 117-20. Abstr. in AES, 9
      (1966), no. 954.

Canterbury Tales

See also: 33, 132, 198, 205, 487, 575, 644, 653.

INTRODUCTION, PROLOGUE

AND *THE MAN OF LAW'S TALE*

See Griffith, pp. 198-201; Crawford, pp. 68-69.

849   BLOOMFIELD, MORTON W. "The Man of Law's Tale: A Tragedy of
Victimization and a Christian Comedy." PMLA, 87 (1972),
384-90. Abstr. in AES, 16 (1972-73), no. 329, and in
MLAA (1972), no. 2682.
Revision and translation of 850, below.

850   BLOOMFIELD, MORTON W. "Il Racconto dell' uomo di legge: la
tragedia di una vittima e la commedia cristiana." SCr,
3 (1969), 195-207.
See 849.

851   BRUNT, ANDREW. "Constance's Covering Her Child's Eyes in
Chaucer's Man of Law's Tale 837f." N&Q, 16 (1969),
87-88. Abstr. in AES, 13 (1969-70), no. 385.

852   CULVER, T. D. "The Imposition of Order: A Measure of Art
in the Man of Law's Tale." YES, 2 (1972), 13-20.

853   DAVID, ALFRED. "The Man of Law vs. Chaucer: A Case in
Poetics." PMLA, 82 (1967), 217-25. Abstr. in AES, 10
(1967), no. 2851.

854   DELASANTA, RODNEY. "And of Great Reverence: Chaucer's Man
of Law." ChauR, 5 (1971), 288-310. Abstr. in AES, 15
(1971-72), no. 695 and in MLAA (1971), no. 2131.

855   FARRELL, ROBERT T. "Chaucer's Use of the Theme of the Help
of God in the Man of Law's Tale." NM, 71 (1970),
239-43.

856   HAMILTON, MARIE P. "The Dramatic Suitability of The Man of
Law's Tale," in 34, pp. 153-63.

857   HARRINGTON, DAVID V. "Chaucer's Man of Law's Tale: Rhetoric
and Emotion." MSpr, 61 (1967), 353-62. Abstr. in AES,
13 (1969-70), no. 1850.

Introduction, Prologue, and the Man of Law's Tale

858   HILL, D. M. "Romance as Epic." ES, 44 (1963), 95-107.
       Brief treatment of the romance structure of the Man of
       Law's Tale on p. 98.

859   *JOHNSON, WILLIAM CLARK, JR. "Chaucer's View of Knowledge: A
       Study of Ambiguity in The Man of Law's Tale." DAI, 33
       (1972), 275A-76A. University of Denver, 1972. 305 pp.

860   *KADAMBI, SHANTHA. "The Man of Law's Constance." EMD, 3
       (1965), 52-56. Cited in PMLAB (1967), no. 5657.
       Inaccessible.

861   LABRIOLA, ALBERT C. "The Doctrine of Charity and the Use of
       Homiletic 'Figures' in the Man of Law's Tale." TSLL, 12
       (1970), 5-14. Abstr. in MLAA (1970), no. 1788.

862   LEFFINGWELL, WILLIAM. "Saints' Lives and the Sultaness: A
       Note on a Perplexing Episode in Chaucer's Man of Law's
       Tale." Thoth, 12 (1971), 29-32.

863   LEWIS, ROBERT ENZER. "Chaucer's Artistic Use of Pope
       Innocent III's De Miseria Humane Conditionis in the Man
       of Law's Prologue and Tale." PMLA, 81 (1966), 485-92.
       Abstr. in AES, 10 (1967), no. 1047.

864   NORMAN, ARTHUR. "The Man of Law's Tale," in 29, pp. 312-23.

865   PAULL, MICHAEL R. "The Influence of the Saint's Legend Genre
       in the Man of Law's Tale." ChauR, 5 (1971), 179-94.
       Abstr. in AES, 15 (1971-72), no. 697 and in MLAA (1971),
       no. 2208.

866   *STERNBERG, IRMA OTTENHEIMER. "The Genre of Chaucer's Man of
       Law's Tale: A Reappraisal." DA, 24 (1964), 5392.
       Vanderbilt University, 1963. 252 pp.

867   STEVENS, MARTIN. "Malkyn in the Man of Law's Headlink."
       LeedsSe, 1 (1967), 1-5.

868   *WATSON, DAVID S. "The Man of Law's Tale: Loss and Separation
       in the Canterbury Tales." DAI, 31 (1971), 4737A-38A.
       State University of New York at Buffalo, 1970. 157 pp.

869   WOOD, CHAUNCEY. "Chaucer's Man of Law as Interpreter."
       Traditio, 23 (1967), 149-90.

See also: 132, 162, 198, 201, 205, 212, 255, 259, 276, 312, 321,
324, 340, 350, 359, 364, 379, 386, 391, 407, 567, 574, 576, 596, 624,

Canterbury Tales

<u>629</u>, 635, <u>640</u>, 646, <u>651</u>, 653, 669, 672, <u>680</u>, <u>745</u>, <u>979</u>, <u>1089</u>, 1284, 1790, 1809, 2156.

The Man of Law's Tale: Source Studies

870   *CORREALE, ROBERT M. "A Critical Edition of the Story of
        Constance in Nicholas Trevet's <u>Les Cronicles</u>: The Source
        of Chaucer's <u>Man of Law's Tale</u>." <u>DAI</u>, 32 (1972), 3946A.
        University of Cincinnati, 1971. 231 pp.

871   LEWIS, ROBERT ENZER. "Glosses to the <u>Man of Law's Tale</u> from
        Pope Innocent III's <u>De Miseria Humane Conditionis</u>." <u>SP</u>,
        64 (1967), 1-16. Abstr. in <u>AES</u>, 10 (1967), no. 3201.

872   PARR, JOHNSTONE. "Chaucer's Semiramis." <u>ChauR</u>, 5 (1970),
        57-61. Abstr. in <u>AES</u>, 15 (1971-72), no. 696 and in <u>MLAA</u>
        (1971), no. 2207.

873   PRATT, ROBERT A. "Chaucer and <u>Les Cronicles</u> of Nicholas
        Trevet," in 29, pp. 303-11.

874   SCHLAUCH, MARGARET. "Chaucer's Constance, Jonah, and the
        <u>Gesta Romanorum</u>." <u>KN</u>, 20 (1973), 305-306.

See also: <u>411</u>, <u>422</u>, <u>423</u>, <u>863</u>, <u>1620</u>.

THE WIFE OF BATH'S PROLOGUE AND TALE

See Griffith, pp. 202-206; Crawford, pp. 69-71.

875   ALBERTINI, VIRGIL R. "Chaucer's Artistic Accomplishment in
        Molding the <u>Wife of Bath's Tale</u>." <u>NwMSCS</u>, 28, iv (1964),
        3-16.

876   ALLEN, JUDSON B. and PATRICK GALLACHER. "Alisoun Through the
        Looking Glass: Or Every Man His Own Midas." <u>ChauR</u>, 4
        (1970), 99-105. Abstr. in <u>MLAA</u> (1970), no. 1742.

877   BAIRD, JOSEPH L. "The 'Secte' of the Wife of Bath." <u>ChauR</u>,
        2 (1968), 188-90. Abstr. in <u>AES</u>, 16 (1972-73), no. 1565.
        See also: 963 and 972 below.

The Wife of Bath's Prologue and Tale

878   BERGERON, DAVID M. "The Wife of Bath and Shakespeare's The
      Taming of the Shrew." UR, 35 (1969), 279-86. Abstr. in
      AES, 13 (1969-70), no. 2552.

879   *BROWN, ERIC DONALD. "Archetypes of Transformation: A Jungian
      Analysis of Chaucer's Wife of Bath's Tale and Clerk's
      Tale." DAI, 33 (1973), 5672A. The Pennsylvania State
      University, 1972. 209 pp.

880   COLMER, DOROTHY. "Character and Class in The Wife of Bath's
      Tale." JEGP, 72 (1973), 329-39. Abstr. in MLAA (1973),
      no. 2804.

881   COTTER, JAMES FINN. "The Wife of Bath and the Conjugal Debt."
      ELN, 6 (1969), 169-72. Abstr. in AES, 14 (1970-71),
      no. 1350.

882   COTTER, JAMES FINN. "The Wife of Bath's Lenten Observance."
      PLL, 7 (1971), 293-97. Abstr. in AES, 15 (1971-72),
      no. 1653 and in MLAA (1971), no. 2126.

883   CURTIS, PENELOPE. "Chaucer's Wyf of Bath." CR, 10 (1967),
      33-45. Abstr. in AES, 14 (1970-71), no. 29.

884   DELASANTA, RODNEY. "Quoniam and the Wife of Bath." PLL, 8
      (1972), 202-206. Abstr. in MLAA (1972), no. 2696.

885   DONALDSON, E. T. "Chaucer, Canterbury Tales, D117: A
      Critical Edition." Spec, 40 (1965), 626-33. Abstr. in
      AES, 10 (1967), no. 665.

886   DUNCAN, EDGAR H. "'Bear on Hand' in The Wife of Bath's
      Prologue." TSL, 11 (1966), 19-33. Abstr. in AES, 10
      (1967), no. 2179.

887   FLEISSNER, ROBERT F. "The Wife of Bath's Five." ChauR,
      8 (1973), 128-32. Abstr. in MLAA (1973), no. 2812.

888   FOX, ALLAN B. "The Traductio on Honde in the Wife of Bath's
      Prologue." NDEJ, 9 (1973), 3-8.

889   GILLAM, D. "'Cast up the Curtyn': A Tentative Exploration
      into the Meaning of the Wife of Bath's Tale," in 63,
      pp. 435-55.

890   GILLIE, CHRISTOPHER. "Women by Chaucer: The Wife of Bath,
      Criseyde," in his Character in English Literature. New
      York: Barnes & Noble, 1965, pp. 41-55.

Canterbury Tales

891   *GUTHRIE, WILLIAM BOWMAN. "The Comic Celebrant of Life." DA, 29 (1969), 3098A. Vanderbilt University, 1968. 315 pp.

892   HALLER, ROBERT S. "The Wife of Bath and the Three Estates." AnM, 6 (1965), 47-64.

893   HAMILTON, ALICE. "Helowys and the Burning of Jankyn's Book." MS, 34 (1972), 196-207. Abstr. in AES, 17 (1973-74), no. 691 and in MLAA (1972), no. 2704.

894   HARWOOD, BRITTON J. "The Wife of Bath and the Dream of Innocence." MLQ, 33 (1972), 257-73. Abstr. in AES, 17 (1973-74), no. 2610 and in MLAA (1972), no. 2707.

895   HASKELL, ANN S. "The St. Joce Oath in the Wife of Bath's Prologue." ChauR, 1 (1966), 85-87. Abstr. in AES, 13 (1969-70), no. 1852.

896   HIGDON, DAVID LEON. "The Wife of Bath and Refreshment Sunday." PLL, 8 (1972), 199-201. Abstr. in MLAA (1972), no. 2709.

897   HOFFMAN, RICHARD L. "Ovid and the Wife of Bath's Tale of Midas." N&Q, 13 (1966), 48-50. Abstr. in AES, 9 (1966), no. 2357.

898   HOLLAND, NORMAN N. "Meaning as Transformation: The Wife of Bath's Tale." CE, 28 (1967), 279-90. Abstr. in AES, 10 (1967), no. 1913.

899   KIESSLING, NICOLAS K. "The Wife of Bath's Tale: D 878-881." ChauR, 7 (1972), 113-17. Abstr. in MLAA (1972), no. 2717.

900   KOBAN, CHARLES. "Hearing Chaucer Out: The Art of Persuasion in the Wife of Bath's Tale." ChauR, 5 (1971), 225-39. Abstr. in AES, 15 (1971-72), no. 713 and in MLAA (1971), no. 2185.

901   LEVY, BERNARD S. "The Wife of Bath's Queynte Fantasye." ChauR, 4 (1970), 106-22. Abstr. in AES, 14 (1970-71), no. 694 and in MLAA (1970), no. 1791.

902   LOOMIS, ROGER S. "The Rimed English Romances," in his The Development of Arthurian Romance. London: Hutchinson, 1963; New York: Norton, 1970, chapter 10, pp. 131-46.

903   MAGEE, PATRICIA ANNE. "The Wife of Bath and the Problem of Mastery." MSE, 3 (1971), 40-45. Abstr. in AES, 17 (1973-74), no. 380.

The Wife of Bath's Prologue and Tale

904   MAHONEY, JOHN. "Alice of Bath: Her 'secte' and 'gentil
       text.'" Criticism, 6 (1964), 144-55.

905   MILLER, ROBERT P. "The Wife of Bath's Tale and Mediaeval
       Exempla." ELH, 32 (1965), 442-56.

906   OVERBECK, PAT TREFZGER. "Chaucer's Good Woman." ChauR, 2
       (1967), 75-94. Abstr. in AES, 16 (1972-73), no. 1571.

907   PARKER, DAVID. "Can We Trust the Wife of Bath?" ChauR, 4
       (1970), 90-98. Abstr. in AES, 14 (1970-71), no. 695 and
       in MLAA (1970), no. 1812.

908   REID, DAVID S. "Crocodilian Humor: A Discussion of Chaucer's
       Wife of Bath." ChauR, 4 (1970), 73-89. Abstr. in AES,
       14 (1970-71), no. 696 and in MLAA (1970), no. 1815.

909   ROWLAND, BERYL. "Chaucer's Dame Alys: Critics in Blunder-
       land?" NM, 73 (1972), 381-95.

910   ROWLAND, BERYL. "Chaucer's The Wife of Bath's Prologue, D
       389." Expl, 24 (1965), Item 14. Abstr. in AES, 11
       (1968), no. 450.

911   ROWLAND, BERYL. "On the Timely Death of the Wife of Bath's
       Fourth Husband." Archiv, 209 (1972), 273-82.

912   ROWLAND, BERYL. "The Wife of Bath's 'Unlawfull Philtrum.'"
       Neophil, 56 (1972), 201-206.

913   SANDERS, BARRY. "Further Puns from the Prologue and Tale of
       the Wife of Bath." PLL, 4 (1968), 192-95.

914   SCHMIDT, A. V. C. "The Wife of Bath's Marital State." N&Q,
       14 (1967), 230-31.
          Refutation of argument by D. S. Silvia, 916 below.

915   SHAPIRO, GLORIA K. "Dame Alice as Deceptive Narrator."
       ChauR, 6 (1971), 130-41. Abstr. in AES, 15 (1971-72),
       no. 2844 and in MLAA (1971), no. 2223.

916   SILVIA, D. S. "Chaucer's Canterbury Tales, D 44a-f." Expl,
       28 (1970), Item 44.
          For an opposing view, see 914.

917   SILVIA, D. S. "The Wife of Bath's Marital State." N&Q, 14
       (1967), 8-10. Abstr. in AES, 10 (1967), no. 2042.

Canterbury Tales

918   SLADE, TONY. "Irony in the Wife of Bath's Tale." MLR, 64
        (1969), 241-47. Abstr. in AES, 13 (1969-70), no. 2184.

919   *SOMERVILLE, ELIZABETH S. "The Application of an Ontological
        Perspective to the Literary Interpretation of Works Drawn
        from Several Periods." DA, 28 (1968), 3158A. Ohio Uni-
        versity, 1967. 180 pp.
        An "existential" reading of the Wife of Bath's Tale.

920   STEINBERG, AARON. "The Wife of Bath's Tale and Her Fantasy
        of Fulfillment." CE, 26 (1964), 187-91. Abstr. in AES,
        8 (1965), no. 978.

921   TALBOT, C. H. "Dame Trot and her Progeny," in 40, pp. 1-14.
        On medieval women doctors and their persecution--
        Chaucer's Dame Trot, Wife of Bath's Tale, III (D) 677.

922   *UNRUE, JOHN CALVIN. "Hali Meidenhad and Other Virginity
        Treatises." DAI, 31 (1971), 5378A. The Ohio State
        University, 1970. 233 p.
        Chaucer's knowledge of virginity treatises as shown in
        the Wife of Bath's Tale.

923   UTLEY, FRANCIS LEE. "Chaucer's Way with a Proverb: 'Allas!
        Allas! That Evere Love was Synne!'" NCarF, 21 (1973),
        98-104. Abstr. in MLAA (1973), no. 2786.

924   VERBILLION, JUNE. "Chaucer's The Wife of Bath's Prologue,
        175." Expl, 24 (1966), Item 58. Abstr. in AES, 11
        (1968), no. 2846.

925   WOOD, CHAUNCEY. "Chaucer's The Wife of Bath's Prologue, D
        576 and 583." Expl, 23 (1965), Item 73. Abstr. in AES,
        11 (1968), no. 437.

926   ZIMBARDO, ROSE A. "Unity and Duality in The Wife of Bath's
        Prologue and Tale." TSL, 11 (1966), 11-18. Abstr. in
        AES, 10 (1967), no. 2178.

See also: 132, 163, 173, 196, 198, 201, 205, 239, 255, 269, 276,
307, 308, 311, 312, 322, 324, 325, 331, 339, 340, 343, 346, 347, 364,
379, 386, 391, 397, 407, 423, 426, 430, 437, 459, 475, 515, 526, 565,
567, 574, 603, 605, 607, 610, 615, 625, 628, 629, 631, 635, 640, 647,
651, 653, 658, 672, 746, 964, 1011, 1162, 1183, 1433, 1658, 1642,
1699, 1750, 1820, 1834, 1839, 2170-71+.

The Wife of Bath's Tale: Source Studies

927   CARY, MEREDITH. "Sovereignty and Old Wife." PLL, 5 (1969),
       375-88.

928   DUNCAN, EDGAR H. "Chaucer's Wife of Bath's Prologue, Lines
       193-828, and Geoffrey of Vinsauf's Documentum." MP, 66
       (1969), 199-211. Abstr. in AES, 13 (1969-70), no. 757.

929   EISNER, SIGMUND. A Tale of Wonder: A Source Study of the
       Wife of Bath's Tale. Wexford, Ireland: J. English,
       1957. 148 pp.
          See Crawford, p. 70.
          Reviews: Claes Schaar, ES, 44 (1963), 360-62.

930   HOFFMAN, RICHARD L. "Ovid and the 'Marital Dilemma' in The
       Wife of Bath's Tale." AN&Q, 3 (1965), 101-102. Abstr.
       in AES, 10 (1967), no. 1558.

931   HOFFMAN, RICHARD L. "Ovid's Argus and Chaucer." N&Q, 12
       (1965), 213-16. Abstr. in AES, 9 (1966), no. 475.

932   HOFFMAN, RICHARD L. "The Wife of Bath as Student of Ovid."
       N&Q, 11 (1964), 287-88. Abstr. in AES, 8 (1965), no. 160.

933   LEVY, BERNARD S. "Chaucer's Wife of Bath, the Loathly Lady,
       and Dante's Siren." Symposium, 19 (1965), 359-73.

934   MUSCATINE, CHARLES. "The Wife of Bath and Gautier's La Veuve,"
       in 47, pp. 109-14.

935   CANCELLED

See also: 397, 400, 416, 680, 681, 876, 893, 896, 897.

THE FRIAR'S PROLOGUE AND TALE

          See Griffith, pp. 207-208; Crawford, pp. 71-72.

936   BAIRD, JOSEPH L. "The Devil in Green." NM, 69 (1968),
       575-78. Abstr. in AES, 15 (1971-72), no. 1647.

937   BAIRD, JOSEPH L. "The Devil's Privetee." NM, 70 (1969),
       104-106.

Canterbury Tales

938   CARRUTHERS, MARY. "Letter and Gloss in the Friar's and
          Summoner's Tales." JNT, 2 (1972), 208-14. Abstr. in
          MLAA (1972), no. 2685.

939   CLINE, RUTH H. "St. Anne." ELN, 2 (1964), 87-89. Abstr. in
          AES, 8 (1965), no. 2904.
             On a reference to St. Anne in Friar's Tale, line 1613.

940   ECKHARDT, CAROLINE D. "Canterbury Tales D 1554: 'Caples
          Thre.'" N&Q, 20 (1973), 283-84. Abstr. in AES, 18
          (1974-75), no. 1038.

941   HATTON, TOM. "Chaucer's Friar's 'Old Rebekke.'" JEGP, 67
          (1968), 266-71. Abstr. in AES, 12 (1969), no. 1560.

942   HENNEDY, HUGH L. "The Friar's Summoner's Dilemma." ChauR,
          5 (1971), 213-17. Abstr. in AES, 15 (1971-72), no. 694.

942.01 KELLOGG, ALFRED L. "A Reading of the Friar's Tale, Line
          1314," in 51, pp. 269-72.
             Reprinted from N&Q, 204 (1959), 190-92.

943   LENAGHAN, R. T. "The Irony of the Friar's Tale." ChauR, 7
          (1973), 281-94. Abstr. in AES, 17 (1973-74), no. 2883
          and in MLAA (1973), no. 2830.

944   MURTAUGH, DANIEL M. "Riming Justice in The Friar's Tale."
          NM, 74 (1973), 107-12.

945   PASSON, RICHARD H. "'Entente' in Chaucer's Friar's Tale."
          ChauR, 2 (1968), 166-71. Abstr. in AES, 16 (1972-73),
          no. 1554.

945.01 RICHARDSON, JANETTE. "Hunter and Prey: Functional Imagery
          in The Friar's Tale," in 37, pp. 155-65.
             Reprinted from EM, 7 (1961), 9-20.

946   STROUD, T. A. "Chaucer's Friar as Narrator." ChauR, 8
          (1973), 65-69. Abstr. in MLAA (1973), no. 2850.

See also: 132, 173, 198, 201, 259, 339, 519, 561, 563, 567, 575,
610, 647, 651, 653, 672, 710, 1820, 2158.

The Friar's Tale: Source Studies

947   CORREALE, ROBERT M. "St. Jerome and the Conclusion of the
          Friar's Tale." ELN, 2 (1965), 171-74. Abstr. in AES, 10
          (1967), no. 1169.

See also: 408.

THE SUMMONER'S PROLOGUE AND TALE

See Griffith, pp. 208-209; Crawford, pp. 72-73.

948   FLEMING, JOHN V. "The Antifraternalism of the Summoner's Tale." JEGP, 65 (1966), 688-700. Abstr. in AES, 10 (1967), no. 2723.

949   FLEMING, JOHN V. "The Summoner's Prologue: An Iconographic Adjustment." ChauR, 2 (1967), 95-107. Abstr. in AES, 16 (1972-73), no. 1564.

950   HARTUNG, ALBERT E. "Two Notes on the Summoner's Tale: Hosts and Swans." ELN, 4 (1967), 175-80. Abstr. in AES, 11 (1968), no. 908.

951   HASKELL, ANN S. "St. Simon in the Summoner's Tale." ChauR, 5 (1971), 218-24. Abstr. in AES, 15 (1971-72), no. 710 and in MLAA (1971), no. 2164.

952   HENNEDY, HUGH L. "The Friar's Summoner's Dilemma." ChauR, 5 (1971), 213-17. Abstr. in MLAA (1971), no. 2169.

953   KASKE, R. E. "Horn and Ivory in the Summoner's Tale." NM, 73 (1972), 122-26.

954   KELLOGG, ALFRED L. "The Fraternal Kiss in the Summoner's Tale," in 51, pp. 273-75. Reprinted from Scriptorium, 7 (1953), 115.

955   LEVITAN, ALAN. "The Parody of Pentecost in Chaucer's Summoner's Tale." UTQ, 40 (1971), 236-46.

956   LEVY, BERNARD S. "Biblical Parody in the Summoner's Tale." TSL, 11 (1966), 45-60. Abstr. in AES, 10 (1967), no. 2181.

957   PEARCY, ROY J. "Chaucer's 'An Impossible' (Summoner's Tale, III, 2231)." N&Q, 14 (1967), 322-25. Abstr. in AES, 11 (1968), no. 986.

Canterbury Tales

958   SEVERS, J. BURKE. "Chaucer's The Summoner's Tale, D 2184-
        2188." Expl, 23 (1964), Item 20. Abstr. in AES, 8 (1965),
        no. 1344.

959   SILVIA, DANIEL S., JR. "Chaucer's Friars: Swans or Swains?
        Summoner's Tale, D 1930." ELN, 1 (1964), 248-50. Abstr.
        in AES, 8 (1965), no. 1945.

960   *SZITTYA, PENN RODION. "'Caimes Kynde': The Friars and the
        Exegetical Origins of Medieval Antifraternalism." DAI,
        33 (1972), 287A-88A. Cornell University, 1971. 293 pp.
        Sets Friar John in the antifraternal tradition.

961   ZIETLOW, PAUL N. "In Defense of the Summoner." ChauR, 1
        (1966), 4-19. Abstr. in AES, 13 (1969-70), no. 1119.

See also: 132, 198, 201, 205, 212, 276, 343, 467, 519, 561, 563,
575, 596, 610, 622, 634, 637, 640, 644, 651, 653, 672, 832, 937, 938,
1658, 1779, 1849.

The Summoner's Tale: Source Studies

962   FLEMING, JOHN. "Chaucer's 'Syngeth Placebo' and the Roman de
        Fauvel." N&Q, 12 (1965), 17-18. Abstr. in AES, 8 (1965),
        no. 2267.

See also: 416, 832, 948, 950.

THE CLERK'S PROLOGUE, TALE, ENVOY AND WORDS OF THE HOST

        See Griffith, pp. 209-13; Crawford, pp. 73-74.

963   BAIRD, JOSEPH L. "Secte and Suit Again: Chaucer and Lang-
        land." ChauR, 6 (1971), 117-19. Abstr. in AES, 15
        (1971-72), no. 2841 and in MLAA (1971), no. 2101.
        See also 877 and 972.

964   CHERNISS, MICHAEL D. "The Clerk's Tale and Envoy, the Wife
        of Bath's Purgatory, and the Merchant's Tale." ChauR,
        6 (1972), 235-54. Abstr. in AES, 16 (1972-73), no. 1566
        and in MLAA (1972), no. 2686.

The Clerk's Prologue, Tale, Envoy and Words of the Host

965   COOK, JAMES WYATT. "Augustinian Neurosis and the Therapy of
      Orthodoxy." Universitas, 2, ii (1964), 51-62. Abstr. in
      AES, 8 (1965), no. 555.
      Walter and Griselda in Augustinian psychology.

966   COVELLA, SISTER FRANCIS DOLORES. "The Speaker of the Wife of
      Bath Stanza and Envoy." ChauR, 4 (1970), 267-83. Abstr.
      in AES, 15 (1971-72), no. 712 and in MLAA (1971), no. 2127.

967   CUNNINGHAM, J. V. "Ideal Fiction: The Clerk's Tale."
      Shenandoah, 19 (Winter, 1968), 38-41. Abstr. in AES, 11
      (1968), no. 3117.

968   FICHTE, JOERG O. "The Clerk's Tale: An Obituary to
      Gentilesse," in 50, pp. 9-16. Abstr. in AES, 18
      (1974-75), no. 739.

969   FRESE, DOLORES WARWICK. "Chaucer's Clerk's Tale: The
      Monsters and the Critics Reconsidered." ChauR, 8 (1973),
      133-46. Abstr. in MLAA (1973), no. 2815.

970   GRENNEN, JOSEPH E. "Science and Sensibility in Chaucer's
      Clerk." ChauR, 6 (1971), 81-93. Abstr. in AES, 15
      (1971-72), no. 2842 and in MLAA (1971), no. 2153.

971   *HACKETT, JOHN P. "Chaucer and the Interpretation of Medieval
      Narrative: an Essay on the Clerk's Tale." DAI, 33
      (1972), 1169A. St. Louis University, 1971. 358 pp.

972   HORNSTEIN, LILLIAN HERLANDS. "The Wyf of Bathe and the
      Merchant: From Sex to 'Secte.'" ChauR, 3 (1968), 65-67.
      Abstr. in AES, 17 (1973-74), no. 681.
      For opposing view, see 963.

973   HOY, MICHAEL. "The Tales of the Prioress and the Clerk," in
      48, pp. 39-59.

974   *HUME, JEANNETTE STOCKTON. "An Essay on the Clerk's Tale."
      DA, 26 (1965), 2184. Yale University, 1965. 172 pp.

975   JAMESON, THOMAS H. "One Up for Clerks." A&S (Winter,
      1964-65), 10-13.

976   KELLOGG, ALFRED L. "The Evolution of the Clerk's Tale: A
      Study in Connotation," in 51, pp. 276-329.

977   LANHAM, RICHARD A. "Chaucer's Clerk's Tale: The Poem Not
      the Myth." L&P, 16 (1966), 157-65. Abstr. in AES, 11
      (1968), no. 200.
      Rejects Lavers' method. See 978.

Canterbury Tales

978   LAVERS, NORMAN. "Freud, The Clerkes Tale, and Literary Crit-
           icism." CE, 26 (1964), 180-87. Abstr. in AES, 8 (1965),
           no. 977.

979   LOGANBILL, DEAN. "The Clerk's Tale and the Man of Law's Tale:
           Chaucer and Godot Waiting for Beckett," in 50, pp. 29-34.
           Abstr. in AES, 18 (1974-75), no. 740.

980   McCALL, JOHN P. "Chaucer and John of Legnano." Spec, 40
           (1965), 484-89. Abstr. in AES, 9 (1966), no. 2116.

981   McCALL, JOHN P. "The Clerk's Tale and the Theme of Obedience."
           MLQ, 27 (1966), 260-69. Abstr. in AES, 10 (1967), no.
           2003.

982   McNAMARA, JOHN. "Chaucer's Use of the Epistle of St. James
           in the Clerk's Tale." ChauR, 7 (1973), 184-93. Abstr.
           in AES, 17 (1973-74), no. 2882 and in MLAA (1973),
           no. 2835.

983   MORROW, PATRICK. "The Ambivalence of Truth: Chaucer's
           Clerkes Tale." BuR, 16, iii (December, 1968), 74-90.
           Abstr. in AES, 12 (1969), no. 1124.

984   ROTHMAN, IRVING N. "Humility and Obedience in the Clerk's
           Tale, with the Envoy Considered as an Ironic Affirmation."
           PLL, 9 (1973), 115-27. Abstr. in AES, 18 (1974-75),
           no. 372 and in MLAA (1973), no. 2843.

985   SCHLEINER, WINFRIED. "Rank and Marriage: A Study of the
           Motif of Woman Willfully Tested." CLS, 9 (1972),
           365-75. Abstr. in MLAA (1972), no. 1361.

986   SPEARING, A. C. "Chaucer's Clerk's Tale as a Medieval Poem,"
           in 363, pp. 76-106.

987   UTLEY, FRANCIS LEE. "Five Genres in the Clerk's Tale."
           ChauR, 6 (1972), 198-228. Abstr. in AES, 16 (1972-73),
           no. 1553 and in MLAA (1972), no. 2742.

See also: 162, 173, 198, 201, 212, 255, 259, 269, 307, 308, 321,
324, 340, 350, 357, 364, 386, 407, 437, 456, 513, 515, 556, 557, 566,
576, 605, 610, 615, 624, 628, 640, 646, 651, 653, 672, 735, 745, 877,
879, 1183, 1635, 2158.

<u>The Clerk's Tale</u>: Source Studies

988   *BETTRIDGE, WILLIAM EDWIN. "Griselda: Aarne-Thompson Tale
        Type 887: Analogues of Chaucer's <u>Clerk's Tale</u>." <u>DA</u>, 27
        (1967), 3005A. The Ohio State University, 1966. 343 pp.

989   SEVERS, J. BURKE. <u>The Literary Relationships of Chaucer's</u>
        <u>Clerkes Tale</u>. Hamden, Connecticut: Archon, 1972.
        371 pp.
          Originally published as <u>YSE</u>, 96, Yale, 1942. See
        Griffith, p. 212.

See also: 984.

THE MERCHANT'S PROLOGUE, TALE, AND *EPILOGUE*

See Griffith, pp. 213-16; Crawford, pp. 74-75.

990   ALTMAN, LESLIE JOAN WOLBARST. "Gesture and Posture in the
        <u>Merchant's Tale</u>: A Study of Chaucer's Narrative Tech-
        nique." <u>DAI</u>, 34 (1974), 1232A. Boston College, 1973.
        40 pp.

991   BAIRD, JOSEPH L. "'Of Marriage, Which We Have on Honde.'"
        <u>AN&Q</u>, 11 (1973), 100-102.

992   BEIDLER, PETER G. "Chaucer's Merchant and the Tale of
        January." <u>Costerus</u>, 5 (1972), 1-25. Abstr. in <u>MLAA</u>
        (1972), no. 2681.

993   *BEIDLER, PETER GRANT. "Chaucer's <u>Merchant's Tale</u> and Its
        Narrator." <u>DA</u>, 29 (1969), 3969A. Lehigh University,
        1968. 310 pp.

994   BEIDLER, PETER G. "The Climax in the <u>Merchant's Tale</u>."
        ChauR, 6 (1971), 38-43. Abstr. in <u>AES</u>, 15 (1971-72),
        no. 1962 and in <u>MLAA</u> (1971), no. 2107.

995   BEIDLER, PETER G. "January, Knight of Lombardy." <u>NM</u>, 72
        (1971), 735-38.

Canterbury Tales

996 BLANCH, ROBERT J., ed. Geoffrey Chaucer: Merchant's Tale.
     With Introduction and Notes. Merrill Casebooks.
     Columbus, Ohio: Charles E. Merrill, 1970. 167 pp.
     Text and ten reprinted articles.

997 BLANCH, ROBERT J. "Irony in Chaucer's Merchant's Tale."
     LHR, 8 (1966), 8-15. Abstr. in AES, 10 (1967), no. 2444.
     Reprinted in 996, pp. 144-49.

998 BROWN, EMERSON LEE, JR. "Allusion in Chaucer's Merchant's
     Tale." DA, 28 (1968), 4118A-19A. Cornell University,
     1967. 194 pp.

999 BROWN, EMERSON, JR. "Hortus Inconclusus: The Significance
     of Priapus and Pyramus and Thisbe in the Merchant's Tale."
     ChauR, 4 (1970), 31-40. Abstr. in AES, 13 (1969-70),
     no. 2862 and in MLAA (1970), no. 1753.

1000 BROWN, EMERSON, JR. "The Merchant's Tale: Januarie's
     'Unlikely Elde.'" NM, 74 (1973), 92-106.

1001 BROWN, EMERSON L., JR. The Merchant's Tale: Why Is May
     Called 'Mayus?'" ChauR, 2 (1968), 273-77. Abstr. in
     AES, 16 (1972-73), no. 1556.

1002 BROWN, EMERSON, JR. "The Merchant's Tale: Why Was Januarie
     Born 'Of Pavye?'" NM, 71 (1970), 654-58.

1003 CHERNISS, MICHAEL D. "The Clerk's Tale and Envoy, the Wife
     of Bath's Purgatory, and the Merchant's Tale." ChauR,
     6 (1972), 235-54. Abstr. in AES, 16 (1972-73), no. 1566
     and in MLAA (1972), no. 2686.

1004 DELANY, PAUL. "Constantinus Africanus and Chaucer's
     Merchant's Tale." PQ, 46 (1967), 560-66. Abstr. in AES,
     15 (1971-72), no. 698.

1005 DELANY, PAUL. "Constantinus Africanus' De Coitu: A Trans-
     lation." ChauR, 4 (1969-70), 55-65. Abstr. in AES, 13
     (1969-70), no. 2863.

1006 DONALDSON, E. TALBOT. "The Effect of the Merchant's Tale,"
     in 39, pp. 30-45.

1007 ECONOMOU, GEORGE D. "Januarie's Sin Against Nature: the
     Merchant's Tale and the Roman de la Rose." CL, 17
     (1965), 251-57. Abstr. in AES, 10 (1967), no. 869.

The Merchant's Prologue, Tale, and Epilogue

1008   ELLIOT, JOHN R., JR. "The Two Tellers of The Merchant's
       Tale." TSL, 9 (1964), 11-17. Abstr. in AES, 9 (1966),
       no. 2768.

1009   FERRIS, SUMNER J. "'Wades Boot': Canterbury Tales E 1424
       and 1684." AN&Q, 9 (1971), 71-72.

1010   FIELD, P. J. C. "Chaucer's Merchant and the Sin Against
       Nature." N&Q, 17 (1970), 84-86. Abstr. in AES, 13
       (1969-70), no. 3192.

1011   HARRINGTON, DAVID V. "Chaucer's Merchant's Tale, 1427-28."
       N&Q, 11 (1964), 166-67. Abstr. in AES, 7 (1964),
       no. 2244.

1012   HARRINGTON, NORMAN T. "Chaucer's Merchant's Tale: Another
       Swing of the Pendulum." PMLA, 86 (1971), 25-31. Abstr.
       in AES, 15 (1971-72), no. 35 and in MLAA (1971), no. 2162.

1013   HARTUNG, ALBERT E. "The Non-Comic Merchant's Tale,
       Maximianus, and the Sources." MS, 29 (1967), 1-25.
       Abstr. in AES, 12 (1969), no. 1249.

1014   HOFFMAN, RICHARD L. "Ovid's Priapus in The Merchant's Tale."
       ELN, 3 (1966), 169-72. Abstr. in AES, 10 (1967),
       no. 1673.

1015   KELLOGG, ALFRED L. "Susannah and the Merchant's Tale," in
       51, pp. 330-37.
          Reprinted from Spec, 35 (1960), 275-79.

1016   MUKHERJEE, MEENAKSHI. "The Merchant's Tale: A Study in
       Multiple Meaning." IJES, 7 (1966), 17-23. Abstr. in
       AES, 16 (1972-73), no. 944.

1017   OTTEN, CHARLOTTE F. "Proserpine: Liberatrix Suae Gentis."
       ChauR, 5 (1971), 277-87. Abstr. in AES, 15 (1971-72),
       no. 699 and in MLAA (1971), no. 2206.

1018   PACE, GEORGE B. "The Scorpion of Chaucer's Merchant's Tale."
       MLQ, 26 (1965), 369-74. Abstr. in AES, 9 (1966),
       no. 3049.

1019   PEETERS, L[EOPOLD]. "Wade, Hildebrand and Brendan." ABäG,
       3 (1972), 25-65.
          Takes issue with Wentersdorf, 1030, below.

Canterbury Tales

1020   PITTOCK, MALCOLM. "The Merchant's Tale." EIC, 17 (1967),
         26-40. Abstr. in AES, 10 (1967), no. 1943.
         Treats tension between tale and teller.

1021   ROBBINS, ROSSELL HOPE. "January's Caress." LHR, 10 (1968),
         3-6. Abstr. in AES, 12 (1969), no. 1911.

1022   ROSENBERG, BRUCE A. "'The Cherry-Tree Carol' and the
         Merchant's Tale." ChauR, 5 (1971), 264-76. Abstr. in
         AES, 15 (1971-72), no. 700 and in MLAA (1971), no. 2216.

1023   SCHROEDER, MARY C. "Fantasy in the Merchant's Tale."
         Criticism, 12 (1970), 167-79. Abstr. in AES, 16
         (1972-73), no. 1557 and in MLAA (1970), no. 1822.

1024   SHORES, DAVID L. "The Merchant's Tale: Some Lay Obser-
         vations." NM, 71 (1970), 119-33.

1025   SMITH, THOMAS NORRIS. "The Garden Image in Medieval Liter-
         ature." DA, 29 (1969), 2685A. The University of
         Connecticut, 1968. 137 pp.

1026   STEVENS, MARTIN. "'And Venus Laugheth': An Interpretation
         of the Merchant's Tale." ChauR, 7 (1972), 118-31.
         Abstr. in AES, 17 (1973-74), no. 2887 and in MLAA (1972),
         no. 2739.

1027   TAYLOR, WILLENE P. "Chaucer's Technique in Handling Material
         in The Merchant's Tale: An Ironic Portrayal of the
         Senex-Amans and Jealous Husband." CLAJ, 13 (1969),
         153-62.

1028   TURNER, W. ARTHUR. "Biblical Women in the Merchant's Tale
         and the Tale of Melibee." ELN, 3 (1965), 92-95. Abstr.
         in AES, 10 (1967), no. 1219.

1029   VON KEISLER, NICOLAI A. "An Aesopic Allusion in the
         Merchant's Tale." ChauR, 6 (1971), 30-37. Abstr. in
         AES, 15 (1971-72), no. 1963 and MLAA (1971), no. 2236.

1030   WENTERSDORF, KARL P. "Chaucer and the Lost Tale of Wade."
         JEGP, 65 (1966), 274-86. Abstr. in AES, 10 (1967),
         no. 129.
         See also Peeters, 1019 above.

1031   WENTERSDORF, KARL P. "Theme and Structure in The Merchant's
         Tale: The Function of the Pluto Episode." PMLA, 80
         (1965), 522-27. Abstr. in AES, 9 (1966), no. 1946.

The Merchant's Prologue, Tale, and Epilogue

1032   WHITE, GERTRUDE M. "'Hoolynesse or Dotage': The Merchant's
           January." PQ, 44 (1965), 397-404. Abstr. in AES, 10
           (1967), no. 3106.
           Reprinted in 996, pp. 116-23.

1033   WICHIRT, ROBERT A. "Chaucer's The Merchant's Tale." Expl,
           25 (1966), Item 32. Abstr. in AES, 11 (1968), no. 2894.

See also: 132, 198, 201, 214, 231, 239, 255, 259, 268, 269, 305,
307, 308, 312, 324, 331, 340, 364, 387, 391, 395, 413, 426, 437, 464,
498, 556, 561, 563, 567, 575, 576, 591, 605, 607, 610, 615, 622, 629,
635, 640, 644, 651, 653, 670, 672, 972, 1183, 1679, 1699, 1768, 1816,
2158.

The Merchant's Tale: Source Studies

1034   BEIDLER, PETER G. "Chaucer's Merchant's Tale and the
           Decameron." Italica, 50 (1973), 266-84. Abstr. in MLAA
           (1973), no. 2798.

1035   GRENNEN, JOSEPH E. "Another French Source for The Merchant's
           Tale." RomN, 8 (1966), 109-12. Abstr. in AES, 14
           (1970-71), no. 1646.

1036   WATKINS, CHARLES A. "Modern Irish Variants of the Enchanted
           Pear Tree." SFQ, 30 (1966), 202-13.
           Twenty-one variants of the Merchant's Tale.

1037   WENTERSDORF, KARL P. "Chaucer's Merchant's Tale and Its
           Irish Analogues." SP, 63 (1966), 604-29. Abstr. in
           AES, 10 (1967), no. 3197.

1038   WENTERSDORF, KARL P. "A Spanish Analogue of the Pear-Tree
           Episode in the Merchant's Tale." MP, 64 (1967), 320-21.
           Abstr. in AES, 11 (1968), no. 2002.

See also: 408, 420, 680, 931, 999, 1004, 1005, 1007, 1013, 1014,
1022, 1029.

Canterbury Tales

THE SQUIRE'S PROLOGUE AND *TALE*

See Griffith, pp. 216-19; Crawford, p. 75.

1039   BERGER, HARRY, JR. "The F-Fragment of the Canterbury Tales:
        Part I." ChauR, 1 (1966), 88-102. Abstr. in AES, 13
        (1969-70), no. 1853.
        See also 1052.

1040   CLARK, JOHN W. "Does the Franklin Interrupt the Squire?"
        ChauR, 7 (1972), 160-61. Abstr. in AES, 17 (1973-74),
        no. 2892 and in MLAA (1972), no. 2687.
        See also 1041.

1041   DUNCAN, CHARLES F., JR. "'Straw for Youre Gentilesse': The
        Gentle Franklin's Interruption of the Squire." ChauR, 5
        (1970), 161-64. Abstr. in AES, 15 (1971-72), no. 708
        and in MLAA (1971), no. 2135.
        See also 1040.

1042   FINKELSTEIN, DOROTHEE. "The Celestial Origin of Elpheta and
        Algarsyf in Chaucer's Squire's Tale." Euroasiatica,
        Folia Philogica AION-SL Suppleta, 4 (1970), 3-13.

1043   FRIEND, ALBERT C. "The Tale of the Captive Bird and the
        Traveler: Nequam, Berechiah, and Chaucer's Squire's Tale."
        M&H, n.s. 1 (1970), 57-65. Abstr. in MLAA (1970),
        no. 1773.

1044   GÖLLER, KARL H. "Chaucers Squire's Tale: 'The knotte of the
        tale,'" in 43, pp. 163-88.

1045   GREENE, RICHARD LEIGHTON. "'Foules of Ravyne' and 'Foules
        Smale' in Chaucer's Squire's Tale." N&Q, 12 (1965),
        446-48. Abstr. in AES, 9 (1966), no. 1905.

1046   HALLER, ROBERT S. "Chaucer's Squire's Tale and the Uses of
        Rhetoric." MP, 62 (1965), 285-95. Abstr. in AES, 9
        (1966), no. 848.

1047   KAHRL, STANLEY J. "Chaucer's Squire's Tale and the Decline
        of Chivalry." ChauR, 7 (1973), 194-209. Abstr. in AES,
        17 (1973-74), no. 2893 and in MLAA (1973), no. 2827.

1048   McCALL, JOHN P. "The Squire in Wonderland." ChauR, 1 (1966),
        103-109. Abstr. in AES, 13 (1969-70), no. 1851.

116

The Words of the Franklin, The Franklin's Prologue and Tale

1049   PEARSALL, D[EREK] A. "The Squire as Story-Teller." UTQ, 34
        (1964), 82-92. Abstr. in AES, 8 (1965), no. 566.

1050   PETERSON, JOYCE E. "The Finished Fragment: A Reassessment
        of the Squire's Tale." ChauR, 5 (1970), 62-74. Abstr.
        in AES, 15 (1971-72), no. 709 and in MLAA (1971), no. 2211.

See also: 33, 132, 198, 201, 276, 312, 340, 364, 386, 391, 426, 455,
498, 541, 580, 640, 660, 672, 1699.

The Squire's Tale: Source Studies

See: 408, 680, 706, 1043.

THE WORDS OF THE FRANKLIN,

THE FRANKLIN'S PROLOGUE AND *TALE*

See Griffith, pp. 219-21; Crawford, pp. 75-76.

1051   BEIDLER, PETER G. "The Pairing of the Franklin's Tale and
        the Physician's Tale." ChauR, 3 (1969), 275-79. Abstr.
        in AES, 13 (1969-70), no. 2550.

1052   BERGER, HARRY, JR. "The F-Fragment of the Canterbury Tales:
        Part II." ChauR, 1 (1967), 135-56. Abstr. in AES, 13
        (1969-70), no. 2869.
        For Part I see 1039.

1053   BÖKER, UWE. "Studien zu Chaucers Franklin's Tale."
        Universitat Regensburg, Dissertation, 1968.
        Contains lengthy review of research.

1054   BURLIN, ROBERT B. "The Art of Chaucer's Franklin." Neophil,
        51 (1967), 55-73. Abstr. in AES, 13 (1969-70), no. 1116.

1055   COLMER, DOROTHY. "The Franklin's Tale: A Palimpsest Reading."
        EIC, 20 (1970), 375-80.
        Reply to Kearney, 1069 below.

1056   DAVID, ALFRED. "Sentimental Comedy in the Franklin's Tale."
        AnM, 6 (1965), 19-27.

117

Canterbury Tales

1057   DONOVAN, MORTIMER J.   The Breton Lay: A Guide to Varieties.
       Notre Dame, Indiana: University of Notre Dame Press,
       1969.   267 pp.
          See especially chapter 4, pp. 173-89, "Chaucer and the
       Franklin's Tale."
          Reviews: Basil Cottle, JEGP, 69 (1970), 304-306;
       G. C. Britton, N&Q, 17 (1970), 317-19; W. H. W. Field,
       MLQ, 31 (1970), 372-73.

1058   GAYLORD, ALAN T. "The Promises in The Franklin's Tale."
       ELH, 31 (1964), 331-65.

1059   GOLDING, M[ALCOLM] R. "The Importance of Keeping 'Trouthe'
       in The Franklin's Tale." MAE, 39 (1970), 306-12. Abstr.
       in AES, 18 (1974-75), no. 741.

1060   GRAY, PAUL EDWARD. "Synthesis and the Double Standard in
       the Franklin's Tale." TSLL, 7 (1965), 213-24.

1061   HATTON, THOMAS J. "Magic and Honor in The Franklin's Tale."
       PLL, 3 (1967), 179-81.

1062   HEYDON, PETER N. "Chaucer and the Sir Orfeo Prologue of the
       Auchinleck MS." PMASAL, 51 (1966), 529-45.

1063   HOWARD, RONNALIE ROPER. "Appearance, Reality, and the Ideal
       in Chaucer's Franklin's Tale." BSUF, 8, iii (Summer,
       1967), 40-44. Abstr. in AES, 14 (1970-71), no. 691.

1064   HUME, KATHRYN. "The Pagan Setting of the Franklin's Tale
       and the Sources of Dorigen's Cosmology." SN, 44 (1972),
       289-94. Abstr. in AES, 17 (1973-74), no. 2248.

1065   HUME, KATHRYN. "Why Chaucer Calls the Franklin's Tale a
       Breton Lai." PQ, 51 (1972), 365-79. Abstr. in MLAA
       (1972), no. 2701.

1066   JOHNSTON, GRAHAME. "Chaucer and the Breton Lays," in Pro-
       ceedings and Papers of the Fourteenth Congress of the
       Australasian Universities Language and Literature Asso-
       ciation Held 19-26 January 1972 at the University of
       Otago, Dunedin, New Zealand. Edited by K. I. D. Maslen.
       Dunedin, New Zealand: AULLA, 1972, pp. 230-41.

1067   JOSEPH, GERHARD. "The Franklin's Tale: Chaucer's Theodicy."
       ChauR, 1 (1966), 20-32. Abstr. in AES, 13 (1969-70),
       no. 1117.

The Words of the Franklin, The Franklin's Prologue and Tale

1068   KEARNEY, ANTHONY [M.]. "The Franklin's Tale." EIC, 21 (1971),
        109-11.
        Reply to Colmer, 1055 above.

1069   KEARNEY, A. M. "Truth and Illusion in The Franklin's Tale."
        EIC, 19 (1969), 245-53. Abstr. in AES, 13 (1969-70),
        no. 750.
        For a reply, see 1055 above.

1070   KELLY, FRANCIS J. "Chaucer's Franklin's Tale, F 942." Expl,
        24 (1966), Item 81. Abstr. in AES, 11 (1968), no. 2866.

1071   KNIGHT, STEPHEN. "Rhetoric and Poetry in the Franklin's Tale."
        ChauR, 4 (1969-70), 14-30. Abstr. in AES, 13 (1969-70),
        no. 2861 and in MLAA (1970), no. 1786.

1072   MANN, LINDSAY A. "Gentilesse and the Franklin's Tale." SP,
        63 (1966), 10-29. Abstr. in AES, 10 (1967), no. 1437.

1073   MILOSH, JOSEPH. "Chaucer's Too-Well Told Franklin's Tale:
        A Problem of Characterization." WSL, 5 (1970), 1-11.
        Abstr. in AES, 13 (1969-70), no. 751.

1074   MUKERJI, N. "Chaucer's Franklin's [Tale] and the Tale of
        Madanasena of Vetalapachisi: A Comparative Study."
        FolkloreC, 9 (1968), 75-85.

1075   PECK, RUSSELL A. "Sovereignty and the Two Worlds of the
        Franklin's Tale." ChauR, 1 (1967), 253-71. Abstr. in
        AES, 14 (1970-71), no. 2938.

1076   PETRICONE, SISTER ANCILLA MARIE, S. C. "The Middle English
        Breton Lays: A Structural Analysis of Narrative Tech-
        nique." DAI, 34 (1973), 1251A-52A. The Catholic Uni-
        versity of America, 1973. 195 pp.

1077   SEVERS, J. BURKE. "Appropriateness of Character to Plot in
        the Franklin's Tale," in 34, pp. 385-96.

1078   STEVENS, MICHAEL. "The Franklin's Tale," in 48, pp. 81-101.

1079   TRIPP, RAYMOND P., JR. "The Franklin's Solution to the
        'Marriage Debate,'" in 50 (PSNLS 1 [1973]), pp. 35-41.
        Abstr. in AES, 18 (1974-75), no. 742.

1080   WOOD, CHAUNCEY. "Of Time and Tide in the Franklin's Tale."
        PQ, 45 (1966), 688-711.
        A study of astrology, magic, and the medieval theory
        of the annual period of the tides.

Canterbury Tales

See also: 132, 162, 173, 187, 190, 196, 198, 201, 212, 225, 233, 239, 255, 259, 276, 307, 312, 324, 339, 340, 350, 364, 379, 386, 387, 391, 576, 603, 605, 607, 610, 615, 621, 628, 631, 635, 640, 651, 658, 660, 662, 672, 740, 1039, 1679, 1824, 1839, 2158.

The Franklin's Tale: Source Studies

1081   WITKE, CHARLES. "Franklin's Tale, F 1139–1151." ChauR, 1
            (1966), 33–36. Abstr. in AES, 13 (1969–70), no. 1118.

See also: 397, 400, 404, 407, 680, 681, 1062, 1064.

THE PHYSICIAN'S TALE

See Griffith, p. 222; Crawford, p. 76.

1082   BRANCA, GERALDINE SESAK. "Experience Versus Authority:
            Chaucer's Physician and Fourteenth-Century Science." DAI,
            32 (1972), 5731A. University of Illinois at Urbana-
            Champaign, 1971. 127 pp.

1083   HANSON, THOMAS B. "Chaucer's Physician as Storyteller and
            Moralizer." ChauR, 7 (1972), 132–39. Abstr. in AES, 17
            (1973–74), no. 2891 and in MLAA (1972), no. 2705.

1084   HOFFMAN, RICHARD L. "Jephthah's Daughter and Chaucer's
            Virginia." ChauR, 2 (1967), 20–31. Abstr. in AES, 15
            (1971–72), no. 34.

1085   HOFFMAN, RICHARD L. "Pygmalion in the Physician's Tale."
            AN&Q, 5 (1967), 83–84.

1086   LONGSWORTH, ROBERT. "The Doctor's Dilemma: A Comic View of
            the Physicians's Tale." Criticism, 13 (1971), 223–33.
            Abstr. in AES, 16 (1972–73), no. 1875 and in MLAA (1971),
            no. 2193.

1087   MIDDLETON, ANNE. "The Physician's Tale and Love's Martyrs:
            'Ensamples Mo Than Ten' as a Method in the Canterbury
            Tales." ChauR, 8 (1973), 9–32. Abstr. in MLAA (1973),
            no. 2836.

Words of the Host, The Pardoner's Prologue and Tale

1088   RAMSEY, LEE C. "'The Sentence of It Sooth Is': Chaucer's
        Physician's Tale." ChauR, 6 (1972), 185–97. Abstr. in
        AES, 16 (1972–73), no. 1562 and in MLAA (1972), no. 2732.

1089   ROWLAND, BERYL. "The Physician's 'Historial Thyng Notable'
        and the Man of Law." ELH, 40 (1973), 165–78. Abstr. in
        MLAA (1973), no. 2845.

1090   USSERY, HULING E. "The Appropriateness of The Physician's
        Tale to Its Teller." PMASAL, 50 (1965), 545–56.

See also: 132, 183, 201, 205, 255, 321, 380, 386, 492, 556, 557, 597,
625, 647, 669, 672, 745, 1051.

The Physician's Tale: Source Studies

See: 680, 1083, 1084, 1088.

WORDS OF THE HOST

(OR INTRODUCTION TO *THE PARDONER'S TALE*),

THE PARDONER'S PROLOGUE AND *TALE*

See Griffith, pp. 222–25; Crawford, pp. 76–78.

1091   ADELMAN, JANET. "That We May Leere Som Wit," in 1106,
        pp. 96–106.

1092   BARAKAT, ROBERT A. "Odin: Old Man of The Pardoner's Tale."
        SFQ, 28 (1964), 210–15.

1093   BARNEY, STEPHEN A. "An Evaluation of the Pardoner's Tale,"
        in 1106, pp. 83–95.

1094   BISHOP, IAN. "The Narrative Art of The Pardoner's Tale."
        MAE, 36 (1967), 15–24. Abstr. in AES, 11 (1968),
        no. 2554.

1095   CALDERWOOD, JAMES L. "Parody in The Pardoner's Tale." ES,
        45, (1964), 302–309. Abstr. in AES, 8 (1965), no. 1962.

Canterbury Tales

1096   CASE, GILBERT A. Geoffrey Chaucer's The Pardoner's Tale.
        Adelaide: Rigby, 1968.
           Not available in the U. S. A.

1097   CONLEE, JOHN W. "The Pardoner's Symbolic Treasure." SHum,
        3 (1972), 1-3.
           Treats the number eight (eight bushels) as a symbol of
        betrayal.

1098   CURRIE, FELICITY. "Chaucer's Pardoner Again." LeedsSE, 4
        (1970), 11-22.

1099   CURTIS, PENELOPE. "The Pardoner's 'Jape.'" CR, 11 (1968),
        15-31. Abstr. in AES, 14 (1970-71), no. 1978.

1100   DAVID, ALFRED. "Criticism and the Old Man in Chaucer's
        Pardoner's Tale." CE, 27 (1965), 39-44. Abstr. in AES,
        9 (1966), no. 1542.

1101   DEAN, CHRISTOPHER. "Salvation, Damnation and the Role of the
        Old Man in the Pardoner's Tale." ChauR, 3 (1968), 44-49.
        Abstr. in AES, 17 (1973-74), no. 688.

1102   DENEEF, A. LEIGH. "Chaucer's Pardoner's Tale and the Irony
        of Misinterpretation." JNT, 3 (1973), 85-96. Abstr. in
        MLAA (1973), no. 2805.

1103   ELLIOTT, CHARLES and R. GEORGE THOMAS. "Two Points of View:
        The Pardoner's Prologue and Tale." AWR, 14 (1964), 9-17.
        Abstr. in AES, 8 (1965), no. 291.

1104   ELLIOTT, RALPH W. V. The Nun's Priest's Tale and The
        Pardoner's Tale. Notes on English Literature. New York:
        Barnes & Noble, 1965. 87 pp.
           Excerpts reprinted in 1106, pp. 23-32.

1105   ELLIOTT, RALPH W. V. "Our Host's 'triacle': Some Obser-
        vations on Chaucer's Pardoner's Tale." REL, 7, ii
        (April, 1966), 61-73. Abstr. in AES, 10 (1967), no. 297.

1106   FAULKNER, DEWEY R., ed. The Pardoner's Tale: A Collection
        of Critical Essays. Twentieth Century Interpretations.
        Englewood Cliffs, New Jersey: Prentice-Hall, 1973.
        127 pp.
           Reprinted critical essays, selected bibliography.

1107   GAFFORD, CHARLOTTE K. "Chaucer's Pardoner and Haze Motes of
        Georgia," in Essays in Honor of Richebourg Gaillard

Words of the Host, The Pardoner's Prologue and Tale

McWilliams. Edited by Howard Creed. Birmingham,
Alabama: Southern College, 1970 [*Birmingham-Southern
College Bulletin, 63, ii (1970)], pp. 9-12.
Reviews (of book): M. A. Owings, SAB, 36, iv
(November, 1971), 93-95.

1108   GRENNEN, JOSEPH E. "'Sampsoun' in the Canterbury Tales:
        Chaucer Adapting a Source." NM, 67 (1966), 117-22.
        Abstr. in AES, 10 (1967), no. 995.

1109   HALVERSON, JOHN. "Chaucer's Pardoner and the Progress of
        Criticism." ChauR, 4 (1970), 184-202. Abstr. in AES,
        14 (1970-71), no. 1979.

1110   HARRINGTON, DAVID V. "Narrative Speed in the Pardoner's
        Tale." ChauR, 3 (1968), 50-59. Abstr. in AES, 17
        (1973-74), no. 689.
        Reprinted in 1106, pp. 33-42.

1111   HARRIS, RICHARD L. "Odin's Old Age: A Study of The Old Man
        in The Pardoner's Tale." SFQ, 33 (1969), 24-38.

1112   HOY, MICHAEL. "The Pardoner's Tale," in 48, pp. 103-31.

1112.01 KELLOGG, ALFRED L. "An Augustinian Interpretation of
        Chaucer's Pardoner," in 51, pp. 245-68.
        Reprinted from Spec, 26 (1951), 465-81.

1113   KELLOGG, ALFRED L. and LOUIS A. HASELMAYER. "Chaucer's
        Satire of the Pardoner," in 51, pp. 212-44.
        Reprinted with revisions from PMLA, 66 (1951), 251-77.

1114   KHINOY, STEPHAN A. "Inside Chaucer's Pardoner?" ChauR, 6
        (1972), 255-67. Abstr. in AES, 16 (1972-73), no. 1559
        and in MLAA (1972), no. 2716.

1115   KIEHL, JAMES M. "Dryden's Zimri and Chaucer's Pardoner: A
        Comparative Study of Verse Portraiture." Thoth, 6
        (1965), 3 12. Abstr. in AES, 9 (1966), no. 2459.

1116   MILLER, CLARENCE H. and ROBERTA BUX BOSSE. "Chaucer's
        Pardoner and the Mass." ChauR, 6 (1972), 171-84.
        Abstr. in AES, 16 (1972-73), no. 1560 and in MLAA (1972),
        no. 2725.

1116.01 MILLER, ROBERT P. "Chaucer's Pardoner, the Scriptural
        Eunuch, and the Pardoner's Tale," in 1106, pp. 43-69.
        Reprinted from Spec, 30 (1955), 180-99.

Canterbury Tales

1117   MITCHELL, CHARLES. "The Moral Superiority of Chaucer's
        Pardoner." CE, 27 (1966), 437-44. Abstr. in AES, 9
        (1966), no. 2197.

1118   NICHOLS, ROBERT E., JR. "The Pardoner's Ale and Cake."
        PMLA, 82 (1967), 498-504. Abstr. in AES, 11 (1968),
        no. 637.

1119   O'NEAL, COTHBURN M. "The Syndrome of Masochism in Chaucer's
        Pardoner: Synopsis of the Pardoner," in Proceedings of
        the Conference of College Teachers of English of Texas,
        vol. 32. Edited by Martin Shockley. Lubbock: Texas
        Technical College, 1967, pp. 18-23.

1120   OSSELTON, N. E. "Chaucer's 'Clumsy Transition' in the
        Pardoner's Tale." ES, 49 (1968), 36-38. Abstr. in AES,
        13 (1969-70), no. 755.

1121   OWEN, NANCY H. "The Pardoner's Introduction, Prologue, and
        Tale: Sermon and Fabliau." JEGP, 66 (1967), 541-49.
        Abstr. in AES, 11 (1968), no. 2223.
        Excerpts reprinted in 1106.

1122   REISS, EDMUND. "The Final Irony of the Pardoner's Tale." CE,
        25 (1964), 260-66.

1123   ROACHE, JOEL. "Treasure Trove in the Pardoner's Tale." JEGP,
        64 (1965), 1-6. Abstr. in AES, 8 (1965), no. 1642.

1124   ROSS, ALAN S. C. "To Go A-Blackberrying." N&Q, 20 (1973),
        284-85. Abstr. in AES, 18 (1974-75), no. 1041.

1125   ROWLAND, BERYL. "Chaucer's Swallow and Dove 'Sittynge on a
        Berne': MilT, I, 3258, PardProl, VI, 397." N&Q, 11
        (1964), 48-49.

1126   SCHMIDT, PHILIP. "Reexamination of Chaucer's Old Man of the
        Pardoner's Tale." SFQ, 30 (1966), 249-55.

1127   SNIPES, KATHERINE. "Intellectual Villains in Dostoyevsky,
        Chaucer and Albert Camus." Discourse, 13 (1970),
        240-50.

1128   STEADMAN, JOHN M. "Chaucer's Pardoner and the Thesaurus
        Meritorium." ELN, 3 (1965), 4-7. Abstr. in AES, 10
        (1967), no. 1202.

Words of the Host, The Pardoner's Prologue and Tale

1129   STEADMAN, JOHN M.   "Old Age and Contemptus Mundi in The
          Pardoner's Tale." MAE, 33 (1964), 121–30.
          Reprinted in 1106, pp. 70–82.

1130   STEWART, DONALD C. "Chaucer's Perplexing Pardoner." CEA, 29,
          iii (1966), 1, 4–6.

1131   TAITT, P. S. "Harry Bailly and the Pardoner's Relics." SN,
          41 (1969), 112–14. Abstr. in AES, 14 (1970–71), no. 347.

1132   TAITT, PETER. "In Defence of Lot." N&Q, 18 (1971), 284–85.
          Abstr. in AES, 15 (1971–72), no. 1651.

1133   TODD, ROBERT E. "The Magna Mater Archetype in The Pardoner's
          Tale." L&P, 15 (1965), 32–40. Abstr. in AES, 9 (1966),
          no. 1709.

1134   TOOLE, WILLIAM B., III. "Chaucer's Christian Irony: The
          Relationship of Character and Action in the Pardoner's
          Tale." ChauR, 3 (1968), 37–43. Abstr. in AES, 17
          (1973–74), no. 690.

See also: 33, 132, 162, 174, 184, 198, 201, 205, 225, 255, 259, 311,
324, 343, 364, 467, 513, 565, 596, 597, 609, 610, 614, 618, 624, 634,
640, 651, 670, 672, 675, 883, 1283, 1620, 1711, 1712, 1753, 1820,
1927, 1975, 2136, 2172–75+.

The Pardoner's Tale: Source Studies

1135   BARAKAT, ROBERT A. "Chaucer's Old Man in the Americas."
          WF, 24 (1965), 33–34. Abstr. in AES, 10 (1967),
          no. 1121.
          Analogues to the ancient wayfarer motif.

1136   HAMER, DOUGLAS. "The Pardoner's Tale: A West-African
          Analogue." N&Q, 16 (1969), 335–36. Abstr. in AES, 13
          (1969–70), no. 1502.

1137   WALKER, WARREN S. "Chaucer's Pardoner's Tale: More
          African Analogues." N&Q, 19 (1972), 444–45. Abstr. in
          AES, 17 (1973–74), no. 2890.

See also: 408, 411, 416, 1108, 1132.

Canterbury Tales

THE SHIPMAN'S PROLOGUE OR *THE EPILOGUE*

OF *THE MAN OF LAW'S TALE* (II [B^1] 1163-1190)

AND *THE SHIPMAN'S TALE*

See Griffith, pp. 225-26; Crawford, p. 78.

1138   ADAMS, GEORGE R. "Chaucer's The Shipman's Tale, 173-177."
        Expl, 24 (1966), Item 41. Abstr. in AES, 11 (1968),
        no. 2168.

1139   COPLAND, MURRAY. "The Shipman's Tale: Chaucer and Boccaccio."
        MAE, 35 (1966), 11-28. Abstr. in AES, 10 (1967), no. 3036.

1140   DELIGIORGIS, S. "Structuralism and the Study of Poetry: A
        Parametric Analysis of Chaucer's Shipman's Tale and
        Parlement of Foules." NM, 70 (1969), 297-306. Abstr. in
        AES, 16 (1972-73), no. 331.

1141   FISHER, RUTH M. "'Cosyn' and 'Cosynage': Complicated Punning
        in Chaucer's Shipman's Tale?" N&Q, 12, (1965), 168-70.
        Abstr. in AES, 9 (1966), no. 463.

1141.01 LAWRENCE, WILLIAM WITHERLE. "Chaucer's Shipman's Tale," in
        58, pp. 190-206.
        Reprinted from Spec, 33 (1958), 56-68.

1142   LEVY, BERNARD S. "The Quaint World of The Shipman's Tale."
        SSF, 4 (1967), 112-18. Abstr. in AES, 10 (1967),
        no. 3449.

1143   McCLINTOCK, MICHAEL W. "Games and the Players of Games: Old
        French Fabliaux and the Shipman's Tale." ChauR, 5 (1970),
        112-36. Abstr. in AES, 15 (1971-72), no. 706 and in
        MLAA (1971), no. 2198.

1144   RICHARDSON, JANETTE. "The Façade of Bawdry: Image Patterns
        in Chaucer's Shipman's Tale." ELH, 32 (1965), 303-13.

See also: 198, 225, 239, 343, 395, 407, 437, 519, 561, 563, 575,
635, 637, 644, 651, 672, 831, 1183, 2158.

The Shipman's Tale: Source Studies

1145   FRIES, MAUREEN. "An Historical Analogue to the Shipman's
        Tale?" Comitatus, 3 (1972), 19-32.

1146   GUERIN, RICHARD. "The Shipman's Tale: The Italian Analogues."
        ES, 52 (1971), 412-19.

1147   HOGAN, MORELAND H., JR. "A New Analogue of the Shipman's
        Tale." ChauR, 5 (1971), 245-46. Abstr. in AES, 15
        (1971-72), no. 705.

1148   NICHOLSON, PETER CHARLES. "The Literary Relations of Chaucer's
        Shipman's Tale." DAI, 34 (1974), 5114A. University of
        Pennsylvania, 1973. 381 pp.

1149   O'BRYANT, JOAN. "Two Versions of The Shipman's Tale from
        Urban Oral Tradition." WF, 24 (1965), 101-103. Abstr.
        in AES, 10 (1967), no. 1122.

See also: 1139.

THE PRIORESS'S HEADLINK, PROLOGUE, AND TALE

See Griffith, pp. 226-28; Crawford, pp. 79-80.

1150   BRENNAN, JOHN P. "Reflections on a Gloss to the Prioress's
        Tale from Jerome's Adversus Jovinianum." SP, 70 (1973),
        243-51. Abstr. in MLAA (1973), no. 2801.

1151   BREWER, D. S. "Children in Chaucer." REL, 5, iii (1964),
        52-60. Abstr. in AES, 8 (1965), no. 894.

1152   *CHITWOOD, GARRETT CLAYTON, JR. "Love and Guilt: A Study of
        Suffering in Selected Medieval Works." DAI, 31 (1971),
        3497A-98A. Case Western Reserve University, 1970.
        375 pp.
            Section on The Prioress's Tale.

1153   *FRANK, MARY HARDY LONG. "The Prioress and the Puys: A Study
        of the Cult of the Virgin and the Medieval Puys in Rela-
        tion to Chaucer's Prioress and Her Tale." DAI, 31 (1970),
        2874A-75A. University of Colorado, 1970. 210 pp.

Canterbury Tales

1154   GAGE, PHYLLIS C. "Syntax and Poetry in Chaucer's Prioress's
        Tale." Neophil, 50 (1966), 252-61. Abstr. in AES, 10
        (1967), no. 2017.

1155   HAWKINS, SHERMAN. "Chaucer's Prioress and the Sacrifice of
        Praise." JEGP, 63 (1964), 599-624. Abstr. in AES, 8
        (1965), no. 1637.

1156   HILL, BOYD H., JR. "The Grain and the Spirit in Medieval
        Anatomy." Spec, 39 (1965), 63-73. Abstr. in AES, 9
        (1966), no. 2114.

1157   HOY, MICHAEL. "The Tales of the Prioress and the Clerk," in
        48, pp. 39-59.

1158   KELLY, EDWARD H. "By Mouth of Innocentz: The Prioress
        Vindicated." PLL, 5 (1969), 362-74.

1159   LANGMUIR, GAVIN I. "The Knight's Tale of Young Hugh of
        Lincoln." Spec, 47 (1972), 459-82. Abstr. in AES, 17
        (1973-74), no. 1581 and in MLAA (1972), no. 2721.
        Shows that the historical Hugh of Lincoln died
        accidentally.

1160   LYONS, JOHN O. "James Joyce and Chaucer's Prioress." ELN,
        2 (1964), 127-32.

1161   O'NEILL, YNEZ VIOLÉ. "A Speculation Concerning the Grain in
        Chaucer's Prioress's Tale." MedH, 12, ii (1968), 185-90.
        Abstr. in AES, 15 (1971-72), no. 36.

1162   PITTOCK, MALCOLM. The Prioress's Tale and The Wife of Bath's
        Tale. Notes on English Literature. Oxford: Blackwell,
        1973. 103 pp.
        For The Prioress's Tale, see pp. 1-41.

1163   RIDLEY, FLORENCE H. The Prioress and the Critics. Berkeley:
        University of California Press, 1965. 51 pp.

1164   *ROBINSON, JAY LUKE. "The Context of Chaucer's Prioresses
        Tale." University of California at Berkeley, Disserta-
        tion, 1962. Cited in MHRA (1964), no. 2219. Listed in
        index but not abstracted in DA, 22 (1962).

1165   RUSSELL, G. H. "Chaucer: The Prioress's Tale," in 59,
        pp. 211-27.

1166   TAYLOR GARY. "Greyn and the Resuscitation of the Little
        Clergeon." SFQ, 34 (1970), 82-89.

Sir Thopas: Prologue and Tale

See also: 132, 162, 174, 183, 198, 201, 214, 255, 259, 276, 321, 340, 364, 491, 556, 640, 646, 651, 669, 670, 672, 715, 745, 1633, 1757, 1886, 1987, 2158.

The Prioress's Tale: Source Studies

See: 1150, 1622.01.

SIR THOPAS: PROLOGUE AND TALE

See Griffith, pp. 228-31; Crawford, p. 80.

1167   BROOKHOUSE, CHRISTOPHER. "Sir Thopas, 901-2." N&Q, 12
          (1965), 293-94. Abstr. in AES, 9 (1966), no. 900.

1168   BURROW, J. A. "'Listeth, Lordes': Sir Thopas, 712 and 833."
          N&Q, 15 (1968), 326-27. Abstr. in AES, 12 (1969),
          no. 492.

1169   BURROW, J. A. "Sir Thopas: An Agony in Three Fits." RES,
          22 (1971), 54-58. Abstr. in AES, 15 (1971-72), no. 707.

1170   BURROW, JOHN. "'Worly under Wede' in Sir Thopas." ChauR,
          3 (1969), 170-73. Abstr. in AES, 13 (1969-70), no. 2551.

1171   GREENE, RICHARD LEIGHTON. "The Hunt Is Up, Sir Thopas:
          Irony, Pun, and Ritual." N&Q, 13 (1966), 169-71. Abstr.
          in AES, 9 (1966), no. 3358.
          See also 1176 below.

1172   HANLEY, KATHERINE, C. S. J. "Chaucer's Horseman: Word-Play
          in the Tale of Sir Thopas." NEMLA Newsl, 2 (1970),
          112-14.

1173   KINDRICK, ROBERT LEROY. "The Unknightly Knight: Anti-
          Chivalric Satire in Fourteenth and Fifteenth Century
          English Literature." DAI, 32 (1972), 5742A. The Uni-
          versity of Texas at Austin, 1971. 223 pp.

1174   LATHAM, MURIEL K. "The Narrative of Sir Thopas and Melibeus:
          Parallels in the Vices and the Virtues." DAI, 34 (1973),
          2568A-69A. The University of New Mexico, 1973. 200 pp.

Canterbury Tales

1175   LUCAS, PETER J. "Towards an Interpretation of Sir Launfal
        with Particular Reference to line 683." MAE, 39 (1970),
        291-300.
           Compares Sir Thopas to Launfal.

1176   ROWLAND, BERYL. "Chaucer's 'Bukke and Hare' (Thop, VII, 756)."
        ELN, 2 (1964), 6-8. Abstr. in AES, 8 (1965), no. 2888.
        See 1171 above.

1177   SCHEPS, WALTER. "Sir Thopas: The Bourgeois Knight, the
        Minstrel and the Critics." TSL, 11 (1966), 35-43. Abstr.
        in AES, 10 (1967), no. 2180.

1178   STANLEY, E. G. "The Use of Bob-Lines in Sir Thopas." NM, 73
        (1972), 417-26.

1179   WILLIAMS, GEORGE. "Chaucer's Best Joke--the Tale of Sir
        Thopas," in 386, pp. 145-51.
           Suggests Sir Thopas is a homosexual.

1180   WOOD, CHAUNCEY. "Chaucer and Sir Thopas: Irony and Con-
        cupiscence." TSLL, 14 (1972), 389-403. Abstr. in MLAA
        (1972), no. 2745.

See also: 132, 188, 201, 239, 364, 426, 436, 437, 510, 575, 640,
647, 660, 672, 1719, 1746, 1799, 1886.

MELIBEUS: HEADLINK AND TALE

See Griffith, pp. 231-32; Crawford, p. 81.

1181   CHRISTMAS, ROBERT ALAN. "Chaucer's Tale of Melibee: Its
        Tradition and Its Function in Fragment VII of the Canter-
        bury Tales." DA, 29 (1969), 3093A. University of South-
        ern California, 1968. 151 pp.

1182   KONAGAYA, YATAKA. "The Tale of Melibeus and Chaucer." SELit,
        42 (1965), 13-18.

1182.01 LAWRENCE, WILLIAM WITHERLE. "Chaucer's Tale of Melibeus," in
        58, pp. 207-17 and excerpts in 62, pp. 133-37.
           Reprinted from Essays and Studies in Honor of Carleton
        Brown. New York: New York University Press, 1940,
        pp. 100-110.

BIBLIOGRAPHY OF CHAUCER, 1964 - 1973

1183   *MATTHEWS, LLOYD JEAN. "The Latent Comic Dimensions of
            Geoffrey Chaucer's Tale of Melibee." DAI, 32 (1972),
            4572A. University of Virginia, 1971. 243 pp.

1184   *OIZUMI, AKIO. "On Collocated Words in Chaucer's Translation
            of Le Livre de Mellibee et Prudence--A Stylistic Com-
            parison of the English Translation with the French Ver-
            sion." SELit, 48, i (1971), 95-108. Cited in PMLAB
            (1972), no. 2727. Abstr. in English in SELit, Eng. no.
            (1972), 196-97.
            In Japanese.

1185   OLSZEWSKA, E. S. "Past and Gone." N&Q, 13 (1966), 209.
            Abstr. in AES, 10 (1967), no. 189.
            The "past and gone" phrase in Melibee.

1186   OWEN, CHARLES A., JR. "The Tale of Melibee." ChauR, 7
            (1973), 267-80. Abstr. in AES, 17 (1973-74), no. 2886
            and in MLAA (1970), no. 2839.

1187   STROHM, PAUL. "The Allegory of the Tale of Melibee." ChauR,
            2 (1967), 32-42. Abstr. in AES, 15 (1971-72), no. 44.

See also: 162, 259, 324, 386, 500, 569, 622, 624, 625, 635, 640,
647, 652, 662, 666, 672, 1028, 1174, 1974.

Melibeus: Source Studies

1188   BÜHLER, CURT F. "The Morgan Manuscript (M 39) of Le Livre
            de Melibee et de Prudence," in 34, pp. 49-54.

1189   HOFFMAN, RICHARD L. "A Newly Acquired Manuscript of
            Albertano of Brescia." LC, 36 (1970), 105-109.

See also: 404, 680, 1181, 1184.

THE MONK'S PROLOGUE AND TALE

See Griffith, pp. 232-35; Crawford, p. 81.

1190   BYERS, JOHN R., JR, "Harry Bailey's St. Madrian." ELN, 4
            (1966), 6-9. Abstr. in AES, 10 (1967), no. 3262.

Canterbury Tales

1191   FRY, DONALD K. "The Ending of The Monk's Tale." JEGP, 71
            (1972), 355-68. Abstr. in MLAA (1972), no. 2700.

1192   HASKELL, ANN SULLIVAN. "The Host's 'Precious Corpus
            Madrian.'" JEGP, 67 (1968), 430-40. Abstr. in AES, 13
            (1969-70), no. 386.

1193   HOFFMAN, RICHARD L. "Ovid and the Monk's Tale of Hercules."
            N&Q, 12 (1965), 406-409. Abstr. in AES, 9 (1966),
            no. 1772.

1194   ORUCH, JACK B. "Chaucer's Worldly Monk." Criticism, 8
            (1966), 280-88.

1195   STRANGE, WILLIAM C. "The Monk's Tale: A Generous View."
            ChauR, 1 (1967), 167-80. Abstr. in AES, 13 (1969-70),
            no. 2864.

1196   TAYLOR, ESTELLE W. "Chaucer's Monk's Tale: An Apology."
            CLAJ, 13 (1969), 172-82.

1197   WATSON, CHARLES S. "The Relationship of the Monk's Tale and
            the Nun's Priest's Tale." SSF, 1 (1964), 277-88. Abstr.
            in AES, 8 (1965), no. 925.

See also: 33, 132, 183, 189, 201, 226, 255, 259, 301, 350, 364, 380,
386, 515, 603, 625, 640, 647, 652, 669, 672, 696, 700, 718, 725, 1108,
1206, 1214, 1735, 2156.

The Monk's Tale: Source Studies

1198   DWYER, R. A. "Some Readers of John Trevisa." N&Q, 14 (1967),
            291-92. Abstr. in AES, 10 (1967), no. 3350.

1199   ROBBINS, ROSSELL H. "A New Chaucer Analogue: The Legend of
            Ugolino." Trivium, 2 (1967), 1-16.

See also: 680, 1193.

THE NUN'S PRIEST'S PROLOGUE, TALE, AND EPILOGUE

See Griffith, pp. 235-38; Crawford, pp. 81-83.

1200   ALLEN, JUDSON BOYCE. "The Ironic Fruyt: Chauntecleer as
Figura." SP, 66 (1969), 25-35.
Considers allegorical interpretations.

1201   BRINDLEY, D. J. "The Mixed Style of the Nun's Priest's Tale."
ESA, 7 (1964), 148-56. Abstr. in AES, 10 (1967), no. 2391.

1202   CHAMBERLAIN DAVID S. "The Nun's Priest's Tale and Boethius's
De Musica." MP, 68 (1970), 188-91. Abstr. in AES, 14
(1970-71), no. 2617.

1203   CLARK, GEORGE. "Chauntecleer and Deduit." ELN, 2 (1965),
168-71.
Comparisons with figures in the Roman de la Rose.

1204   COOK, JAMES W. "The Nun's Priest and the Hebrew Pointer."
AN&Q, 7 (1968), 53-54.
Suggests Chaucer may have known an Anglo-Jewish collec-
tion of beast fables.

1205   DANIELS, EDGAR F. "Chaucer's The Nun's Priest's Tale, B^2,
4054." Expl, 23 (1964), Item 33. Abstr. in AES, 8
(1965), no. 1357.

1206   DELASANTA, RODNEY K. "'Namoore of this': Chaucer's Priest
and Monk." TSL, 13 (1968), 117-32.

1207   DRONKE, PETER. "Chaucer and Boethius' De Musica." N&Q, 13
(1966), 92. Abstr. in AES, 9 (1966), no. 3102.

1208   DUMANOSKI, DIANNE. "A Muse's Eye View of Chaucer." VJ (1964),
50-56.

1209   ELLIOTT, RALPH W. V. "The Nun's Priest's Tale and The Pardoner's Tale. Notes on English Literature. New York:
Barnes & Noble, 1965. 87 pp.

1210   FRIEDMAN, JOHN BLOCK. "The Nun's Priest's Tale: The Preacher
and the Mermaid's Song." ChauR, 7 (1973), 250-66. Abstr.
in AES, 17 (1973-74), no. 2888 and in MLAA (1973),
no. 2816.

Canterbury Tales

1211 *GABBARD, GREGORY NORMAN. "The Animal-Human Double Context in
the Beast Fables and Beast Tales of Chaucer and Henryson."
DA, 29 (1968), 567A-68A. The University of Texas at
Austin, 1968. 236 pp.

1212 *GALLICK, SUSAN LYDIA. "Medieval Rhetoric and Chaucer's Nun's
Priest's Tale." DAI, 33 (1973), 4342A-43A. Indiana
University, 1972. 306 pp.

1213 HARRINGTON, DAVID V. "The Undramatic Character of Chaucer's
Nun's Priest." Discourse, 8 (1965), 80-89.

1214 HATTON, THOMAS J. "Chauntecleer and the Monk, Two False
Knights." PLL, 3 (Summer supplement, 1967), 31-39.

1215 HENNING, STANDISH. "Chauntecleer and Taurus." ELN, 3 (1965),
1-4. Abstr. in AES, 10 (1967), no. 1201.

1216 HIEATT, CONSTANCE B. "The Moral of The Nun's Priest's Tale."
SN, 42 (1970), 3-8. Abstr. in AES, 14 (1970-71), no. 1647.

1217 HOY, MICHAEL. "The Nun's Priest's Tale," in 48, pp. 133-62.

1218 JOSELYN, SISTER M., O. S. B. "Aspects of Form in the Nun's
Priest's Tale." CE, 25 (1964), 566-71. Abstr. in AES,
7 (1964), no. 2046.

1219 KAUFFMAN, CORINNE E. "Dame Pertelote's Parlous Parle."
ChauR, 4 (1970), 41-48. Abstr. in AES, 13 (1969-70),
no. 2865 and in MLAA (1970), no. 1783.

1220 LEVY, BERNARD S. and GEORGE R. ADAMS. "Chauntecleer's
Paradise Lost and Regained." MS, 29 (1967), 178-92.
Abstr. in AES, 12 (1969), no. 1251.

1221 MEREDITH, PETER. "Chauntecleer and the Mermaids." Neophil,
54 (1970), 81-83.

1222 MYERS, D. E. "Focus and 'Moralite' in the Nun's Priest's
Tale." ChauR, 7 (1973), 210-20. Abstr. in AES, 17
(1973-74), no. 2889 and MLAA (1973), no. 2838.

1223 PEARCY, ROY J. "The Epilogue to The Nun's Priest's Tale."
N&Q, 15 (1968), 43-45. Abstr. in AES, 11 (1968),
no. 2567.

1224 PÉREZ, MARTÍN M.[a] JESÚS. "El tono de voz en The Nun's
Priest's Tale de Chaucer." FMod, 6 (1966), 323-27.

134

The Nun's Priest's Prologue, Tale, and Epilogue

1225   RAND, GEORGE I. "The Date of the Nun's Priest's Tale." AN&Q,
        7 (1969), 149-50.

1226   ROBBINS, ROSSELL H. "'Lawriol': CT, B 4153." ChauR, 3
        (1968), 68. Abstr. in AES, 17 (1973-74), no. 687.

1227   ROWLAND, BERYL. "'Owles and Apes' in Chaucer's Nun's Priest's
        Tale, 3092." MS, 27 (1965), 322-25. Abstr. in AES, 12
        (1969), no. 1243.

1228   ROWLAND, BERYL. "'A Sheep That Highte Malle' (NPT, VII,
        2831)." ELN, 6 (1968), 84-87. Abstr. in AES, 14
        (1970-71), no. 1349.

1229   SCHEPS, WALTER. "Chaucer's Anti-Fable: Reductio ad Absurdum
        in the Nun's Priest's Tale." LeedsSE, 4 (1970), 1-10.

1230   SCHRADER, RICHARD J. "Chauntecleer, the Mermaid, and Daun
        Burnel." ChauR, 4 (1970), 284-90. Abstr. in AES, 15
        (1971-72), no. 703 and in MLAA (1971), no. 2222.

1231   *WATKINS, CHARLES ARNOLD. "Chaucer's Nun's Priest's Tale:
        Satire and Solas." DA, 28 (1968), 3653A. The Ohio State
        University, 1967. 118 pp.

1232   WATKINS, CHARLES A. "Chaucer's Sweete Preest." ELH, 36
        (1969), 455-69.

1233   WEIDHORN, MANFRED. "The Anxiety Dream from Homer to Milton."
        SP, 64 (1967), 65-82.
            On the Nun's Priest's Tale, see p. 67.

See also: 112, 132, 198, 201, 205, 212, 213, 215, 222, 224, 225,
232, 239, 246, 255, 259, 276, 277, 308, 312, 324, 343, 356, 364, 391,
425, 430, 441, 453, 459, 498, 515, 554, 575, 576, 610, 613, 621, 622,
634, 635, 640, 647, 651, 652, 672, 696, 1183, 1197, 1711, 1814, 1822,
1823, 1829, 1862, 1994, 2017, 2033, 2040, 2059, 2134, 2135, 2136,
2176-77+.

The Nun's Priest's Tale: Background

1234   *SHALLERS, ALVIN PAUL. "The Renart Tradition in the Literature
        of Medieval England." DAI, 31 (1971), 5374A. The Uni-
        versity of Wisconsin, 1970. 349 pp.

Canterbury Tales

1235 *SPILLEMAECKERS, DIEDERIK LODEWIJK. "Reynard the Fox: The
      Evolution of His Character in Select Medieval Beast Epics."
      DAI, 31 (1970), 2355A-56A. Michigan State University,
      1970. 198 pp.
         Treats five beast epics in various languages. The
      Nun's Priest's Tale is not specifically treated.

1236 VARTY, KENNETH. "The Death and Resurrection of Reynard in
      Medieval Literature and Art." NMS, 10 (1966), 70-93.

1237 VARTY, KENNETH. "The Pursuit of Reynard in Medieval English
      Literature and Art." NMS, 8 (1964), 62-81. Abstr. in
      AES, 8 (1965), no. 2662.
         Background. The Nun's Priest's Tale, pp. 62-63.

1238 VARTY, KENNETH. "Reynard the Fox and the Smithfield
      Decretals." JWCI, 26 (1963), 347-54.

The Nun's Priest's Tale: Source Studies

1239 FLINN, JOHN. Le Roman de Renart dans la littérature
      française et dans les littératures étrangères au moyen
      âge. Toronto: University of Toronto Press, 1963.
      731 pp.
         General discussion of the Nun's Priest's Tale sources,
      pp. 681-88.
         Reviews: Lionel J. Friedman, MLJ, 49 (1965), 329-30;
      Robert Clive Roach, Manuscripta, 9 (1965), 114-15; Lewis
      Thorpe, MAE, 35 (1966), 68-70; D. J. A. Ross, MLR, 61
      (1966), 704-706; P. de Keyser, SpL, 8 (1965), 202-209.

1240 *FLOYD, HARVEY LEROY. "Nigel's Speculum Stultorum: A Study
      in Literary Influences." DAI, 30 (1970), 4432A.
      Vanderbilt University, 1969. 267 pp.

1241 GUERIN, RICHARD. "The Nun's Priest and Canto V of the
      Inferno." ES, 54 (1973), 313-15.

1242 JOHNSTON, EVERETT C. "The Medieval Versions of the Reynard-
      Chanticleer Episode." LangQ, 4, iii-iv (1966), 7-10.

1243 PRATT, R. A. "Chaucer's Adaptation of Three Old French Nar-
      ratives of the Cock and the Fox to Form the Nonnes
      Preestes Tale," in Expression, Communication and Experi-
      ence in Literature and Language. Proceedings of the 12
      Congress of the International Federation for Modern Lan-
      guages and Literatures Held at Cambridge University, 20

The Second Nun's Prologue and Tale

to 26 August 1972 (London). Edited by Ronald G.
Popperwell, pp. 290-92.
  Abstract only.

1244   PRATT, ROBERT A. "Three Old French Sources of Nonnes
        Preestes Tale." Parts I and II. Spec, 47 (1972), 422-44,
        646-68. Abstr. in AES, 17 (1973-74), no. 1579 and in
        MLAA (1972), no. 2731.

1245   STEADMAN, JOHN M. "Champier and the Altercatio Hadriani:
        Another Chaucer Analogue." N&Q, 12 (1965), 170. Abstr.
        in AES, 9 (1966), no. 464.
        Analogue to "Mulier est hominis confusio."

See also: 406, 1202, 1207, 1230.

THE SECOND NUN'S PROLOGUE AND TALE

See Griffith, pp. 239-41; Crawford, p. 83.

1246   *CLOGAN, PAUL M. "The Figural Style and Meaning of The Second
        Nun's Prologue and Tale." M&H, n s, 3 (1972), 213-40.
        Abstr. in MLAA (1972), no. 2689.

1247   *GLASSER, MARC DAVID. "Marriage in Old and Middle English
        Saints' Legends." DAI, 33 (1973), 6356A. Indiana
        University, 1973. 196 pp.
          See chapter 5 on Chaucer's legend of St. Cecilia.

1248   GRENNEN, JOSEPH E. "Saint Cecilia's 'Chemical wedding': The
        Unity of the Canterbury Tales, Fragment VIII." JEGP, 65
        (1966), 466-81. Abstr. in AES, 10 (1967), no. 134.

1249   PECK, RUSSELL A. "The Ideas of 'Entente' and Translation in
        Chaucer's Second Nun's Tale." AnM, 8 (1967), 17-37.

1250   ROSENBERG, BRUCE A. "The Contrary Tales of the Second Nun
        and the Canon's Yeoman." ChauR, 2 (1968), 278-91. Abstr.
        in AES, 16 (1972-73), no. 1567.

See also: 132, 174, 198, 255, 276, 321, 343, 380, 624, 634, 648,
672, 675, 715, 1795.

Canterbury Tales

The Second Nun's Tale: Source Studies

1251   SAYERS, DOROTHY L.   "The Art of Translating Dante." NMS, 9
        (1965), 15-31.
            Brief note on "Hymn to Our Lady" from the Paradiso in-
        corporated into the Second Nun's Tale.

THE CANON'S YEOMAN'S PROLOGUE AND TALE

See Griffith, pp. 241-42; Crawford, p. 83.

1252   ADAMS, GEORGE R.   "The Canon's Yeoman: Alchemist, Confidence
        Man, Artist." EN, 3 (Spring, 1969), 3-14.

1253   DUNCAN, EDGAR H.   "The Literature of Alchemy and Chaucer's
        Canon's Yeoman's Tale: Framework, Theme, and Characters."
        Spec, 43 (1968), 633-56. Abstr. in AES, 16 (1972-73),
        no. 943.

1254   FINKELSTEIN, DOROTHEE.   "The Code of Chaucer's 'Secree of
        Secrees': Arabic Alchemical Terminology in The Canon's
        Yeoman's Tale." Archiv, 207 (1970), 260-76. Abstr. in
        AES, 16 (1972-73), no. 623.

1255   GARDNER, JOHN.   "The Canon's Yeoman's Prologue and Tale: An
        Interpretation." PQ, 46 (1967), 1-17. Abstr. in AES,
        14 (1970-71), no. 1977.

1256   GRENBERG, BRUCE L.   "The Canon's Yeoman's Tale: Boethian
        Wisdom and the Alchemists." ChauR, 1 (1966), 37-54.
        Abstr. in AES, 13 (1969-70), no. 1115.

1257   GRENNEN, JOSEPH E.   "The Canon's Yeoman's Alchemical 'Mass.'"
        SP, 62 (1965), 546-60. Abstr. in AES, 10 (1967),
        no. 1428.

1258   GRENNEN, JOSEPH E.   "Chaucer and the Commonplaces of Alchemy."
        C&M, 26 (1965), 306-33.

1259   GRENNEN, JOSEPH E.   "Chaucer's Characterization of the Canon
        and His Yeoman." JHI, 25 (1964), 279-84. Abstr. in AES,
        7 (1964), no. 1775.

The Canon's Yeoman's Prologue and Tale

1260   HARRINGTON, DAVID V. "Dramatic Irony in the Canon's Yeoman's
        Tale." NM, 66 (1965), 160-66. Abstr. in AES, 9 (1966),
        no. 3070.

1261   HARRINGTON, DAVID V. "The Narrator of the Canon's Yeoman's
        Tale." AnM, 9 (1968), 85-97.

1262   HASKELL, ANN S. "The St. Giles Oath in the Canon's Yeoman's
        Tale." ChauR, 7 (1973), 221-26. Abstr. in AES, 17
        (1973-74), no. 2881 and in MLAA (1973), no. 2824.

1263   HOY, MICHAEL. "The Canon's Yeoman's Tale," in 48, pp. 61-78.

1264   McCRACKEN, SAMUEL. "Confessional Prologue and the Topog-
        raphy of the Canon's Yeoman." MP, 68 (1971), 289-91.
        Abstr. in AES, 14 (1970-71), no. 2615.

1265   OLMERT, K. MICHAEL. "The Canon's Yeoman's Tale: An Inter-
        pretation." AnM, 8 (1967), 70-94. Abstr. in AES, 12
        (1969), no. 1536.

1266   O'REILLY, WILLIAM M., JR. "Irony in the Canon's Yeoman's
        Tale." Greyfriar, 10 (1968), 25-39. Abstr. in AES, 12
        (1969), no. 1536.

1267   REIDY, JOHN. "Chaucer's Canon and the Unity of The Canon's
        Yeoman's Tale." PMLA, 80 (1965), 31-37. Abstr. in AES,
        9 (1966), no. 518.

1268   ROSENBERG, BRUCE ALAN. "Reason and Revelation in the
        Canterbury Tales." DA, 26 (1965), 1654. The Ohio State
        University, 1965. 161 pp.

1269   SANDERS, BARRY. "'Point': Canon's Yeoman's Tale 927." N&Q,
        14 (1967), 325. Abstr. in AES, 11 (1968), no. 987.

1270   WHITTOCK, T. G. "Chaucer's Canon's Yeoman's Tale." Theoria,
        24 (1965), 13-26.

See also: 132, 163, 173, 198, 201, 225, 255, 308, 354, 565, 575,
640, 647, 651, 672, 1248, 1250.

The Canon's Yeoman's Tale: Source Studies

1271   FOLCH-PI, WILLA BABCOCK. "Ramón Llull's Fèlix and Chaucer's
        Canon's Yeoman's Tale." N&Q, 14 (1967), 10-11. Abstr.
        in AES, 10 (1967), no. 2043.

Canterbury Tales

See also: 1253.

THE MANCIPLE'S PROLOGUE AND TALE

See Griffith, pp. 243-44; Crawford, pp. 83-84.

1272   BRODIE, ALEXANDER H. "Hodge of Ware and Geber's Cook:
        Wordplay in the Manciple's Prologue." NM, 72 (1971),
        62-68.

1273   CADBURY, WILLIAM. "Manipulation of Sources and the Meaning
        of the Manciple's Tale." PQ, 43 (1964), 538-48. Abstr.
        in AES, 8 (1965), no. 2322.

1274   CAMPBELL, JACKSON J. "Polonius Among the Pilgrims." ChauR,
        7 (1972), 140-46. Abstr. in AES, 17 (1973-74), no. 2885
        and in MLAA (1972), no. 2684.

1275   GRUBER, LOREN C. "The Manciple's Tale: One Key to Chaucer's
        Language," in 50, pp. 43-50. Abstr. in AES, 18 (1974-75),
        no. 743.

1276   HARWOOD, BRITTON J. "Language and the Real: Chaucer's
        Manciple." ChauR, 6 (1972), 268-79. Abstr. in AES, 16
        (1972-73), no. 1555 and in MLAA (1972), no. 2706.

1277   MUSTANOJA, TAUNO F. "Chaucer's Manciple's Tale, Lines
        311-13," in 30, pp. 250-54.

See also: 132, 201, 212, 231, 255, 445, 498, 635, 647, 672, 745,
1881, 2156, 2158.

The Manciple's Tale: Source Studies

See 408, 422, 680, 1273.

THE PARSON'S PROLOGUE AND *TALE*

See Griffith, pp. 244-46; Crawford, p. 84.

1278   ALLEN, JUDSON BOYCE. "The Old Way and the Parson's Way: An Ironic Reading of the Parson's Tale." JMRS, 3 (1973), 255-71.

1279   BIGGINS, DENNIS. "Canterbury Tales X (1) 424: 'The hyndre part of a she-ape in the fulle of the moone.'" MAE, 33 (1964), 200-203.

1280   DONALDSON, E. TALBOT. "Medieval Poetry and Medieval Sin," in 39, pp. 164-74.

1281   FINLAYSON, JOHN. "The Satiric Mode and the Parson's Tale." ChauR, 6 (1971), 94-116. Abstr. in AES, 15 (1971-72), no. 2843 and in MLAA (1971), no. 2142.

1282   HARGREAVES, HENRY. "Wiclif's Prose." E&S, 19 (1966), 1-17.
        Compares Wiclif's sermons with passages in the Parson's Tale.

1283   MYERS, D. E. "Justesse rationnelle: le 'Myrie Tale in Prose' de Chaucer." MΛ, 78 (1972), 267-86.
        Examines the Parson's Tale in the tradition of the artes praedicandi.

1284   PECK, RUSSELL A. "Number Symbolism in the Prologue to Chaucer's Parson's Tale." ES, 48 (1967), 205-15. Abstr. in AES, 12 (1969), no. 91.

1285   ROWLAND, BERYL. "Chaucer's She-Ape (The Parson's Tale, 424)." ChauR, 2 (1968), 159-65. Abstr. in AES, 16 (1972-73), no. 1561.

1286   SACHS, ARIEH. "Religious Despair in Medieval Literature and Art." MS, 26 (1964), 231-56.
        Brief treatment of the Parson's Tale on pp. 244-45.

1287   SCOTT, P. G. "A Note on the Paper Castle in Sir Gawain and the Green Knight." N&Q, 13 (1966), 125-26.
        Note on the Parson's Tale, Canterbury Tales, X (I), 445.

Canterbury Tales

See also: <u>51</u>, 132, 169, <u>174</u>, 187, <u>201</u>, 221, 239, 255, 259, <u>269</u>, <u>312</u>, 324, <u>343</u>, <u>391</u>, 427, 437, <u>538</u>, 564, <u>566</u>, 569, <u>577</u>, <u>578</u>, 597, <u>613</u>, 625, 629, <u>634</u>, 635, <u>640</u>, 647, 666, 672, 678, 1291, 1292, 1642, 1736.01, 1766, 1784, 1827, 2161.

<u>The Parson's Tale</u>: Source Studies

1288   REGAN, CHARLES LIONEL. "Chaucer's <u>Parson's Tale</u> 1025: A
           Probable Source." <u>N&Q</u>, 11 (1964), 210. Abstr. in <u>AES</u>,
           7 (1964), no. 2483.

1289   SCHMIDT, A. V. C. "Chaucer's 'Philosophre': A Note on <u>The
           Parson's Tale</u>, 534-7." <u>N&Q</u>, 15 (1968), 327-28. Abstr.
           in <u>AES</u>, 12 (1967), no. 493.

1290   WENZEL, SIEGFRIED. "The Source of the 'Remedia' of the
           <u>Parson's Tale</u>." <u>Traditio</u>, 27 (1971), 433-54.

See also: <u>51</u>, 422, 423.

CHAUCER'S RETRACTION

           See Griffith, pp. 246-47; Crawford, p. 85.

1291   CAMPBELL, A. P. "Chaucer's Retraction: Who Retracted What?"
           <u>RUO</u>, 35 (1965), 35-53; <u>HAB</u>, 16 (1965), 75-87. Abstr. in
           <u>AES</u>, 12 (1969), no. 1867.

1292   COLE, E. R. "Chaucer's Retraction and the Parson." <u>UPortR</u>,
           20 (1968), 35-41. Abstr. in <u>AES</u>, 14 (1970-71), no. 1029.

1293   *KESSING, SISTER M. THOMAS, C. S. J. "The Meaning of
           Chaucer's Retraction." St. John's University Disser-
           tation, 1963. Cited in <u>MHRA</u> (1964), no. 2188.

1294   SAYCE, OLIVE. "Chaucer's 'Retractions': The Conclusion of
           the <u>Canterbury Tales</u> and Its Place in Literary Tradition."
           <u>MAE</u>, 40 (1971), 230-48.

See also: <u>201</u>, 324, <u>566</u>, 569, 1717, 1733, 2161.

Longer Works other than
The Canterbury Tales

ANELIDA AND ARCITE

See Griffith, pp. 253-54; Crawford, p. 87.

1295   CHERNISS, MICHAEL D. "Chaucer's Anelida and Arcite: Some
        Conjectures." ChauR, 5 (1970), 9-21. Abstr. in AES, 15
        (1971-72), no. 691 and in MLAA (1971), no. 2120.

1296   WIMSATT, JAMES I. "Anelida and Arcite: A Narrative of
        Complaint and Comfort." ChauR, 5 (1970), 1-8. Abstr. in
        AES, 15 (1971-72), no. 692 and in MLAA (1971), no. 2243.

See also: 163, 193, 194, 243, 246, 255, 285, 289, 333, 369, 386.

Anelida and Arcite: Source Studies

See: 398, 399, 401, 402, 422, 423, 1296.

ASTROLABE

See Griffith, pp. 254-55; Crawford, p. 87.

1297   NAGUCKA, RUTA. The Syntactic Component of Chaucer's
        "Astrolabe." Zeszyty Naukowe Uniwersytetu Jagiellońskiego,
        199 (Kraków), Prace Językoznawcze Zeszyt, 23. Cracow:
        University Jagielloniensis, 1968. 123 pp.

See also: 183, 255, 260, 312, 391, 1993.

Longer Works other than The Canterbury Tales

BOETHIUS

See Griffith, pp. 256-60; Crawford, pp. 87-88.

See: 255, 260, 296, 500, 609, 1679, 1768.

Boethius: Source Studies

1298   *KOTTLER, BARNET. "Chaucer's Boece and the Late Medieval
         Textual Tradition of the Consolatio Philosophiae." DAI,
         31 (1971), 6013A-14A. Yale University, 1953. 189 pp.
         Collates some forty-five manuscripts.

1299   *SILK, EDMUND TAITE. "Cambridge MS Ii 3 21 and the Relation
         of Chaucer's Boethius to Trivet and Jean de Meung." DAI,
         31 (1970), 2355A. Yale University, 1930. 695 pp.

BOOK OF THE DUCHESS

See Griffith, pp. 260-62; Crawford, pp. 88-89.

1300   BERLIN, NORMAND. "Chaucer's The Book of the Duchess and
         Spenser's Daphnaida: A Contrast." SN, 38 (1966), 282-89.
         Abstr. in AES, 10 (1967), no. 1847.

1301   BROUGHTON, BRADFORD B. "Chaucer's Book of the Duchess: Did
         John [of Gaunt] Love Blanche [of Lancaster]?" in Twenty-
         Seven to One: A Potpourri of Humanistic Material Pre-
         sented to Dr. Donald Gale Stillman on the Occasion of His
         Retirement from Clarkson College of Technology by Members
         of the Liberal Studies--Humanities Department Staff,
         1949-1970. Edited by Bradford B. Broughton. Ogdensburg,
         New York: Ryan Press, Inc., 1970, pp. 71-84.

1302   BROWN, JAMES NEIL. "Narrative Focus and Function in The
         Book of the Duchess." MSE, 2, iii (Spring, 1970), 71-79.
         Abstr. in AES, 14 (1970-71), no. 1973.

1303   CARSON, M. ANGELA, O. S. U. "Easing of the 'Hert' in the
         Book of the Duchess." ChauR, 1 (1967), 157-60. Abstr.
         in AES, 13 (1969-70), no. 2860.

1304   CARSON, M. ANGELA, O. S. U. "The Sovereignty of Octovyen in
        the Book of the Duchess." AnM, 8 (1967), 46-58.

1305   CARTIER, NORMAND R. "Froissart, Chaucer and Enclimpostair."
        RLC, 38 (1964), 18-34.

1306   CHERNISS, MICHAEL D. "The Boethian Dialogue in Chaucer's
        Book of the Duchess." JEGP, 68 (1969), 655-65. Abstr.
        in AES, 14 (1970-71), no. 690.

1307   CHERNISS, MICHAEL D. "The Narrator Asleep and Awake in
        Chaucer's Book of the Duchess." PLL, 8 (1972), 115-26.
        Abstr. in MLAA (1972), no. 2674.

1308   CONDREN, EDWARD I. "The Historical Context of the Book of
        the Duchess: A New Hypothesis." ChauR, 5 (1971),
        195-212. Abstr. in AES, 15 (1971-72), no. 693 and in
        MLAA (1971), no. 2124.

1309   DELASANTA, RODNEY. "Christian Affirmation in The Book of the
        Duchess." PMLA, 84 (1969), 245-51. Abstr. in AES, 13
        (1969-70), no. 1500.

1310   DICKERSON, A. INSKIP, JR. "The Book of the Duchess, Line
        480." PBSA, 66, i (1st Qtr., 1972), 51-54. Abstr. in
        AES, 16 (1972-73), no. 1551 and in MLAA (1972), no. 2675.
        Manuscript evidence to support Thynne's inclusion of
        the line.

1311   EBEL, JULIA G. "Chaucer's The Book of the Duchess: A Study
        in Medieval Iconography and Literary Structure." CE, 29
        (1967), 197-206. Abstr. in AES, 11 (1968), no. 1443.

1312   ELDREDGE, LAURENCE. "The Structure of the Book of the Duchess."
        RUO, 39 (1969), 132-51.

1313   FOSTER, EDWARD E. "Allegorical Consolation in The Book of
        the Duchess." BSUF, 11, iv (Autumn, 1970), 14-20. Abstr.
        in MLAA (1971), no. 2144.

1314   FRIEDMAN, JOHN BLOCK. "The Dreamer, the Whelp, and Consola-
        tion in the Book of the Duchess." ChauR, 3 (1969), 145-
        62. Abstr. in AES, 13 (1969-70), no. 2548.

1315   GARDNER, JOHN. "Style as Meaning in the Book of the Duchess."
        Lang&S, 2 (1969), 143-71.

1316   GRENNEN, JOSEPH E. "'Hert-Hunting' in the Book of the Duchess."
        MLQ, 25 (1964), 131-39. Abstr. in AES, 8 (1965), no. 807.

Longer Works other than The Canterbury Tales

1317   *HELSINGER, HOWARD MARK. "The Book of the Duchess and the
        Hunt of the Hart." DAI, 31 (1970), 2878A-79A. Princeton
        University, 1970. 455 pp.

1318   HINTON, NORMAN D. "The Black Death and The Book of the
        Duchess," in 46, pp. 72-78.

1319   KELLOGG, ALFRED L. "Amatory Psychology and Amatory Frustra-
        tion in the Interpretation of the Book of the Duchess,"
        in 51, pp. 59-107.

1320   LUISI, DAVID. "The Hunt Motif in The Book of the Duchess."
        ES, 52 (1971), 309-11.

1321   MALONE, KEMP. "Chaucer's Book of the Duchess: A Metrical
        Study," in 43, pp. 71-95.

1322   MATHEWS, JOHNYE E. "The Black Knight as King of the Castle
        in The Book of the Duchess." SCB, 31 (Winter, 1971),
        200-201. Abstr. in AES, 16 (1972-73), no. 1552 and in
        MLAA (1972), no. 2677.

1323   *MATHEWS, JOHNYE ELIZABETH STRICKLAND. "A Study of The Book
        of the Duchess: Problems in Chaucer's Relationship with
        His Audience." DAI, 30 (1970), 2974A-75A. University
        of Arkansas, 1969. 188 pp.

1324   PECK, RUSSELL A. "Theme and Number in Chaucer's Book of the
        Duchess," in Silent Poetry: Essays in Numerological
        Analysis. Edited by Alastair Fowler. London: Routledge
        and Kegan Paul; *New York: Barnes & Noble, 1970,
        pp. 73-115.

1325   PETERS, F. J. J. "Bo D: Line 47." AN&Q, 8 (1970), 135.

1326   ROBERTSON, D. W., JR. "The Book of the Duchess," in 60,
        pp. 332-40.

1327   ROBERTSON, D. W., JR. "The Historical Setting of Chaucer's
        Book of the Duchess," in Mediaeval Studies in Honor of
        Urban Tigner Holmes, Jr. UNCSRLL, 56. Edited by John
        Mahoney and John Esten Keller. Chapel Hill: University
        of North Carolina Press, 1965, pp. 169-95.

1328   ROWLAND, BERYL. "Chaucer as a Pawn in The Book of the
        Duchess." AN&Q, 6 (1967), 3-5. Abstr. in AES, 13
        (1969-70), no. 2183.

1329   ROWLAND, BERYL. "Chaucer's 'Mistake': The Book of the
       Duchess, Line 455." AN&Q, 4 (1966), 99-100. Abstr. in
       AES, 17 (1973-74), no. 2606.

1330   ROWLAND, BERYL. "The Whelp in Chaucer's Book of the Duchess."
       NM, 66 (1965), 148-60. Abstr. in AES, 9 (1966), no. 3069.

1331   SADLER, LYNN VEACH. "Chaucer's The Book of the Duchess and
       the 'Law of Kinde.'" AnM, 11 (1970), 51-64. Abstr. in
       AES, 17 (1973-74), no. 1904.

1332   SEVERS, J. BURKE. "Chaucer's Self-Portrait in the Book of
       the Duchess." PQ, 43 (1964), 27-39. Abstr. in AES, 8
       (1965), no. 2293.

1333   STEVENS, MARTIN. "Narrative Focus in The Book of the Duchess:
       A Critical Revaluation." AnM, 7 (1966), 16-32.

1334   WILSON, G. R., JR. "The Anatomy of Compassion: Chaucer's
       Book of the Duchess." TSLL, 14 (1972), 381-88. Abstr.
       in MLAA (1972), no. 2678.

1335   WIMSATT, JAMES I. "The Apothesis of Blanche in The Book of
       the Duchess." JEGP, 66 (1967), 26-44. Abstr. in AES,
       10 (1967), no. 2726.

See also: 104, 159, 160, 163, 167, 171, 173, 186, 187, 193, 194,
198, 199, 201, 207, 220, 225, 230, 237, 239, 243, 245, 246, 247, 249,
255, 256, 259, 260, 268, 276, 284, 285, 288, 289, 296, 303, 305, 318,
321, 322, 324, 333, 339, 340, 343, 346, 350, 355, 363, 364, 377, 378,
385, 389, 413, 466, 492, 493, 494, 496, 514, 541, 631, 1679, 1716,
1768, 1776, 1790, 1805, 1816, 1819, 1822, 1838.01, 1849, 1886, 2145.

The Book of the Duchess: Source Studies

1336   CARTIER, NORMAND R. "Le Bleu chevalier de Froissart et Le
       Livre de la duchesse de Chaucer." Romania, 88 (1967),
       232-52.
          See also Wimsatt, 1342, below.

1337   FINLAYSON, JOHN. "The Book of the Duchess: Sources for
       Lines 174, 203-205, 249-253." ELN, 10 (1973), 170-72.
       Abstr. in AES, 17 (1973-74), no. 1577.

1338   MARTIN, JOSEPH BACON, III. "The Medieval Ceyx and Alcyone:
       Ovid's Metamorphoses XI, 407-750, and Chaucer's Book of
       the Duchess." DAI, 33 (1973), 6318A. Duke University,
       1972. 196 pp.

Longer Works other than The Canterbury Tales

1339   TISDALE, CHARLES P. R. "Boethian 'Hert-Huntyng': The Elegiac
        Pattern of The Book of the Duchess." ABR, 24 (1973),
        365-80.

1340   WIMSATT, JAMES. Chaucer and the French Love Poets: The Lit-
        erary Background of The Book of the Duchess. UNCSCL, 43.
        Chapel Hill: University of North Carolina Press, 1968.
        186 pp.
           Reviews: Christopher Brookhouse, Spec, 45 (1970), 186;
        Alan T. Gaylord, JEGP, 69 (1970), 667-71; Albert E.
        Hartung, RR, 61 (1970), 219-20; D. S. Brewer, RES, 22
        (1971), 66-67; Helaine Newstead, RPh, 24 (1970), 349-53;
        Robert M. Jordan, CLS, 8 (1971), 160-63; R. M. Wilson,
        YES, 1 (1971), 216-18.

1341   WIMSATT, JAMES IRVING. "Chaucer's Book of the Duchess and
        Its French Background." DA, 27 (1966), 1041A. Duke
        University, 1963. 414 pp.

1342   WIMSATT, JAMES IRVING. "The Dit dou Bleu Chevalier:
        Froissart's Imitation of Chaucer." MS, 34 (1972),
        388-400. Abstr. in AES, 17 (1973-74), no. 680 and in
        MLAA (1972), no. 2679.
           See also Cartier, 1336 above.

1343   WIMSATT, JAMES. "The Sources of Chaucer's 'Seys and Alcyone.'"
        MAE, 36 (1967), 231-41. Abstr. in AES, 15 (1971-72),
        no. 2256.

See also: 402, 1305, 1306, 1314.

HOUSE OF FAME

        See Griffith, pp. 266-71; Crawford, pp. 90-92.

1344   BENNETT, J. A. W. Chaucer's Book of Fame: An Exposition of
        The House of Fame. Oxford: Clarendon Press, 1968.
        205 pp.
           Excerpts reprinted in 62, pp. 65-70.
           Reviews: TLS (25 July, 1968), p. 782; J. A. Burrow,
        RES, 19 (1968), 424-26; E. Talbot Donaldson, N&Q, 16
        (1969), 147-48; Sylvia Wallace Holton, SN, 41 (1969),
        176-79; Robert M. Jordan, Spec, 44 (1969), 444-46;

House of Fame

Robert Worth Frank, Jr., MP, 68 (1970), 195-98; Wolfgang
Weiss, Ang, 90 (1972), 227-28; P. Mroczkowski, MAE, 39
(1970), 210-15; R. T. Davies, MLR, 65 (1970), 133-35;
John Lawlor, CritQ, 11 (1969), 378-80.

1345   DELANY, SHEILA. "'Ars Simia Naturae' and Chaucer's House of
        Fame." ELN, 11 (1973), 1-5. Abstr. in MLAA (1973),
        no. 2857.

1346   DELANY, SHEILA. "Chaucer's House of Fame: The Poetics of
        Skeptical Fideism." DA, 28 (1967), 1782A-83A. Columbia
        University, 1967. 241 pp.

1346.01 DELANY, SHEILA. Chaucer's House of Fame: The Poetics of
        Skeptical Fideism. Chicago and London: University of
        Chicago Press, 1972. 143 pp.

1347   DELANY, SHEILA. "'Phantom' and the House of Fame." ChauR,
        2 (1967), 67-74. Abstr. in AES, 16 (1972-73), no. 1570.

1348   ELDREDGE, LAURENCE. "Chaucer's Hous of Fame and the Via
        Moderna." NM, 71 (1970), 105-19.

1349   GRENNEN, JOSEPH E. "Science and Poetry in Chaucer's House
        of Fame." AnM, 8 (1967), 38-45.

1350   JOYNER, WILLIAM BALLARD. "'Craft' and 'Sentence' in Chaucer's
        House of Fame." DAI, 32 (1971), 3255A. The University
        of Wisconsin, Madison, 1971. 160 pp.

1351   JOYNER, WILLIAM. "The Journey Motif in Chaucer's House of
        Fame." EngRev, 1 (1973), 28-41.

1352   KOONCE, B. G. Chaucer and the Tradition of Fame: Symbolism
        in The House of Fame. Princeton, New Jersey: Princeton
        University Press; *London: Oxford University Press,
        1966. 293 pp.
           Reviews: R. T. Davies, N&Q, 14 (1967), 263-64;
        H. M. Smyser, Spec, 42 (1967), 536-39; Paul G. Ruggiers,
        MLQ, 29 (1968), 351-54; Douglas Gray, RES, 20 (1969),
        72-74; Helaine Newstead, RPh, 24 (1970), 349-53.

1353   LEYERLE, JOHN "Chaucer's Windy Eagle." UTQ, 40 (1971),
        247-65.

1354   *LYSIAK, ROBERT JOSEPH. "Mythopoetics and Chaucer's Hous of
        Fame." DAI, 34 (1974), 7765A. Ohio University, 1973.
        138 pp.

Longer Works other than The Canterbury Tales

1355   NEWMAN, FRANCIS X. "Hous of Fame, 7-12." ELN, 6 (1968),
        5-12. Abstr. in AES, 14 (1970-71), no. 1351.

1356   SANDERS, BARRY [ROY]. "Love's Crack-up: The House of Fame."
        PLL, 3 (Summer supplement, 1967), 3-13.

1357   SHOOK, LAURENCE K. "The House of Fame," in 60, pp. 341-54.

1358   SIMMONS, J. L. "The Place of the Poet in Chaucer's House of
        Fame." MLQ, 27 (1966), 125-35. Abstr. in AES, 10 (1967),
        no. 983.

1359   *STEVENSON, KAY GILLILAND. "The Structure of Chaucer's House
        of Fame." DAI, 32 (1971), 3272A. Yale University, 1971.
        206 pp.

1360   SUDO, JUN. "A Preliminary Note on the Language of Chaucer's
        House of Fame." KCUJ, 19 (1969), 25-42.

1361   TISDALE, CHARLES P. R. "The House of Fame: Virgilian Reason
        and Boethian Wisdom." CL, 25 (1973), 247-61. Abstr. in
        MLAA (1973), no. 2859.

1362   TRIPP, RAYMOND P., JR. "Chaucer's Psychologizing of Virgil's
        Dido." BRMMLA, 24 (1970), 51-59.

1363   WATTS, ANN C. "'Amor gloriae' in Chaucer's House of Fame."
        JMRS, 3 (1973), 87-113.

1363.01 WILLIAMS, GEORGE. "The Mysterious House of Fame," in 386,
        chapter 6, pp. 105-29.

1364   *WILSON, WILLIAM SMITH, III. "Chaucer's Hous of Fame." DAI,
        31 (1970), 2893A-94A. Yale University, 1960. 151 pp.

1365   WILSON, WILLIAM S. "The Eagle's Speech in Chaucer's House
        of Fame." QJS, 50 (1964), 153-58. Abstr. in AES, 8
        (1965), no. 213.

1366   WILSON, WILLIAM S. "Exegetical Grammar in the House of Fame."
        ELN, 1 (1964), 244-48. Abstr. in AES, 8 (1965),
        no. 1944.

1367   WILSON, WILLIAM S. "Scholastic Logic in Chaucer's House of
        Fame." ChauR, 1 (1967), 181-84. Abstr. in AES, 13
        (1969-70), no. 2870.

1368   ZUCKER, DAVID H. "The Detached and Judging Narrator in
        Chaucer's House of Fame." Thoth, 8 (1967), 3-22. Abstr.
        in AES, 10 (1967), no. 2514.

See also: 160, 163, 165, 167, 173, 185, 186, 193, 194, 198, 199,
201, 207, 212, 225, 226, 230, 237, 239, 243, 245, 246, 247, 249, 255,
259, 260, 276, 284, 285, 288, 296, 303, 305, 308, 318, 321, 325, 333,
340, 347, 350, 355, 364, 369, 377, 383, 385, 386, 387, 389, 466, 514,
609, 1683, 1719, 1768, 1816, 1843, 1973.

House of Fame: Source Studies

1369   DEAN, NANCY. "Ovid's Elegies from Exile & Chaucer's House of
        Fame." HCS, 3 (1966), 75-90.

1370   DELANY, SHEILA. "Chaucer's House of Fame and the Ovide
        moralisé." CL, 20 (1968), 254-64. Abstr. in AES, 13
        (1969-70), no. 30.

1371   MANZALAOUI, MAHMOUD. "English Analogues to the Liber Scalae."
        MAE, 34 (1965), 21-35. Abstr. in AES, 10 (1967),
        no. 3027.

See also: 398, 400, 402, 412, 422, 423, 1353, 1361, 1362.

LEGEND OF GOOD WOMEN

See Griffith, pp. 272-82; Crawford, p. 92.

1372   BAIRD, JOSEPH L. "Jason and His 'Sekte.'" AN&Q, 8 (1970),
        151-52.

1373   FRANK, ROBERT WORTH, JR. Chaucer and the Legend of Good
        Women. Cambridge, Massachusetts: Harvard University
        Press, 1972. 229 pp.
           Reviews: Charles R. Blyth, Spec, 50 (1975), 305-307.

1374   FRANK, ROBERT WORTH, JR. "The Legend of the Legend of Good
        Women." ChauR, 1 (1966), 110-33. Abstr. in AES, 13
        (1969-70), no. 1854.

Longer Works other than The Canterbury Tales

1375　GARDNER, JOHN. "The Two Prologues to the Legend of Good
　　　　Women." JEGP, 67 (1968), 594-611. Abstr. in AES, 13
　　　　(1969-70), no. 387.

1376　LAHOOD, MARVIN J. "Chaucer's The Legend of Lucrece." PQ,
　　　　43 (1964), 274-76. Abstr. in AES, 8 (1965), no. 2314.

1377　*SHANER, MARY CAROL EDWARDS. "An Interpretive Study of
　　　　Chaucer's Legend of Good Women." DAI, 34 (1973),
　　　　739A-40A. University of Illinois, Urbana-Champaign,
　　　　1973. 322 pp.

1378　*SHEA, VIRGINIA ARENS. "Nat Every Vessel al of Gold: Studies
　　　　in Chaucer's Legend of Good Women." DAI, 32 (1972),
　　　　6394A. The University of Connecticut, 1971. 247 pp.

1379　*SMAGOLA, MARY PATRICIA. "'Spek Wel of Love': The Role of
　　　　Woman in Chaucer's Legend of Good Women." DAI, 33
　　　　(1972), 1696A. Case Western Reserve University, 1972.
　　　　139 pp.

1379.01 WILLIAMS, GEORGE. "The Daisy and 'Good Alceste,'" in 386,
　　　　chapter 7, pp. 130-44.

See also: 159, 160, 165, 169, 173, 174, 198, 201, 226, 230, 237,
239, 243, 246, 247, 255, 259, 260, 263, 276, 284, 289, 296, 312,
321, 322, 325, 333, 350, 363, 364, 369, 377, 379, 380, 386, 514, 523,
848, 906, 963, 1558, 1613, 1620, 1621, 1679, 1776, 1838.01, 2036.

Legend of Good Women: Source Studies

1380　CLOGAN, PAUL M. "Chaucer's Cybele and the Liber Imaginum
　　　　Deorum." PQ, 43 (1964), 272-74. Abstr. in AES, 8
　　　　(1965), no. 2313.

1381　CLOGAN, PAUL M. "Chaucer's The Legend of Good Women, 2422."
　　　　Expl, 23 (1965), Item 61. Abstr. in AES, 9 (1966),
　　　　no. 2064.

1382　KNOPP, SHERRON. "Chaucer and Jean de Meun as Self-Conscious
　　　　Narrators: The Prologue to the Legend of Good Women and
　　　　the Roman de la Rose 10307-680." Comitatus, 4 (1973),
　　　　25-39.

1383　*WINSOR, ELEANOR JANE. "A Study in the Sources and Rhetoric
　　　　of Chaucer's Legend of Good Women and Ovid's Heroides."
　　　　DA, 28 (1968), 3161A-62A. Yale University, 1963. 501 pp.

See also: 422, 1376.

PARLIAMENT OF FOWLS

See Griffith, pp. 284-88; Crawford, pp. 93-95.

1384   BAKER, DONALD C. "The Parliament of Fowls," in 60,
        pp. 355-69.

1385   BRADDY, HALDEEN. Chaucer's Parlement of Foules In Its Rela-
        tion to Contemporary Events. Expanded edition. New
        York: Farrar, Straus & Giroux, Octagon Books, 1969.
        120 pp.
            Originally published in 1932. See Griffith, p. 284.

1386   *CASIERI, SABINO. "Osservazioni su The Parlement of Foules,"
        in Studi e ricerche di letteratura inglese e americana,
        1. Edited by Agostino Lombardo. Milano: Ist.
        Editoriale Cisalpino, 1967, pp. 7-19. Cited in PMLAB
        (1967), no. 5613.

1387   CAWLEY, A. C. "Chaucer's Valentine: The Parlement of
        Foules," in 37, pp. 125-39.

1388   CHAMBERLAIN, DAVID. "The Music of the Spheres and The
        Parlement of Foules." ChauR, 5 (1970), 32-56. Abstr.
        in AES, 15 (1971-72), no. 716 and in MLAA (1971), no. 2119.

1389   DEVEREUX, E. J. "John Rastell's Text of The Parliament of
        Fowls." Moreana, 27-28 (1970), 115-20.

1390   *ECONOMOU, GEORGE DEMETRIOS. "The Goddess Natura in Medieval
        Literature." DAI, 31 (1970), 1224A-25A. Columbia
        University, 1967. 296 pp.
            Analyzes the Nature figure in Parliament of Fowls.
        See 1390.01.

1390.01 ECONOMOU, GEORGE DEMETRIOS. The Goddess Natura in Medieval
        Literature. Cambridge, Massachusetts: Harvard Univer-
        sity Press, 1972. 222 pp.
            Based on doctoral dissertation, 1390 above.
            Reviews: TLS (21 September, 1973), p. 1093; VQR, 49
        (Summer, 1973), cxvii.

Longer Works other than The Canterbury Tales

1391   ELDREDGE, LAURENCE. "Poetry and Philosophy in The Parlement
        of Foules." RUO, 40 (1970), 441–59.

1392   GILBERT, A. J. "Chaucer, Grandson, and the 'Turtil Trewe.'"
        N&Q, 19 (1972), 165. Abstr. in AES, 16 (1972–73),
        no. 625.

1393   *HENLEY, ROSALIE DARM. "Chaucer's Parlement of Foules:
        Three Faces of Love." DAI, 32 (1972), 4586A. University
        of Minnesota, 1971. 192 pp.

1394   KELLOGG, A. L. and ROBERT C. COX. "Chaucer's St. Valentine:
        A Conjecture," in 51, pp. 108–45.

1395   KNIGHT, STEPHEN. "The Meaning of The Parlement of Foules."
        SoRA, 2, iii (1967), 223–39. Abstr. in AES, 11 (1968),
        no. 1668.

1396   McCALL, JOHN P. "The Harmony of Chaucer's Parliament."
        ChauR, 5 (1970), 22–31. Abstr. in AES, 15 (1971–72),
        no. 717 and in MLAA (1971), no. 2197.

1397   *MORRIS, FRANCIS J. "Platonic Elements in the Parliament of
        Fowls." PCTEB, 14 (February, 1967), 28–41. Cited in
        MHRA (1967), no. 2565.

1398   *MUCCHETTI, EMIL A. "Hierarchical Modes of Love in Chaucer's
        The Parliament of Fowls." DAI, 33 (1972), 730A. The
        Louisiana State University, 1971. 213 pp.

1399   *PIEHLER, PAUL HERMAN TYNEGATE. "Landscape and Dialogue: A
        Study of Allegorical Tradition in Medieval Literature."
        DA, 26 (1965), 1634–35. Columbia University, 1961.
        200 pp.
            Analyzes the allegory in Parliament of Fowls.

1400   SELVIN, RHODA HURWITT. "Shades of Love in the Parlement of
        Foules." SN, 37 (1965), 146–60. Abstr. in AES, 9
        (1966), no. 1324.

1401   SMITH, FRANCIS J. "Mirth and Marriage in The Parlement of
        Foules." BSUF, 14, i (1973), 15–22. Abstr. in MLAA
        (1973), no. 2863.

1402   UPHAUS, ROBERT W. "Chaucer's Parlement of Foules: Aesthetic
        Order and Individual Experience." TSLL, 10 (1968),
        349–58.

1403   VON KREISLER, NICOLAI. "The Locus Amoenus and Eschatological
        Lore in the Parliament of Fowls 204-10." PQ, 50 (1971),
        16-22. Abstr. in MLAA (1971), no. 2237.

1404   *WENK, LINDA TATELBAUM. "Irresolvable Dichotomies in the
        Twelfth-Century Debate Poem: A Study in Platonic Per-
        spectives." DAI, 33 (1973), 3680A-81A. Cornell Univer-
        sity, 1972. 210 pp.
            Treats Parliament of Fowls briefly in the debate
        tradition.

1405   WILHELM, JAMES J. "The Narrator and His Narrative in Chaucer's
        Parlement." ChauR, 1 (1967), 201-206. Abstr. in AES,
        14 (1970-71), no. 2943.

1405.01 WILLIAMS, GEORGE. "The Parliament of Fowls--A Three-Part
        Mystery," in 386, chapter 5, pp. 82-104.

See also: 33, 160, 163, 167, 173, 193, 194, 198, 199, 201, 202, 207,
212, 225, 230, 231, 237, 239, 243, 245, 246, 247, 249, 255, 256, 259,
260, 284, 285, 287, 296, 303, 305, 308, 318, 321, 328, 333, 340, 343,
350, 353, 355, 359, 365, 369, 377, 378, 385, 386, 389, 391, 412, 437,
457, 466, 541, 1140, 1344, 1586, 1679, 1730, 1764, 1765, 1786, 1798,
1816, 2018, 2178+.

Parlement of Foules: Source Studies

1406   GARBÁTY, THOMAS JAY. "Andreas Capellanus and the Gate in
        the Parlement of Foules." RomN, 9 (1968), 325-30.

1407   VON KREISLER, NICOLAI. "Bird Lore and the Valentine's Day
        Tradition in Chaucer's Parlement of Foules." ChauR, 3
        (1968), 60-64. Abstr. in AES, 17 (1973-74), no. 693.

See also: 1014, 1388, 1392.

TROILUS AND CRISEYDE

See Griffith, pp. 294-310; Crawford, pp. 96-101.

1408   ADAMSON, JANE. "The Unity of Troilus and Criseyde." CR, 14
        (1971), 17-37. Abstr. in AES, 17 (1973-74), no. 2251.

Longer Works other than The Canterbury Tales

1409   apROBERTS, ROBERT P. "The Boethian God and the Audience of
            the Troilus." JEGP, 69 (1970), 425-36. Abstr. in MLAA
            (1970), no. 1744.

1410   apROBERTS, ROBERT P. "Criseyde's Infidelity and the Moral of
            the Troilus." Spec, 44 (1969), 383-402. Abstr. in AES,
            16 (1972-73), no. 946.

1411   *AUBREY, ANNIE. "An Analysis of the Medieval Artes Poetriae
            with a Discussion of Amplification of Character in
            Chaucer's Troilus." DAI, 31 (1971), 3494A. University
            of Cincinnati, 1970. 196 pp.

1412   BARNEY, STEPHEN A. "Troilus Bound." Spec, 47 (1972), 445-58.
            Abstr. in AES, 17 (1973-74), no. 1583 and in MLAA (1972),
            no. 2755.

1413   BARTEL, NEVA A. "Child of Night." BSUF, 6, iii (Autumn,
            1965), 45-50. Abstr. in AES, 11 (1968), no. 1808.

1414   BASU, KAJAL. "The Moral Confusion in Chaucer's Troilus and
            Criseyde." IJES, [4] (1963), 25-47.

1415   BECHTEL, ROBERT B. "The Problem of Criseide's Character."
            SUS, 7, ii (1963), 109-18.

1416   BERRYMAN, CHARLES. "The Ironic Design of Fortune in Troilus
            and Criseide." ChauR, 2 (1967), 1-7. Abstr. in AES, 15
            (1971-72), no. 38.

1417   BESSENT, BENJAMIN R. "The Puzzling Chronology of Chaucer's
            Troilus." SN, 41 (1969), 99-111. Abstr. in AES, 14
            (1970-71), no. 348.

1418   BLOOMFIELD, MORTON W. "Distance and Predestination in
            Troilus and Criseyde," in 31, pp. 201-16.

1419   BLOOMFIELD, MORTON W. "Troilus' Paraclausithyron and Its
            Setting: Troilus and Criseyde V, 519-602." NM, 73
            (1972), 15-24.

1420   BOLTON, W. F. "Treason in Troilus." Archiv, 203 (1966),
            255-62. Abstr. in AES, 11 (1968), no. 3.

1421   BRADDY, HALDEEN. "Chaucer's Playful Pandarus." SFQ, 34
            (1970), 71-81.

156

1422   BRENNER, GERRY. "Narrative Structure in Chaucer's Troilus
        and Criseyde." AnM, 6 (1965), 5-18.

1423   BREWER, DEREK S. "The Ages of Troilus, Criseyde and Pandarus."
        SELit, Eng. no. (1972), 3-13.

1424   BREWER, DEREK S. "Troilus and Criseyde," in 32, chapter 5,
        part 3, pp. 195-228.

1425   BROOKHOUSE, CHRISTOPHER. "Chaucer's Impossibilia." MAE, 34
        (1965), 40-42. Abstr. in AES, 10 (1967), no. 3029.

1426   *BULOW, LORETTA. "Chaucer's Orchestration of the Troilus:
        A Critical Study Based on the Variant Texts." DAI, 31
        (1970), 2868A-69A. Yale University, 1970. 266 pp.

1427   BURJORJEE, D. M. "The Pilgrimage of Troilus's Sailing Heart
        in Chaucer's Troilus and Criseyde." AnM, 13 (1972),
        14-31. Abstr. in MLAA (1972), no. 2758.

1428   CARPENTER, NAN C. "Chaucer's Troilus and Criseyde, III,
        624-628." Expl, 30 (1972), Item 51. Abstr. in MLAA
        (1972), no. 2759.

1429   CARSON, MOTHER ANGELA, O. S. U. "'To Synge a Fool a Masse.'"
        AN&Q, 6 (1968), 135-36.

1430   COGHILL, N. K. "Love and 'Foul Delight': Some Contrasted
        Attitudes," in 53, pp. 141-56.

1431   CONLEE, JOHN W. "The Meaning of Troilus' Ascension to the
        Eighth Sphere." ChauR, 7 (1972), 27-36. Abstr. in AES,
        17 (1973-74), no. 19 and in MLAA (1972), no. 2760.

1432   COOK, ROBERT G. "Chaucer's Pandarus and the Medieval Idea
        of Friendship." JEGP, 69 (1970), 407-24. Abstr. in
        MLAA (1970), no. 1759.

1433   CORRIGAN, MATTHEW. "Chaucer's Failure with Woman: The
        Inadequacy of Criseyde." WHR, 23 (1969), 107-20. Abstr.
        in AES, 13 (1969-70), no. 1855.
            Revision of an article in Paunch, 27 (October, 1966),
        23-38.

1434   CORSA, HELEN S. "Dreams in Troilus and Criseyde." AI, 27
        (1970), 52-65. Abstr. in AES, 14 (1970-71), no. 1981
        and in MLAA (1970), no. 1761.

BIBLIOGRAPHY OF CHAUCER, 1964 - 1973

Longer Works other than The Canterbury Tales

1435   CORSA, HELEN. "Is This a Mannes Herte?" L&P, 16 (1966),
            184-91. Abstr. in AES, 11 (1968), no. 203.

1436   COTTON, MICHAEL E. "The Artistic Integrity of Chaucer's
            Troilus and Criseyde." ChauR, 7 (1972), 37-43. Abstr.
            in AES, 17 (1973-74), no. 20 and in MLAA (1972), no. 2761.

1437   COVELLA, SISTER FRANCIS DOLORES. "Audience as Determinant
            of Meaning in the Troilus." ChauR, 2 (1968), 235-45.
            Abstr. in AES, 16 (1972-73), no. 1573.

1438   DEVEREUX, JAMES A., S. J. "A Note on Troilus and Criseyde,
            Book III, Line 1309." PQ, 44 (1965), 550-52. Abstr. in
            AES, 10 (1967), no. 3118
            Parody of levation prayers.

1439   DI PASQUALE, PASQUALE, JR. "'Sikernesse' and Fortune in
            Troilus and Criseyde." PQ, 49 (1970), 152-63. Abstr. in
            MLAA (1970), no. 1766.

1440   DONALDSON, E. TALBOT. "Criseide and Her Narrator," in 39,
            pp. 65-83.

1440.01 DONALDSON, E. TALBOT. "The Ending of Troilus," in 39,
            pp. 84-101.
            Reprinted from Early English and Norse Studies Presented
            to Hugh Smith. Edited by Arthur Brown and Peter Foote.
            London: Methuen, 1963.

1441   DONALDSON, E. TALBOT. "The Masculine Narrator and Four Women
            of Style," in 39, pp. 46-64.

1442   DOOB, PENELOPE B. R. "Chaucer's 'Corones Tweyne' and the
            Lapidaries." ChauR, 7 (1972), 85-96. Abstr. in MLAA
            (1972), no. 2764.

1443   DRONKE, PETER. "The Conclusion of Troilus and Criseyde."
            MAE, 33 (1964), 47-52.

1444   DURHAM, LONNIE J. "Love and Death in Troilus and Criseyde."
            ChauR, 3 (1968), 1-11. Abstr. in AES, 17 (1973-74),
            no. 695.

1445   DURLING, ROBERT M. The Figure of the Poet in the Renaissance
            Epic. Cambridge, Massachusetts: Harvard University
            Press, 1965. 288 pp.
            Chapter 2, pp. 44-66, focuses on "the rhetorical func-
            tion of the apparent self-contradictions of the Poet and
            of his self-deprecation" in Troilus and Criseyde.

Troilus and Criseyde

1446   ELBOW, PETER. "Two Boethian Speeches in Troilus and Criseyde
       and Chaucerian Irony," in Literary Criticism and Histor-
       ical Understanding: Selected Papers from the English
       Institute. Edited by Phillip Damon. New York and London:
       Columbia University Press, 1967, pp. 85-107.

1447   ERZGRÄBER, WILLI. "Tragik und Komik in Chaucers Troilus and
       Criseyde," in Festschrift für Walter Hübner. Edited by
       Dieter Riesner and Helmut Gneuss. Berlin: Erich Schmidt
       Verlag, 1964, pp. 139-63.

1448   FARINA, PETER M. "Two Notes on Chaucer." LangQ, 10 (1972),
       23-26.
           Note 2. "The Storm Motif in Troilus and Criseyde, III,
       512ff."

1449   FARNHAM, ANTHONY E. "Chaucerian Irony and the Ending of the
       Troilus." ChauR, 1 (1967), 207-16. Abstr. in AES, 14
       (1970-71), no. 2944.

1450   *FINNEGAN, MARY FRANCES. "Comedy in Chaucer's Little Tragedy."
       DAI, 31 (1971), 5359A. University of Denver, 1970.
       254 pp.

1451   FISCHER, RUDOLF. "Die Troilus-Epen von Boccaccio und
       Chaucer," in Zu den Kunstformen des Mittelalterlichen
       Epos. New York: Johnson Reprint Corporation, 1964,
       pp. 217-370.
           Originally published in 1899.

1452   FOWLER, DAVID C. "Love in Chrétien's Lancelot." RR, 63
       (1972), 5-14.
           Comparisons with Troilus and Criseyde.

1453   FRANK, ROBERT W., JR. "Troilus and Criseyde: The Art of
       Amplification," in 55, pp. 155-71.

1454   FREIWALD, LEAH RIEBER. "Swych Love of Frendes: Pandarus and
       Troilus." ChauR, 6 (1971), 120-29. Abstr. in AES, 15
       (1971-72), no. 2847 and in MLAA (1972), no. 2147.

1455   GALLAGHER, JOSEPH E. "Theology and Intention in Chaucer's
       Troilus." ChauR, 7 (1972), 44-66. Abstr. in AES, 17
       (1973-74), no. 21 and in MLAA (1972), no. 2766.

1456   GAYLORD, ALAN T. "Chaucer's Tender Trap: The Troilus and
       the 'Yonge, Fresshe Folkes.'" EM, 15 (1964), 25-42.
       Abstr. in AES, 9 (1966), no. 135.

Longer Works other than The Canterbury Tales

1457   GAYLORD, ALAN T. "Friendship in Chaucer's Troilus." ChauR,
        3 (1969), 239-64. Abstr. in AES, 13 (1969-70), no. 2554.

1458   GAYLORD, ALAN T. "Gentilesse in Chaucer's Troilus." SP, 61
        (1964), 19-34. Abstr. in AES, 8 (1965), no. 1220.

1459   GILL, SISTER ANNE BARBARA. Paradoxical Patterns in Chaucer's
        Troilus: An Explanation of the Palinode. Washington,
        D.C.: The Catholic University of America Press, 1960.
        139 pp.
        See Crawford, p. 98.
        Reviews: D. S. Brewer, ES, 49 (1968), 145-47.

1460   GORDON, IDA L. The Double Sorrow of Troilus: A Study of
        Ambiguities in Troilus and Criseyde. Oxford: Clarendon
        Press, 1970. 163 pp.
        Reviews: TLS (4 September, 1970), p. 977; D. Biggins,
        AUMLA, 35 (1971), 81-83; Charles A. Owen, Jr., MP, 69
        (1971), 63-65; S. S. Hussey, N&Q, 18 (1971), 73-75;
        R. T. Davies, RES, 22 (1971), 468-71; J. R. Simon, EA,
        25 (1972), 319; F. N. M. Diekstra, DQR, 2 (1972), 125-27;
        Janet M. Cowen, YES, 2 (1972), 243-45.

1461   GORDON, IDA L. "The Narrative Function of Irony in Chaucer's
        Troilus and Criseyde," in Medieval Miscellany Presented
        to Eugène Vinaver by Pupils, Colleagues, and Friends.
        Edited by F. Whitehead, A. H. Diverres, and F. E.
        Sutcliffe. Manchester, England: Manchester University
        Press; New York: Barnes and Noble, 1965, pp. 146-56.

1461.01 GORDON, IDA L. "Processes of Characterization in Chaucer's
        Troilus," in Studies in Medieval Literature and Languages
        in Memory of Frederick Whitehead. Edited by W. Rothwell,
        W. R. J. Barron, David Blamires, and Lewis Thorpe.
        Manchester, England: Manchester University Press; New
        York: Barnes and Noble, 1973, pp. 117-31.

1462   GREENFIELD, STANLEY B. "The Role of Calkas in Troilus and
        Criseyde." MAE, 36 (1967), 141-51. Abstr. in AES, 13
        (1969-70), no. 3194.

1463   *GREER, ALLEN WILKINSON. "Chaucer's Troilus and Criseyde:
        The Tragicomic Dilemma." DA, 26 (1966), 4627-28. The
        University of Florida, 1965. 197 pp.

1464   GROSS, LAILA. "Time and the Narrator in Chaucer's Troilus
        and Criseyde." McNR, 19 (1968), 16-26. Abstr. in AES,
        15 (1971-72), no. 2848.

1465   *GROSS, LAILA. "Time in the Towneley Cycle, King Horn, Sir
        Gawain and the Green Knight, and Chaucer's Troilus and
        Criseyde." DA, 29 (1969), 3097A. University of Toronto,
        1967.

1466   GROSS, LAILA. "The Two Wooings of Criseyde." NM, 74 (1973),
        113-25.

1467   GROSSVOGEL, DAVID I. "Chaucer: Troilus and Criseyde," in his
        Limits of the Novel: Evolutions of a Form from Chaucer
        to Robbe-Grillet. Ithaca, New York: Cornell University
        Press, 1968, pp. 44-73.

1468   GUNN, ALAN M. F. "The Polylithic Romance: With Pages of
        Illustrations," in 38, pp. 1-18.
            Treats Troilus, Knight's Tale, Sir Gawain and the Green
        Knight.

1469   *HAFNER, MAMIE. "The Use of Religious Phraseology in Medieval
        Love Poetry: Provençal and French Poems and Chaucer's
        Troilus and Criseyde." DA, 26 (1965), 1632. The Univer-
        sity of Wisconsin, 1965. 242 pp.

1470   HANSON, THOMAS B. "Criseyde's Brows Once Again." N&Q, 18
        (1971), 285-86. Abstr. in AES, 15 (1971-72), no. 1655.

1471   HARVEY, PATRICIA A. "ME. 'Point' (Troilus and Criseyde III,
        695)." N&Q, 15 (1968), 243-44. Abstr. in AES, 11 (1968),
        no. 3309.

1472   HASKELL, ANN S. "The Doppelgängers in Chaucer's Troilus."
        NM, 72 (1971), 723-34.

1473   HATCHER, ELIZABETH R. "Chaucer and the Psychology of Fear:
        Troilus in Book V." ELH, 40 (1973), 307-24. Abstr. in
        MLAA (1973), no. 2866.

1474   HATCHER, ELIZABETH ROBERTA. "Troilus and Criseyde: Chaucer's
        Myth of Love." DAI, 33 (1972), 2327A. Johns Hopkins
        University, 1970. 269 pp.

1475   HEIDTMANN, PETER. "Sex and Salvation in Troilus and Criseyde."
        ChauR, 2 (1968), 246-53. Abstr. in AES, 16 (1972-73),
        no. 1575.

1476   *HERZMAN, RONALD BERNARD. "A Study of Chaucer's Use of Time
        in Troilus and Criseyde." DAI, 30 (1970), 2969A. Univer-
        sity of Delaware, 1969. 184 pp.

Longer Works other than The Canterbury Tales

1477   HILL, BETTY. "On Reading Chaucer." PLPLS-LHS, 14, vi (1971),
        209-20. Abstr. in AES, 16 (1972-73), no. 947.
        On Troilus and Criseyde III, 85-126.

1478   HOFFMAN, NANCY Y. "The Great Gatsby: Troilus and Criseyde
        Revisited," in Fitzgerald/Hemingway Annual, 1971. Edited
        by Matthew J. Bruccoli and C. E. Frazer Clark. Washing-
        ton, D.C.: NCR Microcards Editions, 1971, pp. 148-58.
        Comparisons of a casual nature.

1479   HOWARD, DONALD R. "Courtly Love and the Lust of the Flesh,"
        in 254, chapter 3, pp. 77-160.

1480   HOWARD, DONALD R. "Experience, Language, and Consciousness:
        Troilus and Criseyde, II, 596-931," in 55, pp. 173-92.

1481   HOWARD, DONALD R. "Literature and Sexuality: Book III of
        Chaucer's Troilus." MR, 8 (1967), 442-56. Abstr. in
        AES, 12 (1969), no. 1586.

1482   HUBER, JOHN. "Troilus' Predestination Soliloquy: Chaucer's
        Changes from Boethius." NM, 66 (1965), 120-25. Abstr.
        in AES, 9 (1966), no. 3067.

1483   HUSSEY, S. S. "The Difficult Fifth Book of Troilus and
        Criseyde." MLR, 67 (1972), 721-29. Abstr. in AES, 18
        (1974-75), no. 1364.

1484   ISAACS, NEIL D. "Further Testimony in the Matter of Troilus."
        SLitI, 4, ii (October, 1971), 11-27. Abstr. in AES, 15
        (1971-72), no. 1656.

1485   ISAACS, NEIL D. "On Six and Sevene: Troilus IV, 622."
        AN&Q, 5 (1967), 85-86.

1486   KARARAH, AZZA. "An Approach to Troilus and Criseyde." AUBFA,
        18 (1963), 1-19.

1487   KÄSMANN, HANS. "'I wolde excuse hire yit for routhe':
        Chaucers Einstellung zu Criseyde," in 43, pp. 97-122.

1488   KEAN, P. M. "Chaucer's Dealings with a Stanza of Il
        Filostrato and the Epilogue of Troilus and Criseyde."
        MAE, 33 (1964), 36-46.

1489   KELLY, EDWARD HANFORD. "Myth as Paradigm in Troilus and
        Criseyde." PLL, 3 (Summer supplement, 1967), 28-30.

1490   *KIERNAN, KEVIN SEAN. "The 'In Eched' Method of Narration in
         Chaucer's Troilus." DAI, 32 (1971), 921A. Case Western
         Reserve University, 1970. 220 pp.

1491   *KLINE, AUBREY J., JR. "A Rhetorical Analysis of Chaucer's
         Troilus and Criseyde." DAI, 33 (1973), 4350A. Univer-
         sity of Nevada, Reno, 1972. 177 pp.

1492   KORETSKY, ALLEN C. "Chaucer's Use of the Apostrophe in
         Troilus and Criseyde." ChauR, 4 (1970), 242-66. Abstr.
         in AES, 15 (1971-72), no. 719 and in MLAA (1971),
         no. 2186.

1493   *KORETSKY, ALLEN CURTIS. "Chaucer's Use of Rhetoric in
         Troilus and Criseyde." DA, 28 (1968), 4634A. Univer-
         sity of Toronto, 1967.

1494   KOSSICK, S. G. "Troilus and Criseyde: The Aubades." UES,
         9 (March, 1971), 11-13.

1495   LACKEY, ALLEN D. "Chaucer's Troilus and Criseyde, IV.295-301."
         Expl, 32 (1973), Item 5. Abstr. in MLAA (1973), no. 2868.

1496   LANHAM, RICHARD A. "Opaque Style and Its Uses in Troilus
         and Criseide." SMC, 3 (1970), 169-76.

1497   LEVER, KATHERINE. "Classical Scholars and Anglo-Classical
         Poets." CJ, 64 (1969), 216-18.

1498   LEWIS, C. S. "What Chaucer Really Did to Il Filostrato," in
         his Selected Literary Essays. Edited by Walter Hooper.
         London: Cambridge University Press, 1969, pp. 27-44.
         Reprinted from E&S, 17 (1932), 56-75. Excerpts re-
         printed in 62, pp. 78-87.

1499   LOCKHART, ADRIENNE R. "Semantic, Moral, and Aesthetic Degen-
         eration in Troilus and Criseyde." ChauR, 8 (1973),
         100-18. Abstr. in MLAA (1973), no. 2869.

1500   *LORRAH, JEAN. "The 'Present Eternite' of Chaucer's Troilus
         and Criseyde." DAI, 30 (1969), 688A. The Florida State
         University, 1968. 105 pp.

1501   MACEY, SAMUEL L. "Dramatic Elements in Chaucer's Troilus."
         TSLL, 12 (1970), 301-23. Abstr. in MLAA (1970), no.
         1795.

Longer Works other than The Canterbury Tales

1502   *MALARKEY, STODDARD. "Chaucer's Pandarus: Patterns of Per-
        suasion." DA, 25 (1964), 2983-84. University of Oregon,
        1964. 254 pp.

1503   MANZALAOUI, MAHMOUD. "Roger Bacon's 'In Convexitate' and
        Chaucer's 'In Convers' (Troilus and Criseyde V. 1810)."
        N&Q, 11 (1964), 165-66. Abstr. in AES, 7 (1964),
        no. 2243.

1504   MARKEN, RONALD. "Chaucer and Henryson: A Comparison."
        Discourse, 7 (1964), 381-87. Abstr. in AES, 8 (1965),
        no. 1610.

1505   MARKLAND, MURRAY F. "Pilgrims Errant: The Doubleness of
        Troilus and Criseyde." RS, 33 (1965), 64-77. Abstr. in
        AES, 10 (1967), no. 1806.

1506   MARKLAND, MURRAY F. "Troilus and Criseyde: The Inviola-
        bility of the Ending." MLQ, 31 (1970), 147-59. Abstr.
        in AES, 16 (1972-73), no. 332 and in MLAA (1970),
        no. 1796.

1507   MARTIN, JUNE HALL. Love's Fools: Aucassin, Troilus,
        Calisto, and the Parody of the Courtly Lover. Colección
        Támesis, Serie A: Monografías, 21. London: Tamesis,
        1972. 170 pp.
            Reviews: Stephen Barney, Spec, 49 (1974), 362-64.

1508   *MARTIN, JUNE HALL. "The Problem of Parody and Three Courtly
        Lovers: Aucassin, Troilus, and Calisto." DA, 28 (1968),
        4136A-37A. Emory University, 1967. 223 pp.

1509   MASI, MICHAEL. "Troilus: A Medieval Psychoanalysis." AnM,
        11 (1970), 81-88. Abstr. in AES, 17 (1973-74), no. 1906.

1510   MASUI, MICHIO. "The Development of Mood in Chaucer's
        Troilus, an Approach," in 34, pp. 245-54.

1511   MASUI, MICHIO. "A Mode of Word-Meaning in Chaucer's Lan-
        guage of Love." SELit, Eng. no. (1967), 113-26.
        Love language in Troilus and Criseyde.

1512   *McALPINE, MONICA ELLEN. "A Boethian Approach to the Problem
        of Genre in Chaucer's Troilus and Criseyde." DAI, 33
        (1973), 6877A-78A. The University of Rochester, 1973.
        268 pp.

1513   McCALL, JOHN P. "Troilus and Criseyde," in 60, pp. 370-84.

1514   McNALLY, JOHN J. "Chaucer's Topsy-Turvy Dante." SMC, 2 (1966), 104-10.

1515   MEECH, SANFORD B. Design in Chaucer's Troilus. New York: Greenwood Press, 1969. 541 pp.
          Reprint of 1959 edition. See Crawford, p. 100.
          Reviews: John Leyerle, "The Text and Its Tradition," UTQ, 32 (1963), 205-16.

1516   MILLER, RALPH N. "Pandarus and Procne." SMC, 7, ii (1964), 65-68.

1516.01 MOGAN, JOSEPH J., JR. "Free Will and Determination in Chaucer's Troilus and Criseyde." WSLL, 2 (1969), 131-60.

1517   MOGAN, JOSEPH J., JR. "The Origin and Development of the Story of Troilus and Cressida: A Brief Outline." Bati dil ve Edebiyatlari Arastirmalari Dergisi (Ankara Universitesi), 2 (1969), 123-30.

1518   MOGAN, JOSEPH J., JR. "Further Aspects of Mutability in Chaucer's Troilus." PELL, 1 (1965), 72-77. Abstr. in AES, 9 (1966), no. 504.

1519   MOORMAN, CHARLES. "'Once More Unto the Breach': The Meaning of Troilus and Criseyde." SLitI, 4, ii (October, 1971), 61-71. Abstr. in AES, 15 (1971-72), no. 1657.

1520   *MORTIMER, ANTHONY ROBERT. "The Canzoniere of Petrarch: Selected Poems Translated into English Verse." DAI, 32 (1972), 4624A. Case Western Reserve University, 1972. 218 pp.
          The Canticus Troili in the tradition of Petrarchan translation in England.

1521   *NEWTON, JUDITH MAY. "Chaucer's Troilus: Sir Francis Kynaston's Latin Translation with a Critical Edition of His English and Latin Annotations." DA, 28 (1968), 5026A. University of Illinois, 1967. 460 pp.

1522   *O'CONNOR, CLIVE PATRICK. "A Study of Troilus and Criseyde in the Light of Medieval Legalistic Fictions." DA, 29 (1968), 1876A. State University of New York at Buffalo, 1968. 182 pp.

Longer Works other than The Canterbury Tales

1523   OWEN, CHARLES A., JR. "Mimetic Form in the Central Love
        Scene of Troilus and Criseyde." MP, 67 (1969), 125-32.
        Abstr. in AES, 13 (1969-70), no. 2555.

1524   PECK, RUSSELL A. "Numerology and Chaucer's Troilus and
        Criseyde." Mosaic, 5, iv (1972), 1-29. Abstr. in AES,
        16 (1972-73), no. 1576 and in MLAA (1972), no. 2770.

1525   *PROVOST, WILLIAM GEORGE. "The Structure of Chaucer's
        Troilus and Criseyde." DAI, 31 (1970), 400A. University
        of North Carolina, Chapel Hill, 1969. 219 pp.

1525.01 PROVOST, WILLIAM [GEORGE]. The Structure of Chaucer's
        Troilus and Criseyde. Anglistica, 20. Copenhagen:
        Rosenkilde and Bagger, *1972, 1974. 120 pp. Cited in
        Spec, 49 (1974), 781.

1526   *REEDY, ELIZABETH KATHERINE. "'This Litel Spot of Erthe':
        Time and 'Trouthe' in Chaucer's Troilus and Criseyde."
        DA, 28 (1967), 1057A. Yale University, 1967. 117 pp.

1527   REILLY, ROBERT. "The Narrator and His Audience: A Study of
        Chaucer's Troilus." UPortR, 21, i (Spring, 1969), 23-36.
        Abstr. in AES, 13 (1969-70), no. 1856.

1528   REISS, EDMUND. "Troilus and the Failure of Understanding."
        MLQ, 29 (1968), 131-44. Abstr. in AES, 12 (1969),
        no. 1624.

1529   *RHYS, BRINLEY. "The Role of the Narrator in Chaucer's
        Troilus and Criseyde." DA, 24 (1964), 3327. Tulane
        University, 1963. 138 pp.

1530   ROBBIE, MAY GRANT. "Three-Faced Pandarus." CEJ, 3, i (1967),
        (1967), 47-54.

1531   ROSS, THOMAS W. "Troilus and Criseyde, II, 582-587: A
        Note." ChauR, 5 (1970), 137-39. Abstr. in AES, 15
        (1971-72), no. 720 and in MLAA (1971), no. 2217.

1532   ROWLAND, BERYL. "Pandarus and the Fate of Tantalus." OL,
        24 (1969), 3-16. Abstr. in AES, 13 (1969-70), no. 2871.

1533   RUSSELL, NICHOLAS. "Characters and Crowds in Chaucer's
        Troilus." N&Q, 13 (1966), 50-52. Abstr. in AES, 9
        (1966), no. 2358.

1534   RUTHERFORD, CHARLES S. "Pandarus as Lover: 'A Joly Wo' or
        'Loves Shotes Keene'?" AnM, 13 (1972), 5-13. Abstr. in
        MLAA (1972), no. 2771.

1535   SALTER, ELIZABETH. "Troilus and Criseyde: A Reconsider-
        ation," in 53, pp. 86-106.

1536   SAVILLE, JONATHAN. The Medieval Erotic Alba: Structure as
        Meaning. New York: Columbia University Press, 1972.
        323 pp.
            Includes appendix, "The Alba-Scene in Chaucer's
        Troilus."
            Reviews: Paul Zumthor, Spec, 50 (1975), 747-48.

1537   SCHELP, HANSPETER. "Die Tradition der Alba and die
        Morgenszene in Chaucers Troilus and Criseyde III,
        1415ff." GRM, 46 (1965), 251-61.

1538   *SEYMOUR, EVAN. "Play and Seriousness in Chaucer's Troilus
        and Criseyde." DAI, 34 (1974), 6606A. University of
        Delaware, 1973. 147 pp.

1538.01 SHARROCK, ROGER. "Troilus and Criseyde: Poem of Contin-
        gency," in 37, pp. 140-54.
            Reprinted from EIC, 8 (1958), 123-37. Originally
        titled "Second Thoughts: C. S. Lewis on Chaucer's
        Troilus."

1539   *SHEDD, GORDON MICHAEL. "Amor Dethroned: The Ovidian
        Tradition in Courtly Love Poetry." DA, 26 (1966), 4640.
        The Pennsylvania State University, 1965. 210 pp.

1540   SHEPHERD, G. T. "Troilus and Criseyde," in 35, pp. 65-87.
            Reprinted in 58, pp. 143-63; excerpts reprinted in 62,
        pp. 88-91.

1541   SHIMOSE, MICHIRO. "On the Rivalry Between the Inflectional
        and the Periphrastic Subjunctive in Chaucer's Troilus
        and Criseyde," in 54, pp. 303-16.

1542   *SHORTER, ROBERT NEWLAND. "Boethian Philosophy as the
        Informing Principle in Chaucer's Troilus and Criseyde."
        DA, 26 (1965), 359. Duke University, 1965. 288 pp.

1543   SIDDIQUI, M. NAIMUDDIN. "Troilus and Cressida: Treatment of
        the Theme by Chaucer and Shakespeare." OJES, 4 (1964),
        105-14.

Longer Works other than The Canterbury Tales

1544   *SIMMONS, WILLIAM ARTHUR. "Prologue to a Criticism of Medieval
       Literature." DAI, 32 (1972), 5201A. Duke University,
       1971. 150 pp.
           Chapter 4 analyzes Troilus and Criseyde by principles
       of Cassirer's Philosophy of Symbolic Forms.

1545   SIMS, DAVID. "An Essay at the Logic of Troilus and Criseyde."
       CamQ, 4 (1969), 125-49.

1546   SOMMER, GEORGE J. "The Attitudes of the Narrator in Chaucer's
       Troilus and Criseyde." New York-Pennsylvania MLA News-
       letter (renamed NEMLA), 1, ii (1968), 1-5.

1547   *SOMMER, GEORGE JOSEPH. "The Narrator of the Troilus and
       Criseyde: A Study of the Prohemia and Epilogue." DA, 24
       (1964), 3732-33. Fordham University, 1963. 173 pp.

1548   SOULES, EUGENE HENRI. "Troilus and Criseyde: A Study in
       Chaucer's Narrative Technique." DA, 26 (1966), 6053.
       University of the Pacific, 1966. 204 pp.

1549   SPEARING, A. C. "Chaucer as Novelist," in his Criticism and
       Poetry, 363 above, pp. 96-117.
           1. "Criseyde's Dream" (reprinted in 36, pp. 265-73).
           2. "The Lovers' Parting."

1550   STANLEY, E. G. "Stanza and Ictus: Chaucer's Emphasis in
       Troilus and Criseyde," in 43, pp. 123-48.

1551   STEADMAN, JOHN M. Disembodied Laughter: Troilus and the
       Apotheosis Tradition: A Reexamination of Narrative and
       Thematic Contexts. Berkeley, Los Angeles, London:
       University of California Press, 1972. 190 pp.

1552   STRAUSS, JENNIFER. "Teaching Troilus and Criseyde." SoRA,
       5 (1972), 13-20. Abstr. in AES, 16 (1972-73), no. 1259.

1553   STRAUSS, J[ENNIFER]. "Troilus and Criseyde: The Idea and
       the Poem" (synopsis), in 41, pp. 397-99.

1554   STROHM, PAUL. "Storie, Spelle, Geste, Romaunce, Tragedie:
       Generic Distinctions in the Middle English Troy Narratives."
       Spec, 46 (1971), 348-59.
           Treats Troilus and Criseyde as "tragedie."

1555   STURTEVANT, PETER A. "Chaucer's Troilus and Criseyde, III,
       890." Expl, 28 (1969), Item 5.

1556   *TAKANO, HIDEKUNI. "The Audience of Troilus and Criseyde."
        BFH, 8 (1972), 1-9. Cited in PMLAB (1973), no. 2872.

1557   *TAYLOR, DAVIS. "Style and Character in Chaucer's Troilus."
        DAI, 31 (1970), 1243A. Yale University, 1969. 316 pp.

1558   TAYLOR, WILLENE P. "Supposed Antifeminism in Chaucer's
        Troilus and Cryseyde and Its Retraction in The Legend of
        Good Women." XUS, 9, ii (1970), 1-18. Abstr. in AES, 17
        (1973-74), no. 22.

1559   UENO, NAOZO. Chaucer no Troilus Ron. Tokyo: Nanundo, 1972.
        Study of Troilus and Criseyde in Japanese.

1560   UTLEY, FRANCIS LEE. "Stylistic Ambivalence in Chaucer, Yeats,
        and Lucretius--The Cresting Wave and Its Undertow." UR,
        37 (1971), 174-98. Abstr. in AES, 15 (1971-72), no. 1288.
        See especially pp. 181-92. on Troilus and Criseyde.

1561   VAN, THOMAS A. "Imprisoning and Ensnarement in Troilus and
        The Knight's Tale." PLL, 7 (1971), 3-12. Abstr. in AES,
        14 (1970-71), no. 2618 and in MLAA (1971), no. 2234.

1562   WALKER, IAN C. "Chaucer and Il Filsotrato." ES, 49 (1968),
        318-26. Abstr. in AES, 13 (1969-70), no. 758.

1563   WATTS, ANN CHALMERS. "Chaucerian Selves--Especially Two
        Serious Ones." ChauR, 4 (1970), 229-41. Abstr. in MLAA
        (1971), no. 2239.

1564   WENZEL, SIEGFRIED. "Chaucer's Troilus of Book IV." PMLA,
        79 (1964), 542-47. Abstr. in AES, 8 (1965), no. 1520.

1565   WHITMAN, FRANK H. "Troilus and Criseyde and Chaucer's Dedi-
        cations to Gower." TSL, 18 (1973), 1-11. Abstr. in MLAA
        (1973), no. 2873.

1566   WILLIAMS, GEORGE. "Who Were Troilus, Criseyde, and Pandarus?"
        in 386, chapter 4, pp. 66-81.
            Explores the idea that Troilus and Criseyde reflect
        persons and events of Chaucer's acquaintance. In 386, see
        also pp. 175-95, for "Notes on Troilus and Criseyde."

1567   WOOD, CHAUNCEY. "On Translating Chaucer's Troilus and
        Criseyde, Book III, Lines 12-14." ELN, 11 (1973), 9-14.
        Abstr. in MLAA (1973), no. 2874.

Longer Works other than The Canterbury Tales

See also: 159, 160, 162, 163, 165, 167, 171, 173, 174, 179, 182, 185,
191, 198, 201, 203, 205, 211, 212, 213, 220, 222, 225, 230, 231, 237,
239, 242, 243, 245, 246, 251, 255, 259, 264, 269, 273, 276, 277, 283,
284, 285, 287, 289, 296, 301, 302, 303, 304, 305, 308, 311, 312, 319,
321, 324, 325, 333, 339, 340, 343, 346, 350, 353, 355, 358, 359, 364,
369, 374, 379, 383, 387, 391, 429, 431, 433, 435, 444, 446, 454, 470,
476, 478, 492, 509, 510, 514, 523, 631, 670, 788, 890, 1030, 1602,
1649, 1679, 1683, 1714, 1722, 1733, 1734, 1737, 1740, 1741, 1745,
1759, 1764, 1768, 1773, 1775, 1790, 1800, 1805, 1839, 1837.01, 1838.01,
1880, 1886, 2036, 2137, 2138, 2179-80+.

Troilus and Criseyde: Source Studies

1568   apROBERTS, ROBERT P. "Love in the Filostrato." ChauR, 7
        (1972), 1-26. Abstr. in AES, 17 (1973-74), no. 18 and
        in MLAA (1972), no. 2754.

1569   ARNTZ, SISTER MARY LUKE, S. N. D. "'That Fol of Whos Folie
        Men Ryme.'" AN&Q, 3 (1965), 151-52. Abstr. in AES, 10
        (1967), no. 1571.

1570   BOATNER, JANET WILLIAMS. "Criseyde's Character in the Major
        Writers from Benoît Through Dryden: The Changes and Their
        Significance." DAI, 31 (1971), 4705A. The University of
        Wisconsin, Madison, 1970. 254 pp.

1571   DAVIS, NORMAN. "The Litera Troili and English Letters." RES,
        16 (1965), 233-44. Abstr. in AES, 10 (1967), no. 1057.

1572   DE VRIES, F. C. "In Chaucer's Workshop: Two Boethian Pas-
        sages in Troilus and Criseyde" (synopsis), in 41,
        pp. 383-85.

1573   DE VRIES, F. C. "Troilus and Criseyde, Book III, Stanza 251,
        and Boethius." ES, 52 (1971), 502-507. Abstr. in AES,
        17 (1973-74), no. 694.

1574   FRY, DONALD K. "Chaucer's Zanzis and a Possible Source for
        Troilus and Criseyde, IV, 407-413." ELN, 9 (1971),
        81-85.

1575   GARBÁTY, THOMAS. "The Pamphilus Tradition in Ruiz and
        Chaucer." PQ, 46 (1967), 457-70. Abstr. in AES, 15
        (1971-72), no. 718.

1576   HOFFMEISTER, GERHART. Petrarkitische Lyrik. SM, 119.
        Stuttgart: Metzler, 1973. 107 pp.

Troilus and Criseyde

See pp. 45–46 for brief references to the influence of the Petrarchan lyric on Troilus and Criseyde.

1577   KEAN, P. M. "Chaucer's Dealings with a Stanza of Il
        Filostrato and the Epilogue of Troilus and Criseyde."
        MAE, 33 (1964), 36–46.

1578   KELLOGG, ALFRED L. and WALLER B. WIGGINTON. "How Dares Col-
        laborated with Dictys," in 51, pp. 146–54.

1579   KELLOGG, ALFRED L. "On the Tradition of Troilus's Vision of
        the Little Earth," in 51, pp. 199–211.

1580   *MIESZKOWSKI, GRETCHEN BUCKELMUELLER. "The Reputation of
        Criseyde: 1155–1500." DA, 27 (1966), 459A. Yale Uni-
        versity, 1966. 253 pp.

1581   MIESZKOWSKI, GRETCHEN. The Reputation of Criseyde: 1155–
        1500. Transactions of the Connecticut Academy of Arts
        and Sciences, 43 (1971), pp. 71–153. Hamden, Connecticut:
        Archon Books, 1971.

1582   PIATKOWSKI, ADELINA. "Circulatia temei Troilus si Cressida
        din antichitate pina in secolul al XVII-lea" [The Migra-
        tion of the Troilus and Cressida Theme from Ancient Times
        to the XVIIth Century]. SLUB, 14 (1969), 11–24.

1583   WALKER, IAN C. "Chaucer and Il Filostrato." ES, 49 (1968),
        318–26.

1584   WITLIEB, BERNARD L. "Chaucer's Elysian Fields (Troilus IV,
        789F)." N&Q, 16 (1969), 250–51. Abstr. in AES, 13
        (1969–70), no. 1503.

1585   YOUNG, KARL. The Origin and Development of the Story of
        Troilus and Criseyde. New York: Gordian Press, 1968.
        195 pp.
           Harvard Dissertation, published in 1908. See Griffith,
        p. 310.

See also: 398, 399, 400, 402, 404, 408, 412, 413, 421, 422, 423,
1411, 1434, 1439, 1443, 1446, 1451, 1453, 1482, 1488, 1498, 1512,
1514, 1515, 1523, 1539, 1542, 1551, 1562, 1837.01.

Lyrics and Shorter Poems

GENERAL

1586   FRANÇON, MARCEL. "Note on Chaucer's Roundels and his French
        Models." AION-SG, 9 (1966), 195-97.

1587   *HAYES, JOSEPH JOHN. "The Court Lyric in the Age of Chaucer."
        DAI, 34 (1974), 4205A-06A. Indiana University, 1973.
        306 pp.

1588   *MERRILL, RODNEY HARPSTER. "Formal Elements in the Late
        Medieval Courtly Love Lyric." DAI, 31 (1971), 4172A.
        Stanford University, 1970. 580 pp.
            Compares love lyrics of Petrarch with those of Chaucer.

1589   *PRASAD, PRAJAPATI. "The Order of Complaint: A Study in
        Medieval Tradition." DA, 26 (1966), 3930. The Univer-
        sity of Wisconsin, 1965. 359 pp.

1590   REISS, EDMUND. "Dusting off the Cobwebs: A Look at Chaucer's
        Lyrics." ChauR, 1 (1966), 55-65. Abstr. in AES, 13
        (1969-70), no. 1121.

1591   ROBBINS, ROSSELL HOPE. "The Lyrics," in 60, pp. 313-31.

See also: 105, 193, 242, 255, 316.

AN A B C

1592   KLINEFELTER, RALPH A. "Chaucer's An A B C, 25-32." Expl,
        24 (1965), Item 5. Abstr. in AES, 11 (1968), no. 443.

1593   *ROGERS, WILLIAM ELFORD. "Image and Abstraction: Six Middle
        English Religious Lyrics." DAI, 31 (1971), 6023A. Uni-
        versity of North Carolina, Chapel Hill, 1970). 199 pp.

1594   *ZBOZNY, FRANK T.   "The Metrical Structure of Chaucer's
        A B C." DAI, 31 (1970), 2359A. University of Pittsburgh,
        1970. 151 pp.

See also: 85, 96, 174, 193, 194, 220, 242, 500, 1590, 1790.

THE COMPLAINT OF CHAUCER TO HIS PURSE

1595   FERRIS, SUMNER. "The Date of Chaucer's Final Annuity and of
        the Complaint to His Empty Purse." MP, 65 (1967), 45-52.

1596   FINNEL, ANDREW J.   "The Poet as Sunday Man: The Complaint of
        Chaucer to His Purse." ChauR, 8 (1973), 147-58. Abstr.
        in MLAA (1973), no. 2765.

1597   SCOTT, FLORENCE R.   "A New Look at The Complaint of Chaucer
        to His Empty Purse." ELN, 2 (1964), 81-87. Abstr. in
        AES, 8 (1965), no. 2903.

See also: 242, 2136, 2164, 2178.

THE COMPLAINT OF MARS

        See Griffith, pp. 282-83; Crawford, p. 93.

1598   HULTIN, NEIL C.   "Anti-Courtly Elements in Chaucer's Complaint
        of Mars." AnM, 9 (1968), 58-75.

1599   LAIRD, EDGAR S.   "Astrology and Irony in Chaucer's Complaint
        of Mars." ChauR, 6 (1972), 229-31. Abstr. in AES, 16
        (1972-73), no. 1569 and in MLAA (1972), no. 2746.

1600   LAIRD, EDGAR S.   "Chaucer's Complaint of Mars, Line 145:
        'Venus valaunse.'" PQ, 51 (1972), 486-89. Abstr. in
        MLAA (1972), no. 2747.

1601   MERRILL, R. H.   "Chaucer's Broche of Thebes: The Unity of
        The Complaint of Mars and The Complaint of Venus," in
        Literary Monographs. Edited by Eric Rothstein. Madison,

Lyrics and Shorter Poems

        Wisconsin: University of Wisconsin Press, 1973, vol. 5,
        pp. 1-61.

1602   *STORM, MELVIN G., JR. "Chaucer's Poetic Treatment of the
        Figure of Mars." DAI, 34 (1973), 742A. University of
        Illinois, Urbana-Champaign, 1973. 136 pp.

1603   WILLIAMS, GEORGE. "What is the Complaint of Mars?" in 386,
        chapter 3, pp. 56-65.
          Argues that Mars appears to be a record of an episode
        in the life of John of Gaunt.

See also: 105, 193, 194, 276, 285, 305, 312, 319, 359, 391, 402,
413, 1588.

Mars: Source Studies

1604   DEAN, NANCY. "Chaucer's Complaint, a Genre Descended from
        the Heroides." CL, 19 (1967), 1-27.

THE COMPLAINT OF VENUS

1605   WILLIAMS, GEORGE. "Many Sondry Werkes," in 386, chapter 9,
        pp. 152-66.

See also: 402, 500, 1601.

A COMPLAINT TO HIS LADY

See: 193, 194.

THE COMPLAINT UNTO PITY

See: 105, 193, 194, 1744.

ENVOY TO SCOGAN

1606   DAVID, ALFRED. "Chaucer's Good Counsel to Scogan." ChauR, 3 (1969), 265-74. Abstr. in AES, 13 (1969-70), no. 2553.

See also: 105, 2178.

THE FORMER AGE

See Griffith, p. 264; Crawford, p. 90.

See also: 422.

FORTUNE

See: 83, 94, 105.

GENTILESSE

See: 94, 658.

LAK OF STEDFASTNESSE

1607   CROSS, J. E. "The Old Swedish Trohetsvisan and Chaucer's Lak of Stedfastnesse--A Study in a Mediaeval Genre." Saga Book, 16 (1965), 283-314.

See also: 33, 2136, 2164, 2178.

Lyrics and Shorter Poems

TO ROSEMOUNDE

1608   ROBBINS, ROSSELL H. "Chaucer's To Rosemounde." SLitI, 4, ii
        (October, 1971), 73-81.

See also: 105, 242, 1590, 2178.

TRUTH

1609   LAMPE, DAVID E. "The Truth of a 'Vache': The Homely Homily
        of Chaucer's Truth." PLL, 9 (1973), 311-14.

See also: 94, 105.

WOMANLY NOBLESSE

See: 1880.

Apocrypha, Lost Works,
and Works of Doubtful Authorship

GENERAL

1610   ROBBINS, ROSSELL H. "The Chaucerian Apocrypha," in A Manual of the Writings in Middle English, 1051-1500. General editor, Albert E. Hartung. Hamden, Connecticut: Shoe String Press, 1973, volume 4, chapter 11, pp. 1061-1101. See also, pp. 1286-1303 for bibliography.

EQUATORIE OF PLANETIS

See 255, 260.

GAMELYN

1611   DANIEL, NEIL. "A Metrical and Stylistic Study of The Tale of Gamelyn," in 38, pp. 19-32.

See also: 1694, 1719.

Gamelyn: Source Studies

1612   LOOMIS, LAURA HIBBARD. Medieval Romance in England: A Study of the Sources and Analogues of the Non-Cyclic Metrical Romances. New edition with bibliographical index. New York: Burt Franklin, 1960, 1969. 358 pp.

Apocrypha, Lost Works, and Works of Doubtful Authorship

> Originally published in 1924. See Griffith, p. 89: Hibbard, Laura Alandis. For a study of Gamelyn, see pp. 156-63.

MAUDELEYNE

1613   McCALL, JOHN P. "Chaucer and the Pseudo Origen De Maria Magdalena: A Preliminary Study." Spec, 46 (1971), 491-509. Abstr. in AES, 17 (1973-74), no. 1582.

MERCILES BEAUTE

See: 1586, 2178.

PLOWMAN'S TALE

1614   ASTON, MARGARET. "Lollardy and the Reformation: Survival or Revival?" History, 49 (1964), 149-70. Abstr. in AES, 8 (1965), no. 2012.
        The interest of sixteenth century reformers in Lollardy and the inclusion of the spurious Plowman's Tale in editions of Chaucer.

1615   WAWN, ANDREW N. "Chaucer, Wyclif, and the Court of Apollo." ELN, 10 (1972), 15-20.

1616   WAWN, ANDREW N. "The Genesis of The Plowman's Tale." YES, (1972), 21-40.

See also: 1744.

PROVERBS

1617   PACE, GEORGE B. "The Chaucerian Proverbs." SB, 18 (1965), 41-48. Abstr. in AES, 9 (1966), no. 286.

Of The Wreched Engendrynge of Mankynde

THE ROMAUNT OF THE ROSE

1618   ANDO, SHINSUKE. "The Language of The Romaunt of the Rose
        (Fragment A), with Particular Reference to Chaucer's
        Relationship to Middle English Provincial Poetry."
        SELit, Eng. no. (1970), 63-74.

1619   MATHEW, GERVASE. "Ideals of Friendship," in 53, pp. 45-53.
        See especially pp. 50-52.

See also: 185, 239, 255, 260, 296, 308, 364, 461, 500, 541, 1390,
1390.01, 1679, 1860.

Romaunt: Source Studies

See: 123, 1748.

OF THE WRECHED ENGENDRYNGE OF MANKYNDE

1620   *LEWIS, ROBERT ENZER. "Chaucer and Pope Innocent III's De
        miseria humane conditionis." DA, 25 (1965), 7246-47.
        University of Pennsylvania, 1964. 451 pp.
            Includes text of probable manuscript used by Chaucer.

1621   LEWIS, ROBERT ENZER. "What Did Chaucer Mean by Of the
        Wreched Engendrynge of Mankynde?" ChauR, 2 (1968),
        139-58. Abstr. in AES, 16 (1972-73), no. 1572.

Backgrounds

GENERAL BACKGROUNDS INCLUDING HISTORICAL,

AND PHILOSOPHIC BACKGROUNDS

See Griffith, pp. 314-29; Crawford, pp. 102-109.

1622   ALEXANDER, JAMES W. "The Becket Controversy in Recent
        Historiography." JBS, 9, ii (1970), 1-26.
        Review of scholarship.

1622.01 ANDERSON, M[ARY] D[ESIREE]. A Saint at Stake: The Strange
        Death of William of Norwich, 1144. London: Faber and
        Faber, 1964. 231 pp.
        Note on the Prioresse's Tale, p. 63.

1623   BAKER, TIMOTHY. Medieval London. New York, Washington:
        Praeger, 1970. 260 pp.
        Reviews: Martin Weinbaum, Spec, 46 (1971), 362; TLS
        (25 June, 1971), pp. 745-46.

1624   BARBER, RICHARD. The Knight and Chivalry. New York:
        Charles Scribner's Sons, 1970. 393 pp.
        Reviews: W. R. Thomson, WHR, 25 (1971), 363-365; TLS
        (16 April, 1971), p. 440.

1625   BARTSOCAS, CHRISTOS S. "Two Fourteenth Century Greek
        Descriptions of the Black Death." JHM, 21 (1966),
        394-400.

1626   BEAN, J. M. W. The Decline of English Feudalism, 1215-1540.
        Manchester, England: Manchester University Press; New
        York: Barnes and Noble, 1968. 347 pp.
        Reviews: *D. L. Bethell, Tablet (26 October, 1968),
        p. 1062; Alan Rogers, HistT, 18 (1968), 735-37; Fred A.
        Cazel, Jr., AHR, 74 (1969), 967-68.

BIBLIOGRAPHY OF CHAUCER, 1964 - 1973

General Backgrounds/Historical, Philosophic Backgrounds

1627   BELLAMY, J. G. The Law of Treason in England in the Later
        Middle Ages. Cambridge Studies in English Legal History.
        Cambridge, England; New York: Cambridge University Press,
        1970. 284 pp.
            Based on the author's thesis, University of Nottingham.

1628   BERESFORD, MAURICE [WARWICK]. New Towns of the Middle Ages:
        Town Plantation in England, Wales, and Gascony. New York
        and Washington: Praeger, 1967. 690 pp.
            Reviews: John H. Mundy, Spec, 44 (1969), 446-48;
        Gordon Godfrey, ContempR (October, 1967), pp. 219-20;
        W. C. Hoskins, Listener, 79 (15 February, 1968), p. 215;
        TLS (6 June, 1968), p. 573; R. H. Hilton, History, 53
        (1968), 255; Helen Rosenau, ArchR, 144 (December, 1968),
        466.

1628.01 BISHOP, MORRIS. The Horizon Book of the Middle Ages. Edited
        by Norman Kotker. New York: American Heritage; Toronto:
        McClelland and Stewart, 1968. 416 pp., 260 illustrations,
        some in color.

1629   BOASE, T. S. R. Death in the Middle Ages: Mortality, Judge-
        ment and Remembrance. Library of Medieval Civilization.
        London: Thames and Hudson, 1972. 144 pp., 109 plates.

1630   BOWSKY, WILLIAM M., ed. The Black Death: A Turning Point in
        History. European Problem Studies. New York: Holt,
        Rinehart and Winston, 1971. 128 pp.

1631   BRUNDAGE, JAMES A. Medieval Canon Law and the Crusader.
        Madison: The Wisconsin University Press, 1969. 264 pp.
            Treats crusaders as pilgrims. Contains a bibliography.
            Reviews: John W. Baldwin, Spec, 46 (1971), 131-33.

1632   COBBAN, ALAN B. The King's Hall Within the University of
        Cambridge in the Later Middle Ages. Cambridge Studies in
        Medieval Life and Thought, Third Series, I. Cambridge,
        England: Cambridge University Press, 1969. 371 pp.,
        8 plates.
            Reviews: Franklin J. Pegues, Spec, 48 (1973), 557-58;
        *C. I. Konigsberg, Tablet, (26 April, 1969), p. 416; TLS
        (26 June, 1969), p. 708; J. R. L. Highfield, MAE, 39
        (1970), 70-73.

1633   COOK, RAYMOND A. "The Influence of the Black Death on
        Medieval Literature and Language." KFLQ, 11 (1964), 5-13.

1634   DAHMUS, JOSEPH. William Courtenay, Archbishop of Canterbury,
        1381-1396. University Park, Pennsylvania; London:
        Pennsylvania State University Press, 1966. 341 pp.

Backgrounds

> Reviews: Dorothy Bruce Weske, Spec, 43 (1968), 501-503;
> John Fines, HistT, 17 (1967), 565-66; L. J. Daly, Manu-
> scripta, 11 (1967), 115; John T. McNeill, CH, 36 (1967),
> 219-21; F. R. H. DuBoulay, EHR, 83 (1968), 827-28; May
> McKisack, History, 53 (1968), 84.

1635 *DEAN, JAMES. "The World Grows Old: The Significance of a
      Medieval Idea." DAI, 32 (1972), 6924A. The Johns Hopkins
      University, 1971. 490 pp.

1635.01 DELORT, ROBERT. Life in the Middle Ages. Translated by
      Robert Allen. New York: Universe Books for Edita
      Lausanne, 1972, 1973. 345 pp. Plates.

1636 DENHOLM-YOUNG, N. History and Heraldry, 1254 to 1310: A
      Study of the Historical Value of the Rolls of Arms.
      Oxford: Clarendon Press; New York: Oxford University
      Press, 1965. 193 pp.
        Reviews: Gerard J. Brault, Spec, 41 (1966), 318-20;
      P. J. Jones, NSt (6 August, 1965), p. 192; TLS
      (23 December, 1965), p. 1194; Fred A. Cazel, Jr., AHR,
      71 (1966), 536-37; M. MacLagan, EHR, 81 (1966), 811-12;
      I. J. Sanders, History, 50 (1965), 352.

1637 DERRY, T. K. and M. G. BLAKEWAY. The Making of Britain:
      Life and Work to the Close of the Middle Ages. London:
      Murray, 1968. 220 pp., 16 plates.
        A popular survey. See especially chapter 14, pp. 180-95,
      "The England of The Canterbury Tales and Paston Letters."

1638 DESTOMBES, MARCEL, ed. Mappemondes, A. D. 1200-1500.
      Catalogue préparé par la Commission des Cartes Anciennes
      de l'Union Géographique Internationale. Monumenta
      Cartographica Vetustioris Aevi, 1; Imago Mundi, Supple-
      ment, 4. Amsterdam: N. Israel, 1964. 354 pp., plates.
        Reviews: Curt F. Bühler, Spec, 41 (1966), 738-39.

1638.01 DU BOULAY, F. R. H. and CAROLINE M. BARRON, eds. The Reign
      of Richard II: Essays in Honour of May McKisack. London:
      University of London, The Athlone Press; New York:
      Oxford University Press, 1971. 351 pp.
        Fourteen essays by various hands.
        Reviews: Joel T. Rosenthal, Spec, 48 (1973), 741-43;
      TLS (7 July, 1972), p. 778.

1639 EVANS, JOAN, ed. The Flowering of the Middle Ages. New York:
      McGraw-Hill; *London: Thames and Hudson, 1966. 360 pp.,
      631 illustrations (192 in color).

General Backgrounds/Historical, Philosophic Backgrounds

Essays by various hands on medieval life.
Reviews: David Knowles, Listener, 76 (1966), 543-44;
TLS (15 September, 1966), p. 856.

1640   FINES, JOHN. Who's Who in the Middle Ages. London: Blond,
        1970. 230 pp.

1641   *GILLESPIE, DAVID SOUTHARD. "The Changing Outlook of
        Chaucerian England." DAI, 32 (1971), 3188A-9A. Michigan
        State University, 1971. 312 pp.

1642   GREEN, V[IVIAN] H[UBERT] H[OWARD]. Medieval Civilization in
        Western Europe. London: Edward Arnold, 1971. 426 pp.
        3 fold-out maps.

1642.01 HALE, J. R., J. R. L. HIGHFIELD and B. SMALLEY, eds. Europe
        in the Late Middle Ages. Evanston, Illinois: North-
        western University Press, 1965. 520 pp.
        Sixteen essays on various subjects.

1643   HARDING, ALAN. The Law Courts of Medieval England. Histor-
        ical Problems: Studies and Documents, 18. London:
        George Allen and Unwin; New York: Barnes and Noble, 1973.
        201 pp.
        Includes thirty documents, edited and translated into
        English. See especially chapter 3, pp. 86-123, "English
        Law Courts in the Later Middle Ages."
        Reviews: TLS (15 June, 1973), p. 668.

1644   HAY, DENYS. Europe in the Fourteenth and Fifteenth Centuries.
        A General History of Europe, 5. New York: Holt,
        Rinehart and Winston, 1966. 430 pp.
        Reviews: TLS (12 January, 1967), p. 33; TLS (3 August,
        1967), p. 710; G. A. Holmes, EHR, 83 (1968), 591; John
        Le Patourel, History, 53 (1968), 256.

1645   HEER, FRIEDRICH. The Intellectual History of Europe. Trans-
        lated from German by Jonathan Steinberg. Cleveland and
        New York: The World Publishing Company, 1966. 566 pp.
        Originally published in Stuttgart: W. Kohlhammer
        Verlag, 1953.

1646   HERLIHY, DAVID, ed. Medieval Culture and Society. New York:
        Walker and Co.; New York and London: Harper and Row,
        1968. 425 pp.
        A documentary history. See Part Three, I, 3, for
        modern English translation of the General Prologue.

Backgrounds

1647   HEWITT, H. J. The Organization of War under Edward III,
       1338-62. Manchester, England: Manchester University
       Press; New York: Barnes and Noble, 1966. 215 pp.
       Reviews: TLS (6 October, 1966), p. 920; John Beeler,
       AHR, 72 (1967), 555-56; M. R. Powicke, Spec, 42 (1967),
       739-40; E. L. G. Stones, History, 52 (1967), 317-18;
       Fritz Trautz, HZ, 212, H. 1 (1971), 133-34; *A. Gerlich,
       Erasmus, 21 (1970), 250.

1648   HUSSEY, MAURICE. "Chaucer's England," in 258, chapter 2,
       pp. 28-55.

1649   *INGHAM, MURIEL BRIERLEY. "Some Fifteenth-Century Images of
       Death and Their Background." DA, 28 (1968), 4132A-33A.
       University of California, Riverside, 1967. 193 pp.

1650   JEWELL, HELEN M. English Local Administration in the Middle
       Ages. Newton Abbot, Devon, England: David & Charles;
       New York: Barnes & Noble, 1972. 238 pp.
       Reviews: W. O. Ault, Spec, 49 (1974), 567; TLS
       (19 January, 1973), p. 62.

1651   JOHANSEN, BØRGE V. Fra Chaucers Tid 1327-1400. København:
       Nyt Nordisk Forlag; *Arnold Busck, 1965. 260 pp.
       Study in Danish of political and intellectual currents
       and domestic activities of the fourteenth century.

1652   JONES, RICHARD H. The Royal Policy of Richard II: Abso-
       lutism in the Later Middle Ages. New York: Barnes and
       Noble, 1968. 205 pp.
       Reviews: TLS (30 May, 1968), p. 554; Margaret Hastings,
       AHR, 74 (1969), 969-70; J. J. N. Palmer, History, 53
       (1968), 405; W. H. Dunham, Jr., Spec, 44 (1969), 466-67.

1653   JONES, THOMAS M., ed. The Becket Controversy. Major Issues
       in History. New York: John Wiley, 1970. 173 pp.

1654   KEEN, M[AURICE] H[UGH]. England in the Later Middle Ages.
       London: Methuen, 1973. 593 pp.
       Reviews: *A. Leguai, Erasmus, 25 (1974), 429-31; TLS
       (20 April, 1973), p. 436.

1655   KEEN, MAURICE. A History of Medieval Europe. New York,
       Washington: Frederick A. Praeger, 1968. 318 pp.
       Introductory study. See especially section 4,
       pp. 195-281 covering c. 1330-c. 1460.
       Reviews: *D. L. Douie, Tablet (18 May, 1968), p. 499;
       TLS (5 February, 1971), p. 141.

General Backgrounds/Historical, Philosophic Backgrounds

1656   KEEN, MAURICE H. The Laws of War in the Late Middle Ages.
        Toronto: University of Toronto Press, 1965. 302 pp.
        Reviews: Richard A. Newhall, Spec, 40 (1965), 732-34;
        P. J. Jones, NSt, (6 August, 1965), p. 192; Economist
        (10 April, 1965), pp. 198-99; TLS (18 March, 1965),
        p. 211; Fredric L. Cheyette, AHR, 71 (1966), 538-39;
        Richard Vaughan, MAE, 34 (1965), 279-81; R. Allen Brown,
        EHR, 81 (1966), 816; Denys Hay, History, 51 (1966),
        77-78.

1657   *KESTEVEN, G. R., pseud. The Peasants' Revolt. Studies in
        English History. London: Chatto and Windus, 1965.
        94 pp. Cited in MHRA (1965), no. 2389.

1658   KNAPP, BRUCE. "A Note on Roses and Wheels." Comitatus, 1
        (1970), 43-46.

1659   KNOWLES, DAVID. Thomas Becket. Stanford, California:
        Stanford University Press, 1971. 194 pp.
        Reviews: Charles R. Young, Spec, 47 (1972), 779-81;
        TLS (9 April, 1971), p. 428.

1660   CANCELLED

1661   LEFF, GORDON. Paris and Oxford Universities in the
        Thirteenth and Fourteenth Centuries: An Institutional
        and Intellectual History. New Dimensions in History,
        Essays in Comparative History. New York, London: John
        Wiley, 1968. 339 pp.
        Reviews: C. G. Boyce, AHR, 74 (1968), 139-40; C. M. D.
        Crowder, QQ, 75 (1968), 546-47; TLS (2 January, 1969),
        p. 19; VQR, 44 (1968), clxxii; Pearl Kibre, Spec, 44
        (1969), 642-46.

1662   LEWIS, C. S. The Discarded Image. Cambridge, England:
        Cambridge University Press, 1964. 240 pp.
        Reviews: TLS (16 July, 1964), p. 632; Helen Gardner,
        Listener, 72 (1964), 97; John Holloway, Spect (5 June,
        1964), p. 760; Alec Vidler, NYHTB (26 July, 1964), p. 3;
        D. C. Allen, ELN, 2 (1964), 133-35; R. T. Davies, N&Q,
        11 (1964), 350-51; Michel Poirier, EA, 18 (1965), 67-68;
        Albert Howard Carter, ChCen, 82 (January, 1965), 55-56;
        Jerome Taylor, Thought, 40 (1965), 291-93; E. Catherine
        Dunn, CHR, 51 (1965), 87-88; Edward Grant, Isis, 56
        (1965), 99-100; John Burrow, EIC, 15 (1965), 207-11;
        Marie Pascale Bon, Moreana, 23 (1969), 113-15; Karl
        Heinz Göller, Archiv, 205 (1969), 71-72; SCN, 24 (1968),
        59.

Backgrounds

1663   LOBEL, MARY DOREEN, ed. Historical Towns: Maps and Plans of
         Towns and Cities in the British Isles, with Historical
         Commentaries, from Earliest Times to 1800. London:
         Lovell Johns-Cook, Hammond and Kell Organization, 1969;
         Baltimore, Maryland: The Johns Hopkins Press, 1970.
         n.p.
             Includes eight towns with colored maps.
             Reviews: Urban T. Holmes, Spec, 45 (1970), 309-10.

1664   LOOMIS, ROGER SHERMAN. A Mirror of Chaucer's World.
         Princeton, New Jersey: Princeton University Press, 1965.
         n.p., 179 illustrations.
             Reviews: TLS (10 March, 1966), p. 194; Margaret Willy,
         Eng, 16 (1966), 61-62; Margaret Twycross, MAE, 36 (1967),
         191-95; Douglas Gray, N&Q, 14 (1967), 106; Francis Lee
         Utley, Spec, 42 (1967), 540-42; Connoisseur, 165 (1967),
         197.

1665   LYMAN, THOMAS W. "The Pilgrimage Roads Revisited." Gesta,
         8, ii (1969), 30-44.

1666   MATHEW, GERVASE. The Court of Richard II. London: John
         Murray, 1968. 238 pp., 29 plates.

1667   McFARLANE, K[ENNETH] B[RUCE]. Lancastrian Kings and Lollard
         Knights. Edited by J. R. L. Highfield and G. L. Harriss.
         Oxford: Clarendon Press; New York: Oxford University
         Press, 1972. 261 pp.
             Reviews: J. M. W. Bean, Spec, 49 (1974), 582-84.

1668   McFARLANE, K. B. The Nobility of Later Medieval England:
         The Ford Lectures for 1953 and Related Studies. Oxford:
         Clarendon Press; New York: Oxford University Press,
         1973. 367 pp.

1669   *McLAY, ALAN DRUMMOND. "A Comparative Study of the Life of
         St. Thomas of Canterbury by John of Salisbury and Other
         Contemporary Latin Lives." DAI, 30 (1969), 1143A. The
         University of Wisconsin, 1969. 707 pp.

1670   MURRAY, PATRICK. "Thomas Becket of Canterbury: Eight
         Hundred Years On." Studies, 59 (1970), 68-80.
             Treats the career of Thomas à Becket.

1671   MYERS, A. R. England in the Late Middle Ages. The Pelican
         History of England, 4. Harmondsworth: Penguin, 1966,
         1972. 282 pp.

Bibliography of Chaucer, 1964 - 1973

General Backgrounds/Historical, Philosophic Backgrounds

1672   MYERS, A. R. London in the Age of Chaucer. The Centers of
         Civilization Series. Norman: University of Oklahoma
         Press, 1972. 247 pp.

1673   NEWTON, A. P., ed. Travel and Travellers of the Middle Ages.
         The History of Civilization. New York: Barnes and Noble,
         1968. 227 pp., 8 plates.

1674   *OAKESHOTT, RONALD EWART. The Sword in the Age of Chivalry.
         London: Lutterworth Press, 1964. 152 pp. Cited in MHRA
         (1964), no. 2088.

1675   OBERMAN, HEIKO AUGUSTUNUS, ed. Forerunners of the Reforma-
         tion: The Shape of Late Medieval Thought. New York:
         Holt, Rinehart, & Winston, 1966. 343 pp.
           Includes translated selections from Medieval Writers.
           Reviews: Richard Luman, Spec, 43 (1968), 748-50.

1676   O'DONOVAN, PATRICK. "Becket, the Suspect Martyr." Critic,
         29 (1971), 28-36.

1677   PAIN, NESTA. The King and Becket. London: Eyre and
         Spottiswoode, 1964. 272 pp.
           Reviews: TLS (18 June, 1964), p. 526.

1678   PALMER, J[OHN] J[OSEPH] N[ORMAN]. England, France and
         Christendom, 1377-99. London: Routledge and Kegan Paul;
         *Chapel Hill: University of North Carolina Press, 1972.
         282 pp.
           Reviews: VQR, 49 (1973), xxxviii; TLS (21 July, 1972),
         p. 850.

1679   PEARSALL, DEREK A. and ELIZABETH SALTER. Landscapes and
         Seasons of the Medieval World. Toronto: University of
         Toronto Press, 1973. 267 pp., 66 illustrations.

1680   POUNDS, NORMAN J[OHN] G[REVILLE]. An Historical Geography
         of Europe, 450 B. C. - A. D. 1330. Cambridge University
         Press, 1973. 489 pp.
           See especially chapter 5, "Europe in The Early Four-
         teenth Century."
           Reviews: TLS (24 August, 1973), p. 975.

1681   QUELLER, DONALD E. The Office of the Ambassador in the
         Middle Ages. Princeton, New Jersey: Princeton Univer-
         sity Press, 1967. 264 pp.
           Reviews: Helene Wieruszowski, Spec, 44 (1969), 489-91;
         Giles Constable, AHR, 73 (1968), 1500-501; Marshall W.

Backgrounds

Baldwin, *Manuscripta*, 12 (1968), 109-110; Pierre Chaplais, *History*, 53 (1968), 403-404.

1682   RAFTIS, J. A., C. B. S. "Changes in an English Village after the Black Death." *MS*, 29 (1967), 158-77.

1683   ROBERTSON, D. W., JR. *Chaucer's London*. New York: John Wiley and Sons, 1968. 251 pp.
        Reviews: Richard H. Jones, *AHR*, 75 (1969), 107-108; May McKisack, *History*, 54 (1969), 267; *Giovanni Cherubini, *Archivio storico italiano*, 129 (1971), disp. 4, pp. 538-40; Martin M. Crow, *Spec*, 46 (1971), 539-42; R. M. Wilson, *YES*, 1 (1971), 216-18.

1684   RÖRIG, FRITZ. *The Medieval Town*. Translated by D. J. A. Matthew. Berkeley: University of California Press, 1967. 208 pp.
        Reviews: *TLS* (6 June, 1968), p. 573; J. K. Hyde, *EHR*, 84 (1969), 160-61; Edward Miller, *History*, 53 (1968), 400-401; *VQR*, 44 (1968), lxxvi.

1685   RUNCIMAN, STEVEN. "The Decline of the Crusading Ideal." *SewR*, 79 (1971), 498-513.

1686   RUSSELL, JEFFREY BURTON. *Witchcraft in the Middle Ages*. Ithaca; London: Cornell University Press, 1972. 403 pp.

1687   SANDQUIST, T. A. "The Holy Oil of St. Thomas Becket," in *Essays in Medieval History Presented to Bertie Wilkinson*. Edited by T. A. Sandquist and M. R. Powicke. Toronto: University of Toronto Press, 1969, pp. 330-44.

1688   SERRAILLIER, IAN. *Chaucer and His World*. London: Lutterworth Press, 1967; New York: Walck, 1968. 45 pp., 70 plates.

1689   SHREWSBURY, J[OHN] F[INDLAY] D[REW]. *A History of Bubonic Plague in the British Isles*. Cambridge, England: Cambridge University Press, 1970. 670 pp.
        Reviews: C. R. Young, *SAQ*, 70 (1971), 435-36.

1690   SMALLEY, BERYL. *The Becket Conflict and the Schools: A Study of Intellectuals in Politics in the Twelfth Century*. Oxford: Basil Blackwell; *Totowa, New Jersey: Rowman and Littlefield, 1973. 271 pp.
        Based on the Ford Lectures at Oxford, 1967. Concerns the Becket conflict; the use of Biblical allegorization for political purposes.
        Reviews: *TLS* (7 September, 1973), p. 1035.

BIBLIOGRAPHY OF CHAUCER, 1964 - 1973

General Backgrounds/Historical, Philosophic Backgrounds

1691   SMITH, SIR SYDNEY ARMITAGE. John of Gaunt. New York:
        Barnes & Noble, 1964. 518 pp., illustrated.
        New issue of 1904 edition.

1692   STEVENSON, LLOYD G. "The Black Death." Ventures, 5 (1965),
        36-40.

1693   STOREY, R. L. Chronology of the Medieval World, 800-1491:
        The Events of Six Centuries Year by Year. New York:
        David McKay, 1973. 717 pp.
          Primary reference work on political, economic, reli-
        gious, historical, artistic, literary developments in the
        Middle Ages.
          Reviews: TLS (16 February, 1973), p. 189.

1694   THIÉBAUX, MARCELLE. "The Medieval Chase." Spec, 42 (1967),
        260-74.
          References to the Tale of Gamelyn.

1695   TIERNEY, BRIAN and SIDNEY PAINTER. Western Europe in the
        Middle Ages, 300-1475. New York: Alfred A. Knopf,
        1970, 1974. 581 pp.
          Revision of Sidney Painter's History of the Middle Ages,
        1953. See Crawford, p. 106.

1696   TURNER, HILARY L. Town Defences in England and Wales: An
        Architectural and Documentary Study, A. D. 900-1500.
        London: John Baker; Hamden, Connecticut: Archon Books,
        1971. 246 pp., 24 plates.
          Reviews: John Beeler, Spec, 47 (1972), 814-16; TLS
        (18 June, 1971), p. 717.

1697   ULLMANN, WALTER. A History of Political Thought: The Middle
        Ages. Harmondsworth: Penguin Books, 1965; reprinted,
        1968; with revisions, 1970. 247 pp.

1698   URRY, WILLIAM G. Canterbury under the Angevin Kings. Uni-
        versity of London Historical Studies, 19. London: The
        Athlone Press, University of London; New York: Oxford
        University Press, 1967. 530 pp.
          Reviews: R. H. Rouse, Spec, 43 (1968), 751-53; *David
        Knowles, Tablet (9 September, 1967), p. 944; Economist
        (2 September, 1967), pp. 794-95; C. R. Young, AHR, 73
        (1968), 1498-99; TLS (25 April, 1968), p. 416; C. R.
        Cheney, MAE, 37 (1968), 229-31; *J. E. Sayers, JSA
        (October, 1968), 430.

Backgrounds

1699   *VAN AMEYDEN VAN DUYM, HIDDE H.   "Chaucer and the Low Countries."
       DAI, 31 (1971), 4137A-38A.   The University of Nebraska,
       1970.   203 pp.

1700   WEINBERG, JULIUS R.   A Short History of Medieval Philosophy.
       Princeton, New Jersey: Princeton University Press, 1964.
       304 pp.
          Reviews: W. S. Debenham, LJ (15 September, 1964),
       p. 3318; V. J. Bourke, Spec, 40 (1965), 373-74; J. F.
       Benton, AHR, 70 (1965), 841-42; TLS (14 January, 1965),
       p. 33; J. F. Ross, JP, 62 (1965), 229-39; Marion G. Fry,
       QQ, 72 (1965), 584-85; Richard Koehl, PPR, 26 (1966),
       613-14; E. A. Moody, PhR, 75 (1966), 407-409; *G. Leff,
       JTS (October, 1965), 532; J. F. Wippel, CHR, 52 (1966),
       448-49.

1701   WEISHEIPL, JAMES A., O. P.   "Curriculum of the Faculty of
       Arts at Oxford in the Early Fourteenth Century." MS, 26
       (1964), 143-85.

1702   WIERUSZOWSKI, HELENE.   The Medieval University: Masters,
       Students, Learning.   Princeton; London: Van Nostrand,
       Anvil Books, 1966.   207 pp.
          See pp. 155-62 on The University of Oxford.

1703   WILLIAMS, GWYN A.   Medieval London from Commune to Capital.
       University of London Historical Studies, 11.   London:
       University of London, Athlone Press; New York: Oxford
       University Press, 1963.   391 pp.
          Reviews: Martin Holmes, Listener, 69 (1963), 1084;
       TLS (28 June, 1963), p. 474; Martin Weinbaum, Spec, 39
       (1964), 372-73; Fritz Trautz, HZ, 198 (1964), 764-65.

1704   WINSTON, RICHARD.   Thomas Becket.   London: Constable, 1967.
          Reviews: Eleanor Duckett, MassR, 9 (1968), 800-802;
       Bernhard W. Scholz, Spec, 44, (1969), 330-32.

1705   WOLFFE, B[ERTRAM] P[ERCY].   The Royal Demesne in English
       History: The Crown Estate in the Governance of the Realm
       from Conquest to 1509.   Athens, Ohio: Ohio University
       Press, 1971.   324 pp.
          Reviews: Margaret Hastings, Spec, 49 (1974), 171-74.

1706   WOOD, CHARLES T.   The Age of Chivalry, Manners and Morals,
       1000-1450.   New York: Universe Books, 1970.   176 pp.
          Reviews: Norton Downs, Spec, 46 (1971), 412-13.

Literary and Aesthetic Backgrounds

1707   WRIGHT, JOHN KIRTLAND. The Geographical Lore of the Time of
        the Crusades. A Study in the History of Medieval Science
        and Tradition in Western Europe. Introduction by
        Clarence J. Glacken. New York: Dover; London:
        Constable, 1965.
            Originally published in 1925. See Griffith, p. 362.

1708   ZIEGLER, PHILIP. The Black Death. New York: The John Day
        Co.; *Harper & Row, 1971. 319 pp.

See also: 58, 232, 237, 249, 258, 273, 339, 694, 726, 734, 1159,
1327, 1385, 1844.

LITERARY AND AESTHETIC BACKGROUNDS

1709   ACKERMAN, ROBERT W. Backgrounds to Medieval English Litera-
        ture. New York: Random, 1966. 189 pp.
            General, undergraduate.

1710   ACKERMAN, ROBERT W. "Middle English Literature to 1400," in
        The Medieval Literature of Western Europe: A Review of
        Research. Edited by John H. Fisher. New York University
        Press for The Modern Language Association of America,
        1966, chapter 11, pp. 110-22 (on Chaucer).
            Chiefly twentieth century scholarship up to 1959.

1711   ALLEN, JUDSON BOYCE. The Friar as Critic: Literary Attitudes
        in the Later Middle Ages. Nashville, Tennessee:
        Vanderbilt University Press, 1971. 187 pp.
            Reviews: Bernhard Harder, Clio, 1 (1972), 95-99;
        Virginia Shea Noto, HSL, 4 (1972), 183-85; Robert Emmett
        Finnegan, Mosaic, 5 (1972), 185-89.

1712   ANDERSON, GEORGE K. The Legend of the Wandering Jew.
        Providence: Brown University Press, 1965. 489 pp.
            See especially pp. 31-32 on the Pardoner's Tale.

1713   ARMANDI, GABRIELE. "Il cinema come pretesto." FLett, 48:44
        (1972), 18.
            Review of Pasolini's Italian film version of the
        Canterbury Tales. See 2157 below.

1714   ASKEW, MELVIN W. "Courtly Love: Neurosis as Institution."
        Psychoanalytic Review, 52 (1965), 19-29. Abstr. in AES,
        9 (1966), no. 2004.

Backgrounds

1715   AUERBACH, ERICH. <u>Literary Language & its Public in the Late
        Latin Antiquity and in the Middle Ages</u>. Translated from
        German by Ralph Manheim. Bollingen Series, 74. New York:
        Pantheon Books; London: Routledge and Kegan Paul, 1965.
        405 pp.
            Reviews: Tony Stoneburner, <u>E-W</u>, 2 (1966), 193-97;
        M. Winterbottom, <u>History</u>, 51 (1966), 68-69.

1716   *BADESSA, RICHARD PAUL. "Literary Conventions of Courtly
        Love." <u>DA</u>, 28 (1968), 4114A. Indiana University, 1967.
        269 pp.
            Treats the <u>Book of the Duchess</u>.

1717   BAIRD, LORRAYNE YATES. "The Status of the Poet in the Middle
        Ages and the Problem of Anonymity." <u>DAI</u>, 30 (1970),
        3422A-23A. University of Kentucky, 1969. 240 pp.

1718   *BARON, F. XAVIER and JUDITH M. DAVIS. "<u>Amour Courtois</u>," The
        Medieval Ideal of Love: A Bibliography. Louisville:
        University of Louisville, 1973. 34 pp. Cited in <u>PMLAB</u>
        (1973), no. 1086.

1719   BAUGH, ALBERT C. "The Middle English Romance: Some Ques-
        tions of Creation, Presentation, and Preservation."
        <u>Spec</u>, 42 (1967), 1-31.

1720   *BENSON, CARL DAVID. "The Medieval English History of Troy."
        <u>DAI</u>, 31 (1971), 6539A. University of California,
        Berkeley, 1970. 258 pp.

1721   BETHURUM, DOROTHY, ed. <u>Critical Approaches to Medieval
        Literature</u>. New York: Columbia University Press, 1960.
        186 pp.
            See Crawford, pp. 18-19.
            Reviews: P. Mertens-Fonck, <u>MA</u> 70 (1964), 135-37.

1722   BLAICHER, GÜNTHER. "Über das Lachen im englischen
        Mittelalter." <u>DVLG</u>, 3 (1970), 508-29.

1722.01 BLAKE, N. F. "Late Medieval Prose," in 32, pp. 371-402.

1723   BLANCH, ROBERT J. "The Origins and Use of Medieval Color
        Symbolism." <u>IJSym</u>, 3 (1972), 1-5.
            Notes opposite symbolic values for primary colors and
        in the late Middle Ages, tints and secondary colors.

1724   BOLTON, W. F. "The Conditions of Literary Composition in
        Medieval England," Introduction in 32, pp. ix-xxxvii.

Literary and Aesthetic Backgrounds

1724.01*BOSSY, MICHEL-ANDRÉ RAOUL. "The Prowess of Debate: A Study
of a Literary Mode, 1100-1400." DAI, 31 (1971), 6540A-41A.
Yale University, 1970. 284 pp.

1725   BRAULT, GERARD J. Early Blazon: Heraldic Terminology in the
Twelfth and Thirteenth Centuries with Special Reference
to Arthurian Literature. Oxford, England: Clarendon
Press; New York: Oxford University Press, 1972. 327 pp.,
3 plates.
Reviews: M. A. Stones, Spec, 49 (1974), 319-20; TLS
(18 August, 1972), p. 966.

1726   *BRIANS, PAUL EDWARD. "Medieval Literary Parody." DA, 29
(1969), 4449A. Indiana University, 1968. 252 pp.
Includes "little-known anti-courtly love parodies" by
Chaucer and others.

1727   *BRODNAX, MARY MARGARET O'BRYAN. "Medieval Analogues of
Paradise Lost." DA, 29 (1969), 2667A. Texas Christian
University, 1968. 171 pp.

1728   *BRODY, SAUL NATHANIEL. "The Disease of the Soul: A Study in
the Moral Associations of Leprosy in Medieval Literature."
DAI, 32 (1971), 379A-80A. Columbia University, 1968.
218 pp.

1729   BROWN, DANIEL RUSSELL and WILLIAM N. HARLOWE. "Myth Criticism and Medieval Literature." BSUF, 11, iv (Autumn,
1970), 3-13.

1730   *BRUMBLE, HERBERT DAVID, III. "Genius and Other Related Allegorical Figures in the De Planctu Naturae, the Roman de
la Rose, the Confessio Amantis, and the Faerie Queene."
DAI, 31 (1971), 4113A. The University of Nebraska, 1970.
139 pp.

1730.01 BRUYNE, EDGAR DE. The Esthetics of the Middle Ages. Translated by E. B. Hennessy. New York: Ungar, 1969.
340 pp.
Reviews: F. J. Kovach, JHP, 8 (1970), 470; G. W. Olsen,
Thought, 44 (1969), 610-11; G. Boas, JAAC, 29 (1970),
131-32.

1730.02 CAENEGEM, R. C. VAN and F. L. GANSHOF. Kurze Quellenkunde
des Westeuropäischen Mittelalters: Eine typologische,
historische und bibliographische Einfürung. Göttingen,
Germany: Vandenhoeck & Ruprecht, 1964. 365 pp.
Reviews: Gray C. Boyce, Spec, 41 (1966), 188-89.

Backgrounds

1731   *CHAPIN, DIANA DERBY. "Metamorphosis as Punishment and Reward:
        Pagan and Christian Perspectives." DAI, 32 (1972), 6369A.
        Cornell University, 1971. 205 pp.

1732   CHYDENIUS, JOHAN. The Symbolism of Love in Medieval Thought.
        CHLSSF, 44:1. Helsinki: Helsingfors, 1970. 68 pp.

1733   COTTLE, BASIL. The Triumph of English, 1350-1400. History
        and Literature. New York: Barnes and Noble; *London:
        Blandford, 1969. 318 pp., 16 plates.
            Reviews: TLS (10 July, 1969), p. 762; A. Hudson, RES,
        22 (1971), 110-11.

1734   *COVO, JACQUELINE. The Lake of Darkness: Marine Imagery in
        Relation to Themes of Disruption in Medieval Poetry."
        DA, 28 (1967), 2205A. Brandeis University, 1967. 196 pp.

1735   DICKINS, BRUCE. "The Nine Unworthies," in Medieval Literature
        and Civilization: Studies in Memory of G. N. Garomsway.
        London: University of London, Athlone Press, 1969,
        pp. 228-32.

1736   DIEKSTRA, F. N. M. A Dialogue Between Reason and Adversity:
        A Late Middle English Version of Petrarch's De Remediius.
        New York: Humanities Press, 1968. 185 pp.
            Examines the influence of Petrarch in fourteenth-
        century England.
            Reviews: A. J. Bliss, SN, 41 (1969), 466-70; Donald
        McCluskey, GL, 10 (1970), 31-33; Anne Leyland, ES, 52
        (1971), 547-50; P. M. Vermeer, DQR, 1 (1971), 56-57.

1736.01 DONAHUE, CHARLES. "Patristic Exegesis in the Criticism of
        Medieval Literature," in 1679, pp. 61-82.
            See also 1791 below.

1736.02 DONALDSON, E. TALBOT. "Medieval Poetry and Medieval Sin,"
        in 39, pp. 164-74.

1737   DONALDSON, E. TALBOT. "The Myth of Courtly Love." Ventures,
        5 (1965), 16-23. Abstr. in AES, 9 (1966), no. 2139.
            Reprinted in 39, pp. 154-63.

1738   *DOOB, PENELOPE BILLINGS REED. "Ego Nabugodonosor: A Study
        of Conventions of Madness in Middle English Literature."
        DAI, 31 (1970), 1755A-56A. Stanford University, 1970.
        581 pp.
            Published, 1738.01 below.

BIBLIOGRAPHY OF CHAUCER, 1964 - 1973

Literary and Aesthetic Backgrounds

1738.01 DOOB, PENELOPE B. Nebachadnezzar's Children: Conventions of
Madness in Middle English Literature. New Haven: Yale
University Press, 1974. 264 pp.
Revised dissertation, 1738 above.

1739　DRONKE, PETER. Medieval Latin and the Rise of European Love-
Lyric. 2 vols. Oxford: Clarendon Press, 1965; second
edition, 1968. 626 pp.
See especially vol. 1: Problems and Interpretations.
Reviews: David Blamires, MLR, 62 (1967), 301-304.

1740　DRONKE, PETER. The Medieval Lyric. Modern Languages and
Literature. London: Hutchinson, 1968. 266 pp.
Reviews: Stephen Manning, Spec, 45 (1970), 125-27.

1741　DRONKE, PETER. Poetic Individuality in the Middle Ages: New
Departures in Poetry 1000-1150. Oxford: Clarendon Press,
1970. 244 pp.
Minimizes the importance of topoi.
Reviews: TLS (23 April, 1971), pp. 475-76; J. B.
Friedman, ELN, 9 (1972), 199-203; W. T. H. Jackson,
Spec, 47 (1972), 529-32.

1742　DUBOIS, MARGUERITE-MARIE. La littérature anglaise du moyen
âge, (500-1500). Paris: Presses universitaires, 1962.
174 pp.
Introductory study. Includes a chapter on Chaucer.
Reviews: A. C. Cawley, MLR, 59 (1964), 447-48;
D. S. Brewer, ES, 51 (1970), 59.

1743　ECONOMOU, GEORGE D. "The Character Genius in Alan de Lille,
Jean de Meun, and John Gower." ChauR, 4 (1970), 203-10.

1744　*ELLIOTT, THOMAS JOSEPH. "Complaint as a Middle English
Genre: A Survey of the Tradition Culminating in the
School of Piers Plowman." DAI, 31 (1971), 4116A. The
University of Michigan, 1970. 211 pp.

1745　EVANS, W. O. "'Cortaysye' in Middle English." MS, 29 (1967),
143-57.

1746　*EVARTS, PETER G. "Themes, Motifs, and Formulae in the Tail-
Rhyme Romances." DAI, 32 (1972), 6372A-73A. Wayne State
University, 1969. 367 pp.

1747　FISHER, JOHN H. John Gower: Moral Philosopher and Friend of
Chaucer. New York University Press, 1964; London:
Methuen, 1965. 387 pp.

Backgrounds

Reviews: Martin M. Crow, Spec, 43 (1968), 146-50; John Lawlor, CritQ, 8 (1966), 187.

1748   FLEMING, JOHN V. The Roman de la Rose: A Study in Allegory and Iconography. Princeton, New Jersey: Princeton University Press, 1969. 272 pp.
        Reviews: Alfred David, ELN, 9 (1971), 134-39; Alan M. F. Gunn, MP, 69 (1971), 57-59; William Calin, Spec, 47 (1972), 311-13.

1749   FLETCHER, ANGUS. Allegory: The Theory of a Symbolic Mode. Ithaca, New York: Cornell University Press, 1964. 430 pp.
        Reviews: Harold Bloom, YR, 54 (1964), 143-49; Manfred Mackenzie, EIC, 14 (1964), 397-401; TLS (10 June, 1965), pp. 465-66; W. H. Halewood, JEGP, 64 (1965), 712-14; Terence Hawkes, RN, 18 (1965), 340-42; Geoffrey Bullough, ELN, 4 (1966), 157-60; Russell Fraser, MLR, 62 (1967), 298-99; A. P. Frank, MP, 64 (1967), 382-84; W. D. Matthews, RPh, 20 (1967), 557-63; J. D. Peacock, RES, 18 (1967), 100-101; R. Hollander, SoQ, 4 (1968), 756-62; G. MacG., Personalist, 47 (1966), 139.

1750   FRIEDMAN, JOHN BLOCK. "Eurydice, Heurodis, and the Noon-Day Demon." Spec, 41 (1966), 22-29.

1751   FRIEDMAN, JOHN BLOCK. Orpheus in the Middle Ages. Cambridge, Massachusetts: Harvard University Press; *London: Oxford University Press, 1970. 263 pp.
        Reviews: Michael Masi, Cithara, 10 (1971), 105-108; AmRecG, 38 (1972), 230-32.

1752   GALLO, ERNEST. The Poetria Nova and its Sources in Early Rhetorical Doctrine. De Proprietatibus litterarum, Series Maior, 10. The Hague, Paris: Mouton, 1971. 241 pp.
        Text, translation, and commentary.
        Reviews: James J. Murphy, Spec, 49 (1974), 116-18; Traugott Lawler, Spec, 48 (1973), 750-54.

1753   GATTO, LOUIS C. "The Blood Theology of Medieval English Literature." SMC, 2 (1966), 84-92.
        See note on the Pardoner's relics, p. 91.

1754   GIAMATTI, A. BARTLETT. The Earthly Paradise and the Renaissance Epic. Princeton, New Jersey: Princeton University Press, 1966. 374 pp.
        Reviews: Bernard F. Huppé, Spec, 42 (1967), 527-29; Frances Yates, NYRB (23 February, 1967), pp. 26-28;

Literary and Aesthetic Backgrounds

G. R. Hibbard, N&Q, 15 (1968), 115–16; John L. Lievsay, CLS, 4 (1968), 331–34; Alan Bullock, RenQ, 20 (1967), 31–35; B. Rajan, MLR, 64 (1969), 125–26; Louise George Clubb, RPh, 22 (1969), 650–54; Michael N. Nagler, CL, 21 (1969), 377–79; L. M. Ferrari, Italica, 44 (1967), 368–71; J. C. Garrett, AUMLA, 29 (1968), 82–83; A. A., Personalist, 50 (1969), 416–17.

1755   GLUNZ, HANS H. Die Literarästhetik des europäischen Mittelalters: Wolfram-Rosenroman-Chaucer-Dante. Second edition. Frankfurt: Klostermann, 1963. 623 pp., plates.
        Originally published in 1937. See especially Part III. "Ars Rhetorica."
        Reviews: Marianne Wynn, MLR, 59 (1964), 152–53.

1756   GOLDIN, FREDERICK. The Mirror of Narcissus in the Courtly Love Lyric. Ithaca, New York: Cornell University Press, 1967. 286 pp.
        Reviews: Louise Vinge, RPh, 22 (1969), 574–81; Stephen Manning, Spec, 44 (1969), 181–82.

1757   GRADON, PAMELA. Form and Style in Early English Literature. London: Methuen, 1971, 1973. 408 pp.
        Reviews: J. J. Anderson, CritQ, 15 (1973), 186–87.

1757.01*GRAEFFE, LOTTE BURCHARDT. "The Child in Medieval Literature from 1200 to 1400." DA, 29 (1968), 869A. The University of Florida, 1965. 223 pp.
        The child in romances, ballads, saints' lives, and in Chaucer.

1758   GRANSDEN, ANTONIA. "Realistic Observation in Twelfth-Century England." Spec, 47 (1972), 29–51.

1758.01 GRAY, DOUGLAS. "Later Poetry: The Courtly Tradition," in 32, pp. 312–70.

1759   GREEN, D. H. "Irony and the Medieval Romance." FMLS, 6 (1970), 49–64.

1760   *GREENFIELD, CONCETTA CARESTIA. "Studies in Fourteenth and Fifteenth Century Poetics." DAI, 32 (1971), 5183A–84A. University of North Carolina at Chapel Hill, 1971. 296 pp.

1761   GRIMM, REINHOLD R. "Die Paradiesesehe: Eine erotische Utopie des Mittelalters," in Getempert und gemischet für

Backgrounds

Wolfgang Mohr zum 65. Geburtstag vom seinen Tübinger
Schülern. GAG, 65. Hrsg. von Franz Hundsnurscher und
Ulrich Müller. Göppingen: Kümmerle, 1972, pp. 1-25.

1761.01 GROS LOUIS, KENNETH R. R. "Robert Henryson's Orpheus and
Eurydice and the Orpheus Traditions of The Middle Ages."
Spec, 41 (1966), 643-55.

1762   HAKUTANI, YOSHINOBA. "The Doctrine of Courtesy in Certain
Medieval Writings." Discourse, 13 (1970), 259-74.

1763   *HALLMUNDSSON, MAY N. "A Collection of Materials for a Study
of the Literary Scene at the End of the 14th Century."
DAI, 31 (1971), 4120A. New York University, 1970. 144 pp.

1764   *HAMMIL, CARRIE ESTHER. "The Celestial Journey and the Harmony
of the Spheres in English Literature, 1300-1700." DAI,
33 (1972), 2326A. Texas Christian University, 1972.
226 pp.
Treats the dream of Scipio.

1765   *HANSON-SMITH, ELIZABETH ANN. "Be Fruitful and Multiply: The
Medieval Allegory of Nature." DAI, 33 (1972), 2892A.
Stanford University, 1972. 416 pp.

1766   HARMS, WOLFGANG. Homo viator in bivio: Studien zur
Bildlichkeit des Weges. MAE, 21. München: Fink, 1970.
320 pp.

1767   HATTON, THOMAS J. "Nature as Poet: Alanus de Insulis' The
Complaint of Nature and the Medieval Concept of Artistic
Creation." Lang&S, 2 (1969), 85-91.

1768   HEITMANN, KLAUS. "Orpheus im Mittelalter." AKG, 45 (1963),
253-94.

1769   HELLMAN, ROBERT and RICHARD O'GORMAN. Fabliaux: Ribald Tales
from the Old French. New York: Thomas Y. Crowell, 1965.
201 pp.
Reviews: Francis Lee Utley, Spec, 42 (1967), 533-35.

1770   *HELMING, VERNON PARKER. "Medieval Pilgrimages and English
Literature to A. D. 1400." DAI, 31 (1970), 2826A. Yale
University, 1937. 817 pp.

1771   HOLLAND, WILLIAM E. "Formulaic Diction and the Descent of a
Middle English Romance." Spec, 48 (1973), 89-109.

BIBLIOGRAPHY OF CHAUCER, 1964 - 1973

Literary and Aesthetic Backgrounds

1772   HOWARD, DONALD R[OY]. "Medieval Poems and Medieval Society."
       M&H, n.s. 3 (1972), 99-115.

1773   HOWARD, DONALD R. The Three Temptations: Medieval Man in
       Search of the World. Princeton, New Jersey: Princeton
       University Press; *Oxford University Press, 1966. 328 pp.
          Reviews: R. M. Wilson, Eng, 16 (1966), 106-107; John
       Gardner, JEGP, 66 (1967), 249-54; Traugott F. Lawler,
       MLJ, 51 (1967), 225-27; R. T. Davies, RES, 18 (1967),
       236-37; S. M. Jeremy Finnegan, MP, 65 (1967), 60-62;
       Robert Kellogg, SAQ, 66 (1967), 117-18; Douglas Gray,
       N&Q, 15 (1968), 150-51.

1774   JACKSON, W[ILLIAM] T[HOMAS] H[OBDELL]. "Allegory and Alle-
       gorization." RS, 32 (1964), 161-75.

1775   JACKSON, W. T. H. Medieval Literature: A History and a
       Guide. New York: Macmillan; London: Collier-Macmillan,
       1966. 287 pp.
          Reviews: Sister M. Patricia Forrest, DrCrit, 9 (1966),
       163.

1776   JACOBS, NICOLAS. "Alliterative Storms: A Topos in Middle
       English." Spec, 47 (1972), 695-719.

1777   *JANKOFSKY, KLAUS. Darstellungen von Tod und Sterben in
       Mittelenglischer Zeit: Untersuchung literarischer Texte
       und historische Quellen. Berlin: Selbstverl., 1970;
       Duluth: University of Minnesota Book Stores, 1970.
       294 pp. Dissertation, Universitat des Saarlandes. Cited
       in PMLAB (1971), no. 2009.

1778   JAUSS, HANS-ROBERT. "Allegorese, Remythisierung und neuer
       Mythos: Bemerkungen zur christlichen Gefangenschaft der
       Mythologie im Mittelalter," in Terror und Spiel: Probleme
       der Mythenrezeption. Hrsg. von Manfred Fuhrmann.
       München: Fink, 1971, pp. 187-209.

1779   *JEFFREY, DAVID LYLE. "Franciscan Spirituality and Popular
       Middle English Poetry." DAI, 30 (1969), 1138A. Prince-
       ton University, 1968. 504 pp.

1780   *KAMINSKA, ALEXANDRA BARBARA. "Literary Confessions from 1215
       through 1550: Development in Theme and Form of French,
       German, and English Confessions from the Fourth Lateran
       Council through the Reformation." DAI, 33 (1972), 2332A.
       University of Maryland, 1972. 218 pp.

Backgrounds

1781   KELLY, DOUGLAS. "Theory of Composition in Medieval Narrative
        Poetry and Geoffrey of Vinsauf's Poetria Nova." MS, 31
        (1969), 117-48.

1782   KELLY, HENRY ANSGAR. "The Metamorphoses of the Eden Serpent
        During the Middle Ages and Renaissance." Viator, 2
        (1971), 301-28.

1783   KER, W[ILLIAM] P[ATON]. Medieval English Literature. New
        Impression with bibliographical notes by Pamela Gradon.
        London: Oxford University Press, 1969. 143 pp.
          Originally published in 1912, reprinted in 1962. See
        Griffith, p. 67.

1783.01 KOZIOL, HERBERT. "Bemerkungen zu einigen mittelenglischen
        Erziehungslehren." NM, 73 (1972), 162-71.

1784   KOZIOL, HERBERT. "Zu kritischen und satirischen Äusserungen
        über Kleidung in der älteren englischen Literatur," in
        Literatur-Kultur-Gesellschaft in England und Amerika:
        Aspekte und Forschungsbeiträge. Hrsg. von Gerhard
        Müller-Schwefe und Konrad Tuzinski. Friedrich Schubel
        zum 60. Geburtstag. Frankfurt: Diesterweg, 1966,
        pp. 145-56.

1785   LADNER, GERHART B. "Homo Viator: Mediaeval Ideas on Aliena-
        tion and Order." Spec, 42 (1967), 233-59.
          On pilgrimage topoi and traditions.

1786   *LAMPE, DAVID ELWOOD. "Middle English Debate Poems: A Genre
        Study." DAI, 30 (1970), 3910A-11A. The University of
        Nebraska, 1969. 164 pp.

1787   *LEO, DIANA THOMAS. "The Concept of the Hero in the Middle
        English Verse Romances." DAI, 31 (1971), 6558A. Uni-
        versity of Pittsburgh, 1970. 297 pp.

1788   LEWIS, C[LIVE] S[TAPLES]. Studies in Medieval and Renais-
        sance Literature. Collected by Walter Hooper. Cambridge,
        England: Cambridge University Press, 1966. 205 pp.
          Chapter 3, "Imagination and Thought in the Middle Ages,"
        is reprinted in 58, pp. 46-66.
          Reviews: Douglas Bush, CE, 28 (1966), 254-55; Graham
        Hough, Listener, 76 (1966), 245-47; TLS (14 July, 1966),
        p. 616; R. M. Wilson, Eng, 16 (1966), 106-107; John
        Burrow, EIC, 17 (1967), 89-95; Jean-Pierre Barricelli,
        IQ, 10 (1967), 102-105; John Mulryan, Cithara, 7 (1968),
        76-77; Dieter Mehl, Archiv, 205 (1969), 68-70.

Literary and Aesthetic Backgrounds

1789   LOUIS, KENNETH R. R. GROS.   See 1761.01.

1790   *LURIA, MAXWELL SIDNEY. "The Christian Tempest: A Symbolic
          Motif in Medieval Literature." DA, 26 (1966), 5439.
          Princeton University, 1965. 335 pp.

1791   MALINA, MARILYN. "A Note on Charles Donahue's Account of the
          Exegetical Tradition." AnM, 12 (1971), 126-29.
             See 1679, pp. 61-82, for Donahue's article, "Patristic
          Exegesis in the Criticism of Medieval Literature," or see
          1736.01.

1792   MANN, NICHOLAS. "Petrarch's Role in Humanism." Apollo, 94,
          i (September, 1971), 176-83.

1792.01 MATHEW, GERVASE. "Marriage and Amor Courtois in Late Four-
          teenth-Century England," in 58, pp. 104-11. Reprinted
          from Essays Presented to Charles Williams. Oxford Uni-
          versity Press, 1947, pp. 128-35.

1793   MATTHEWS, WILLIAM, ed. Medieval Secular Literature: Four
          Essays. California University Center for Medieval and
          Renaissance Studies. Contributions, 1. Berkeley:
          University of California Press; London: Cambridge Uni-
          versity Press, 1965. 97 pp.
             Reviews: June Hall Martin, CL, 18 (1966), 186-89;
          D. D. R. Owen, FMLS, 2 (1966), 281-86; R. T. Davies, MLR,
          62 (1967), 693-94; Patricia M. Gathercole, RR, 59 (1968),
          41; Lionel J. Friedman, RPh, 23 (1970), 349-51.

1794   McALINDON, T. "Comedy and Terror in Middle English Litera-
          ture: The Diabolical Game." MLR, 60 (1965), 323-32.
          Abstr. in AES, 9 (1966), no. 1757.

1795   *McMASTER, HELEN NEILL. "The Legend of St. Cecilia in Middle
          English Literature." DAI, 31 (1970), 2350A. Yale Uni-
          versity, 1936. 264 pp.

1796   *MEANS, MICHAEL HUGH. "The Consolatio Genre in Middle English
          Literature." DA, 29 (1968), 875A. The University of
          Florida, 1963. 167 pp.

1797   MOORE, ARTHUR K[EISTER]. Contestable Concepts of Literary
          Theory. Baton Rouge: Louisiana State University Press,
          1973. 241 pp.

1798   MOORE, ARTHUR K. "Medieval English Literature and the
          Question of Unity." MP, 65 (1968), 285-300. Abstr. in
          AES, 12 (1969), no. 951.

Backgrounds

1799   MOORMAN, CHARLES. A Knyght There Was: The Evolution of the
        Knight in Literature. Lexington: University of Kentucky
        Press, 1967. 178 pp.
          Reviews: William Matthews, Spec, 43 (1968), 525-27.

1800   MÜLLER, ULRICH. "Ovid 'Amores' - alba, tageliet: Typ und
        Gegentyp des 'Tageliedes' in der Liebesdichtung der Antike
        und des Mittelalters." DVLG, 45 (1971), 451-80.

1801   MURPHY, JAMES J[EROME]. Medieval Rhetoric: A Select Bibliog-
        raphy. Toronto Medieval Bibliographies, 3. Toronto:
        University of Toronto Press, 1971. 116 pp.
          Reviews: John Conley, M&H, n.s., 4 (1973), 189-93.

1802   MURPHY, JAMES J. "Rhetoric in Fourteenth-Century Oxford."
        MAE, 34 (1965), 1-20.

1803   MURPHY, JAMES J., ed. Three Medieval Rhetorical Arts.
        Berkeley: University of California Press, 1971. 258 pp.
          Reviews: Beryl Rowland, AN&Q, 10 (1972), 77-78; John
        Conley, M&H, n.s., 4 (1973), 189-93.

1804   MUSTANOJA, TAUNO F. "The Suggestive Use of Christian Names
        in Middle English Poetry," in 55, pp. 51-76.

1805   NEWMAN, F. X., ed. The Meaning of Courtly Love. Papers of
        the First Annual Conference of the Center for Medieval
        and Early Renaissance Studies, March 17-18, 1967. Albany,
        New York: State University of New York Press, 1968.
        112 pp.
          Reviews: Charles Muscatine, Spec, 46 (1971), 747-50;
        R. M. Wilson, YES, 1 (1971), 216-18; Constance S. Wright,
        ELN, 9 (1972), 203-205; Joan M. Ferrante, RR, 63 (1972),
        42-43.

1806   NIMS, MARGARET F., ed. and trans. Poetria Nova of Geoffrey
        of Vinsauf. Toronto: Pontifical Institute of Mediaeval
        Studies, 1967. 110 pp.
          Reviews: SCN, 25 (1968), 84; Herbert Grabes, Ang, 87
        (1969), 449-51.

1807   *NOLL, DOLORES LOUISE. "The Love Universe in Late-Medieval
        English and Scottish Allegorical Love Poetry." DAI, 30
        (1969), 2493A. University of Kentucky, 1965. 335 pp.

1808   *OWEN, TREVOR ALLEN. "Julius Caesar in English Literature
        from Chaucer through the Renaissance." DA, 27 (1967),
        3847A. University of Minnesota, 1966. 368 pp.

BIBLIOGRAPHY OF CHAUCER, 1964 - 1973

Literary and Aesthetic Backgrounds

1809 *PAULL, MICHAEL RAY. "The Figure of Mahomet in Middle English
Literature." DAI, 30 (1970), 3915A-16A. University of
North Carolina at Chapel Hill, 1969. 268 pp.

1810 *PAYEN, M. Les Origines de la courtoise dans la littérature
Française médiévale. Littérature du Moyen Age. Paris:
Centre de Documentation Universitaire, 1966. 2 vols.
Cited in Spec, 41 (1966), 789.

1811 PEARSALL, DEREK. "The Development of Middle English Romance."
MS, 27 (1965), 91-116.

1812 PERELLA, NICHOLAS JAMES. The Kiss, Sacred and Profane: An
Interpretative History of Kiss Symbolism and Related
Religio-Erotic Themes. Berkeley and Los Angeles: Univer-
sity of California Press, 1969. 356 pp.
    Reviews: George Fenwick Jones, Spec, 45 (1970), 682-84;
A. J. Smith, RenQ, 23 (1970), 279-82; John V. Fleming,
Italica, 48 (1971), 497-99; Lionel J. Friedman, MLQ, 33
(1972), 181-83.

1813 *PETTY, GEORGE RAYMOND, JR. "Middle English Topical Poetry:
A Catalog and Survey." DA, 28 (1967), 1083A. New York
University, 1967. 536 pp.

1814 *PICHASKE, DAVID RICHARD. "The Reynardian Tradition in Medieval and Renaissance English Literature." DAI, 30
(1970), 3953A. Ohio University, 1969. 205 pp.

1815 *PICKREL, PAUL MURPHY. "Religious Allegory in Medieval England: An Introductory Study Based on the Vernacular
Sermon Before 1250." DA, 25 (1964), 3557. Yale University, 1944. 156 pp.

1816 PIEHLER, PAUL. The Visionary Landscape: A Study in Medieval
Allegory. London: Edward Arnold; Montreal: McGill-
Queen's University Press, 1971. 178 pp.
    A psychological approach.
    Reviews: A. C. Cawley, ELN, 10 (1972), 142-44; Sheila
Delany, WCR, 6 (1972), 79-81; Kenneth A. Bleeth, Spec,
47 (1972), 138-41.

1817 *PLUMMER, JOHN FRANCIS, III. "The Continental Love Song Tradition and a Critical Theory for Middle English Love
Lyrics." DAI, 32 (1972), 5197A. Washington University,
1971. 213 pp.

Backgrounds

1818   RABY, F. J. E.   "Nuda Natura and Twelfth-Century Cosmology."
        Spec, 43 (1968), 72-77.

1819   REISS, EDMUND.   "Number Symbolism and Medieval Literature."
        M&H, n.s., 1 (1970), 161-74.

1820   REVARD, CARTER.   "The Lecher, the Legal Eagle, and the Papelard
        Priest: Middle English Confessional Satires in MS. Harley
        2253 and Elsewhere," in 46, pp. 54-71.

1821   ROBBINS, ROSSELL HOPE.   "Middle English Misunderstood:
        Mr. Speirs and the Goblins." Ang, 85 (1967), 270-81.
            Analyzes methods of John Speirs in Chaucer the Maker
        (Crawford, p. 28; Griffith, p. 77).

1822   RICHMOND, VELMA BOURGEOIS.   Laments for the Dead in Medieval
        Narrative. Duquesne Studies, Philological Series, 8.
        Pittsburgh, Pennsylvania: Duquesne University Press,
        1966. 199 pp.
            Reviews: M. Alexiou, MLR, 64 (1969), 376; M. W.
        Bloomfield, Spec, 43 (1968), 535.

1823   RICKARD, PETER, ALAN DEYERMOND, DEREK BREWER, DAVID BLAMIRIS,
        PETER KING and MICHAEL LAPRIDGE, translators, with an
        afterword by Derek Brewer. Medieval Comic Tales.
        Totowa, New Jersey: Rowman and Littlefield, 1973.   171 pp.
            Reviews: Meg Twycross, "Bawdy Snatchers," TLS
        (13 December, 1974), p. 1407.

1824   RUMBLE, THOMAS C.   The Breton Lays in Middle English.   Detroit:
        Wayne State University Press, 1965.   299 pp.
            Anthology with introduction.   Includes Franklin's Tale,
        pp. 229-59; bibliography, pp. 268-69.
            Reviews: Brinley Rhys, SewR, 75 (1967), 337-45; Roger
        Sherman Loomis, Spec, 41 (1966), 366-68.

1825   RUSSELL, JEFFREY B.   "Courtly Love as Religious Dissent."
        CHR, 51 (1965), 31-44.

1826   RYDING, WILLIAM W.   Structure in Medieval Narrative.   De
        proprietatibus litterarum, Series Maior, 12.   The Hague
        and Paris: Mouton, 1971.   177 pp.
            Reviews: Morton W. Bloomfield, Spec, 48 (1973), 584-87.

1827   SACHS, ARIEH.   "Religious Despair in Mediaeval Literature and
        Art." MS, 26 (1964), 231-56.

BIBLIOGRAPHY OF CHAUCER, 1964 - 1973

Literary and Aesthetic Backgrounds

1828   SALTER, ELIZABETH. "Medieval Poetry and the Figural View of Reality" (Sir Israel Gollancz Memorial Lecture, British Academy, 54 1968) from Proceedings of the British Academy, 44. London: Oxford University Press, 1970, 30 pp. (pp. 73-92).
Reviews: Stella Brook, YES, 2 (1972), 234-35.

1829   SANDS, DONALD B. "Reynard the Fox as Pícaro and Reinaerts Historie as Picaresque Fiction." JNT, 1 (1971), 137-45.

1830   SCAGLIONE, ALDO D. Nature and Love in the Late Middle Ages. Berkeley and Los Angeles: University of California Press, 1963. 260 pp.
See Crawford, p. 111.
Reviews: Charles Witke, Spec, 40 (1965), 545-47; Gray C. Boyce, RN, 17 (1964), 210-11; Glauco Cambon, MLQ, 25 (1964), 493-94; Richard H. Green, MLN, 79 (1964), 58-70; Louise G. Clubb, RPh, 18 (1965), 362-65; J. M. Ferrante, RR, 56 (1965), 59-60; Elio Gianturco, CL, 17 (1965), 367; Charles S. Singleton, "The Uses of the Decamerone," MLN, 79 (1964), 71-76.

1831   CANCELLED

1832   SCHLAUCH, MARGARET. "Realism and Convention in Medieval Literature." KN, 11 (1964), 3-12.

1833   SCHLAUCH, MARGARET. "Rhetorical Doctrine and Some Aspects of Medieval Narrative." KN, 18 (1971), 353-64.

1834   SCHMITT, CHARLES B. "Theophrastus in the Middle Ages." Viator, 2 (1971), 251-70.

1835   SCHOECK, R. J. "On Rhetoric in Fourteenth-Century Oxford." MS, 30 (1968), 214-25.

1836   *SCHREIBER, EARL GEORGE. "The Figure of Venus in Late Middle English Poetry." DAI, 31 (1970), 767A. University of Illinois, 1969. 154 pp.

1837   SHEPHERD, GEOFFREY. The Nature of Alliterative Poetry in Late Medieval England. Sir Israel Gollancz Memorial Lecture. Proceedings of the British Academy, 56. London and New York: Oxford University Press, 1971. 22 pp.

1837.01*SIMMONS, WILLIAM ARTHUR. "Prologue to a Criticism of Medieval Literature." DAI, 32 (1972), 5201A. Duke University, 1971. 150 pp.

205

Backgrounds

> Uses Cassirer's Philosophy of Symbolic Forms as point
> of departure. See chapter 4 on Troilus and Criseyde.

1838   *SINCLAIR, LEON RUSSELL, JR. "The Evidence for an Aesthetic
        Theory in Fourteenth-Century Vernacular Poetry." DAI,
        31 (1970), 1772A-73A. University of Washington, 1970.
        201 pp.

1838.01 SPEARING, A. C. "The Art of Poetry," in his Criticism and
        Medieval Poetry, 363 above, chapter 3, pp. 51-75.

1838.02 STEADMAN, JOHN M. "'Courtly Love' as a Problem of Style,"
        in 43, pp. 1-33.

1839   STEVENS, JOHN. Medieval Romance: Themes and Approaches.
        New York: Hilary House; London: Hutchinson, 1973.
        255 pp.

1840   STEWART, STANLEY. The Enclosed Garden: The Tradition and
        the Image in Seventeenth-Century Poetry. Madison,
        Milwaukee, Wisconsin; London: University of Wisconsin
        Press, 1966. 240 pp.
            Reviews: Margaret Carpenter, JEGP, 66 (1967), 141-43;
        P. G. Stanford, SCN, 25 (1967), 30-31; R. Wilcher, MLR,
        63 (1968), 188-89; Rosemary Freeman, RES, 18 (1967),
        467-68; Vivian de Sola Pinto, RenQ, 20 (1967), 66-68;
        Harold Toliver, MP, 65 (1968), 383-84; E. A. Newcomb,
        Criticism, 10 (1968), 88-90; H. M. Richmond, CL, 22
        (1970), 81-85.

1840.01 THOSS, DAGMAR. Studien zum locus amoenus im Mittelalter.
        Wiener Romanistische Arbeiten, 10. Vienna, Stuttgart:
        Wilhelm Braunmüller, 1972. 199 leaves.
            Vienna dissertation.

1841   TOBIN, FRANK. "Concupiscentia and Courtly Love." RomN,
        14 (1972), 387-93.

1842   TUVE, ROSEMOND. Allegorical Imagery: Some Mediaeval Books
        and Their Posterity. Princeton, New Jersey: Princeton
        University Press; London: Oxford University Press, 1966.
        461 pp.
            Reviews: TLS (8 September, 1966), p. 827; Graham
        Hough, Listener, 76 (1966), 245-47; R. M. Wilson, Eng,
        15 (1966), 106-107; John Burrow, EIC, 17 (1967), 89-95;
        R. E. Kaske, Spec, 42 (1967), 196-99; William H. Halewood,
        JAAC, 26 (1967), 267-68; Angus Fletcher, YR, 56 (1967),
        453-57; William Matthews, RenQ, 20 (1967), 345-47;

Literary and Aesthetic Backgrounds

J. A. W. Bennett, ELN, 5 (1967), 52-57; Urban T. Holmes,
Manuscripta, 11 (1967), 55-56; Don Cameron Allen, JEGP,
66 (1967), 118-20; Richard A. Green, CL, 19 (1967), 83-86;
O. B. Hardison, CLS, 4 (1967), 327-29; J. Norton-Smith,
RES, 18 (1967), 305-308; John M. Steadman, MLQ, 29 (1968),
99-105; Chauncey Wood, ShakS, 4 (1969), 439-43.

1843   TWYCROSS, MEG. The Medieval Anadyomene: A Study in Chaucer's
        Mythography. Medium Aevum Monographs, n.s., 1.   Oxford:
        Basil Blackwell, for the Society for the Study of Medi-
        eval Languages and Literature, 1972. 119 pp.
        Iconographic and mythographic traditions of Venus.

1844   VAN CAENEGEM, R. C. and F. L. GANSHOF. See 1730.02, for
        Library of Congress listing of Van Caenegem's name.

1845   VINAVER, EUGÈNE. "From Epic to Romance." BJRL, 46 (1964),
        476-503.

1846   VINAVER, EUGÈNE. The Rise of Romance. Oxford: Clarendon
        Press, 1971. 168 pp., 14 plates.
           Reviews: R. T. Davies, RES, 23 (1972), 463-66;
        Morton W. Bloomfield, Spec, 48 (1973), 584-87.

1847   VINGE, LOUISE. The Narcissus Theme in Western European
        Literature up to the Early 19th Century. Translated
        by Robert Dewsnap and Nigel Reeves. Lund: Gleerups,
        1967. 463 pp.
           Reviews: Stephen Manning, Spec, 44 (1969), 181-82;
        J. Donovan, MLR, 63 (1968), 924-25; Dietrich Briesemeister,
        Archiv, 205 (1968), 202-204; Bruce Harbert, MAE, 37 (1968),
        341-44; R. O. Jones, BHS, 45 (1968), 254-55; R. M.
        Ogilvie, RES, 19 (1968), 215-17; G. S. Rousseau, CJ, 64
        (1968), 76-77; Jean Seznec, FS, 23 (1969), 49-51;
        Roswitha Wisniewski, JEGP, 68 (1969), 471-72; PQ, 47
        (1968), 350; Emmanuel Hatzantonis, CL, 21 (1969), 181-83;
        Leo Weinstein, CLS, 7 (1970), 128-31; *M. Beller, OL, 24
        (1972), 315; Alfred Foulet, RR, 61 (1970), 45-50;
        F. Goldin, RPh, 23 (1969), 220; J. C. Van Meurs, ES, 50
        (1969), 614-18; *J. Barthels, RLV, 36 (1970), 553.

1848   WENZEL, SIEGFRIED. "The Pilgrimage of Life as a Late Medi-
        eval Genre." MS, 35 (1973), 370-88.

1849   WHITE, BEATRICE. "Medieval Beasts." E&S, 18 (1965), 34-44.

1849.01 WHITE, BEATRICE. "Poet and Peasant," in 1638.01, pp. 58-74.

Backgrounds

1850   *WHITEBOOK, BUDD BERGOVOY. "Individuals: Eccentricity and
            Inwardness in English and French Romance, 1170-1400."
            DAI, 32 (1971), 3275A-76A. Yale University, 1971.
            323 pp.

1851   WHITING, BARTLETT JERE with the collaboration of HELEN
            WESCOTT WHITING. Proverbs, Sentences, and Proverbial
            Phrases from English Writings Mainly Before 1500.
            Cambridge, Massachusetts: Harvard University Press; The
            Belknap Press, 1968. 784 pp.
              Reviews: Albert C. Friend, Spec, 44 (1969), 674-76;
            TLS (24 July, 1969), p. 794; A. C. Baugh, JEGP, 68 (1969),
            688-89; P. W. Rogers, QQ, 76 (1969), 361-62; E. G. Stanley,
            N&Q, 17 (1970), 187-88; Norman Davis, MAE, 41 (1972),
            164-68; Helmut Gneuss, Ang, 88 (1970), 529-31; A. G. Rigg,
            RES, 22 (1971), 326-33.

1852   WILLIAMS, ARNOLD. "Medieval Allegory: an Operational
            Approach." PMMLA, 1 (1969), 77-84.

1852.01 WILLIAMS, D. J. "Alliterative Poetry in the Fourteenth and
            Fifteenth Centuries," in 32, pp. 107-58.

1853   WILSON, R[ICHARD] M[IDDLEWOOD]. The Lost Literature of Medi-
            eval England. Second edition. New York: Cooper Square,
            1969; London: Methuen, 1970. 286 pp.
              Originally published in 1952. See Griffith, p. 98.
              Reviews: J. R. Simon, EA, 25 (1972), 48-49; E. G.
            Stanley, N&Q, 19 (1972), 282.

1853.01 WOOLF, ROSEMARY. "Later Poetry: The Popular Tradition," in
            32, pp. 263-311.

1854   WOLPERS, THEODOR. Die englische Heiligenlegende des
            Mittelalters: Eine Formgeschichte des Legendenerzählens
            von der spätantiken lateinischen Tradition bis zur Mitte
            des 16. Jahrhunderts. Buchreihe der Anglia, 10.
            Tübingen: Niemeyer, 1964. 485 pp.
              Survey of saints' legends in England.
              Reviews: Erwin Mayer, MAE, 35 (1966), 266-69; Charlotte
            D'Evelyn, Spec, 42 (1967), 213-17.

1855   *ZACHER, CHRISTIAN KEELER. "Curiositas and the Impulses for
            Pilgrimage in Fourteenth-Century English Literature."
            DAI, 30 (1970), 4429A. University of California,
            Riverside, 1969. 223 pp.

Social Backgrounds

See also: 32, 164, 173, 182, 248, 254, 255, 257, 274, 351, 363, 366, 374, 388, 645, 858, 1025, 1152, 1247, 1411, 1536, 1588.

SOCIAL BACKGROUNDS

See Griffith, pp. 330–42; Crawford, pp. 110–12.

Bibliographic Sources

1856   SOCIAL SCIENCES AND HUMANITIES INDEX (Formerly International
        Index). Edited by J. Doris Dart. New York: The
        H. W. Wilson Company. Vols. 19-, 1966-.

1856.01 SOCIAL SCIENCES CITATION INDEX. Philadelphia, Pennsylvania:
        Institute for Scientific Information, 1971-.

Studies

1857   AULT, WARREN O. "The Village Church and the Village Commu-
        nity in Medieval England." Spec, 45 (1970), 197–215.

1858   BARBER, RICHARD. The Knight and Chivalry. London:
        Longmans, Green; New York: Scribner's, 1970. 393 pp.
        Reviews: *Vincent Cronin, BW (27 December, 1970),
        p. 3; Williell R. Thomson, WHR, 25 (1971), 363–65.

1859   BARON, SALO WITTMAYER. A Social and Religious History of the
        Jews: Late Middle Ages and Era of European Expansion,
        (1200–1650). 15 vols. Second edition. New York and
        London: Columbia University Press; Philadelphia, Penn-
        sylvania: Jewish Publication Society of America, 1967.
        Originally published in 1952. See Vol. XI: Citizen
        or Alien Conjurer; XII: Economic Catalyst.

1860   BEAN, J. M. W. "'Bachelor' and Retainer." M&H, n.s. 3
        (1972), 117–31.
        Treats the bachelors of John of Gaunt.

1861   BELLAMY, JOHN. Crime and Public Order in England in the
        Later Middle Ages. Studies in Social History. London:
        Routledge & Kegan Paul; Toronto: University of Toronto
        Press, 1973. 236 pp.
        Reviews: TLS (15 June, 1973), p. 668.

209

Backgrounds

1862   BENNETT, H[ENRY] S[TANLEY]. Life on the English Manor.
        Second edition. Cambridge, England: Cambridge Univer-
        sity Press, 1967. 364 pp.
        Originally published in 1937.

1863   BROOKE-LITTLE, JOHN. Knights of the Middle Ages: Their
        Armour and Coats of Arms. London: Hugh Evelyn, 1966.
        32 pp., 12 color plates.
        See especially V. "John of Gaunt."

1864   DELORT, ROBERT. Life in the Middle Ages. Translated by
        Robert Allen. Lausanne, Switzerland: Edita, 1971, 1973.
        345 pp., illustrated.
        Survey of classes of medieval society, domestic peasant
        life and servitude, warrior aristocrats, public health,
        daily life, the village church.
        Reviews: D. Douglas, TLS (1 November, 1974), p. 1237.

1865   DU BOULAY, F. R. H. The Lordship of Canterbury: an Essay on
        Mediaeval Society. New York: Barnes and Noble; London:
        Nelson, 1966. 432 pp., 4 plates.
        Reviews: Michael M. Sheehan, Spec, 44 (1969), 277-80;
        B. F. Harvey, EHR, 83 (1968), 337-38; Edward Miller,
        History, 52 (1967), 316-17; Harold J. Grimm, RenQ, 21
        (1968), 72-73; J. R. L. Highfield, MAE, 37 (1968), 111-12;
        G. R. C. Davis, HistT, 17 (1967), 135-36; Hermann Jakobs,
        HZ, 208 (1969), 204-205; R. H. Hilton, EconHistR, 20
        (1967), 161-63.

1866   ENGLISH RURAL LIFE IN THE MIDDLE AGES. Bodleian Picture Book,
        14. Oxford, England: Bodleian Library, 1965. 10 pp.,
        illustrated.

1867   GREEN, THOMAS A. "Societal Concepts of Criminal Liability
        for Homicide in Mediaeval England." Spec, 47 (1972),
        669-94.

1868   HASTINGS, MARGARET. Medieval European Society, 1000-1450.
        New York: Random House, 1971.
        General introductory study.

1869   HEERS, JACQUES. L'Occident aux XIVe et XVe siècles: Aspects
        économique et sociaux. 2e édition. Nouvelle Clio:
        L'Histoire et ses problèmes, 23. Paris: Presses
        Universitaires de France, 1963. 408 pp., 11 maps.
        See Crawford, p. 114.

Social Backgrounds

Reviews: Richard D. Face, Spec, 39 (1964), 536-37;
Ralph E. Giesey, AHR, 69 (1964), 503-504.

1870 HODGETT, GERALD A. J. A Social and Economic History of
Medieval Europe. London: Methuen, 1972. 246 pp.
Reviews: TLS (6 April, 1973), p. 401; David Herlihy,
Spec, 50 (1975), 129.

1871 HOWARD, DONALD R. "Medieval Poems and Medieval Society."
M&H, n.s. 3, (1972), 99-131.

1872 JONES, W. R. "Image of the Barbarian in Medieval Europe."
CSSH, 13 (1971), 376-407.

1873 MATHEW, GERVASE. "The International Court Culture," in 1666,
pp. 284-90.

1874 MEAD, W[ILLIAM] E[DWARD]. The English Medieval Feast. Second
edition. London: Allen and Unwin, 1967. 272 pp.
Reviews: Maryellen Hains, AbFS, 6 (1968), 42.

1875 PUGH, RALPH B[ERNARD]. Imprisonment in Medieval England.
Cambridge, England, and New York: Cambridge University
Press, 1968. 434 pp., 6 plates.
Reviews: Donald W. Sutherland, Spec, 45 (1970), 157-59;
*D. Bethell, Tablet (5 July, 1969), p. 667; Michael
Borrie, Spect (27 December, 1968), pp. 913-14; G. D. G.
Hall, MAE, 39 (1970), 73-74.

1876 ROSEN, GEORGE. "The Mentally Ill and the Community in Western and Central Europe During the Late Middle Ages and
the Renaissance." JHM, 19 (1964), 377-88.

1877 ROSENTHAL, JOEL T[HOMAS]. The Purchase of Paradise: Gift
Giving and the Aristocracy, 1307-1485. Studies in Social
History. London: Routledge & Kegan Paul; Toronto:
University of Toronto Press, 1972. 183 pp., 14 tables,
1 map.
Reviews: J. R. Lander, Spec, 49 (1974), 754-58; TLS
(1 September, 1972), p. 1018.

1878 RUSSELL, JOSIAH C. "Effects of Pestilence and Plague, 1315-
1385." CSSH, 8 (1966), 464-83.
With a reply by Sylvia L. Thrupp.

1879 RUSSELL, J. C. "Recent Advances in Mediaeval Demography."
Spec, 40 (1965), 84-101.

Backgrounds

1880   SCHELP, HANSPETER. "Nurture: Ein mittelenglischer
            Statusbegriff." Ang, 83 (1965), 253-70.

1881   SCHLAUCH, MARGARET. English Medieval Literature and its
            Social Foundations. London: Oxford University Press,
            1967. 380 pp.
              Originally published in 1956. See Crawford, p. 27.
              Reviews: Rossell Hope Robbins, Archiv, 205 (1969),
            489-94.

1882   SHEEHAN, MICHAEL M. "The Formation and Stability of Marriage
            in Fourteenth-Century England: Evidence of an Ely
            Register." MS, 33 (1971), 228-63.

1883   TAYLOR, DUNCAN. Living in England: Chaucer's England.
            London; New York: Roy, 1968. 248 pp.
              Originally published in 1959. General, popular intro-
            duction on domestic affairs.

1884   THRUPP, SYLVIA L[ETTICE], ed. Change in Medieval Society:
            Europe North of the Alps, 1050-1500. New York: Appleton-
            Century-Crofts, 1964. 336 pp.
              See especially S. Guerchberg, "The Controversy over the
            Alleged Sowers of the Black Death in the Contemporary
            Treatises on Plague." pp. 208-24.
              Reviews: TLS (19 August, 1965), p. 721.

1885   TITOW, J. Z. English Rural Society, 1200-1350. Historical
            Problems: Studies and Documents, 4. London: George
            Allen and Unwin; New York: Barnes and Noble, 1969.
            217 pp.
              Includes translations of twenty documents.
              Reviews: J. A. Raftis, Spec, 45 (1970), 330-32.

1886   WHITMORE, SISTER MARY ERNESTINE. Medieval English Domestic
            Life and Amusements in the Works of Chaucer. New York:
            Cooper Square, 1972. 290 pp.
              Catholic University of America dissertation, originally
            published in 1937.

See also: 254, 695, 740, 1646, 1772.

ECONOMIC BACKGROUNDS

See Griffith, pp. 343-45; Crawford, pp. 113-15.

1887   AULT, W[ARREN] O[RTMAN]. Open-Field Farming in Medieval
        England: A Study of Village By-Laws. London: George
        Allen and Unwin; New York: Barnes and Noble, 1972.
        183 pp.

1888   BRIDBURY, A. R. "The Black Death." EconHistR, 26 (1973),
        577-92.

1889   DUBY, G[EORGES]. "The Agrarian Life of the Middle Ages."
        EconHistR, 21 (1968), 159-65.
          Review of The Cambridge Economic History of Europe, I.
        See 1903 below.

1890   *DUBY, GEORGES. L'économie rurale et la vie des campagnes
        dans l'occident médiévale (France, Angleterre Empire,
        IXe - XVe siècles). Essai de synthèse et perspectives
        de recherches. Paris: Aubier-Éditions Montaigne, 1962.
        2 vols., 822 pp.
          Reviews: John H. Mundy, Spec, 39 (1964), 313-16;
        Robert Sabatino Lopez, Spec, 39 (1964), 503-505.

1890.01 DUBY, GEORGES. Rural Economy and Country Life in the
        Medieval West. Translated by Cynthia Postan. Columbia:
        University of South Carolina Press, 1968. 615 pp.,
        illustrated.

1891   HYAMS, PAUL R. "The Origins of a Peasant Land Market in
        England." EconHistR, 23 (1970), 18-31.

1892   JAMES, MARGERY KIRKBRIDE. Studies in the Medieval Wine Trade.
        Edited by Elspeth M. Veale. Oxford: Clarendon Press;
        *New York: Oxford University Press, 1971. 249 pp.
          Reviews: Sylvia L. Thrupp, Spec, 48 (1973), 369-70;
        TLS (11 February, 1972), p. 165.

1893   JONES, P. J. "Economic Organization and Policies in the
        Middle Ages." EconHistR, 17 (1965), 570-78.
          Review of The Cambridge Economic History of Europe,
        III. See 1904 below.

Backgrounds

1894   LLOYD, T. H. The Movement of Wool Prices in Medieval England.
        The Economic History Review Supplements, 6. London and
        New York: Cambridge University Press, for the Economic
        History Society, 1973. 81 pp.
           Reviews: TLS (18 May, 1973), p. 561.

1895   LOPEZ, ROBERT S[ABATINO]. The Commercial Revolution of the
        Middle Ages, 950-1350. The Economic Civilization of
        Europe. Englewood Cliffs, New Jersey: Prentice Hall,
        1971. 188 pp.
           Reviews: Richard D. Face, Spec, 48 (1973), 381-83.

1896   LYON, BRYCE and A. E. VERHULST. Medieval Finance: A Com-
        parison of Financial Institutions in Northwestern
        Europe. Providence, Rhode Island: Brown University
        Press, 1967. 100 pp.
           Reviews: Raymond De Roover, AHR, 73 (1968), 1493;
        Thomas N. Bisson, Spec, 43 (1968), 740-43.

1897   CANCELLED

1898   MISKIMIN, HARRY A. The Economy of Early Renaissance Europe
        1300-1460. Englewood Cliffs, New Jersey: Prentice-Hall,
        1969. 189 pp.
           Reviews: Sylvia L. Thrupp, Spec, 46 (1971), 174-75.

1899   NORTH, DOUGLASS C. and ROBERT PAUL THOMAS. "Rise and Fall of
        the Manorial System: a Theoretical Model." JEconHist,
        31 (1971), 771-803.

1900   OSCHINSKY, DOROTHEA. Walter of Henley and Other Treatises on
        Estate Management and Accounting. Oxford: Clarendon
        Press, 1971. 528 pp.
           Reviews: J. A. Raftis, Spec, 48 (1973), 174-76.

1901   PLATT, COLIN. The Monastic Grange in Medieval England: A
        Reassessment. New York: Fordham University Press, 1969.
        272 pp.
           Emphasis on Cistercians.

1902   CANCELLED

1903   POSTAN, M[ICHAEL] M[OISSEY], ed. The Agrarian Life of the
        Middle Ages. Second edition. Cambridge Economic History
        of Europe, I. London and New York: Cambridge University
        Press, 1966. 887 pp.
           Reviews: see 1889 above.

1904 POSTAN, M. M., et al, eds. Economic Organization and
Policies in the Middle Ages. Cambridge Economic History
of Europe, III. London and New York: Cambridge University Press, 1963. 709 pp.
  See Crawford, p. 115.
  Reviews: Robert Sabatino Lopez, Spec, 39 (1964),
503-506; see 1893 above.

1905 POSTAN, M. M. Essays on Medieval Agriculture and General
Problems of the Medieval Economy. Cambridge University
Press, 1973. 302 pp.

1906 POSTAN, M. M. "Investment in Medieval Agriculture."
JEconHist, 27 (1967), 576-87.

1907 POSTAN, M. M. The Medieval Economy and Society: An Economic
History of Britain in the Middle Ages. London:
Weidenfeld and Nicolson; Baltimore: Penguin Books, 1972.
269 pp.

1908 POSTAN, M. M. Medieval Trade and Finance. Cambridge,
England: Cambridge University Press, 1973. 388 pp.

1909 CANCELLED

1910 SALZMAN, L[OUIS] F[RANCIS]. English Industries of the Middle
Ages. London: Pordes, 1964.
  Originally published in 1923. See Griffith, p. 345.

1911 SALZMAN, L. F. English Trade in the Middle Ages. London:
Pordes, 1964. 58 pp.
  Originally published in 1931. See Griffith, p. 345.

1912 SLICHER VAN BATH, B. H. The Agrarian History of Western
Europe, A. D. 500-1850. Translated by Olive Ordish.
London: Edward Arnold; *New York: St. Martin's Press,
1963. 373 pp.
  Reviews: John T. Schlebecker, AHR, 70 (1964), 116-17;
*K. L. A., Agriculture, 70 (1963), 552; TLS (16 January,
1964), p. 44; Eric Kerridge, History, 50 (1965), 138-39;
Folke Dovring, JEconHist, 25 (1965), .295-97; David
Herlihy, CHR, 52 (1966), 403.

1913 SLICHER VAN BATH, B. H. Yield Ratios, 810-1820. A. A. G.
Bijdragen, 10. Wageningen, Netherlands: Afdeling
Agrarische Geschiedenis Landbouwhogeschool, 1963. 264 pp.
  Reviews: Bryce Lyon, Spec, 41 (1966), 187-88; Eric
Kerridge, History, 50 (1965), 138-39.

Backgrounds

1914   SMITH, R[EGINALD] A[NTHONY] L[ENDON]. Canterbury Cathedral
        Priory: A Study in Monastic Administration. Cambridge
        Studies in Economic History. Cambridge, England and New
        York: Cambridge University Press, 1969. 237 pp.
            The economic aspects of medieval monasticism.
            Reviews: *U. Dirlmeier, Erasmus, 23 (1972), 113.

1915   TITOW, J. Z. Winchester Yields: A Study in Medieval Agri-
        cultural Productivity. Cambridge, England and New York:
        Cambridge University Press, 1972. 159 pp.
            Reviews: J. A. Raftis, Spec, 50 (1975), 158-59; TLS
        (14 July, 1972), p. 822.

1916   UNWIN, GEORGE. The Gilds and Companies of London. Fourth
        edition, with a new introduction by William F. Kahl.
        New York: Barnes & Noble, 1964. 447 pp.
            First published in 1908.
            Reviews: *P. W. Filby, LJ (10 October, 1964), p. 3733;
        Brian Spencer, Listener, 72 (2 July, 1964), pp. 26-28.

1917   VEALE, ELSPETH M. The English Fur Trade in the Later Middle
        Ages. Oxford, England: Clarendon Press; *New York:
        Oxford University Press, 1966. 263 pp.
            Reviews: Alice Beardwood, Spec, 42 (1967), 764-65;
        R. H. Hilton, N&Q, 14 (1967), 72-73; Howard L. Adelson,
        Manuscripta, 11 (1967), 170-72; Sylvia L. Thrupp, AHR,
        72 (1967), 1372-73; T. S. Willan, History, 52 (1967),
        192-93; J. L. Bolton, EconHistR, 20 (1967), 163-64.

                    RELIGIOUS BACKGROUNDS

            See Griffith, pp. 346-55; Crawford, pp. 116-19

1918   ASTON, MARGARET. Thomas Arundel: A Study of Church Life in
        the Reign of Richard II. Oxford: Clarendon Press; New
        York: Oxford University Press, 1967. 470 pp., 17 plates.
            Reviews: B. Wilkinson, Spec, 43 (1968), 688-89; John
        Fines, HistT, 17 (1967), 565-66; TLS (20 July, 1967),
        p. 641; J. F. A. Mason, N&Q, 15 (1968), 306-307; F. R. H.
        DuBoulay, EHR, 84 (1969), 115-16; J. J. N. Palmer,
        History, 53 (1968), 84-85; *M. Deanesly, CQR, 168 (1968),
        114; Kathleen Major, JEH, 19 (1968), 247-48; *H. S.
        Offler, JTS, 19 (1968), 358.

1919 BARRACLOUGH, GEOFFREY. The Medieval Papacy. New York:
Harcourt, Brace and World, 1968. 216 pp., illustrated.
Reviews: James A. Brundage, Spec, 45 (1970), 115-16.

1920 *BEALE, WALTER HENRY, III. "The Medieval Topic of Active and
Contemplative Life." DAI, 32 (1972), 6365A-66A. The
University of Michigan, 1971. 274 pp.

1921 BENSON, ROBERT L[OUIS]. The Bishop-Elect: A Study in
Medieval Ecclesiastical Office. Princeton, New Jersey:
Princeton University Press, 1968. 447 pp.
Reviews: Peter Herde, Spec, 45 (1970), 455-57; Charles
R. Young, SAQ, 68 (1969), 437; Richard E. Sullivan,
Manuscripta, 15 (1971), 36-38.

1922 BOYD, BEVERLY [MARY]. Chaucer and the Liturgy. Philadelphia:
Dorrance, 1967. 95 pp.
For reviews, see 174.

1923 BOWERS, R. H. "A Middle-English Anti-Mendicant Squib." ELN,
1 (1964), 163-64.

1924 BRAUDE, PEARL F. "'Cokkel in oure Clene Corn': Some Implications of Cain's Sacrifice." Gesta, 7 (1968), 15-28.

1925 BRAUNFELS, WOLFGANG. Monasteries of Western Europe: The
Architecture of the Orders. Princeton, New Jersey:
Princeton University Press, 1969; London: Thames and
Hudson, 1972. 263 pp.
See especially chapter 8, "The English Cathedral Mon-
asteries."

1926 BROOKE, CHRISTOPHER. Medieval Church and Society: Collected
Essays. London: Sidgwick & Jackson; *New York: New
York University Press, 1971. 256 pp., 4 plates.
See especially, pp. 121-38, "Thomas Becket."

1927 CAMERON, KENNETH WALTER. The Pardoner and His Pardons.
Hartford, Connecticut: Transcendental Books, 1965.
80 pp.
Includes texts of indulgences circulating in England
on the eve of the Reformation.

1928 CAPLAN, HARRY. "The Four Senses of Scriptural Interpretation
and the Mediaeval Theory of Preaching," in his Of
Eloquence: Studies in Ancient and Mediaeval Rhetoric.
Edited by Anne King and Helen North. Ithaca and London:
Cornell University Press, 1970, pp. 93-104.
Reprinted from Spec, 4 (1929), 282-90.

Backgrounds

1929   *CHYDENIUS, JOHAN. Medieval Institutions and the Old Testa-
          ment. Societas Scientiarum Fennica, Commentationes
          Humanarum Litterarum, 37, 2. Helsinki: Helsingfors,
          1965. 140 pp. Cited in Spec, 46 (1971), 413.
             Reviews: K. F. Morrison, Spec, 41 (1966), 731-32.

1930   *COLEMAN, JANET. "Sublimes et Litterati: The Audience for
          the Themes of Grace, Justification and Predestination,
          Traced from the Disputes of the 14th Century Moderni to
          the Vernacular Piers Plowman. DAI, 32 (1971), 382A.
          Yale University, 1970. 231 pp.

1931   DALY, LOWRIE J[OHN], S. J. Benedictine Monasticism, Its
          Formation and Development Through the 12th Century. New
          York: Sheed and Ward, 1965. 390 pp.

1932   DIETER, OTTO A. "Arbor Picta: The Medieval Tree of
          Preaching." QJS, 51 (1965), 123-44.

1933   DOMONKOS, L[ESLIE] S[TEVE] and R. J. SCHNEIDER, eds. Studium
          Generale. Studies offered to Astrik L. Gabriel by his
          former students at the Mediaeval Institute, University of
          Notre Dame, on the occasion of his election as an Honorary
          Doctor of the Ambrosiana in Milan. Texts and Studies in
          the History of Mediaeval Education, 11. Notre Dame,
          Indiana: The Mediaeval Institute, University of Notre
          Dame, 1967. 284 pp.
             See especially Bernard A. Grendreau, "The Unity of the
          Mediaeval Intellectual Attitude," pp. 55-107.

1934   ERB, PETER C. "Vernacular Material for Preaching in MS
          Cambridge University Library Ii. III. 8." MS, 33
          (1971), 63-84.

1935   FUNKENSTEIN, AMOS. "Basic Types of Christian Anti-Jewish
          Polemics in the Later Middle Ages." Viator, 2 (1972),
          373-82.

1936   HAIR, PAUL, ed. Before the Bawdy Court: Selections from
          church court and other records relating to the correction
          of moral offences in England, Scotland and New England,
          1300-1800. London: Elek; *New York: Barnes & Noble,
          1972. 271 pp.
             Includes 600 extracts dealing with cases involving
          sexual misdemeanors.
             Reviews: TLS (5 January, 1973), p. 22.

Religious Backgrounds

1937   HALE, J[OHN] R[IGBY], J. R[OGER] L. HIGHFIELD and B[ERYL]
       SMALLEY, eds. Europe in the Late Middle Ages. Evanston,
       Illinois: Northwestern University Press, 1965. 521 pp.
         See especially essays by B. Smalley and E. F. Jacob.
         Reviews: George Holmes, Listener (14 October, 1965),
       p. 592; *David Knowles, Tablet (9 October, 1965), p. 1120;
       TLS (7 October, 1965), p. 901; *K. B. McFarlane, NSt
       (10 June, 1966), p. 849; A. R. Myers, HistT, 16 (1966),
       67-68; Gaines Post, AHR, 71 (1966), 1314-15; Economist
       (15 January, 1966), p. 208; Denys Hay, EHR, 82 (1967),
       117-19; A. R. Myers, History, 51 (1966), 212; *QR, 304
       (1966), 99.

1938   HALL, D[ONALD] J[OHN]. English Mediaeval Pilgrimage. London:
       Routledge and Kegan Paul, 1965; *Bath, England: Cedric
       Chivers, 1973. 246 pp., illustrated.
         See chapter 6, "Saint Thomas Becket of Canterbury,"
       pp. 130-65.
         Reviews: TLS (12 May, 1966), p. 408.

1939   HEATH, PETER. The English Parish Clergy on the Eve of the
       Reformation. Studies in Social History. London:
       Routledge & Kegan Paul; Toronto: University of Toronto
       Press, 1969. 262 pp.
         Reviews: J. W. McKenna, Spec, 46 (1971), 517-18.

1940   HELL, VERA and HELLMUT HELL. The Great Pilgrimage of the
       Middle Ages: The Road to St. James of Compostela.
       Translated from the German by Alisa Jaffa, with Intro-
       duction by Sir Thomas Kendrick. London: Barrie and
       Rockliff, 1966. 275 pp., illustrated.

1940.01 HILL, ROSALIND. "'A Chaunterie for Soules': London
       Chanteries in the Reign of Richard II," in 1638.01,
       pp. 242-55.

1941   HUSSEY, MAURICE. "The Church," in 258, chapter 3, pp. 56-88.

1942   *JAMES, MAX HUBERT. "Pre-Chaucerian and Chaucerian Concern
       with Providence: The Question of Providence Examined in
       Representative Theologians and Poets Before Chaucer and
       as a Major Preoccupation in Chaucer's Poetry." DA, 29
       (1968), 604A. Claremont Graduate School and University
       Center, 1967. 355 pp.

1943   JONES, W. R. "Saints in Service: the Political and Cultural
       Implications of Medieval Hagiolatry." Cithara, 10 (1970),
       33-44.

Backgrounds

1944   KARLEN, ARNO. "The Homosexual Heresy." ChauR, 6 (1971),
        44-63.

1945   *KELLY, THOMAS DANIEL. "Medieval Poems of the Cross and
        Crucifixion." DA, 28 (1968), 5020A. Princeton Univer-
        sity, 1967. 257 pp.

1946   KNOWLES, DAVID. Christian Monasticism. New York: McGraw-
        Hill, 1969. 253 pp.

1947   KNOWLES, DAVID, FATHER. The Episcopal Colleagues of
        Archbishop Thomas Becket; being the Ford Lectures
        delivered in The University of Oxford in Hilary term,
        1949. Cambridge, England: Cambridge University Press,
        1970. 190 pp.

1948   KNOWLES, DAVID. From Pachomius to Ignatius: A Study in the
        Constitutional History of the Religious Orders. Oxford:
        Clarendon Press, 1966. 105 pp.

1949   KNOWLES, DAVID with DIMITRI OBOLENSKY. The Middle Ages. The
        Christian Centuries, 2. New York: McGraw-Hill, 1968.
        551 pp., and 72 pp. of plates.
          Reviews: Anselm G. Biggs, O. S. B., Spec, 46 (1971),
        160-62.

1950   *KONRAD, ROBERT. "Das himmlische und das irdische Jerusalem
        im mittelalterlichen Denken: mystische Vorslettung und
        geschichtliche Wirkung," in Speculum Historiale:
        Geschichte im Spiegel von Geschichtsschreibung und
        Geschichtsdeutung. Johannes Spörl aus Anlass seines
        sechzigsten Geburtstages dargebracht von Weggenossen,
        Freunden und Schülern. Freiburg, München: Karl Alber,
        1965, pp. 523-40. Cited in PMLAB (1967), no. 4652.

1951   LAMPE, G[EOFREY] W[ILLIAM] H[UGO], ed. The West from the
        Fathers to the Reformation. The Cambridge History of the
        Bible, II. Cambridge, England; New York: Cambridge
        University Press, 1969. 575 pp.
          Reviews: James S. Preus, Spec, 45 (1970), 307-308;
        Joseph F. Kelly, Thought, 45 (1970), 630-32.

1952   LEA, HENRY CHARLES. The Inquisition of the Middle Ages: Its
        Organization and Operation. An abridgement by Margaret
        Nicholson. New York: The MacMillan Company, 1961; *New
        York: Harper and Row, 1969. 920 pp.
          Based on the three volume Inquisition of the Middle
        Ages, 1955.

1953   LEFF, GORDON. Heresy in the Later Middle Ages: The Relation
       of Heterodoxy to Dissent c. 1250-c. 1450. New York:
       Barnes and Noble, *Manchester University Press, 1967.
       2 vols., 414 pp.; 407 pp.
          Reviews: Paul P. Bernard, AHR, 74 (1968), 140-41;
       H. S. Offler, EHR, 84 (1969), 572-76; Richard Harrington,
       JHP, 8 (1970), 205-11; James Crompton, MAE, 38 (1969),
       99-107; *D. L. Douie, Tablet (6 January, 1968), p. 11;
       TLS (25 January, 1968), p. 84; Albert C. Shannon, CHR,
       56 (1970), 356-58.

1954   LERNER, ROBERT E. The Heresy of the Free Spirit in the Later
       Middle Ages. Berkeley: University of California Press,
       1972. 272 pp.
          Reviews: Eleanor L. McLaughlin, Spec, 49 (1974),
       747-51; TLS (27 October, 1972), p. 1295.

1955   LOGAN, F. DONALD. Excommunication and the Secular Arm in
       Medieval England: A Study in Legal Procedure from the
       Thirteenth to the Sixteenth Century. Studies and Texts,
       15. Toronto: Pontifical Institute of Mediaeval Studies,
       1968. 239 pp.
          Reviews: Donald W. Sutherland, Spec, 45 (1970),
       145-47.

1956   *MARSHALL, ROBERT DOYLE. "Dogmatic Formalism to Practical
       Humanism: Changing Attitudes Towards the Passion of
       Christ in Medieval English Literature." DA, 25 (1965),
       5910. The University of Wisconsin, 1965. 258 pp.

1957   MOORMAN, JOHN [RICHARD HUMPIDGE]. A History of the Fran-
       ciscan Order from its Origins to the Year 1517. Oxford:
       Clarendon Press; New York: Oxford University Press,
       1968. 654 pp.
          Reviews: Lester K. Little, AHR, 74 (1969), 1269-71;
       J. H. L. Highfield, MAE, 38 (1969), 336-38; Fr. Geldon
       Gal, Cithara, 8 (1969), 66-68.

1957.01 MURPHY, JOHN C., O. F. M. "The Early Franciscan Studium at
       the University of Paris," in 1933, pp. 159-203.

1958   OWST, G[ERALD] R[OBERT]. Literature and Pulpit in Medieval
       England. Second edition. Oxford: Blackwell; New York:
       Barnes and Noble, 1961. 614 pp.
          See Crawford, p. 118.
          Reviews: Leonard Boyle, O. P., MAE, 33 (1964), 227-30.

Backgrounds

1959   PFAFF, R. W. New Liturgical Feasts in Later Medieval England.
        Oxford, England: Clarendon Press; New York: Oxford
        University Press, 1970. 161 pp.
            Reviews: Massey H. Shepherd, Jr., Spec, 46 (1971),
        750-51; Joseph Crehan, S. J., MAE, 40 (1971), 311-12.

1960   POWER, EILEEN. Medieval English Nunneries c. 1275 to 1535.
        New York; London: Hafner, 1964.
            New issue of the 1922 edition. See Griffith, p. 352.

1961   REICHER, REV. ROBERT A. "A Study of Medieval Anti-Semitism."
        BaratR, 2 (1967), 27-31.

1962   ROTH, REV. FRANCIS [XAVIER], O. S. A. The English Austin
        Friars, 1249-1538. Cassiciacum, Studies in St. Augustine
        and the Augustinian Order, 6, American Series. New York:
        Augustinian Historical Institute, 1966. Vol. I: History.
        673 pp.
            Published jointly with Augustiniana, vols. 8-16
        (1958-66). See Crawford, p. 119.
            Reviews: William A. Hinnebusch, O. P., Spec, 43 (1968),
        537-39.

1963   RUSSELL, JEFFREY BURTON. Dissent and Reform in the Early
        Middle Ages. Publications of the Center for Medieval and
        Renaissance Studies, 1. Berkeley and Los Angeles: Uni-
        versity of California Press, 1965. 323 pp.
            Reviews: Richard E. Sullivan, Spec, 42 (1967), 187-89;
        Marshall W. Baldwin, AHR, 71 (1966), 1305-306; *David
        Knowles, Tablet (25 June, 1966), p. 729; Walter L.
        Wakefield, CH, 35 (1966), 365; H. E. J. Cowdrey, History,
        52 (1967), 67-68; Gordon Leff, MAE, 36 (1967), 100-101;
        *C. N. L. Brooke, JTS, 18 (1967), 256; *CQR, 167 (1966),
        536.

1964   RUSSELL, JEFFREY B., ed. Religious Dissent in the Middle
        Ages. Major Issues in History. New York, London,
        Sydney, Toronto: John Wiley & Sons; *Ithaca, New York:
        Cornell University Press, 1971. 172 pp.

1965   RUSSELL, JEFFREY BURTON. Witchcraft in the Middle Ages.
        Cornell University Press, 1972. 403 pp.
            Reviews: Lawrence F. Barman, Manuscripta, 17 (1973),
        38-40; Richard Cavendish, Folklore, 83 (1972), 345-46.

1966   SMALLEY, BERYL. The Study of the Bible in the Middle Ages.
        Notre Dame: University of Notre Dame Press, 1964.
        428 pp.

Reprint of the 1952 second edition. See Griffith,
p. 353.
Reviews: N&Q, 11 (1964), 322.

1967   SNYDER, SUSAN. "The Left Hand of God: Despair in Medieval
        and Renaissance Tradition." SRen, 12 (1965), 18-59.

1968   SOUTHERN, R[ICHARD] W[ILLIAM]. Western Society and the Church
        in the Middle Ages. The Pelican History of the Church,
        2. Harmondsworth and Baltimore: Penguin, 1970. 376 pp.

1969   TIERNEY, BRIAN. Origins of Papal Infallibility, 1150-1350:
        A Study on the Concepts of Infallibility, Sovereignty
        and Tradition in the Middle Ages. Studies in the History
        of Christian Thought, 6. Leiden: E. J. Brill, 1972.
        306 pp.
        Reviews: TLS (6 October, 1972), p. 1201.

1970   TUBACH, FREDERIC C. Index Exemplorum: A Handbook of Medieval
        Religious Tales. FF Communications 86, 204. Helsinki:
        Suomalainen Tiedeakatemia, Academia Scientiarum Fennica,
        1969. 530 pp.
        Includes Chaucerian tale sources.
        Reviews: Francis Lee Utley, Spec, 47 (1972), 557-61;
        *Fabula, 12 (1973), 289; Reino Virtanen, SFQ, 35 (1971),
        361-62; John Gage Allee, JAF, 85 (1972), 276-78.

1971   WAKEFIELD, WALTER L[EGGETT] and AUSTIN P. EVANS, eds. and
        transs. Heresies of the High Middle Ages. Records of
        Civilization, Sources and Studies, 81. New York and
        London: Columbia University Press, 1969. 879 pp.
        Reviews: Marjorie Reeves, MAE, 39 (1970), 232-35; VQR,
        46 (1970), lxxi; Aaron W. Godfrey, Lit Arts, 39 (1971),
        78-80; *R. L. Jones, JSA, 4 (1971), 254; Jeffrey Burton
        Russell, Spec, 45 (1970), 333-35.

1972   WENZEL, SIEGFRIED. "The Seven Deadly Sins: Some Problems of
        Research." Spec, 43 (1968), 1-22.

1973   WENZEL, SIEGFRIED. The Sin of Sloth: "Acedia" in Medieval
        Thought and Literature. Chapel Hill: University of
        North Carolina Press, 1960, 1967. 280 pp.
        Reviews: F. C. deVries, Neophil, 53 (1969), 101-103;
        S. Neuijen, ES, 50 (1969), 605-607; *Paulus Engelhardt,
        Arcadia, 4 (1969), 91-93; Donald R. Howard, Spec, 43
        (1968), 758-61; John P. McCall, JEGP, 67 (1968), 296-97.

Backgrounds

1974   WENZEL, SIEGFRIED. "The Three Enemies of Man." MS, 29
        (1967), 47–66.

1975   WILLIAMS, ARNOLD. "Some Documents on English Pardoners,
        1350–1400," in Mediaeval Studies in Honor of Urban
        Tigner Holmes, Jr. UNCSRLL, 56. Edited by John Mahoney
        and John Esten Keller. Chapel Hill: University of North
        Carolina Press, 1965, pp. 197–207.

1976   WOOD–LEGH, K[ATHLEEN] L[OUISE]. Perpetual Chantries in
        Britain. Cambridge, England; New York: Cambridge Univer-
        sity Press, 1965. 368 pp.
            Reviews: Dorothy Bruce Weske, Spec, 42 (1967), 768–69;
        J. C. Dickinson, MAE, 36 (1967), 104–105; F. R. H.
        DuBoulay, EHR, 82 (1967), 376–77; Susan Wood, History,
        53 (1968), 85–86; Kenneth A. Strand, RN, 19 (1966),
        369–71; *R. Brooke, JTS, 18 (1967), 260; Richard Luman,
        JR, 47 (1967), 273.

1977   ZWEIG, PAUL. The Heresy of Self–Love: A Study of Subversive
        Individualism. New York, London: Basic Books, 1968.
        283 pp.
            On narcissism in Western literature.
            Reviews: Basil Willey, CritQ, 11 (1969), 87–88.

See also: 258, 420, 618, 669, 715, 969, 982, 1527, 1686.

SCIENTIFIC BACKGROUNDS

        See Griffith, pp. 356–62; Crawford, pp. 120–25

1978   BEAUJOUAN, GUY, YVONNE POULLE–DRIEUX et JEANNE–MARIE DUREAU-
        LAPEYSSONNIE. Médecine humaine et vétérinaire à la fin
        du moyen âge. Publications du Centre de Recherches
        d'Histoire et de Philologie de la IVe Section de l'École
        pratique des Hautes Études, Series IV, 2. Geneva:
        Librairie Droz; Paris: Librairie Minard, 1966. 487 pp.
            Reviews: William D. Sharpe, Spec, 43 (1968), 119–21.

1979   BIBLIOGRAPHY OF THE HISTORY OF MEDICINE, 1 (1965)––.
        Bethesda, Maryland: National Library of Medicine, U.S.
        Department of Health, Education and Welfare, 1966.
        300 pp.

Scientific Backgrounds

An annual bibliography containing a section, "Literature and Medicine," arranged by countries.
Reviews: William D. Sharpe, Spec, 43 (1968), 123.

1980   BULLOUGH, VERN L. The Development of Medicine as a Profes-
        sion: The Contribution of the Medieval University to
        Modern Medicine. Basel: S. Karger; New York: Hafner,
        1966. 133 pp.
        Note on Chaucer's Physician, pp. 94-95.
        Reviews: Morris H. Saffron, Spec, 44 (1969), 448-50.

1981   CLAY, ROTHA MARY. The Mediaeval Hospitals of England. New
        York: Barnes and Noble, 1966. 379 pp.
        Originally published in 1909. Contains a chapter on
        leprosy.

1981.01 CROMBIE, A. C. "Science in Medieval England," in 58,
        pp. 88-103. Reprinted from "Science" in Medieval England.
        Edited by Austin Lane Poole. New edition. Oxford: The
        Clarendon Press, 1958, Vol. II, pp. 584-604.

1982   *DESTOMBES, M. "La diffusion des instruments scientifiques du
        haut moyen âge au XVe siècle." JWH, 10 (1966), 31-51.
        Cited in 11, 20, p. 483.

1983   EASTWOOD, BRUCE S. "Mediaeval Empiricism: The Case of
        Grosseteste's Optics." Spec, 43 (1968), 306-21.

1984   CANCELLED

1985   GRAHAM, THOMAS F[RANCIS]. Medieval Minds: Mental Health in
        the Middle Ages. London: Allen and Unwin, 1967. 112 pp.,
        8 plates.
        Note on Chaucer, p. 63.

1986   GRANT, EDWARD. "Medieval and Seventeenth Century Conceptions
        of an Infinite Void Space Beyond the Cosmos." Isis, 60
        (1969), 39-60.

1987   HILL, BOYD H., JR. "The Grain and the Spirit in Mediaeval
        Anatomy." Spec, 40 (1965), 63-73.
        Treats the Prioress's Tale and Arcite's wound in the
        Knight's Tale.

1988   *LAIRD, EDGAR STOCKTON. "The Exposicion of Astrology." DA,
        27 (1967), 3873A. Rutgers University, 1966. 141 pp.

1989   CANCELLED

BIBLIOGRAPHY OF CHAUCER, 1964 - 1973

Backgrounds

1990   *LINDEN, STANTON JAY. "Alchemy and the English Literary
            Imagination: 1385-1633." DAI, 33 (1973), 3591A-92A.
            University of Minnesota, 1971. 338 pp.

1991   MacKINNEY, LOREN. Medical Illustrations in Medieval Manu-
            scripts. Berkeley: University of California Press, 1965.
            280 pp., plates.
                Reviews: E. A. Hammond, BHM, 40 (1966), 481-82;
            Florence McCulloch, Spec, 41 (1966), 755-57.

1992   NEWTON, ROBERT R. Medieval Chronicles and the Rotation of the
            Earth. Baltimore and London: The Johns Hopkins Univer-
            sity Press, 1972. 842 pp.
                Treats mentions of solar and lunar eclipses in medieval
            records.
                Reviews: Nicholas H. Steneck, Spec, 49 (1974), 365-68;
            TLS (22 September, 1972), p. 1124.

1993   NORTH, J. D. "The Astrolabe." SciAmer, 23 (1974), 96-106.

1993.01 OGILVY, J. D. A. "The Stirrup and Feudalism." CSSLL, 10
            (1966), 1-13.
                Questions Lynn White's conclusions in 2002 below.

1994   ROBBINS, ROSSELL HOPE. "Medical Manuscripts in Middle
            English." Spec, 45 (1970), 393-415.
                On the use of astrology and herbs in medicine. Contains
            an occasional reference to Chaucer.

1995   *SIEGEL, RUDOLPH E. Galen on Sense Perception: His Doctrines,
            Observations and Experiments on Vision, Hearing, Smell,
            Taste, Touch and Pain, and their Historical Sources.
            Basel, Switzerland; New York: S. Karger, 1970. 216 pp.
                Reviews: E. D. Phillips, ClassR, 23 (1973), 90-91;
            *F. Lasserre, Erasmus, 22 (1971), 815.

1996   *SIEGEL, RUDOLPH E. Galen's System of Physiology and Medicine:
            An Analysis of His Doctrines & Observations on Bloodflow,
            Respiration, Tumors & Internal Disease. Basel:
            S. Karger, 1968. 431 pp.
                Reviews: E. D. Phillips, ClassR, 21 (1971), 370-71.

1997   TALBOT, C[HARLES] H. Medicine in Medieval England. Chicago:
            University of Chicago Press, 1966; *London: Oldbourne,
            1967. 222 pp., 8 plates.
                Various references to Chaucer.
                Reviews: Morris H. Saffron, Spec, 44 (1969), 670-71;
            TLS (11 January, 1968), p. 42.

1998   TEMKIN, OWSEI. Galenism: Rise and Decline of a Medical
          Philosophy. Cornell Publications in the History of
          Science. Ithaca, New York and London: Cornell Univer-
          sity Press, 1973. 257 pp., illustrated.

1999   WALLACE, WILLIAM A. Causality and Scientific Explanation.
          Vol. 1: Medieval and Early Classical Science. Ann Arbor:
          The University of Michigan Press, 1972. 299 pp.
            Reviews: David C. Lindberg, Spec, 50 (1975), 161-63;
          TLS (26 April, 1974), p. 453.

2000   WEISHEIPL, JAMES A. "Classification of the Sciences in
          Medieval Thought." MS, 27 (1965), 54-90.

2001   WHITE, LYNN, JR. "Cultural Climates and Technological
          Advance in the Middle Ages." Viator, 2 (1971), 171-201.

2002   WHITE, LYNN, JR. Medieval Technology and Social Change.
          Oxford: Clarendon Press; New York: Oxford University
          Press, 1962. 204 pp., 10 plates.
            See Crawford, p. 125, and 1993.01 above.
            Reviews: L. Carrington Goodrich, JAOS, 83 (August/
          September, 1963), 384; Marshall Clagett, Spec, 39 (1964),
          359-65.

2002.01 WHITE, LYNN. "Technology and Invention in the Middle Ages,"
          in 58, pp. 67-87. Reprinted from Spec, 15 (1940),
          141-56.

2003   WHITE, LYNN, JR. "Medieval Uses of Air." SciAmer, 223 (1970),
          92-100.
            Organs, windmills, air screws.

2004   WINNY, JAMES. "Chaucer's Science," in 258, chapter 6,
          pp. 153-84.

See also: 258, 317, 323, 583, 745, 921, 1005, 1082, 1258, 1349.

ARTISTIC BACKGROUNDS

See Griffith, pp. 363-68; Crawford, pp. 126-30.

Bibliographic Sources

2005   ART INDEX. Edited by David J. Patten. New York: The
          H. W. Wilson Co. Vols. 14 (1964)--.

Backgrounds

Studies

2006   ANDERSON, M[ARY] D[ÉSIRÉE]. Drama and Imagery in English
        Medieval Churches. Cambridge, England and New York:
        Cambridge University Press, 1963. 259 pp., illustrated.
          Reviews: Rosalie B. Green, Spec, 41 (1966), 725-26;
        Moelwyn Merchant, Apollo, 81 (1965), 506-507; C. F.
        Pitman, Connoisseur, 156 (August, 1964), 287-88;
        *T. Edwards, Tablet (8 February, 1964), p. 157; TLS
        (27 February, 1964), p. 157; W. O. Hassall, MAE, 33
        (1964), 241-42; VQR, 40 (1964), clxx; *Alex Helm,
        Folklore, 75 (1964), 136-38.

2007   AURENHAMMER, HANS. Lexikon der Christlichen Ikonographie.
        Vienna: Brüder Hollinek. Bd. 1 (1959)--.
          Reviews: Philipp P. Fehl, JAAC, 19 (1960), 239-40;
        JAAC, 21 (1962), 96-98; JAAC, 28 (1969), 100-101.

2008   BLUMENKRANZ, BERNHARD. Le juif médiéval au miroir de l'art
        chrétien. Paris: Études Augustiniennes, 1966. 158 pp.

2009   BOYD, BEVERLY. Chaucer and the Medieval Book. San Marino,
        California: Huntington Library, 1973. 176 pp.

2010   CLIFTON-TAYLOR, ALEC. The Cathedrals of England. *London:
        Thomas and Hudson, 1967; New York: Association Press,
        1970. 288 pp.
          Reviews: TLS (17 October, 1968), p. 1168; W. J. S.,
        Connoisseur, 169 (October, 1968), p. 115; ArchR, 143
        (June, 1968), 411.

2011   *DE GAIFFIER, BAUDOUIN. Études critiques d'hagiographie et
        d'iconologie. Subsidia Hagiographica, 43. Brussels:
        Société des Bollandistes, 1967. 532 pp., 31 plates.
          Reviews: Spec, 44 (1969), 332-33.

2012   EGBERT, VIRGINIA WYLIE. The Mediaeval Artist at Work.
        Princeton, New Jersey: Princeton University Press,
        1967. 93 pp., 54 illustrations.
          Reviews: Daniel V. Thompson, Spec, 43 (1968), 708;
        Mojmír S. Frinta, ArtB, 51 (1969), 292-93; Leslie W.
        Jones, AHR, 74 (1968), 128-29; Walter Oakeshott, MAE, 38
        (1969), 110-11; Hans Huth, ArtJ, 27 (1968), 442; John
        Beckwith, Apollo, 90 (1969), 267-68.

2013   *ENGLISH BOOK ILLUSTRATION, 966-1846. 1: Illuminated Manu-
        scripts. London: Trustees of the British Museum, 1965.
        Cited in Spec, 41 (1966), 204.

Artistic Backgrounds

2014   FRISCH, TERESA G. Gothic Art, 1140-c.1450. Sources and
        Documents in the History of Art Series. Englewood Cliffs,
        New Jersey: Prentice-Hall, 1971. 191 pp.

2015   GRABAR, ANDRÉ. Christian Iconography: A Study of its Origins.
        The A. W. Mellon Lectures in the Fine Arts. Bollingen
        Series, XXV, 10. Princeton, New Jersey: Princeton Uni-
        versity Press, 1969.
            Reviews: Aaron W. Godfrey, LitArts, 38 (1970), 76-77.

2016   HARVEY JOHN [HOOPER]. The Mediaeval Architect. London:
        Wayland Publishers; *New York: St. Martin's Press, 1972.
        296 pp.
            Reviews: Lon R. Shelby, Spec, 49 (1974), 340-42.

2017   KIRSCHBAUM, ENGELBERT, S. J., et al. Lexikon der christlichen
        Ikonographie. Rome, Freiburg, Basel, Vienna: Herder,
        1968-74. Bd. 1 (1968)--.
            In progress, Bds. 1-4 (complete): Allgemeine
        Ikonographie, Bds. 5--: Ikonographie der Heiligen.

2018   KLINGENDER, FRANCIS [DONALD]. Animals in Art and Thought to
        the End of the Middle Ages. Edited by Evelyn Antal and
        John Harthan. Cambridge, Massachusetts: The M. I. T.
        Press; *London: Routledge and Kegan Paul, 1971. 608 pp.
            Reviews: Gerhart B. Lander, Spec, 50 (1975), 732-38;
        *J. Gardner, The New York Times (9 April, 1972), p. 27;
        TLS (18 August, 1972), p. 966; *L. De Paor, Studio Inter-
        national (March, 1972), p. 133; JAAC, 30 (1972), 569.

2019   MAHLER, ANNEMARIE. "Art and Visual Imagery: A Methodology
        for the Study of Medieval Styles." YCGL, 21 (1972), 7-14.

2020   MÂLE, EMILE. L'art religieux de la fin du moyen âge en France:
        étude sur l'iconographie du moyen âge et sur ses sources
        d'inspiration. Sixième édition. Paris: Librairie Armand
        Colin, 1969. 516 pp., 265 illustrations.
            First published in 1905.

2021   MARTINDALE, ANDREW. Gothic Art from the Twelfth to Fifteenth
        Century. Praeger World of Art Series. New York and
        Washington: Frederick A. Praeger, 1967. 287 pp., 206
        illustrations.
            Reviews: Earnle Money, ContempR, 211 (December, 1967),
        273-74; TLS (8 February, 1968), p. 124.

2022   MARTINDALE, ANDREW. The Rise of the Artist in the Middle
        Ages and Early Renaissance. London: Thames and London,
        1972. 144 pp., 90 plates.

Backgrounds

Reviews: *Mens en Mel, 27 (1972), 381; R. M. Quinn,
ArQ, 29 (1973), 79-81.

2023   MEYER-BAER, KATHI. Music of the Spheres and the Dance of
Death: Studies in Musical Iconology. Princeton, New
Jersey: Princeton University Press, 1970. 403 pp.,
174 illustrations.
Reviews: Morton W. Bloomfield, Spec, 46 (1971),
172-74; John Hollander, RenQ, 24 (1971), 239-40.

2024   MITCHELL, SABRINA. Medieval Manuscript Painting. London:
Weidenfeld and Nicolson, 1964; New York: Viking Press,
1965. 47 pp., 176 plates.

2025   PARKES, M[ALCOLM] B[ECKWITH]. English Cursive Book Hands,
1250-1500. Oxford Palaeographical Handbooks. Oxford,
England: Clarendon Press, 1969. 56 pp., 24 plates.
Reviews: Ruth J. Dean, Spec, 46 (1971), 177-80; J. E.
Fagg, MAE, 40 (1971), 212-14; Janet Backhouse, Library,
26 (1971), 67-68; Frederick G. Emmison, RenQ, 24 (1971),
391-92; Braxton Ross, MP, 69 (1972), 250-52; *P. D. A.
Harvey, JSA, 4 (1972), 539.

2026   PICKERING, F. P. Literature and Art in the Middle Ages.
London: Macmillan, 1970. 384 pp.
Translated from the German, originally published as
Literatur und darstellende Kunst im Mittelalter, 1966.
Anti-Robertsonian: objects to using one medium as
metaphor for another.
Reviews: Julia Ebel, CE, 33 (1972), 609-12.

2027   PRITCHARD, V[IOLET]. English Medieval Graffiti. London and
New York: Cambridge University Press, 1967. 208 pp.,
229 illustrations.
Scattered references to Chaucer.
Reviews: David Kunzle, Spec, 45 (1970), 318-21; TLS
(22 February, 1968), p. 188; J. A. W. B., MAE, 39 (1970),
77-78; George Henderson, BurM, 110, Part 2 (1968), 705;
Theo Stemmler, Ang, 86 (1968), 377-79.

2028   RANDALL, LILIAN M. C. Images in the Margins of Gothic
Manuscripts. California Studies in the History of Art,
4. Berkeley and Los Angeles: University of California
Press, 1966. 243 pp., 739 illustrations.
Reviews: Meyer Schapiro, Spec, 45 (1970), 684-86; TLS
(16 February, 1967), p. 120; J. J. G. Alexander, Library,
23 (1968), 149-50; Nicholas Barker, BC, 17 (1968), 85-92;
W. O. Hassall, MAE, 37 (1968), 102-104; Constantine G.
Christofides, RPh, 21 (1968), 559-60; Lucy Freeman

Artistic Backgrounds

Sandler, ArtB, 52 (1970), 95-96; L. M. J. Delaissé, JAAC, 27 (1968), 109-110; Philippe Verdier, ArtJ, 27 (1967), 104-106; Carl Nordenfalk, BurM, 109 (1967), 418-21.

2029   RÉAU, LOUIS.   Iconographie de l'art chrétien.   Paris: Presses universitaires de France, 1955-59; Reprinted, 1974.   3 vols, in 6.   3243 pp.

2030   REMNANT, G. L.   A Catalogue of Misericords in Great Britain. With an Essay on their Iconography by M. D. Anderson. Oxford, England: Clarendon Press; New York: Oxford University Press, 1969.   261 pp., 48 plates.
        Reviews: Lilian M. C. Randall, Spec, 45 (1970), 159-62; W. O. Hassall, MAE, 39 (1970), 76-77.

2031   ROBB, DAVID M[ETHENY].   The Art of the Illuminated Manuscript. Cranbury, New Jersey: A. S. Barnes; London: Thomas Joseloff, 1973.   356 pp., illustrated.
        Reviews: TLS (3 May, 1974), p. 480; *J. Canaday, The New York Times (2 December, 1973), p. 90.

2032   ROWLAND, BERYL.   Animals with Human Faces: A Guide to Animal Symbolism. Knoxville: University of Tennessee Press, 1973.   211 pp.
        Treats the medieval symbolic associations of real and imaginary animals.
        Reviews: Joan Owen, LJ, 98 (August, 1973), 2301; VQR, 50 (Spring, 1974), lx; Choice, 11 (July/August, 1974), 742.

2033   SALTER, ELIZABETH.   "Medieval Poetry and the Visual Arts." E&S, 22 (1969), 16-32.
        Questions recent examinations of Chaucer's poetry in reference to aesthetics of Gothic art.

2034   SALVINI, ROBERTO.   Medieval Sculpture: A History of Western Sculpture. Greenwich, Connecticut: New York Graphic Society, 1969.   308 pp., 350 plates.
        Reviews: TLS (3 December, 1971), p. 1495; Nicholas Hall, Connoisseur, 179 (February, 1972), 140.

2035   SALZMAN, L[OUIS] F[RANCIS].   Building in England down to 1540: A Documentary History. Second edition. Oxford, England: Clarendon Press; New York: Oxford University Press, 1958. 653 pp., 21 illustrations.
        Originally published in 1952, 1958.
        Reviews: Carl F. Barnes, Jr., ArtB, 51 (1969), 303-304.

Backgrounds

2036   SCHERER, MARGARET R[OSEMAN]. The Legends of Troy in Art and
           Literature. New York and London: Phaidon Press for the
           Metropolitan Museum of Art, 1963.   322 pp., 190 figures.
           Reviews: M. I. Finley, NST (28 February, 1964),
           p. 338; TLS (16 April, 1964), p. 315; Reynold Higgins,
           BurM, 106 (1964), 469.

2036.01*STEINEM, WOLFRAM VON DEN. Homo Caelestis: Das Wort der Kunst
           im Mittelalter. Bern und Munich: Francke, 1965. 2 vols.,
           339 pp., 298 plates.
           Reviews: Alfred Neumeyer, ArtB, 49 (1967), 71-72.

2037   TRIVICK, HENRY H. The Craft and Design of Monumental Brasses.
           London: John Baker; New York: Humanities Press, 1969.
           152 pp., 85 plates.
           Reviews: Norton Downs, Spec, 47 (1972), 147; M. D.
           Anderson, ArchR, 146 (December, 1969), 482; Robert E.
           Tully, LitArts, 38 (1970), 77-79.

2038   TRIVICK, HENRY [H]. The Picture Book of Brasses in Gilt.
           New York: Charles Scribner's Sons, 1972. 33 pp., 106
           plates.
           Reviews: TLS (24 September, 1971), p. 1155.

2039   TUVE, ROSEMOND. "Notes on the Virtues and Vices." Part 1,
           JWCI, 26 (1963), 264-303; Part, 2, JWCI, 27 (1964),
           42-72.

2040   VARTY, KENNETH. Reynard the Fox: A Study of the Fox in
           Medieval English Art. Leicester, England: Leicester
           University Press, 1967. 169 pp., 96 plates.
           Reviews: Francis Lee Utley, Spec, 44 (1969), 498-501;
           TLS (22 February, 1968), p. 188; John Fox, MLR, 64 (1969),
           131-32; D. J. A. Ross, MAE, 37 (1968), 337-41; George
           Henderson, BurM, 110, Part 2 (1968), 705; Lilian M. C.
           Randall, Apollo, 87 (1968), 480-82; M. Dominica Legge,
           FS, 23 (1969), 51-52; P. M. Vermeer, ES, 52 (1971),
           545-47.

2041   VON DEN STEINEM, WOLFRAM. See 2036.01

2042   WOOD, MARGARET. The English Mediaeval House. London:
           Phoenix House, 1965. 478 pp.
           Reviews: Martin Holmes, Listener, 74 (1965), 244;
           Urban T. Holmes, Spec, 41 (1966), 381-83; R. H. C. Davis,
           History, 51 (1966), 73-74; P. Faulkner, MedArch, 10
           (1967), 231-33.

See also: 226, 1748, 1843.

MUSIC BACKGROUNDS

Bibliographic Sources

2043   HUGHES, ANDREW. Medieval Music: The Sixth Liberal Art.
        Toronto Medieval Bibliographies, 4. Buffalo, New York:
        University of Toronto Press, 1974.
        Includes a few items on Chaucer.

2044   THE MUSIC INDEX: A Subject-Author Guide to Current Music
        Periodical Literature. Edited by Florence Kretzschmar.
        Detroit: Information Coordinators, Inc. Vol. 16
        (1964)--.

2045   RÉPERTOIRE INTERNATIONAL DES SOURCES MUSICALES. München:
        G. Henle Verlag (for la Société Internationale de
        Musicologie and l'Association Internationale des
        Bibliothèques Musicale), 1960--.
          Still in progress, RISM provides a catalogue of musical
        works and writings about music from all countries from
        the earliest records up to 1800.

Studies

2046   APEL, WILLI. Harvard Dictionary of Music. Second edition,
        revised, enlarged. Cambridge, Massachusetts: Belknap
        Press of Harvard University Press, 1969. 950 pp.
          First edition, 1944.
          Reviews: John H. Baron, New Republic (31 January,
        1970), pp. 22-24; Charles Rosen, NYRB (26 February, 1970),
        pp. 11-15; TLS (16 October, 1970), p. 1204; B. H. Haggin,
        "Music and Ballet Chronicle," HudR, 24 (1971), 495-98;
        A. Hyatt King, MusT, 111 (1970), 1221-23.

2047   APEL, WILLI. The History of Keyboard Music to 1700. Trans-
        lated and revised by Hans Tischler. Bloomington:
        Indiana University Press, 1972. 894 pp.
          Translation of Geschichte der Orgel-und Klaviermusik
        bis 1700. Bärenreiter, 1967. See parts 1, 3 and 4,
        pp. 19-32, on the organ in the early Middle Ages.
          Reviews: H. F., M&L, 54 (1973), 345.

Backgrounds

2048   APFEL, ERNST. "Volkskunst und Hochkunst in der Musik des
        Mittelalters." ArchMus, 25 (1968), 81-95.

2049   BACHMANN, WERNER. The Origins of Bowing and the Development
        of Bowed Instruments up to the Thirteenth Century. Trans-
        lated by Norma Deane. London and New York: Oxford
        University Press, 1969. 193 pp., 97 plates.
          German title: Die Anfänge des Streichinstrumentenspiels,
        1964. A rich collection of iconographic materials. See
        note on Chaucer, p. 128.
          Reviews: M. R., M&L, 51 (1970), 309-10; Guy Oldham,
        MusT, 112 (1971), 33-34; Joan Rimmer, Notes, 28 (1971),
        45-48.

2050   BEDBROOK, G. S. "The Problem of Instrumental Combination in
        the Middle Ages." RBelgeMus, 25 (1971), 53-67.
          Contains notes on the symbolism of musical instruments,
        pp. 59-60.

2051   BESCOND, ALBERT-JACQUES. Le Chant Grégorien. Collection de
        l'Institut International d'Études Comparatives de la
        Musique publiée sous le patronage du Conseil International
        de la Musique. Les Traditions Musicales, 6. Paris:
        Buchet/Chastel, 1972. 318 pp., 29 plates.
          A "popular" approach to the origins and history of the
        Gregorian chant in medieval times and later.
          Reviews: Spec, 48 (1973), 434.

2052   BESSELER, HEINRICH and PETER GÜLKE. Schriftbild der
        Mehrstimmigen Musik. Musikgeschichte in Bildern, III,
        Musik des Mittelalters und der Renaissance, Lfg. 5.
        Leipzig: VEB Deutscher Verlag für Musik, 1974. 183 pp.,
        illustrated.
          Covers note-writing from c. 1000 to 1610.
          Reviews: R. K., SchweizMus, 114 (1974), 253.

2053   *BETTS, JANE COLVILLE. "The Marriage of Music and Rhetoric:
        A Study of the Use of Classical Rhetoric as a Rationale
        for Musical Innovation During the Middle Ages and the
        Renaissance." DAI, 33 (1972), 2315A-16A. University of
        Minnesota, 1972. 296 pp.

2054   BLACKBURN, BONNIE J. "Te Matrem Dei Laudamus: A Study in
        the Musical Veneration of Mary." MusQ, 53 (1967),
        53-76.

Music Backgrounds

2055   BLADES, JAMES. "Percussion Instruments of the Middle Ages
        and Renaissance: Their History in Literature and Painting."
        EarlyMus, 1 (1973), 11-18.
          List of instruments described with accompanying
        illustrations.

2056   BLOM, ERIC. Grove's Dictionary of Music and Musicians.
        Fifth edition. New York: St. Martin's Press, 1954.
        9 vols. Supplement to the Fifth edition, 1961.

2057   BOWLES, EDMUND A. "Eastern Influences on the Use of Trumpets
        and Drums During the Middle Ages." AnuMus, 26 (1971),
        3-28.

2058   BOWLES, EDMUND. "The Guitar in Medieval Literature." GuitarR,
        29 (1966), 2-7.

2059   BOWLES, EDMUND A. "Musical Instruments in the Medieval
        Corpus Christi Procession." AMS, 17 (1964), 251-60.
          Contains a short passage (p. 259) on the symbolism of
        musical instruments.

2060   BOWLES, EDMUND A. "A Performance History of the Organ in
        the Middle Ages." Diap, 61 (January, 1970), 13-14.
          Contains a note on the Nun's Priest's Tale.

2061   BOWLES, EDMUND A. "The Symbolism of the Organ in the Middle
        Ages: A Study in the History of Ideas," in 2082,
        pp. 27-39.

2062   *BUTTS, THOMAS E. "Bagpipes in Medieval Music." AmR, 14
        (1973), 43-45. Cited in MI (August, 1973), 25.
          For reply, see J. S. Upton, Letters to the Editor, AmR,
        14 (1973), 148-52.

2063   *BUTTS, THOMAS E. "The Use of Instruments in the Church and
        Liturgical Events of the Middle Ages." AmR, 13 (1972),
        6-9. Cited in MI (April, 1972), 41.

2064   CALDWELL, JOHN. "The Organ in the Medieval Latin Liturgy,
        800-1500." RMA, 93 (1966-67), 11-24.

2065   CARPENTER, NAN COOKE. Music in the Medieval and Renaissance
        Universities. Norman, Oklahoma: Oklahoma University
        Press, 1958. 407 pp.
          Notes on Chaucer, pp. 81-82.
          Reviews: *Muzyka, 8 (1963), 75-77.

Backgrounds

2066   *CHAMBERLAIN, DAVID STANLEY. "Music in Chaucer: His Knowl-
       edge and Use of Medieval Ideas About Music" (Vols. I and
       II). DA, 27 (1967), 3834A. Princeton University, 1966.
       833 pp.

2067   CHAMBERLAIN, DAVID S. "Philosophy of Music in the Consolatio
       of Boethius." Spec, 45 (1970), 80-97.

2068   *COLLINS, FLETCHER, JR. "Chaucer's Understanding of Music."
       DAI, 31 (1970), 2338A. Yale University, 1934. 213 pp.
       Includes glossary of musical terms and instruments.

2069   *CORBIN, SOLANGE. L'Église à la conquête de sa musique.
       Paris: Gallimard, 1960. 309 pp. Cited in MI (1968),
       p. 359.
          Evans (below) notes that the work is a valuable intro-
       duction to the Gregorian chant, especially literary
       sources of the history of early Christian music. It
       enables us to trace the changing attitude of the Church
       toward music, and the evolution of the "professional"
       singer.
          Reviews: Paul Evans, AMS, 21 (1968), 101-102.

2070   FREEMAN, MICHAEL. "The World of Courtly Love." R&MM, 4
       (1973), 226-28.
          See 2091 below.

2071   GALLO, F. ALBERTO. "Astronomy and Music in the Middle Ages:
       the Liber introductorius by Michael Scot." MusDisc, 27
       (1974), 5-9.

2072   GALLO, F. ALBERTO. "Philological Works on Musical Treatises
       of the Middle Ages: a Bibliographical Report." ActaMus,
       44 (1972), 78-101.
          Examines "recent text editions and studies of the manu-
       script tradition of medieval musical treatises."

2073   GOLDRON, ROMAIN. Byzantine and Medieval Music: St. Sophia
       to Notre Dame. Translated by Doris C. Dunning. History
       of Music, 2. Garden City, New York: Doubleday, 1968.
       116 pp.
          Valuable for the illustrations.
          Reviews: *IntMus, 66 (1968), 14; David L. Meeker,
       MusEdJ, 54 (May, 1968), 76-77; Eugene Helm, Notes, 25
       (1969),485-87.

2074   GOLDRON, ROMAIN. Minstrels and Masters: The Triumph of
       Polyphony. Translated by J. V. Williams. History of

Music, 3. Garden City, New York: Doubleday, 1968.
103 pp.
Valuable for the illustrations.
Reviews: Eugene Helm, Notes, 25 (1969), 485–87;
David L. Meeker, MusEdJ, 54 (May, 1968), 76–77.

2075   *HAMMERSTEIN, REINHOLD. Die Musik der Engel: Untersuchungen
zur Musik und Musikanschauung des Mittelalters. Bern und
München: Francke Verlag, 1962. 303 pp., 144 plates.
Dahlhaus below notes that Hammerstein examines the
topos of the song of the angels in patristic writing,
legends, hymns, literature, and art.
Reviews: *NZ, 125 (1964), 364–66; Carl Dahlhaus, MF,
18 (1965), 332; *Mens en Mel, 23 (1968), 61–62; *Svensk
Tid, 45 (1963), 192–97; *Slov Hud, 13 (1969), 272–74.

2076   HARMAN, ALEC. Mediaeval and Early Renaissance Music. London:
Rockliff, 1958; *New York: Schocken, c. 1962, 1969.
268 pp.
Reviews: SatR, 52 (29 November, 1969), p. 49.

2077   HARRISON, FRANK L[LEWELLYN]. "Tradition and Innovation in
Instrumental Usage, 1100-1450," in 2082 below, pp. 319–35.
Treats church instruments and secular instruments.

2078   *HEYDE, HERBERT. "Trompete und Trompetenblasen im europäischen
Mittelalter." Leipzig Dissertation, 1965. Abstr. in MF,
19 (1966), 57–58.

2079   HOLMGREN, ILENE. "Problems in Tracing the History of Medieval
Musical Instruments Through Art." AmOrg, 53 (1970),
22–24.

2080   HUGHES, DOM ANSELM and GERALD ABRAHAM, eds. Ars Nova and the
Renaissance, 1300–1540. New Oxford History of Music, 3.
London and New York: Oxford University Press, 1960.
565 pp.
See Crawford, p. 128. Occasional references to Chaucer
throughout.
Reviews: *JChurchMus, 6 (1964), 13–14.

2081   *HUGLO, MICHEL. Les Tonaires: Inventaire, analyse, comparaison.
Publications de la Société française de Musicologie,
Troisième Série, 2. Paris: Heugel, 1971. 487 pp.
Reviews: Kenneth Levy, Spec, 49 (1974), 125–26; Ruth
Steiner, MusQ, 58 (1972), 672; F. Alberto Gallo, ActaMus,
44 (1972), 78–101 (see p. 83).

Backgrounds

2082   LaRUE, JAN, ed. Aspects of Medieval and Renaissance Music:
        A Birthday Offering to Gustave Reese. New York:
        W. W. Norton; *New York, London: Oxford University Press,
        1966. 908 pp.
           Reviews: William S. Newman, Notes, 23 (1966), 259-63;
        J. A. W., M&L, 48 (1967), 266-67; Frank Harrison, MusT,
        108 (1967), 515-17; *MF, 22 (1969), 91; *GalpinSJ, 23
        (1970), 156-60; *Zvuk, 101 (1970), 63-64.

2083   LIPPMAN, EDWARD A. "The Place of Music in the System of
        Liberal Arts," in 2082, pp. 545-59.

2084   MACHABEY, A., SR. "Notions scientifiques disséminées dans
        les textes musicologiques du moyen âge." MusDisc, 17
        (1963), 7-20.

2085   *MACKEY, JULIE REICH. "Medieval Metrical Saints' Lives and
        the Origin of the Ballad." DA, 29 (1969), 2162A.
        University of Pennsylvania, 1968. 278 pp.
           Proposes that saints' lives served as models for the
        ballads.

2086   MAILLARD, JEAN. "The Many Faces of Medieval Musicology."
        StudiesMus, 4 (1970), 1-18.
           Includes supplement: six medieval songs, edited by
        Jean Maillard. English translation by Brian Willis.

2087   *McKINNON, JAMES WILLIAM. "The Church Fathers and Musical
        Instruments." DA, 28 (1967), 1837A. Columbia University,
        1965. 317 pp.
           Argues that musical instruments early became symbols of
        debauchery and lust.

2088   McKINNON, JAMES W. "The Meaning of the Patristic Polemic
        Against Musical Instruments." Current Mus, 1 (1965),
        69-82.
           On the association of musical instruments with lust.

2089   McKINNON, JAMES W. "Musical Instruments in Medieval Psalm
        Commentaries and Psalters." AMS, 21 (1968), 3-20.
           Examines literary, allegorical, and iconographic
        evidence of the use of musical instruments in medieval
        liturgical music, and questions the validity of this
        evidence.

2090   MORE, MOTHER THOMAS. "The Performance of Plainsong in the
        Later Middle Ages and the Sixteenth Century." RMA, 92
        (1965-66), 121-34, and 4 plates.

2091   *MÜLLER-HEUSER, FRANZ. Vox humana, ein Beitrag zur
       Untersuchung der Stimmästhetik des Mittelalters. Kölner
       Beiträge zur Musikforschung, 26. Regensburg: Gustav
       Bosse Verlag, 1963. 191 pp. Cited in MI (1964), 558 and
       MI (1966), 612.
          Reviews: Mens en Mel, 19 (1964), 318; Reinhold
       Hammerstein, MF, 18 (1965), 447-49; *Ars Organi, 21
       (1973), 1895.

2092   MUNROW, DAVID. "Courtly Love and the World of Music:
       Guillaume de Machaut and his Age." R&MM, 4 (1973),
       229-33.
          See 2070 above.

2093   PINON, ROGER. "Philologie et folklore musical: les
       instruments de musique des pâtres au moyen âge et à la
       Renaissance." Jahrbuch für Volksliedforschung, 14 (1969),
       197-213.
          Treats various musical instruments in literature.

2094   RAJECZKY, B[ENJAMIN]. "Europäische Volksmusik und Musik des
       Mittelalters." StudiaMus, 15 (1973), 201-204.

2095   RASTALL, RICHARD. "Some English Consort-Groupings of the
       Late Middle Ages." M&L, 55 (1974), 179-202.
          Notes on Chaucer's references to instruments in the
       Canterbury Tales, p. 185.

2096   RASTALL, RICHARD. "Minstrelsy, Church, and Clergy in
       Medieval England." RMA, 97 (1970-71), 83-98.

2097   REANEY, GILBERT. "The Question of Authorship in the Medieval
       Treatises on Music." Mus Disc, 18 (1964), 7-17.

2098   REMNANT, MARY. "Opus Anglicanum." GalpinSJ, 17 (1964),
       111-13.
          Notes on musical instruments in medieval English
       embroidery: bagpipes played by shepherds; various instru-
       ments played by angels.

2099   REMNANT, MARY. "Rebec, Fiddle and Crowd in England." RMA,
       95 (1968-69), 15-28.

2100   REMNANT, MARY. "Rebec, Fiddle and Crowd in England: Some
       Further Observations." RMA, 96 (1969-70), 149-50.

2101   RIEMANN, HUGO. Polyphonic Theory from the Ninth to the
       Sixteenth Century. History of Music Theory, I, II.

Backgrounds

Translated with a preface, commentary and notes by
Raymond H. Haggh. Lincoln: Nebraska University Press,
1962. 451 pp.
Originally published in German, Geschichte der
Musiktheorie, 1898; second edition, 1921.
Reviews: Lawrence A. Gushee, AMS, 17 (1964), 395-400.

2102 ROBERTSON, ALEC and DENIS STEVENS, eds. The Pelican History
of Music. Vol. 1: Ancient Forms to Polyphony. Vol. 2:
Renaissance and Baroque. Baltimore: Pelican; *London,
Cassell, 1960, 1962, 1963.
General survey.
Reviews: *MusEvents, 20 (1965), 27; *MusTcr, 44 (1965),
371.

2103 *SANDERS, ERNEST HELMUT. "Medieval English Polyphony and its
Significance for the Continent." DA, 28 (1968),
3707A-08A. Columbia University, 1963. 467 pp.
Reviews: J. E. Maddrell, CurrentMus, 9 (1969), 209-12.

2104 SANDERS, ERNEST H[ELMUT]. "Die Rolle der englischen
Mehrstimmigkeit des Mittelalters in der Entwicklung von
Cantus-firmus-Satz und Tonalitätsstruktur. ArchMus, 24
(1967), 24-53.

2105 SEAY, ALBERT. Music in the Medieval World. Prentice-Hall
History of Music Series. Englewood Cliffs, New Jersey:
London: Prentice-Hall, 1965. 182 pp.
Introductory digest.
Reviews: Martin Picker, AmChoralR, 8, ii (December,
1965), 18-19; John W. Barker, AmRecG, 32 (1965), 266-68;
Leo Treitler, JRME, 14 (1966), 235-36; E. T., M&L, 47
(1966), 160-61; *Mus&Mus, 14 (1966), 63; *MusJ, 24 (1966),
90; Leonard Ellinwood, Notes, 23 (1966), 59; Michel
Huglo, RdeMus, 52 (1966), 123; Peter Gülke, MF, 21 (1968),
108-109; *AmR, 9 (1968), 80.

2106 SMITS VAN WAESBERGHE, JOSEPH. Musikerziehung: Lehre und
Theorie im Mittelalter. Musikgeschichte in Bildern, 111,
Musik des Mittelalters und der Renaissance, Lfg. 3. Hrsg.
von Heinrich Besseler und Werner Bachmann. Leipzig:
VEB Deutscher Verlag für Musik; *Mainz: B. Schott, 1969.
213 pp.
F. A. Gallo, 2071 above, p. 83, notes that the
work "... gives a useful and accurate choice of reproduc-
tions from medieval manuscripts containing texts on
musical theory." See, for example, p. 182, for connections between music and astronomy.

Music Backgrounds

Reviews: *ME, 24 (1970), 95; *Mens en Mel, 25 (1970),
349; *MH, 21 (1970), 190; *Mus in Schule, 21 (1970),
139-40; *Mus u Ges, 20 (1970), 709-11; Musica, 24 (1970),
492; Michel Huglo, RdeMus, 56 (1970), 232-34; *NZ, 132
(1971), 43-45; *AmR, 13 (1972), 64; *VNM, 22 (1971),
289-93; *SvenskTid, 53 (1971), 139-40.

2107   SMITS VAN WAESBERGHE, JOSEPH, et al., eds. The Theory of
Music from the Carolingian Era up to 1400. Vol. 1:
Descriptive Catalogue of Manuscripts. Repertoire Inter-
national des Sources Musicales. München-Duisburg: G.
Henle Verlag, 1961, 1968. 155 pp.
Reviews: *SvenskTid, 45 (1963), 215.

2108   SMOJE, DUJKA. "La harpe médiévale." CarnetMus, 3 (January,
1972), 6-7; 4 (March, 1972), 14-16.

2109   SPRUIT, JOP E. Van Vedelaars, trommers en pijpers. Utrecht:
Oosthoek, 1969. 141 pp.
General study of medieval "Spielmann."

2110   STEVENS, DENIS. "Music in Honor of St. Thomas of Canterbury."
MusQ, 56 (1970), 311-45.
Contains note on Chaucer, p. 344.

2111   STRUNK, OLIVER, ed. Source Readings in Music History. Vol.
1: Antiquity and the Middle Ages. New York: W. W.
Norton, 1965. 192 pp.
Standard reference work. See especially chapter 3,
"Music as a Liberal Art," (on Boethius), pp. 79-86 and
chapter 4, "Musical Theory in the Middle Ages,"
pp. 103-90.
Reviews: *Clavier, 5 (1966), 14; William C. Holmes,
Notes, 22 (1966), 1234.

2112   TISCHLER, HANS. "Coordination of Separate Elements: Chief
Principle of Medieval Art." OrbisMus, 2 (1973-74),
67-82.

2113   VAN DER WERF, HENDRIK. The Chansons of the Troubadours and
Trouvères. Utrecht: Oosthoek, 1972. 166 pp.
Reviews: J. A. W., M&L, 54 (1973), 215-17; Leila
Birnbaum, Notes, 30 (1973), 44-47; Albert Seay, MusQ,
60 (1974), 306-11.

Backgrounds

2114   WINTERNITZ, EMANUEL. Musical Instruments and Their Symbolism
        in Western Art. New York: W. W. Norton, 1967. 240 pp.,
        96 plates.
          On pp. 129-36 is reprinted "Bagpipes for the Lord,"
        from The Metropolitan Museum of Art Bulletin, 16 (1958),
        276-86.

2115-
2125   CANCELLED

242

Dictionaries and Indexes

See Griffith, pp. 3-4; Crawford, p. 131.

2126   *DE WEEVER, JACQUELINE ELINOR. "A Dictionary of Classical,
        Mythological and Sideral Names in the Works of Geoffrey
        Chaucer." DAI, 32 (1972), 4559A. University of
        Pennsylvania, 1971. 246 pp.

2127   DILLON, BERT. "A Dictionary of Personal, Mythological,
        Allegorical, and Astrological Proper Names and Allu-
        sions in the Works of Geoffrey Chaucer." DAI, 33 (1973),
        5118A-19A. Duke University, 1972. 435 pp.

2127.01 DILLON, BERT. A Chaucer Dictionary: Proper Names and Allu-
        sions Excluding Place Names. Edited by Joseph Katz.
        Boston, Massachusetts: G. K. Hall, 1974. 283 pp.

2128   GREAVES, PAUL. Grammatica Anglicana, 1594. English Lin-
        guistics Collection of Facsimile Reprints, 169. Menston,
        Yorks: Scolar, 1969. 75 pp.
            Includes very brief Chaucer glossary.

2129   ROBBINS, ROSSELL HOPE and JOHN L. CUTLER. Supplement to the
        Index of Middle English Verse. Lexington, Kentucky:
        University of Kentucky Press, 1965, 1966. 580 pp.
            Reviews: Morton W. Bloomfield, Spec, 42 (1967),
        548-50; Val M. Bonnell, AN&Q, 4 (1966), 138-40;
        E. G. Stanley, N&Q, 13 (1966), 309-310; R. M. Wilson,
        MLR, 61 (1966), 659-60; *Raymond C. Sutherland, PBSA,
        60 (1966), 233; Norman Davis, RES, 18 (1967), 444-48;
        Sylvia Wallace Holton, SN, 38 (1966), 360-62; Helmut
        Gneuss, Archiv, 207 (1970), 64-65; A. A. Prins, ES, 52
        (1971), 57-58.

2129.01 ROSS, THOMAS W. Chaucer's Bawdy. New York: Dutton, 1972.
        256 pp.
            Reviews: Paul E. Beichner, NDEJ, 8 (1972), 52-54.

Dictionaries and Indexes

2129.02 SCOTT, A. F. Who's Who in Chaucer. New York: Taplinger
Publishing Co., 1974. 156 pp.
A glossary of characters appearing in Chaucer.

See also: 60, 332.01, 1970, 2068.

Recordings, Films, and Filmstrips

DISTRIBUTORS

NICEM   National Information Center for Educational Media, University of Southern California, Los Angeles, California 90007.

DISTRIBUTORS: RECORDINGS

BOW   Stanley Bowmar Company, 4 Broadway, Valhalla, New York 10595.

CAED   Caedmon Records, Inc., 505 Eighth Avenue, New York, New York 10018. Catalog, 1973.

CAP   Capitol Records, Inc., Hollywood and Vine Street, Hollywood, California.

DGG   Deutsche Grammophon Gesellschaft, Hamburg, Germany.

DOV   Dover Publications, Inc., 180 Varick Street, New York, New York 10014.

EAV   Educational Audio-Visual, 29 Marble Avenue, Pleasantville, New York 10570.

EE   Everett/Edwards, Inc., P. O. Box 1060, Deland, Florida 32720. Catalog (1975-76), n.p.

EYE   Eyegate House, Inc., 146-01 Archer Avenue, Jamaica, New York 11435.

FSR   Folkways/Scholastic Records, 50 West 44th Street, New York, New York 10036.

HM   Houghton Mifflin Co., One Beacon Street, Boston, Massachusetts 02107.

BIBLIOGRAPHY OF CHAUCER, 1964 - 1973

Recordings, Films, and Filmstrips

IMP Imperial Film Co., Inc., 4404 S. Florida Avenue, Lakewood, Florida 33803.

LL Listening Library, 1 Park Avenue, Old Greenwich, Connecticut 06870.

MHT McGraw-Hill Textfilms, 330 W. 42nd Street, New York, New York 10036.

NCTE National Council of Teachers of English, 508 South Sixth Street, Champaign, Illinois 61820.

TU Tapes Unlimited, Division of Education Unlimited, 1300 1 Puritan Avenue, Detroit, Michigan 48227.

DISTRIBUTORS: FILMS AND FILMSTRIPS

CEA Carmen Educational Associates, Pine Grove, Ontario, Canada.

DUFOUR DuFour Editions, Inc., Booksellers & Publishers, Chester Springs, Pennsylvania 19425.

EAV Educational Audio Visual, 29 Marble Avenue, Pleasantville, New York 10570.

EBEC Encyclopedia Britannica, Educational Corporation, 425 North Michigan Avenue, Chicago, Illinois 60611.

GA Guidance Associates, P. O. Box 5, Pleasantville, New York 10570.

HRW Holt, Rinehart and Winston, 383 Madison Avenue, New York, New York 10017.

IFB International Film Bureau, Inc., 332 South Michigan Avenue, Chicago, Illinois 60604.

PATED Pathescope Educational Films, 71 Weyman Avenue, New Rochelle, New York 10802.

UMTV University of Michigan Television Center, 400 South Fourth Street, Ann Arbor, Michigan 48103.

BIBLIOGRAPHIC SOURCES

2130   COOVER, JAMES and RICHARD COLVIG. _Medieval and Renaissance_
        Music on Long-Playing Records. Detroit: Information
        Service, 1964. 134 pp.
          Reviews: Klaus Speer, _Notes_, 22 (1966) 1235-36; *_MF_,
        20 (1967), 84-85; *_AmR_, 10 (1969), 90; *_Consort_, 23
        (1966), 192-94; *_Must_, 115 (1974), 571-72.

2131   DANKER, FREDERICK E. "Teaching Medieval English Literature:
        Texts, Recordings and Techniques." _CE_, 32 (1970), 340-57.

2132   LIBRARY OF CONGRESS CATALOG--_Motion Pictures and Filmstrips:_
        A Cumulative List of Works Represented by Library of
        Congress Printed Cards. Washington, D.C.: The Library
        of Congress, 1968--.

2133   LIBRARY OF CONGRESS CATALOG--_Music and Phonorecords: A_
        Cumulative List of Works Represented by Library of
        Congress Printed Cards. Washington, D.C.: The Library
        of Congress, 1963--.

2134   LIBRARY OF CONGRESS CATALOGS: _Films and Other Materials for_
        Projection. Washington: Library of Congress, 1974
        (for 1973).

2134.01 LIBRARY OF CONGRESS CATALOGS--_Music: Books on Music and_
        Sound Recordings. Washington, D.C.: Library of Congress,
        1974 (for 1973)--.

2135   NICEM. _Index to Educational Audio Tapes_. Second edition.
        1972.

2136   NICEM. _Index to 16mm Educational Films_. Fourth edition.
        3 vols. 1967.

2137   NICEM. _Index to 35 mm Educational Filmstrips_. Second
        edition. New York: R. R. Bowker, 1970.

2138   NICEM. _Index to Educational Records_. Second edition.
        1972.

2139   NICEM. _Index to Educational Slides_. First edition.
        1973.

Recordings, Films, and Filmstrips

CHAUCER: GENERAL BACKGROUNDS

Recordings

2140   *BORNSTEIN, DIANE. A History of the English Language. CAED.
        LC 73-750641. TC 3008 3-12" LPs; CDL 53008 cassettes
        (3). Cited and annotated in CAED catalog (1973), p. 16.

2141   *BURNS, RAYMOND S. Understanding Chaucer and The Canterbury
        Tales. A Lecture. Phonodisc. PC 3375. LL, 1970.
        Cited in 2133 (1968-72), p. 96 and in 2133 (1970), p. 463.

2142   *CHAUCER. 1 7/8 Audiotape stereo cassette. World Writers
        Series. LL. Cited and annotated in 2135, p. 222.

2143   *CHAUCER: A KNIGHT. 1 7/8 Audiotape cassette. Survey of
        English Poetry Series. TU. Cited and annotated in 2135,
        p. 222.

2144   *CHAUCER TO SPENSER, SHAKESPEARE TO MILTON. 33 1/3 rpm 12"
        record. Secondary Poetry Library - A Series. IMP.
        Cited and annotated in 2138, p. 196.

2145   KNAPP, DANIEL and NIEL K. SNORTUM. The Sounds of Chaucer's
        English. RL20-8. NCTE, 1967.
          Instructional recording with study pamphlet. Excerpts
        from Book of the Duchess, Parliament of Fowls, Troilus
        and Criseyde, The General Prologue, The Knight's Tale,
        The Reeve's Tale, The Wife of Bath's Tale, The Pardoner's
        Tale, The Nun's Priest's Tale.

2146   *MEDCALF, STEPHEN. Chaucer: The Art of Self-Consciousness.
        Cassette Lecture. British Literature Series, 3001. EE,
        1975. Cited in EE catalog.

Films and Filmstrips

2147   *CHAUCER. Filmstrip. 36 frames, black and white, 35 mm.
        Pictorial Biographies Series; LC no: FIA67-401. DUFOUR,
        1968. Cited and annotated in 2137, p. 225.

2148   *CHAUCER'S CANTERBURY PILGRIMS. Filmstrip. 35 frames, color,
        35 mm. EAV, 1963. Cited and annotated in 2132 (1969,
        for 1968), p. 51.

The Canterbury Tales

2149   *CHAUCER'S CANTERBURY PILGRIMS. Sound filmstrip with record.
       35 frames, color, 35 mm and phonodisc, 2 sides. EAV,
       1970. Cited and annotated in 2132 (1971), p. 70 and in
       2137, p. 225.

2150   *CHAUCER'S ENGLAND--WITH A SPECIAL PRESENTATION OF THE PAR-
       DONER'S TALE. Motion picture. 30 minutes, color/black
       and white, 16 mm. EBEC, 1958. Cited and annotated in
       2136, p. 180.

2151   *CHAUCER'S TALE. Motion picture. 30 minutes, sound, color,
       16 mm. Argo Sight and Sound, London, 1968; HRW, 1970.
       Cited and annotated in 2136, p. 180.

2152   *FROM EVERY SHIRES ENDE: THE WORLD OF CHAUCER'S PILGRIMS.
       Motion picture. 38 minutes, sound, color, 16 mm. Made
       by Mary Kirby and Naomi Diamond. Pilgrim Films, London.
       IFB, 1969. Cited and annotated in 2132 (1971 for 1970),
       p. 170.

2153   *GEOFFREY CHAUCER. Filmstrip. 57 frames, color, 35 mm and
       phonotape, 17 minutes. Great Writers of the British
       Isles, 1. PATED, 1969. Cited and annotated in 2132
       (1970), p. 174.

2154   *GEOFFREY CHAUCER: POET AND PILGRIM. Sound filmstrips. Part
       1, 68 frames and part 2, 69 frames, color, 35 mm; 2
       phonodiscs, 4 sides, 33 1/3 rpm, or phonotape in cassette.
       GA, 1970. Cited and annotated in 2132 (1971), p. 156.

2155   *THE TIME, THE LIFE, THE WORKS OF GEOFFREY CHAUCER. Sound
       filmstrip. 52 frames, color, 35 mm, and phonodisc,
       33 1/3 rpm, 2 sides, 12". Study Unit Series. EAV, 1968.
       Cited and annotated in 2132 (1969), p. 361.

THE CANTERBURY TALES

Recordings

2156   *THE CANTERBURY TALES. Four records, mono. British Broad-
       casting Corporation Production. DOV.
          99701-4, The Prologue; 99702-2, The Monk's Tale; The
       Nun's Priest's Tale; 99703-0; The Reeve's Tale; The
       Manciple's Tale; 99704-9, The Man of Law's Preamble and
       Tale. Cited in 2131, pp. 348-49 and in Dover catalog.

Recordings, Films, and Filmstrips

2157   *MEDCALF, STEPHEN. The Canterbury Tales. Cassette Lecture.
           British Literature Series, 3003. EE, 1975. Cited in
           EE catalog.

See also: 2140, 2141, 2166, 2183.

Films

2158   *THE CANTERBURY TALES. 10 motion pictures, 30 minutes each,
           sound, black and white, 16 mm; also issued on video tape.
           MUTV, 1967.
                Includes 1. The Pardoner's Prologue and Tale; 2. The
           Knight's Tale; 3. The Shipman's Tale; 4. The Prioress'
           Tale; 5. The Wife of Bath's Tale; 6. The Friar's Tale;
           7. The Clerk's Tale; 8. The Merchant's Tale; 9. The
           Franklin's Tale; 10. The Nun's Priest's Tale and The
           Manciple's Tale. Cited and annotated in 2132 (1969, for
           1968), p. 45.

2159   *PASOLINI, PIER-PAOLO. I Racconti de Canterbury.
                Italian film version of The Canterbury Tales, 1972.
                Reviews: A. Gabrielle, FLett, 48 (1972), 18 (1713
           above).

See also: 2148, 2149, 2153, 2183.

                          GENERAL PROLOGUE

Recordings

2160   *CHAUCER, GEOFFREY: THE CANTERBURY PILGRIMS. Phonodisc.
           33 1/3 rpm, 12", 2 sides. SLPM 139, 380. DGG, 1968.
           Cited and annotated in 2133 (1969 for 1968), p. 78.
                Reviews: F. E. Danker, 2130 above, p. 349.

2161   *CHAUCER, GEOFFREY: THE CANTERBURY TALES GENERAL PROLOGUE,
           IN MIDDLE ENGLISH. LC R65-999. TC 1151 1-12" LP; CDL
           51151 cassette; CT2 1151 2-track open reel tape. CAED.
           Cited in CAED catalog (1973), p. 16.
                J. B. Bessinger, Jr. reads General Prologue, Prologue
           to the Parson's Tale, Chaucer's Retraction.
                Reviews: F. E. Danker, 2131 above, pp. 348-49.

2162   *CHAUCER, GEOFFREY: PROLOGUE TO THE CANTERBURY TALES. Hough-
           ton Mifflin Literary Masters LP Program. HM.
             Read in Middle English by Nevill Coghill, Norman Davis,
           and John Burrow. Cited in 2138, p. 274.

2163   *CHAUCER, GEOFFREY: THE PROLOGUE TO THE CANTERBURY TALES AND
           THE NUN'S PRIEST'S TALE. Argo RG 401, 466. Argo Record
           Company, 1964, 1966.
             Read in Middle English by Nevill Coghill, Norman Davis,
           and John Burrow. Cited in 2131, pp. 348-49.

2164   *CHAUCER: READINGS FROM CANTERBURY TALES. 33 1/3 rpm,
           monaural, 12" record. FSR.
             Victor L. Kaplan reads selections from The Canterbury
           Tales: General Prologue, The Pardoner's Tale, The Nun's
           Priest's Tale, Complaint of Chaucer to his Purse, Lack of
           Steadfastness. Cited in 2138, p. 196.

2165   *CHAUCER'S CANTERBURY PILGRIMS. 33 1/3 rpm, monaural, 12"
           record. EAV. Cited and annotated in 2138, p. 196.

2166   *GEOFFREY CHAUCER. 33 1/3 rpm, monaural, 12" record. BOW.
             Nevill Coghill and Norman Davis read from the Canterbury
           Tales, General Prologue, and Pardoner's Tale. Cited in
           2138, p. 274.

See also: 2145, 2156, 2181.

Filmstrips

2167   *CHAUCER'S PROLOGUE. Part 1. Filmstrip. 43 frames, black
           and white, 35 mm. English Literature Series. CEA, 1971.
           Common Ground Filmstrips, Harlow, England, 1948. Cited
           and annotated in 2134, p. 106.

2168   *CHAUCER'S PROLOGUE. Part 2. Filmstrip. 40 frames, color,
           35 mm. English Literature Series. CEA, 1971. Common
           Ground Filmstrips, Harlow, England, 1948. Cited and
           annotated in 2134, p. 106.

See also: 2158, 2181.

Recordings, Films, and Filmstrips

THE KNIGHT'S TALE

Recording - see: 2145.

Film - see: 2158.

THE MILLER'S TALE

Recordings

2169   *TWO CANTERBURY TALES IN MIDDLE ENGLISH: THE MILLER'S TALE
        AND THE REEVE'S TALE. CAED. LC R67-2715. TC 1223
        1-12" LP; CDL 51223 cassette.
          Read by J. B. Bessinger, Jr. Cited in CAED catalog
        (1973), p. 16.
          Reviews: F. E. Danker, 2131 above, pp. 348-49.

See also: 2174, 2175, 2181.

THE REEVE'S TALE

Recording - see: 2145, 2156, 2169, 2181.

THE MAN OF LAW'S PREAMBLE AND TALE

Recording - see: 2156

THE WIFE OF BATH'S TALE

Recordings

2170   *EARLY ENGLISH POETRY. Recording. FSR. Folkways, FL 9851.
          Reviews: F. E. Danker, 2131 above, p. 347.

2171   *THE WIFE OF BATH, IN MODERN ENGLISH. CAED. LC R61-1759.
        TC 1102 1-12" LP; CDL 51102 cassette. Cited in CAED
        catalog (1973), p. 16.
            Reviews: F. E. Danker, 2131 above, p. 348.

See also: 2145, 2155, 2181.

Films - see: 2155, 2158.

THE FRIAR'S TALE

Film - see: 2158.

THE CLERK'S TALE

Film - see: 2158.

THE MERCHANT'S TALE

Film - see: 2158.

THE FRANKLIN'S TALE

Film - see: 2158.

THE PARDONER'S PROLOGUE AND TALE

Recordings

2172   *GEOFFREY CHAUCER: TWO CANTERBURY TALES, IN MIDDLE ENGLISH.
        33 1/3 rpm, monaural, 12" record. EYE.

Recordings, Films, and Filmstrips

> Robert Ross reads The Pardoner's Prologue and Tale and The Nun's Priest's Tale. Cited in 2138, p. 274.

2173   TWO CANTERBURY TALES IN MIDDLE ENGLISH: THE PARDONER'S PRO-
        LOGUE AND TALE, AND THE NUN'S PRIEST'S TALE. CAED. LC
        RA55-275. TC 1008 1-12" LP; CDL 51008 cassette. Cited
        in CAED catalog (1973), p. 16.
        Reading by Robert Ross.
        Reviews: F. E. Danker, 2131 above, p. 348.

2174   *GEOFFREY CHAUCER: TWO CANTERBURY TALES, IN MODERN ENGLISH:
        THE PARDONER'S TALE AND THE MILLER'S TALE. CAED. 33 1/3
        rpm, monaural record. EYE.
        The Pardoner's Tale read by Michael MacLiammoir; The
        Miller's Tale, by Stanley Holloway. Modern English trans-
        lation by Theodore Morrison. Cited in 2138, p. 274.

2175   *CHAUCER, GEOFFREY: TWO CANTERBURY TALES IN MODERN ENGLISH:
        THE PARDONER'S TALE AND THE MILLER'S TALE. CAED. LC
        R66-1803. TC 1130 1-12" LP.
        The Pardoner's Tale read by Michael MacLiammoir; The
        Miller's Tale, by Stanley Holloway. Modern English trans-
        lation by Theodore Morrison. Cited in CAED catalog (1973),
        p. 16.
        Reviews: F. E. Danker, 2131 above, p. 348.

See also: 2145, 2164, 2166.

Films — see: 2150, 2158, 2177.

THE SHIPMAN'S TALE

Film — see: 2158.

THE PRIORESS'S TALE

Film — see: 2158.

THE MONK'S TALE

Recording - see: 2156.

THE NUN'S PRIEST'S TALE

Recordings

2176   *CHAUCER, GEOFFREY: THE NUN'S PRIEST'S TALE FROM THE
          CANTERBURY TALES. Houghton Mifflin Literary Masters LP
          Program. HM.
            Read in Middle English by Nevill Coghill, Norman Davis,
          Lena Davis, and John Burrow. Cited in 2138, p. 274.

See also: 2145, 2156, 2163, 2164, 2172, 2173.

Filmstrips

2177   *CHAUCER'S NUN'S PRIEST'S AND PARDONER'S TALES. Filmstrip.
          51 frames, black and white, 35 mm. English Literature
          Series. CEA, 1971. Common Ground Filmstrips, Harlow,
          England, 1949.
            Background materials for The Nun's Priest's Tale, The
          Pardoner's Tale. Cited in 2134, p. 106.

See also: 2158.

THE MANCIPLE'S TALE

Recording - see: 2156.

Film - see: 2158.

PROLOGUE TO THE PARSON'S TALE

Recording - see: 2161.

Recordings, Films, and Filmstrips

RETRACTION

Recording - see: 2161.

BOOK OF THE DUCHESS

Recording - see: 2145.

THE PARLIAMENT OF FOWLS

Recordings

2178   THE PARLIAMENT OF FOWLS AND SIX OTHER POEMS. CAED. LC
        R67-3730. TC 1226 1-12" LP; CDL 51226 cassette. Cited
        in CAED catalog (1973), p. 16.
            J. B. Bessinger, Jr. reads <u>Parliament of Fowls</u>, <u>Merci-</u>
        <u>less Beauty</u>, <u>To Rosamund</u>, <u>Lack of Steadfastness</u>, (includ-
        ing Envoy to Henry IV), <u>To his Scribe Adam</u>, <u>Envoy to</u>
        <u>Scogan</u>. Includes text in Middle English.

See also: 2145.

TROILUS AND CRISEYDE

Recordings

2179   *CHAUCER, GEOFFREY: TROILUS AND CRISEYDE. The English Poets
        from Chaucer to Yeats. Argo ZPL 1003-1004, 1971. Also,
        HM. Houghton Mifflin Literary Masters LP Program.
            Two-record set with complete text. Excerpts of <u>Troilus</u>
        <u>and Criseyde</u> read in Middle English by Gary Watson,
        Prunella Scales, Richard Marquand, Derek Brewer, and
        Peter Orr. Cited in 2134.01 (1973), p. 134.

2180   *MEDCALF, STEPHEN. Troilus and Criseyde. Cassette Lecture.
        British Literature Series, 3002. EE, 1975. Cited in
        EE catalog.

Musical Settings and Adaptations

See also: 2145.

TO ROSEMOUNDE

Recording - see: 2178.

TO HIS SCRIBE ADAM

Recording - see: 2178.

THE COMPLAINT OF CHAUCER TO HIS PURSE

Recording - see: 2164, 2178.

LAK OF STEDFASTNESSE

Recording - see: 2164, 2178.

ENVOY TO SCOGAN

Recording - see: 2178.

MERCILES BEAUTE

Recording - see: 2178.

MUSICAL SETTINGS AND ADAPTATIONS

2181   CANTERBURY TALES. A Musical. Book by Martin Starkie and
        Nevill Coghill based on Coghill's translation from
        Chaucer. Music by Richard Hill and John Hawkins. Lyrics
        by Nevill Coghill. 33 1/3 rpm record, stereo. The
        Canterbury Company, 1969. CAP, SW-229.

Recordings, Films, and Filmstrips

       Stage versions of <u>General Prologue</u>, <u>Miller's Tale</u>, <u>Reeve's Tale</u>, <u>Wife of Bath's Tale</u>, featuring popular medieval lyrics adapted by Coghill and set to modern pop music with medieval rhythms and harmonies. See 195 above.

2182   *MILHAUD, DARIUS. Cantate sur des poèmes de Chaucer. Piano-vocal score. English and French. Cantate sur des poèmes de Chaucer; pour choeurs mixtes et orchestre. Adaptation française de Darius Milhaud. Paris: Au Ménestral, 1963. Cited in 2133 (1963), p. 173.

2183   *TRIMBLE, LESTER. Four Fragments from The Canterbury Tales by Geoffrey Chaucer. High voice and flute, clarinet, harpsichord (piano). New York: C. F. Peters Corporation, 1967. Cited in 2133, p. 96.

Author Index

AUTHOR INDEX

Rosenberg, Bruce Alan, 55, 648,
    1022, 1250, 1268
Rosenthal, Joel Thomas, 1877
Ross, Alan S. C., 1124
Ross, Thomas W., 341, 1531,
    2129.01
Roth, Rev. Francis Xavier,
    O. S. A., 1961
Rothman, Irving N., 984
Rotzler, Willy, 649
Roucaute, Danielle, 650
Rowland, Beryl, 60, 342, 343,
    344, 345, 346, 347, 757, 829
    830, 909, 910, 911, 912,
    1089, 1125, 1176, 1227, 1228,
    1285, 1328, 1329, 1330, 1532,
    2032
Ruff, Joseph Russell, 514
Ruggiers, Paul G., 417, 651, 652,
    760
Rumble, Thomas C., 794, 1824
Runciman, Steven, 1685
Russell, G. H., 1165
Russell, Jeffrey Burton, 1686,
    1825, 1963, 1964, 1965
Russell, Josiah C., 1878, 1879
Russell, Nicholas, 1533
Rutherford, Charles S., 1534
Rutledge, Sheryl P., 653
Ryding, William W., 1826
Rydland, Kurt, 654

Sabin, Marie Noonan, 515
Sachs, Arieh, 1286, 1827
Sadler, Lynn Veach, 1331
Saito, Mother Masako, R. S. C. J.,
    655
Salter, Elizabeth, 348, 1535,
    1679, 1828, 2033
Salvini, Roberto, 2034
Salzman, Louis Francis, 1910,
    1911, 2035
Sampson, Gloria Marie Paulik,
    656
Sams, Henry W. (Festschrift),
    840
Samuels, M. L., 510
Sanders, Barry Roy, 657, 913,
    1269, 1356
Sanders, Ernest Helmut, 2103,
    2104

Sandquist, T. A., 1687
Sands, Donald B., 1829
Sarno, Ronald A., S. J., 349
Saville, Jonathan, 1536
Sayce, Olive, 1294
Sayers, Dorothy L., 1251
Scaglione, Aldo D., 1830
Scattergood, V. J., 472
Schaar, Claes, 350, 473
Schaefer, Willene, 658
Schelp, Hanspeter, 1537, 1880
Scheper, George Louis, 351
Scheps, Walter, 474, 1177, 1229
Scherer, Margaret Roseman, 2036
Schildgen, Brenda Deen, 659
Schirmer, Ruth, 352
Schirmer, Walter F. (Festschrift),
    43
Schlauch, Margaret, 353, 475,
    517, 874, 1832, 1833, 1881
Schlauch, Margaret (Festschrift),
    34
Schleiner, Winfried, 985
Schmidt, A. V. C., 795, 914, 1289
Schmidt, Philip, 1126
Schmitt, Charles B., 1834
Schneider, R. J., 1933
Schoeck, Richard J., 354, 1835
Schrader, Richard J., 1230
Schreiber, Earl George, 1836
Schroeder, Mary C., 1023
Schulz, Herbert C., 97
Schulz, Max F., 61
Schweitzer, Edward C., Jr., 758
Scott, Florence R., 1597
Scott, Kathleen L., 751
Scott, P. G., 1287
Scrivner, Buford, Jr., 355
Seay, Albert, 2105
Selvin, Rhoda Hurwitt, 1400
Sequeira, Isaac, 725
Serraillier, Ian, 1688
Severs, Jonathan Burke, 659.01,
    660, 958, 989, 1077, 1332
Seymour, Evan, 1538
Shallers, Alvin Paul, 1234
Shaner, Mary Carol Edwards, 1377
Shapiro, Gloria K., 915
Sharma, Govind Narayan, 356
Sharrock, Roger, 1538.01
Shea, Virginia Arens, 1378

272

AUTHOR INDEX

Subject Index

Aarne-Thompson Yale Type 887, 988

ABC, An, 1592-1594+

Absolutism, 1652

Adversus Jovinianum, See Epistola Adversus Jovinianum

Aesop, 1029

African Analogues, 1136, 1137

Alanus de Insulis, 412, 1743, 1767

Alba, 1536, 1537, 1800

Albertano of Brescia, Ms., 1189

Alchemy, 1252, 1253, 1254, 1256, 1257, 1258, 1990

Algarsyf (Elpheta and), 1042

Allegory, 118, 164, 209, 251, 256, 274, 288, 357, 388, 413, 628, 1187, 1313, 1399, 1690, 1730, 1748, 1749, 1765, 1774, 1778, 1807, 1815, 1816, 1842, 1852, 2127

Alliterative Poetry, 1837, 1852.01

Altercatio Hadriani, the, 1245

Amorous complaint, 192

Anagogue, 248

Anatomy, medieval, 1156, 1987

Ancient Mariner, The, 455

Ancient wayfarer motif, 1135

ANELIDA AND ARCITE, 1295-1296+; Source Studies, 398-402, 422, 423, 1296

Animals, 342, 343, 453, 727, 757, 764, 1018, 1176, 1211, 1235, 1243, 1407, 1849, 2018, 2032; see also "Beast Fables"

Anne of Bohemia, 376

Anne, St., 939

Anti-feminist tradition, 329, 330, 1558

Antifraternalism, 948, 954, 960

Apocrypha, Lost Works, and Works of Doubtful Authorship (attributed to Chaucer), 20.01, 1610, 1611-1621

Appearance and reality, theme of, 793, 1063, 1069

April date of The Canterbury Tales, 678

Arabic influences, 408, 1254

Archetype, 248, 655, 879

Architecture, medieval, 1925, 2016, 2035, 2042

Archpriest of Hita, see Ruiz, Juan

Argus, 785, 931

Arnold, Matthew, 62, 280

Ars Nova, 2084

Artes Poetriae, 1411

Artes Praedicandi, 634

Arundel, Thomas, 1918

Ascham, 707

ASTROLABE, 1297+

Astrology, 390, 391, 392, 586, 697, 1080, 1599, 1988, 1993, 2127

Astronomy, 313, 323, 359, 1992, 2074

Aubade, 1494

Auchinleck Ms., 1062

Augustan scholarship, 424

Augustine, St., 965, 1962

Austin friars, 1962

Autobiographical fallacy, 275

277